DISRUPTED KNOWLEDGE

Studies in Critical Social Sciences Book Series

Haymarket Books is proud to be working with Brill Academic Publishers (www.brill.nl) to republish the *Studies in Critical Social Sciences* book series in paperback editions. This peer-reviewed book series offers insights into our current reality by exploring the content and consequences of power relationships under capitalism, and by considering the spaces of opposition and resistance to these changes that have been defining our new age. Our full catalog of *SCSS* volumes can be viewed at https://www.haymarketbooks .org/series_collections/4-studies-in-critical-social-sciences.

DISRUPTED KNOWLEDGE

Scholarship in a Time of Change

EDITED BY
TINA SIKKA, GARETH LONGSTAFF AND STEVE WALLS

Haymarket Books
Chicago, IL

First published in 2023 by Brill Academic Publishers, The Netherlands
© 2023 Koninklijke Brill NV, Leiden, The Netherlands

Published in paperback in 2024 by
Haymarket Books
P.O. Box 180165
Chicago, IL 60618
773-583-7884
www.haymarketbooks.org

ISBN: 979-8-88890-232-5

Distributed to the trade in the US through Consortium Book Sales and
Distribution (www.cbsd.com) and internationally through Ingram Publisher
Services International (www.ingramcontent.com).

This book was published with the generous support of Lannan Foundation,
Wallace Action Fund, and the Marguerite Casey Foundation.

Special discounts are available for bulk purchases by organizations and
institutions. Please call 773-583-7884 or email info@haymarketbooks.org for more
information.

Cover design by Jamie Kerry and Ragina Johnson.

Printed in the United States.

Library of Congress Cataloging-in-Publication data is available.

Contents

Acknowledgements

First and foremost, we would like to thank each of the authors for their contributions, their patience, and their enthusiasm for the project. This is a unique project that brings together a departmental team of academic scholars, activists and creative thinkers and it does so through the lens of the 2020 pandemic. It uses this as a prism or portal into how disruption can generate possibility and it affirms this as a group of people we would like to badge as 'The Newcastle School'. We would also like to extend thanks to our editors for their support throughout the process – their kind and practical guidance has really helped us to develop and complete this project and its ambition. The completion of this edited collection is both a stopping and a starting point. Its ideas and their relationship to 'disrupted knowledge' emerged from discussions, anecdotes, and encounters both in person and across the new world that we found ourselves in during the 2020 pandemic. Zoom and Teams calls, Whatsapp groups and good old fashioned phone calls have underpinned this project and the potentials and possibilities that can emerge from moments of disruption, anxiety, and uncertainty. As editors and both at the start and the end of this project we found ourselves sitting around Tina's kitchen table working out the final parts of what we really wanted this book to do and to say and we hope that this becomes apparent as you engage with it. Finally, this book is an attempt to revive and sustain critical thinking, subordination, resistance, and desire and is dedicated to anyone and everyone that has tried to think beyond the limits of what they are told.

Notes on Contributors

James Barker
is a Ph.D. candidate in Music and Media at Newcastle University. His Ph.D. research explores the potential of queer reading as a strategy to assert LGBTQ+ belonging in country music, using Dolly Parton as a case study. He is a proud queer country scholar, but more broadly his work explores the ways artists, audiences and songs navigate, shape and challenge ideas of musical genre, using a queer theoretical framework. In addition to his academic research, he has worked as a journalist focusing on championing LGBTQ+ voices in country, Americana and roots music.

David Bates
is Lecturer in Media and Cultural Studies at Newcastle University. His research interests are race and racism in media and political discourse, and media history. His most recent research, examining political discussions of immigration in the Labour Party, has recently been published in *Critical Discourse Studies*; his other research on immigration and asylum has appeared in journals such as the *Journal of Community and Applied Social Psychology*, *Refugee Review* and *PLATFORM: Journal of Media and Communication*. Prior to working as an academic and lecturer, he worked in the voluntary sector.

Alexander D. Brown
is Leverhulme Early Career Fellow at Liverpool University. His interests are in the politics of memory, ideology studies and the history of state socialism. From 2019 to 2022, he was AHRC Research Associate at Newcastle University on the research project: "Knowing the Secret Police: Secrecy and Knowledge in East German Society". The project looked at the GDR's Ministry for State Security ('Stasi') from the perspective of ordinary citizens. His current work is on Jewish antifascists and Holocaust memory in the German Democratic Republic. A monograph about the Paul Merker affair in German state-mandated memory is forthcoming.

Briony A. Carlin
is an early career researcher interested in art, affect and feminist new materialist epistemologies. She has recently obtained her Ph.D. from Newcastle University with a thesis entitled 'Bindings, Boundaries and Cuts: Relating Agency and Ontology in Photobook Encounters'. She has a background as a museum practitioner and previously worked as Assistant Curator of

Photographs at the Victoria and Albert Museum, London. She is working on developing publications from her doctoral research, alongside a postdoctoral project exploring relationships between identity, experience and knowledge cultures in field-based research.

Deborah Chambers

is Professor of Media and Cultural Studies, Newcastle University. Intersecting sociology and media/communication studies, her research centres on digital technologies and everyday life: the role of digital and smart technologies in household dynamics; mobile media apps and mediated intimacies; media cultures and everyday life. She is currently researching cybersecurity and online harms (EPSRC project). Her books include *A Sociology of Family Life: Change and Diversity in Intimate Relations* (Polity Press 2022); *Cultural Ideals of Home: The Social Dynamics of Domestic Space* (Routledge 2020), *Changing Media, Homes & Households* (Routledge 2016); *Social Media and Personal Relationships* (Palgrave 2013).

Abbey Couchman

is a Ph.D. candidate in Media and Cultural Studies at Newcastle University. Her Ph.D. research explores the negotiation of masculinity and performance in relation to perceived risk in mobile and online dating, within the context of heightened societal anxieties. Her research aims to understand men's anxiety as a social and cultural phenomenon, building upon foundational psychological concepts such as anxiety, self-esteem and narcissism. In addition to her research, she continues her contributions to academic scholarship in her advisement in Academic Quality at University Campus of Football Business (UCFB).

Richard Elliott

is a cultural musicologist with a particular interest in popular musics of the world. He is the author of the books *Fado and the Place of Longing: Loss, Memory and the City* (2010), *Nina Simone* (2013), *The Late Voice: Time, Age and Experience in Popular Music* (2015), *The Sound of Nonsense* (2018) and *DJs do Guetto* (2022). He has also published articles and reviews on popular music, literature, consciousness, memory, nostalgia, place and space, affect, language and technology. He is Senior Lecturer in Music at the International Centre for Music Studies at Newcastle University, where he specialises in courses related to popular music.

Joss Hands

is Reader in Critical Theory at Newcastle University, his research explores the relationship between digital media and politics through the lens of critical theory. His publications include @ *is for Activism: Dissent, Resistance and Rebellion in a Digital Culture*, Pluto Press (2011) and *Gadget Consciousness: Collective Thought, Will and Action in the Age of Social Media*, Pluto Press (2019). He recently contributed to and edited a special issue of *Javnost: The Public* on 'Pandemic Publics' (2022).

Chris Haywood

is a Reader in Critical Masculinity Studies at Newcastle University. His current work *Sex, Clubs: Recreational Sex, Fantasies and Cultures of Desire* (Palgrave) investigates the relationships between hetero-eroticism and heteronormativity within UK sex clubs. More specifically, it explores in the context of the growing demand for leisure sex a range of areas that includes women's sexual excess, post-masculinities, the fetish and commodification of black bodies and transgressive sex. His previous work includes *Men, Masculinity and Contemporary Dating* (Palgrave) and as the co-author of *The Conundrum of Masculinity* (Routledge).

Sarah Hill

is a Lecturer in Media and Cultural Studies at Newcastle University. Her research interests are broadly situated within feminist media studies, girl studies, and disability studies. Her current research explores disabled young women's online self-representation practices and her work has been published in the journals *Girlhood Studies and Feminist Media Studies*. She is also the author of *Young Women, Girls and Postfeminism in Contemporary British Film* (2020), published by Bloomsbury Academic.

Gareth Longstaff

is a Lecturer in Media and Cultural Studies at Newcastle University. His research is connected to queer theory, history, archiving, and the contours of how this relates to gay male sexuality, celebrity, and pornography and the self. In his book *Celebrity, Pornography, and the Politics of Desire* (2023, Bloomsbury) he engages and applies this approach to self-representational media, pornography/sexual representation, and digital/networked archives of desire. Dr Longstaff has been involved with AHRC and ESRC research projects allied to queer archives and the prodcution of desire. He has also published on pornography, celebrity, HIV & AIDS, desire and self in journals such as *Porn Studies, Persona Studies, The Journal of Bodies, Sexualities & Masculinities, Culture, Health and Sexuality,* and *The Journal of Celebrity Studies.*

Altman Yuzhu Peng

is currently Assistant Professor in Intercultural Communication at the University of Warwick and obtained his Ph.D. from Newcastle University. His research interests lie at the intersections of Critical Discourse Studies, Feminism, Media and Cultural Studies, and Public Relations. He is the author of *A Feminist Reading of China's Digital Public Sphere* (Palgrave 2020) and has published 20 scholarly articles in *Asian Journal of Communication, Convergence, Critical Discourse Studies, Chinese Journal of Communication, Feminist Media Studies, International Feminist Journal of Politics, International Journal of Communication, Journal of Gender Studies, Media International Australia, Social Semiotics*, and *Television & New Media.*

Joanne Sayner

is Senior Lecturer in Cultural and Heritage Studies. Her research expertise is in the politics of remembering in contemporary culture. Her work bridges cultural studies, memory studies, heritage studies, gender studies and media studies. It addresses both tangible and intangible heritage in terms of contemporary memory cultures, with a particular focus on the UK and German contexts since the Second World War. Her publications include: *Reframing Antifascism: Memory, Genre and the Life Writings of Greta Kuckhoff* (Palgrave 2013); *Women Without A Past? German Autobiographical Writings and Fascism* (Rodopi 2007).

Tina Sikka

is Reader in Technoscience and Intersectional Justice in the School of Arts and Culture at Newcastle University, UK. Her current research includes the critical and intersectional study of science, applied to climate change, bodies, and health, as well as research on consent, sexuality, and restorative justice. Her most recent book, *Sex, Consent, and Justice: A New Feminist Framework* (2021), offers a novel approach to sexual ethics and transformative justice using case studies from #MeToo, while her previous book, *The Ethics of Geoengineering: Climate Change and Feminist Empiricism* (2018), draws on feminist science studies to explore the science underpinning solar climate engineering. She has published articles in such noted journals as *The Nordic Journal in Feminist and Gender Research*; *The Journal of the Swiss Anthropological Association*; *Capitalism, Nature, Socialism*; *Social Identities: Journal for the Study of Race, Nation, and Culture*; and *Food, Culture, Society.*

Steve Walls

is a Lecturer in Media and Cultural Studies at Newcastle University. Employing a variety of critical and cultural theory his research and pedagogical expertise explores the historical and contemporary landscapes of advertising and consumption, fashion communications, masculinities and sexuality, social media and representation, work and leisure. He has previously published *Examining Male Service Work: Gendered and Sexualised Aesthetics* (2012, Lambert Academic Publishing) and his most recent projects include *Critical Approaches to Promotional Cultures* (Palgrave Macmillan, 2023) and edited collection *Re-Fashioning the Fashion Sector? Resilience and Evolution* (Intellect/ University of Chicago, 2023).

Michael Waugh

is a lecturer in Media and Cultural Studies at Newcastle University, with a Ph.D. from Anglia Ruskin University. His research explores fandom and identity in digital spaces, with particular focus on popular music, television and comics, and he leads the module Popular Culture, Media & Identity at Newcastle. He has published in journals such as *Popular Music* and *Critical Studies in Television* and contributed a chapter about experimental producer Arca to *Mute Records: Artists, Business, History*. He is currently writing a chapter for a forthcoming anthology about hip hop, to be published by Cambridge University Press in 2023. He co-organised a series of talks titled "Sound Salon" at Somerset House alongside Jennifer Walshe and Adam Harper (2017) and was a guest speaker at Berlin's 3hd Festival (2016), while his research was the subject of a one-off radio show ("The Internet State of Mind") on German station WDR (2017). He has written press releases for albums by musicians including Arca, KUČKA and Derek Piotr.

Introduction: *'Then, There and Everywhere'* – Situating Disrupted Knowledge

Tina Sikka, Gareth Longstaff and Steve Walls

To say the last two years (2021–2022) have been materially and affectively unexpected, challenging, and traumatic is an understatement. World events, private tragedies, and drastic transformations to work practices has left many of us working in higher education (HE) especially those of us who are marginalised, unable to cope. This has led to high rates of attrition as well as staff redundancies despite stable, or even increasing, rates of student enrolment.

The pandemic has also led to those remaining in the university system, operating under varying levels of precarity, to step back, re-evaluate our priorities, rethink our relation to scholarship, and reassess how we 'do' research. It is on this basis that the spark for this collection first emerged. Specifically, we wanted to find a way to engage solidaristically with people working around and with us – some of whom we had not seen for months – in order to: one, revivify our departmental research culture; two, find ways to connect and affirm with colleagues and their evolving research; three, create a repository of the innovative and productively '(dis)connected' scholarship that characterised this time of isolation, stress, and disorientation; and four, cultivate a better understanding of how the unforeseen events of late and resulting changes have transformed the research being done by this group of scholars in a discipline of 'disrupted knowledge' that is diverse, politically-engaged, and social-justice oriented.

Our subject area, Media, Cultural, and Heritage (MCH), as the departmental website explains,

> brings together longstanding staff groupings associated with highly successful research and teaching programmes in Cultural Studies, Media Studies, Journalism, Public Relations, Digital Cultural Communication and Participation, and Museum, Gallery and Heritage Studies, alongside new provision in the area of Film Practice. MCH focuses on public culture, broadly defined, undertaking socially-relevant research and providing education that maximises graduates' critical and professional skills, and their experiences and understandings of cultural sector contexts.

While this summation is generally accurate, it does not quite reflect the uniqueness of our combined research and its productively disruptive approach to the intersections of mediated cultures and the nuances of cultural heritage. As a relatively newly formed entity, we aim to study culture in all of its forms where culture is understood as a sociomaterial assemblage of changing technologies, media forms, institutions, genres, power relations, representational and symbolic forms, intersectional identities, policies, practices, interests, values, and norms. This approach has provided us with the leeway to study everything from social media and political polarisation, to cultural memory and conflict, with an emphasis on the changing intersections between class, race, sexuality and gender. Many of us also build on political economic work to examine how culture is produced, expressed, transformed, and disseminated locally, nationally, and transnationally. Furthermore, many of us are both fascinated and dismayed by practices of neoliberalism and their socio-political effects on everyday life and culture. The monetised, marketised and branded power that everything and anything can now contain has become simultaneously powerful *and* precarious in a pandemic and post-pandemic setting. Here we see that disparate discourses associated with the human body and sexual desire, sustainability and the climate crisis, political ideologies allied to race and social justice, and human suffering through war are all digitally and algorithmically maintained and promoted for individually minded consumers to customise, control and comment on. Within these spaces we witness the reification and materiality of 'disrupted knowledge' as it is lived, captured, edited and shared. It is through this kind of curiosity, urgency and interdisciplinarity that has allowed for staff examining the cultures of science (Sikka 2018; 2021) to work and teach seamlessly alongside those studying sexuality and the body (Longstaff 2019, 2020), promotion and consumption (Walls, 2012), memory (Mason, Galani, Lloyd and Sayner, 2018) and disability (Hill 2017). The most important thread that draws our scholarship together is a shared interest in cultivating a society of just outcomes, sociomaterial equality, inclusive scholarship. and open expression and imagination. Happily, we have managed, through our combined work, to cultivate a balance between the material and the discursive by approaching culture as constituted by 'material discourses' wherein concerns about material inequality are addressed alongside with, and in synergistic relation to, the study of ideology, hegemony, symbolic violence, and relations of power (Berlant 2011; Mouffe 2014; Beetz and Schwab 2018; Foucault 2019; Bourdieu 2003; Gramsci 2000; Marsh and Tan 1999; Fuchs and Mosco 2015).

This book reflects important work being done by our faculty on and around the pandemic and in light of intersecting 'disruptions' including #BlackLivesMatter, political extremism, the commodification of LGBTQ lives and social media influence. Together, it provides an epistemological snapshot of how scholars in one subject area, and housed within the Humanities and Social Sciences at Newcastle University, had their research upturned and transformed during 2021–2022. We argue that 'taking' an epistemological snapshot of current research is significant for the contribution it makes to posterity and historical record keeping as well as encouraging collective reflection and acting as a means through which to cultivate transformative, forward looking change. The cultural impact and disruption felt by the pandemic made us stop and reflect – during this time we feel an intense and startling level of loss, trauma, isolation, panic, and anxiety and we experienced this in terrifyingly real ways. Yet we also felt an intense and startling level of love, understanding, empathy, intimacy, generosity and community in ways which we had not witnessed before. It was through various discussions (via zoom, teams, whatsapp, messenger, or even over the good old fashioned telephone) that this intersection of feeling afraid and affirmed by those that we worked with and cared for that we asked contributors to produce a chapter that reflected something they had been working on, thinking about, or intended to study further as a result of the pandemic and/or related disruptions. Their submission should also, we requested, reflect work they believed was important to disseminate now and that they were particularly passionate about. What emerged from this request, is a reflective, resonant, and engaging set of chapters that concretizes our school's research culture. It will thus take the reader on a journey through a number of interrelated subject areas. While the themes and issues addressed are diverse, *they converge on the need for an engaged citizenry, revived solidaristic politics, anti-colonial and anti-racist action, community engagement, a social justice ethos, and a feminist ethic of care.*

This is reflected in chapters that, for example, engage in unpacking changing conceptions of consumerism, sexual desire, disability and mediated self-representations (vis-à-vis girls) during the pandemic; the ongoing cultivation of a mediated pandemic self, an isolated pandemic self, a self-reflective pandemic self and an entrepreneurial self; the rise of the phenomenon of 'truth twisting', the politics of populism, intellectual self-defence within the university system; and the evolution of conflicting consumer, ethical and moral practices in light of the confluence of inconsistent government direction, neoliberal capitalism, and Covid restrictions. Significantly, not all of these chapters take on or address the pandemic directly despite it being the most obvious shared experience. The pandemic, however, does act as a 'zeitgeist', a common inflection point, a forceful agent pushing our interests, concerns, and projects in some directions rather than others. This collection essentially aims to use the pandemic as a way to reflect on and engage fully with emergent concerns. It functions as an experiential, emotional, epistemological and methodological crossing point where the initial shudder and shock of disruption can

energise and shape new forms of knowledge, value and desire. David Bates'
chapter, for example, examines changing notions of race as it relates to Brexit,
immigration, and agitation around colonial statues, while another, by Brown
and Sayner, examines post-1990 reconstructions of the Stasi's archives as read
through the lens of nationality and citizenship, controversy and truth, media
(fiction and non), co-construction, and the process of making sense of the
recent past. While not Covid-specific, these chapters emerged out of forces
and flows shaped by the pandemic and thereby share concerns including
changing forms of protest, the material concerns of the public, and the politics of truth.

Thus, there are two ways in which we justify the existence of such a collection
and offer a 'holding' rationale for the chapters as they appear. The first comes
from a place of interdisciplinary de-institutionalisation. We feel strongly that
the rise of departments with an explicit trans and interdisciplinary approach to
scholarship, like ours, have lacked edited collections and texts that mirror the
epistemological messiness which, we argue, offers students, academics, and
other readers an approach to knowledge production that reflects real -world
unfoldings and enfoldings. Such a collection also allows readers, alongwith the
text, to co-produce their own productive synergies and construct narratives
that enable them to think across academic disciplines. As will be made evident, in this particular collection we have chosen focally diverse chapters the-
matically held together by shared understanding (e.g. power and justice) while
grappling with sweeping social, political, scientific, and cultural disruptions.
These chapters are temporally and topically connected while being methodologically and spatially diverse.

Our advice to the reader is to act as an 'agential cutter',that is, to immerse
themselves in the assemblage of chapters that constitute this collection and, in
doing so, enact their own co-produced and contingent resolution or narrative
for which they are responsible. This approach, borrowed from new materialism,
encourages readers to enact agential cuts "in different ways, at different points
in time, with different ends in view, in picking out for attention, and action,
different features" (Shotter 2014, p. 308; Barad 2007). This kind of 'assemblage
thinking' reflects the interdisciplinarity of this text while also holding fast to
shared thematic elements. More so the reader might approach the chapters
and the edited collection as something that is not yet here. This resembles the
'queerness [that] is not yet here' in José Esteban Muñoz *Cruising Utopia* (2009,
p. 1). Like this utopic queerness, disrupted knowledge might follow Muñoz's
hopeful vision and be felt 'as the warm illumination of a horizon imbued with
potentiality [...] as an ideality that can be distilled from the past and used to
imagine a future'(ibid). Furthermore, we suggest that as you encounter and

engage with this collection, you reject the confines of the *'here and now'* and instead 'strive in the face of the here and now's totalising rendering of reality, to think and feel a *then and there* (ibid)'. It may be in this pleasurably disruptive space of *then and there* that 'other ways of being in the world' are possible and where 'an insistence on potentiality or [the] concrete possibility for another world' (ibid) occurs in response to the disruptive forms of knowledge and experience that we map.

The second rationale, briefly, relates to a novel 'snapshot' methodology, mentioned above, in which we encourage the production of such collections which are temporally and spatially focused, interdisciplinary, and reflects current issues and concerns within a particular institutional space (Hall, Jones, and Thomson, 2010; Thomson and Hall, 2016). We hope more scholarship of this sort will be generated going forward, as it depicts an innovative kind of representational practice – one that is needed during times of flux and change.

The collection begins with Steve Walls who sets the cultural and conceptual 'scene' of disruption that the Covid-19 pandemic brought to the everyday experiences of neoliberal 'consumer-citizens' through the critical lens of social class and shopping practices. He examines the ways in which hasty and unforeseen government restrictions and regulations were presented to neoliberal consumers already familiar with notions of individualised adaption, agency and entrepreneurialism. It was in this pandemic setting that the tensions between consumer flexibility, restriction, greed and selfishness merged with those of an apparent selflessness, affinity and affirmation towards others. Here, we saw the emergence of the 'hero-consumer' through the incentivised 'Eat Out to Help Out' scheme and its promotion through government and mass media rhetoric. Walls argues that such incentives reify and reiterate the intrinsically 'class-based materiality of experiences of lockdown'. By these means, the social anxieties (and pleasures) proliferated by pandemic and waves of lockdown are framed by individual and collective 'consumer-citizen' responses to changes and restrictions to their lives. Through the use of vectors of socialising ('Pubs'), shopping ('Primark') and eating ('Pasta-Making Machines') Walls reveals the excesses and divisive issues allied to these ordinary and mundane objects and spaces of 'Pubs, Primark & Pasta-Making Machines' place emphasis on class-based and consumerist inequalities and conflicts. It is through this tension, during this unprecedented and uncanny period in history, that we also see a disruptive form of knowledge emerging, one which correlates with a collectively contradictory and confusing rhetoric across government, social media and those practices of safety, risk and respect that all of us as consumer-citizens became absorbed by.

Deborah Chambers, in her chapter, evaluates claims surrounding the myriad ways in which Covid-19 is said to have reconfigured established modalities of social connectivity in light of the increased use of home-based digital technologies. Chambers chronicles the rise of so-called 'postdigital socialities' and the intensification of the 'postdigital phase of domestic mediatization' over the last two years, describing them as scopic, visual, and home-bound. She makes the case that these technologies hold potential despite the concomitant rise of abusive and extreme content as well as other 'frictions' of encoded racial and gender bias and increased corporate control. Chambers points out that many of these technologies, Zoom and social media among them, "enabled householders to overcome the lack of physical closeness during lockdowns and cope with isolation by keeping in touch, remotely, with friends and family" (Chambers 2023, xx). The chapter concludes with the observation that the 'thickening' of current trends might augur more permanent trends including a different role for digital technologies in our lives as novel forms of visual home-bound connectivity develop. Similarly scrutinising the medicalised sphere, Tina Sikka's chapter skilfully exposes the materialisation of racialised difference through medical technology. At a time where medical treatment needs to be agile, Sikka highlights the racialised assumptions and biases that inform medical technological developments and associated diagnostic/treatment regimes. Using the Pulse Oximeter as a case study, Sikka's chapter illustrates how notions of racialised difference are *built-into* medical technology through their very design; the subsequent inequity in access to accurate diagnostics and treatment; and finally, how the Pulse Oximeter reinforces essentialist racialisation through artificially 'collapsing' notions of phenotypical variation and genotypical difference. Employing a new materialist approach, Sikka advocates for a more critically reflexive medical praxis to facilitate the de-geneticisation of race while allowing for appropriate non-racialised adjustments (i.e. where adjusting for skin colour becomes as socio-materially insignificant as adjusting for height). Similarly, associated medical research/technological development strategies need to address the invisibility and neglect of specific populations when developing technology at the level of design. Enveloping this critically reflexive praxis, Sikka argues that we must embed the experiences of racialised groups in order to comprehend the complex assemblages of culture, race, and health technologies.

Joss Hands' chapter further develops a critique of the assault upon critical scholarship and the agenda-setting involved in the social construction of knowledge informed by rightwing populism. His chapter explores strategies of manipulation employed through historical fascism and examines how they map against contemporary populist tendencies through 'truth-twisting' and divisive manoeuvring. Hands unpicks three specific cultural accelerants that cultivate growing levels of intolerance and hostility: first, the increasing colonisation of online networks by the extreme right; second, the seepage of these discourses into mainstream politics and media; and finally, the global Covid-19 pandemic. Across these strands, hostility is mobilised against a specific theme – 'wokeness'. As a distorted perception of advocacy for the rights of the marginalised, to be 'woke' is to appear ridiculously extreme. Hands explores how these distortions have informed educational policy and the toxification of higher education. In this sense, universities were represented in the media as 'stasi-like' settings (Somerville, 2022), by encouraging students to police their maskless peers and by providing a new 'liberal elite' target after having vanquished pro-European foes through Brexit. The chapter concludes with a salient commentary on critical pedagogy: for moving knowledge forward without necessarily maintaining 'balanced' views.

David Bates continues the discussion on race through the lens of cultural studies and critical race theory. Highlighting the need to sustain scrutiny, Bates uses the backdrop of the UK's 'culture wars' emboldened through the pandemic context and Black Lives Matter movement. Following the 'disruptive' power of the Black Lives Matter protests in the UK, the chapter begins by scrutinising the Commission on Race and Ethnic Disparities (CRED) report into state level institutional racism. The chapter then uses a social media critical discourse analysis to illuminate and unpack discourses of race, national identity and heritage in a Facebook discussion group. Bates explains how British colonialism can become unproblematically folded into notions of *Britishness* and to reveal the discursive silencing of political activism. This silencing involves the active construction of BLM protest as unnecessary and disruptive violence, while sanitising/denying the cultural and state-sanctioned violence woven into British Imperialist history. Such views resonate with government rhetoric in the form of opposition to critical race theory, hidden histories and the social construction of knowledge associated with the British Colonial elite's status (and statues) in light of revelations as to their involvement with the global slave trade.

Altman Yuzhu Peng turns his attention to the exponential rise in discussions surrounding Traditional Chinese Medicine (TCM) as a treatment for Covid-19 patients on social media in China. Using a discourse analysis of online posts, Peng's chapter explains that support for such treatments are more closely aligned with the user's pre-existing political views than one might think. Peng chronicles debates around TCM intersects with public health policy, nationalism, tradition, and global power politics and homes to show how this played out in novel ways on the social media knowledge sharing app, Zhihu. Peng's data and analysis reveals significant tensions in the deployment of scientific language, the intromission of experts onto these channels, the significance of heritage and tradition (often acting as an ideological test), and the professed superiority of the Chinese political system. together, these tensions reflect a significant overlap between TCM advocates and government supporters. Peng argues that the politicisation of medicine is a primary feature of this techno-political ecosystem which does not bode well for public health.

The next chapter, "The Stasi as a site of institutionalised memory and knowledge", written by Alexander D. Brown and Joanne Sayner, reflects the shift in how both scholars conceptualise and examine state power and authority in their historical work. This shift is due, in large part, to the impact of Covid-19 which altered how they accessed data and developed new epistemic priorities. The chapter examines the construction of the German Stasi as a site of insti-tutional memory constituted (unequivocally) by evil and danger which, the authors argue, requires another look given the release of new archival documen-tation. Brown and Sayner draw attention to the functioning of state ideology in post-war Germany. They argue that this specific case, the further opening of the Stasi Archives, demands a further re-evaluation of fascism versus anti-fascism, the Stasi, the GDR, and a wider rethinking of 'how one remembers'. This focus foregrounds questions around access to information, gatekeeping, the public versus private spheres, mediatised narrative formation, and national memory which will also inevitably inform how we will construct our memory of the past few years. This chapter produces synergies with other contributors' shared concern with (state) power and the social construction of knowledge such as those by Bates, Hands and Peng.

Sarah Hill's chapter steers the collection towards a consideration of subjec-tive and self-presentational forms of desire. Titled "(Not) being the 'cool disa-bled person': Queering/ cripping postfeminist girlhood on social media", Hill draws on crip theory, postfeminism, and drag performance art to demonstrate how young, disabled women have manifested disability and empowering forms of self-representation on social media. This process took on heightened significance for these women during the height of the pandemic. Hill refers to this as a process of 'queering/cripping' or resisting ideals of postfeminist girlhood and draws on a case study – semi-structured interviews and social media analysis with a young person, named Ali (pseudonym) – to show how Instagram's technological affordances have been used in ways that make 'invis-ible' disability visible and legible while also queering/ cripping postfeminist girlhood. Gareth Longstaff's chapter, 'Self, Self, Self' – Masculine modes of sex-ual self-representation and the disruptive politics of jouissance on OnlyFans. com' also considers the disruptive potentials of queer desire and visibility. He builds on the history of mediation and the platformisation of social relations over the past decade – particularly as a result of the pandemic during which labour and sexual sociality has migrated to online spaces. Specifically, Longstaff draws on cultural criticism, psychoanalysis, and a critique of entrepreneurial neoliberalism to examine the intersections of sexual desire, labour, and gay masculinity on the platform OnlyFans.com. He makes the case that OnlyFans.com represents "a space where those who are seeking out desire through forms of jouissance are persuaded into associating with a yearning for proximity, intimacy, and reciprocity" (Longstaff 2023, xx). However, he argues that this platform also cultivates a form of neoliberal sexual selfhood that, as exemplified by the sexual persona of OnlyFans.com star Josh Moore, transforms the self into a commodity rather than the embodiment of deferred pleasure offered by jouissance, the Real, and the Symbolic Other. Longstaff concludes, however, that a more hedonic and capacious form of sexual relationality is possible and is exemplified by Moore's ability to draw on more enigmatic forms of signification that simultaneously 'disrupt' neoliberal capital and reified gay male jouissance.

On a similar level, the digital sphere used as a 'decanted' space to contain the overflow of 'lockdown' activities is explored in Abbey Couchman's chapter. Couchman looks at the gendered politics of health regulation during the pandemic and the complex intersection of masculine performativity and 'risk' in online dating practice. Couchman explores discursive constitutions of masculine subjectivities and the challenges, tensions and resistance encountered through digital intimacy against the backdrop of the global pandemic. Couchman highlights the ways in which digital dating apps and the pandemic contextualise the material inconsistencies of contemporary masculinities. Whereas these dating apps and technology facilitate shifts in intimacy towards the digital and destabilise notions of the physical 'hook-up', they continue to illustrate conventional gendered norms in terms of hegemony and 'networked misogyny'. The chapter explains that these phenomena are frequently heightened by challenges to masculinities through romantic rejection during times of 'crisis' or social upheaval. Exposed as vulnerable and 'fragile', in the face of a potentially debilitating/deadly virus, masculine resistance to safety regulations and 'risky' practices highlight the need for broader socio-cultural understandings with attempts to regulate and promote public health.

Chris Haywood explores UK Sex Clubs to push this argument further and into a disruptive and subversive space where new methodological and analytical possibilities are framed by the possibilities of promiscuity, queer intimacies and desires. Here, he claims that the pandemic initiated an 'epistemological jolt' which, in turn, generated a 'broader fear, anxiety and frustration' folded into the pleasures, desires, and possibilities of the sex club as both a social *and* a sexual space. In this bold and innovative chapter, Haywood discusses how the pandemic impacted sex clubs and their initial responses as commercial enterprises. He then contours this enquiry ethnographically to critically analyse how the pandemic appeared to exacerbate particular 'cultures of desire' (Cornwall 1997) that were evinced in complex exchanges of 'social intimacy, scopophilic touching and visceral physical connections'. Through these spaces and bodily, embodied and affective ways of being and becoming, desire and sexuaity is disrupted and affirmed. The fieldwork used in Haywood's chapter provides excerpts from the ethnographies which, in themselves can be 'troubling and disruptive'. They resemble and formulate a deliberately disruptive methodological approach that Haywood terms 'ethnopornographic'. Using this approach as a portal into these spaces of desire, as well as a mode of epistemological and methodological disruption, he argues that disruptions can often operate productively through enigmatic forms of emersion, new forms of sexual exchange and belonging.

Michael Waugh's chapter guides the idea of disruption towards another (auto)ethnographic space which also challenges notions of desire, anxiety, isolation and belonging. He uses his own personal experiences of escapism through media during the 2020 lockdowns and singles out his obsession with the American TV show *Twin Peaks* as a catalyst for becoming absorbed and lost in the 'epitextual materials' of YouTube videos, blog posts, forums, and podcasts allied to the show. For Waugh, during a period of intense isolation and profound self-reflection, it was the *Diane* podcast (2016-) and its episode-by-episode breakdown of *Twin Peaks'* three seasons (1990–1991; 2017) and the film *Twin Peaks: Fire Walk With Me* (1992) that provided him with an 'intimate parasocial experience' as well as a sense of epistemological empowerment through disruption. In this way, with the *Diane* podcast as his pivot, Waugh explores the auto-ethnographic and philosophical tensions between mediated forms of manipulation and real-world sociality, using the premise that 'the identity foundations on which new relationships are built can be every bit as sturdy online as off' (Baym, 2010, p. 121). Waugh argues that media allow for a form of solace, comfort and affirmation that can genuinely help our wellbeing and, as a space of 'disrupted knowledge', our (and his) scholarly integrity and productivity. Continuing to explore the intimacy and comfort produced by various media, James Barker, Richard Elliott and Gareth Longstaff collaboratively explore the use of 'evocative objects' (Bollas, 1987, 2009; Turkle, 2007) in the lyrical stylings of US country/pop music star Taylor Swift. Within Swift's 'sonic-lyrical regimes' (Tragaki, 2020), the materiality of affect is realised. The authors delicately unpack the use of evocative objects as a narrative device linked to specific genres such as country and pop music. This unpacking exemplifies an intensive form of neoliberal capitalism in which media and art forms, as well as emotional intimacies, become entangled with material culture and objects. In a detailed analysis of albums *folklore* and *evermore* the chapter draws attention to the rich Swiftian tapestry that induces an affective response in listeners. The authors argue that this occurs through the intensity and ordinary nature of the objects and experiences in Swift's songs which create a 'something-ness' that connects listeners in a myriad of meaningful ways. The cultural phenomenon of 'cottagecore' is used as a prism here through which to view the complex intersections between neoliberal capitalism, nostalgia, and social consciousness within Swift's lyrics and subsequent merchandising. Finally, the chapter develops a poignant critical reading of Taylor Swift's music and a potential queer reading/reworking of her song 'betty'. This represents an affective strategy employed by LGBTQ+ listeners of Swift who situate the song within ordinary experiences of coming out, queer longing and 'unrequited love' (Kircher, 2020). However, the authors highlight the apparent tension between these queer affective intensities which are ultimately commodified and monetised as a cultural form.

In the final chapter of the collection Briony A. Carlin presents a moving and contemplative autoethnographic account of her own experiences of working on a paint-by-numbers of a landscape painting by Paul Cézanne (which also graces our front cover) during 2020. Like Waugh, she reflects on this as a "time when my physical, social and creative worlds were constrained by pandemic lockdowns" (Carlin 2023, xx). Yet rather than finding solace and calm in a podcast, she finds it in a particular method of painting. Carlin's identifies this process as a form of autoethnographic writing which merges with 'a more-than-human apparatus, one that works simultaneously as an instrument of making knowledge, and artefact of unreliable knowledge 'making'. She delineates the act of painting-by-numbers using feminist, posthuman, and new materialist theories by enigmatically and disruptively considering both via her own ontological perceptions about nature and art. It is here that 'memory, affect, anxiety, time, frustration, boredom, imagination, intuition and other historically marginalised non-hegemonic forms of knowing in academia' are folded into one another. In Carlin's work, the banal process of painting by numbers informs ontological and epistemological ways of dispersing and unlocking new possibilities for slow and assiduous research. In turn, this can point towards unforeseen, discrete and subtle forms of knowledge-making and ways of disrupting knowledge which are always 'there, then and everywhere'.

References

Barad, K. (2007) *Meeting the universe halfway*. Durham: Duke University Press.

Baym, N.K. (2010), *Personal connections in the digital age*. Cambridge: Polity Press.

Beetz, J., and Schwab, V. (2018) 'Conditions and relations of (re) production in Marxism and Discourse Studies', *Critical Discourse Studies* 15(4), pp. 338–350.

Berlant, L. (2011) *Cruel Optimism*. Durham: Duke University Press.

Bollas, C. (1987) *The shadow of the object: Psychoanalysis of the Unthought Known*. London: Free Association Books.

Bollas, C. (2009) *The evocative object world*. London: Routledge.

Bourdieu, P. (2003) 'Symbolic violence', in R. Célestin, E.F. DalMolin, and I. De Courtivron, (eds.) *Beyond French feminisms: debates on women, culture and politics in France 1981–2001*. New York: Palgrave Macmillan. pp. 23–26.

Cornwall, R. (1997) 'The Social Articulation of Desire', In A. Gluckman, and B. Reed, (eds), *Homo Economics: Capitalism, Community, and Lesbian and Gay Life*, London: Routledge, 89–122.

Foucault, M. (2019) *Discourse and truth and parresia*. Chicago: University of Chicago Press.

Fuchs, C. and Mosco, V. (2015) *Marx and the political economy of the media*. Leiden: Brill.

Gramsci, A. (2000) *The Gramsci reader: selected writings, 1916–1935*. New York: New York University Press.

Hall, C., Jones, K. and Thomson, P. (2010) 'Snapshots, illustrations and portraits: looking again at presenting research findings', in P. Thomson, and J. Sefton-Green (eds.) *Researching creative learning: methods and issues*. London: Routledge, pp. 126–145.

Hill, S. (2017) 'Exploring Disabled Girls' Self-representational Practices Online', *Girlhood Studies* 10(2), pp. 114–130. https://doi.org/10.3167/ghs.2017.100209.

Kircher, M. M. (2020, July 29). Taylor Swift's songs can be as gay as you want them to be. Vulture. https://www.vulture.com/2020/07/taylor-swifts-songs-can-be-as-gay-you-wantthem-to-be.html.

Longstaff, G. (2019) "Bodies that splutter'–theorizing jouissance in bareback and chemsex porn', *Porn Studies* 6(1), pp. 74–86.

Longstaff, G. (2020) 'Detached desires'-resituating pornographic and celebrity persona online', *Persona Studies* 6(1), pp. 9–11.

Marsh, D. and Tant. T. (1999) *Marxism and social science*. Chicago: University of Illinois Press.

Mason, R., Galani, A., Lloyd, K., and Sayner, J. (2018) 'Experiencing mixed emotions in the museum: Empathy, affect, and memory in visitors' responses to histories of migration", in L. Smith, M. Wetherell, and G. Campbell (eds.). *Emotion, affective practices, and the past in the present*. London: Routledge, pp. 124–148.

Mouffe, C. (2014) 'Democratic politics and conflict: An agonistic approach'. *Política Común* 9, pp. 17–29.

Muñoz, J-E. (2009) *Cruising utopia: The then and there of queer futurity.* New York and London: New York University Press.

Shotter, J. (2014) 'Agential realism, social constructionism, and our living relations to our surroundings: Sensing similarities rather than seeing patterns', *Theory & Psychology* 24(3), pp. 305–325.

Sikka, T. (2018) *Climate technology, gender, and justice: The standpoint of the vulnerable.* New York: Springer.

Sikka, T. (2021) 'Personalised nutrition: studies in the biogenetics of race and food', *Social Identities* 27(3), pp. 359–376.

Somerville, E. (2022) "Dozens of universities ignore easing of Covid mask rules". *The Telegraph*, 12 March 2022.

Thomson, P. and Hall, C. (2016) *Place-based methods for researching schools.* London: Bloomsbury Publishing.

Tragaki, D. (2020) 'Acoustemologies of rebetiko love songs', in F. Riedel, and J. Torvinen (eds.) *Music as atmosphere: collective feelings and affective sounds.* London: Routledge. pp. 184–201.

Turkle, S. (ed.) (2007) *Evocative objects: things we think with.* Cambridge, MA: The MIT Press.

Walls, S. (2012) *Examining Male Service Work: Gendered and Sexualised Aesthetics.* Saarbrucken: Lambert Academic Publishing.

CHAPTER 1

'Pubs, Primark & Pasta-Making Machines': Social Class, the 'Covidiot' and Neoliberal Narratives of Consumer Practice

Steve Walls

1   Introduction

The centrality of consumption to the UK economy and the implications of consumer practice to well-being (and even survival) has never been more pronounced and tangible than through the lens (and extreme measures) of 'lockdown'. This chapter explores class-based narratives and practices during 'Lockdown 1.0' until the easing of restrictions and so-called 'freedom day' on 19th July 2021 in the UK. In this context, constructions of consumer habits/practices appear to oscillate along a neoliberal spectrum – reifying the restraint, sacrifice and adaptability of 'enterprising subjects' (du Gay, 1996) while also pathologizing and devaluing the stupidity, excess and immobility of classed 'others' (Bourdieu, 1986; Skeggs, 1997, 2004; Waquant, 2000; Haylett, 2001; Sayer, 2005, Jensen, 2012). As such, the UK lockdowns saw consumers framed simultaneously as adaptable, enterprising 'hero' consumers and risky, irresponsible deviants.

Political and media discourses surrounding consumption throughout the pandemic reveal socio-structural inequities that 'ordered' and categorised individual consumers and broader consumer groups according to class dynamics. These discourses highlight the often competing/contrasting constructions of worth, value and 'lack' tied to social class that have been documented elsewhere through media and representation (Tyler 2008; Tyler & Bennett, 2010; Raisborough, Frith & Klein, 2013; Nayak & Keehily, 2014). The active construction of 'responsible' citizen-consumers and the co-constitution of the 'covidiot' through media and government rhetoric showcase how neoliberal discursive regimes produce subjects of unequal worth (Reicher, 2020; Foster & Feldman, 2021). These regimes legitimised and sanctified the 'flexible' and 'mobile' (Adkins, 2002) consumer spaces and practices of the middle-classes (such as online wine-tasting, 'book to shop' and premium delivery services, restaurants and dining outside the home) while sanctioning and pathologizing those of the working/lower classes. In the latter case here, Pubs and budget fashion retailer Primark provide the focus of discussion as the media reinforced a neo-liberal politics of class disgust (Hancock, 2004; Skeggs, 2004; Lawler, 2005). The 'excessive', unregulated and selfish qualities of the working classes were actively produced as a form of contextualised 'poverty porn' (Jensen, 2014) through reporting of localised outbreaks of coronavirus cases linked to pubs, underground 'quarantine raves' and 'Covidiots' as contemporary 'folk devils' (Cohen, 1972).

The writing of this chapter was embedded within the 'disruption' of the UK lockdown context but also simultaneously highlights the 'disruptive' nature of consumption and consumers framed within antinomies of safety/risk, citizenship/hedonism, collective/individual. Situating the knowledge (Haraway, 1991) here also highlights the disruptive nature of my own personal experience of lockdown – as a 40 year-old male and 'clinically vulnerable' as defined by the UK government at the start of the pandemic. The capacity to conduct fieldwork or experience lockdown consumer behaviour held their own risks and my own research process had to adapt along the trajectory of other social research throughout the lockdown period – using media texts and limited colloquial experiential contexts where appropriate (like many, I quickly switched to predominantly online shopping for non-essential items, wherever possible). The resulting chapter is a critical reflection upon the ways in which media texts from various sources framed the often competing and contradictory discourses surrounding consumption, consumer practice and consumers themselves. Post-structural perspectives from theorists such as Foucault, (1977; 1978), Bourdieu (1986), Skeggs (1997; 2004; 2005) Adkins (2002) and Jensen (2012; 2014) inform the following discussion and serve to highlight the political economy of neo-liberal constructions of consumer culture and consumer-citizens within the UK pandemic context. The chapter is structured around loosely defined stages of the UK lockdown context between March 2020–July 2021. This schema does not deny the many complexities/intricacies of the lockdown context, but merely serves as a tool to facilitate analysis and provide some sense of the temporal and cultural journey through the pandemic within the UK. This journey reveals neoliberal discursive and regulatory mechanisms governing/producing consumers and their behaviour as either 'heroic' or pathological on the basis of social class dynamics.

Within this timeline, specific examples are drawn upon to illustrate the discursive production of asymmetric class relations – in particular, the characterisations of the worthwhile, 'mobile' middle-class consumer-citizen (Adkins, 2002; Skeggs, 2004) and the excessive, irresponsible, pathologized working-class 'other' (Bourdieu, 1986; Skeggs, 1997, 2004; Waquant, 2000; Haylett, 2001; Sayer, 2005, Jensen, 2012). Discussion below argues that the historical processes of 'othering' the working and lower classes can be neatly folded into a more recent stigmatised identity arising from the UK lockdown context – the 'covidiot'. These constructions are framed here through government rhetoric, public policy and media representations. Case study examples draw upon the notions of 'enterprising' consumerism, and citizen-consumer in the context of the 'Eat-Out-to-Help-Out' government initiative. Within this dynamic, we also have the service worker, 'fixed' in situ to facilitate the 'heroic' activity of the 'sovereign consumer' (du Gay, 1996) and suffer the 'hidden injuries of service work' (Walls, 2012). The second half of the chapter explores anxiety/ disgust over the clustering of coronavirus cases attributed to zones/sites associated with working class identities. These sites/spaces here include the anxiety surrounding alcohol consumption, the pub and the excessive shopping habits of the 'hordes' hitting budget retailer Primark once non-essential retail restrictions were lifted. All of the above examples highlight the ways neoliberal logic categorises individuals according to 'value' and how this intersects with notions of citizenship *through* consumption practices. Such mechanisms point towards the continuing materiality of inequality and privilege that frame narratives of consumer behaviour, morality and worth during the pandemic.

2   Enterprising Subjects, 'Hero-Consumers' and 'Consumer-Citizenship'

2.1   *The Enterprising 'Lockdown Subject'*

During the UK lockdowns we saw a raft of media reports highlighting the enterprising genius of local business and the efforts of consumers to support them. Shop windows converted into 'vending machines' for shoppers to select items from outside, that would be subsequently delivered to their homes, 'shopping bubble' appointments created to reduce social contact, voucher schemes developed to save local business until lockdown was lifted and online wine-tasting classes through platforms such as Zoom. These types of strategies are quite clearly demarcated as desirable, adaptable, enterprising activities of middle-class business owners and consumer-subjects. The ability to 'support' local business (and ultimately save the struggling economy) through spending money, reserves this form of citizenship for those who have the means to participate. Similarly, the capacity to support through buying vouchers to redeem later also pre-supposes a consumer that has disposable income to spare, or be realised at a later date, and does not need to feed/clothe the family in the immediate here and now. In contrast to the problematic nature of pub-drinking as we will see later in the chapter, by comparison, the phenomenon of 'at-home' drinking through online 'tasting' sessions was seen as entrepreneurial capitalism, playfulness and adaptability while providing a context for amusement, diversion and 'mobility' of middle-class subjects. By the very nature of the exclusivity of premium alcohol beverages (wine, gin, cocktail ingredients etc), the product itself remains heavily classed and generally quite expensive, thus excluding specific groups from participation. However, with the added dimension of knowledge acquisition here (through the 'tasting' online and stay-at-home mixology), middle-class consumer subjects are able to exhibit and accrue 'symbolic capital' (Bourdieu, 1986) as citizen-consumers supporting local business and also as 'enterprising selves' (du Gay, 1996), demonstrating their 'mobility'/flexibility (Adkins, 2002; Skeggs, 2004) in adapting to lockdown situations. This was clearly reflected in the characterisation and data shared by bastion of 'middle' England: department store *John Lewis*. According to the retailer, 'huge spikes' in product sales were recorded for cocktail ingredients (Tequila and cocktail liqueurs), exercise-equipment (weights, yoga and pilates 'gear') and pasta-making machines during the first lockdown (Poulter, 2020). All of this signals a sense of playfulness, novelty and enterprise attached to consumption for pleasure over necessity – something specific to those enjoying the benefits of well-paid, non-precarious work and the flexibility that increased spending power affords. John Vine, Buyer at Waitrose said 'With pubs and bars shut, we have seen the rise of the "have-a-go" bartender at home … [p]eople are shopping for more unusual ingredients to make that perfect drink for staying in' (ibid). Similarly, the UK lockdown saw a massive surge in coffee-machine sales (up by 412% to over £2bn in 2020) as the middle-class 'café-rati' became 'at-home-Baristas' (Thompson, 2020). These machines are generally expensive with online electrical goods retailer AO's three best-selling coffee-machines of 2020 having an average RRP of over £1299, £1085 and £629 (ibid). The 'at-home-barista' and the Waitrose shopper above show flexibility in circumnavigating limited access and product shortages through superior spending power. Purchasing expensive ingredients and equipment to 'make their own' lattes, pasta and cocktails at home highlights the privileged position and alternate experiences of lockdown structured by class. The middle-class domestic sphere in this context becomes the site through which neoliberal logic determines lockdown experience and capacity for maintaining consumer activity when products and services are heavily restricted. Such constructions reinforce and reflect the value attributed to the self-contained, stay-at-home barista, cocktail-maker, fitness enthusiast and resourceful culinary experimenter. When confronted with 'lack', 'excellent individuals' (du Gay, 1996) – those with material and cultural resources – find 'flexible' ways to adapt to avoid 'going without'. This flexible domestic-sphere and equally mobile consumer-subject provide the context through which social class contours experience of 'risk' and lockdown. Elsewhere, fellow middle-class icon Marks & Spencer introduced a 'Book and Shop' service to allow for the more orderly management of socially distanced shopping and provide a safer environment for their consumers, avoiding the risk, inconvenience and disruption that over-crowding and massive queues pose (Clark, 2020). The above representations and experiences stand in stark contrast to the negative portrayal and limited access to products/services of those who are less privileged. A case that can be further underlined when we consider supermarkets and online grocery shop-ping. In contrast to their more expensive competitors, budget supermarket chains Lidl and Aldi do not have online shopping services. During 2020 Aldi began trialling 'click and collect' as well as home delivery via Deliveroo, but only at a limited number of stores (Butler, 2021). The complete lack of option-ality determined by material inequalities, structures the consumer habits of those who can only afford to buy groceries at the likes of Lidl and Aldi. As such, these consumers cannot exhibit a 'flexible' or 'mobile' consumer subjectivity because they lack the material resources to do so and the service provision at that price point does not extend to digital platformisation.

2.2   The 'Consumer-Citizen' and 'Hero-Consumer'

Towards the end of the most severe lockdown period in terms of restrictions we see a massive shift in discourse, policy and public attitude that further entrenched the 'hidden injuries' (Sennett & Cobb, 1993) of class-based lock-down consumption. On May 10th, 2020, Government messaging adapted from 'stay home, protect the NHS, save lives' to the revised 'stay alert, control the virus, save lives'. A relatively small alteration in wordage but a monumental shift in terms of responsibility and agency. The propaganda here involves a subtle mechanism, but one which remains heavily politicised. The notion of 'control' – that individuals 'control' the virus through what they do, how they behave and their own practices, as opposed to government responsibility to protect citizens from a virus that thrives upon social contact and the inevi-table death toll of an open society with relatively densely populated areas. These 'densely populated areas' include our cityscapes, supermarkets and shopping malls – places designed to attract and operate with large numbers of people confined in relatively small streets, buildings, and retail outlets. Around a month later, on June 15th, non-essential shops reopened and a week later on June 23rd, Prime Minister Boris Johnson announced the relaxation of restrictions and 2m social distancing rule. Drivers behind the change in pub-lic health policy and subsequent lifting of lockdown measures included calls to 'restart' the economy and growing 'lockdown fatigue'. It is at this point in the UK lockdown where the illusion of 'control' over the virus further integrates neo-liberal logic. Self-regulating, 'responsible' subjects and 'hero' consumers (Binkley, 2003) will save the economy and ultimately the lives of fellow citizens through returning to the high streets while observing appropriate hygiene and social -distancing measures. In an attempt to boost the national economy, Government policy sought to promote the heroic citizen-consumer narrative through the 'Eat-Out-to-Help-Out' initiative (EOHO). The policy was heralded as welcome relief for restaurants, pubs, cafes and bars across the UK. The scheme allowed customers to receive a 50% discount (subsidised by the UK government) on food or non-alcoholic drinks to eat-in, up to a maximum of £10 per customer. The offer was available every Monday, Tuesday and Wednesday between 3rd and 31st August 2020 aiming to boost parts of the hospitality sector and encourage consumers to eat out. According to a House of Commons briefing paper the scheme included 78,116 participating outlets with a total amount of £840 million paid under the scheme – £340 million more than the forecast (Hutton, 2020). In total, this included over 160 million meals for a population clearly keen to take advantage of the discounted prices, enjoy some semblance of 'normality' and contribute to the 'collective effort' of supporting the British economy and struggling businesses. EOHO is a clear example of 'social capital': 'features of social organization, such as trust, norms, and networks, that can improve the efficiency of society by facilitating coordinated actions' (Putnam, et al 1993, p. 167, cited in Bjørnskov & Sønderskov, 2013, p. 1225) employed at the policy level. This maps closely with social class as networks of support are 'most present in communities that are already better off' (Felici, 2020). This enshrines notions of the idealised middle-class consumer-citizen – flexible, mobile, autonomous, ethical – within neoliberal lockdown logic. In this way, the middle-class is represented as more skilled than lower class groups at regulating themselves and rebuilding the economy in lieu of coronavirus. Parallels may be drawn here with how Jensen (2012) frames 'austerity chic' within the neoliberalising logic associated with the global recession 2009–10. Jensen argues that 'new thrift' discourses during periods of austerity allowed those with material resources and competence to transform everyday survival practices of those 'living on the breadline' into 'aesthetic pleasures and art-forms' (2012, p. 15). This kind of 'mobility' in relation to everyday praxis leads to a materialist privileging of those with resources, where consumer activities (such as EOHO) become a 'heroic' act and 'duty' rather than 'risky' self-indulgence.

Such practices tie-in to middle-class conspicuous consumption through respectable and valued forms of dining out in public, away from the domestic sphere, where the labour involved in food preparation, cooking and cleaning is displaced onto (mainly low-paid) service sector employees and middle-class patrons can be waited-on (... as heroes should be) by serving staff. This contrasts with the often pathologised representation and anxieties surrounding pubs and alcohol consumption at various points throughout the UK lockdowns that will be discussed in the next section. There are echoes here of Marxist Feminist traditions (i.e. Rowbotham, 1973) that point towards domestic labour provided by the wife in the home as fuelling the productive power of the husband outside in the capitalist economy. In this pandemic context, we can see the service labour of the hospitality staff as allowing the middle-class, work-from-home professional, to achieve some respite from the amalgamation of home and workplace within the domestic sphere. In this sense, the hospitality worker forced into the workplace, does not have the same choices (or indeed value) as the middle-class diner who chooses to eat out. Such dynamics highlight the 'hidden injuries of service work' in advanced consumer cultures (Walls, 2012), whereby service sector employees in retail and hospitality face power-asymmetries as part of customer service professions and under the logic of the 'sovereign consumer' (du Gay, 1996). These 'injuries' occur at the level of subjectivity where specific subject positions enjoy privilege over others and their interests, behaviours and practices given greater priority. However, as the above example indicates, such asymmetry can become a source of physical risk when increasing levels of social contact and potential exposure to Covid-19 are part of frontline service labour. A physical risk that is a 'choice' of the agentic middle-class consumer, but which is imposed upon those in low-paid service sector employment during the EOHO scheme. Consumer practices are inevitably class-based in the sense that material resources determine how much we can consume, how often and at what price point. Bourdieu (1986) goes even further to highlight the way these become inscribed upon the body through 'taste' and 'habitus'. However, these practices need to be enabled through the service provision of frontline workers and the EOHO scheme accentuates the privileging of respectable middle-class 'hero- consumers' above the safety or choice of service workers 'fixed' by the conditions of their employment. An imposition of privileging consumer over worker and prioritising pleasure over risk that is highlighted in the way that the EOHO scheme was conceived in the first place, positively received at its inception but later criticised for exacerbating the spread of coronavirus. Preliminary evidence even suggests that areas with a higher uptake of EOHO experienced a sharp rise in new Covid-19 infections a week after the scheme began, with between 8–17% of new cases attributed to the scheme, and these same 'higher uptake' areas also exhibited a decline in coronavirus infections a week after the scheme ended (Fetzer, 2020).

3   Pubs, Primark and 'Covidiots': Neoliberalism and Lockdown
       Regulation

3.1   *The 'Covidiot' as Contemporary 'Folk Devil'*

It is within the context of the transitional period above that we see a marked
shift in public discourse. We saw a rise in the numbers of those behaving
irresponsibly – referred to by some as 'covidiots' – contemporary 'folk devils'
(Cohen, 1972) emblematic of selfish, indulgent, 'risky', stupid and unregulated
individuals placing other's safety and national interest in jeopardy. These
covidiots gathered in large numbers and refused to observe 'common sense'
hygiene practices such as mask-wearing and reduced social contact. The tone
of Downing Street political briefings remained overwhelmingly supportive
of the British Public (often in direct contrast to what the data and statistics
were telling us about social interaction and virus spread at the time). However,
there was an increasing element of warning/threat creeping into the political
messaging ever since the easing of restrictions. Despite no longer being a legal
requirement (in England) to wear a face mask in public from the 19th of July,
Boris Johnson and other MPs (notably, newly-appointed health secretary Sajid
Javid and vaccines minister Nadhim Zahawi) all mentioned issues of 'responsibility', 'citizenship' and 'caution' in order to maintain a trajectory out of the
pandemic (Merrick, 2021). With 'opening-up' there was an inevitability of rise
in case numbers of coronavirus. However, this rise was politically framed as
somehow 'controllable' or potentially mitigated through responsible citizenship and self-regulatory consumption practices. The following sections serve
to illustrate how the representation of the 'covidiot' in two different contexts
across British media can be understood in relation to neoliberal class dynamics.

3.2   *The 'Drink' Problem*

One of the strongest connections between consumption and the spread of
coronavirus is the way in which alcohol consumption and the night-time
economy became demonised for spreading Covid-19. Elsewhere, research
has explored alcohol consumption during pandemic lockdowns and 'worries'
(Alpers et al, 2021; Callinan et al, 2021) as well as increasing forms of 'heavy
drinking' (Rossow et al 2021). As pubs re-opened they became the focus of
media and government scrutiny as the basis of creating coronavirus 'clusters'
(Speare-Cole, 2020; BBC News, 2020). These clusters were often cited in connection with fears over imposing localised lockdowns yet remained somehow
diametrically 'opposed' to the incentivised gathering indoors that the EOHO
scheme encouraged. Preston city council even launched a glibly titled 'don't
kill granny' campaign targeting the 'young' and supporting the granting of

increased local authority power to close pubs at the centre of coronavirus outbreaks (Sharman, 2020). Amidst a surge in coronavirus cases following easing
of lockdown and the EOHO scheme, the Prime Minister announced numerous
times that *pubs* would shut in order to keep schools open and on September
22nd 2021 his conservative government imposed a 10pm curfew on pubs as
late-night drinking was seen as too 'risky' with patrons becoming potentially
more inebriated, relaxed and ultimately failing to observe the regulations
over 'hands, space, face'. Connections between danger, risk, disease, hygiene
and the working-class can be tracked elsewhere throughout history (Brown,
2009; Siena, 2019). The polarity between the incentivised EOHO scheme and
the active naming of 'pubs' as 'risky', virus-spreading spaces can perhaps be
attached to similar anxieties concerning the classed and gendered stereotype of the 'lager lout' and longstanding 'moral panics' over the 'evils of drink'
(Jayne et al, 2011 cited in Thurnell-Read, 2013, para 5.1). Popularised during the
1980s and 1990s, the figure of the lager lout provided a social function in acting
as a 'conduit' for anxieties regarding the 'unbounded body, manifest through a
lack of control and, particularly vomiting in public ... read as symptomatic of
a wider lack of concern for social propriety' (Thurnell-Read, 2013, para 5.3). By
way of extension, the 'undisciplined' drunken body of the lager lout became an
easy target for public and government surveillance during the UK lockdown.
Regimes of regulation and 'discipline' (Foucault, 1977) such as the 10pm curfew or exclusion of alcoholic beverages from the EOHO scheme highlight the
very tangible nature of these perceptions of risk and 'risky' bodies. Yet alcohol
is not the determining feature of pathologisation here, it is the concern over
the excessive and abject working class drinking spaces/cultures. This is highlighted by Thurnell-Read (2013) through the obsessive depiction of:

> excesses of appetite evident in [the] night-time economy ... mounds of
> takeaway packets, scattered chips and dropped kebabs; an iconography
> that speaks of the lack of restraint ... men who have failed to control
> their body in passing out, vomiting or in being perpetrator or victim of
> alcohol-fuelled aggression.
>
> para 5.4–5.5

By contrast, the middle-class 'real-ale drinker' or the Hipster craft beer enthusiast are the source of alternative forms of denigration – based on self-contained
failure to regulate body shape, pretentious snobbery and generational contes-
tations over 'authenticity' within the middle-class itself (Thurnell-Read, 2013;
le Grand, 2020). All of these stereotypes may be connected to gendered alcohol consumption. However, the key difference is that 'danger' and 'risk' posed

by the undisciplined, uncontained and permeable body of the working-class 'lager lout' is especially pronounced as the basis for societal anxiety during Covid-19 lockdowns. As such, we can begin to understand the asymmetric distinctions between incentivised gathering from the EOHO scheme and the 'super-spreader' status that pubs and working-class drinkers seemingly accrued in government rhetoric, regulatory measures and media representation during the pandemic.

These practices indicate the ways in which consumer behaviour became a neoliberal political tool within the pandemic context. Rather than maintaining the same approach adopted at the start of the lockdown, the UK government shifted the burden of responsibility over to the public. Coronavirus rates had 'peaked and troughed' throughout the UK lockdowns. The reasons for increases in cases are multiple and complex. More transmissible variant 'Delta' (and later Omicron) exacerbate the situation. However, many national 'spikes' coincided with easing of restrictions across, settings, institutions and contexts. Politicians were quick to stress that should coronavirus cases begin to increase, that 'freedoms' would be curbed in a regressive move. So, we see the Prime Minister point out that he will not hesitate to close pubs in order to keep schools open, that irresponsible consumer behaviour will lead to further restrictions, and that consumers would be the cause of this rather than acknowledge the inevitability of upsurges in case numbers following increasing levels of social contact and often unclear government messaging. This line of argument also completely bypasses the fact that schools and universities were some of the worst spaces/settings in terms of coronavirus transmission rates once restrictions began to ease. Instead, specific 'bad choices' made by 'irresponsible others' were the target of regulatory sanction and disdain. Earlier discussion in the chapter has already highlighted how these 'bad choices' and irresponsibility are traditionally attributed to the lower classes.

The cultural implications of this type of neoliberalising discourse are severe. As mentioned above, the term 'covidiots' was coined fairly early-on in the pandemic. This label reflects the moral judgements imposed by commentators upon those who refuse to adhere to safety advice and regulations, whether through ignorance, nihilism or stupidity. This involves an oversimplified production of 'disciplined' (Foucault, 1977) responsible, self-regulating subjects on the one hand and those who cannot (or will not) conform on the other. The creation of this category suggests that Cohen's concept of 'folk devils' coined in the 1970s remains strong to this day. Pub 'Covidiots' in this case, are rule-breakers and risk-takers. They potentially place the lives of the vulnerable at risk and also fuel the spread of a virus, crippling communities, the country, and the world. 'Covidiots', characterised in relation to their ignorance and behavioural deviance, jeopardise the easing of lockdown restrictions and subsequently prevent the rest of society (or localised areas) from enjoying personal freedoms any sooner. In the UK, (and elsewhere as noted by Trottier, Huang & Gabdulhakov, 2021) the acts of the few, were seen as dominating the many, and responsible citizens were routinely encouraged to police the rule-breaking activities of others through 'sousveillance' strategies (Mann, Nolan & Wellman, 2003). The pub-going covidiot was a trope frequently seen across British media and used to illustrate the futility of attempts to regulate the unruly lower classes (Stafford, 2020; Davies, 2020; Speirs, 2021). The covidiot thus becomes a folk devil in the sense of providing a more contained and tangible target for which the public can focus their anger, anxiety and frustration during lockdown uncertainty and upheaval. However, the category of the 'covidiot' serves to unify and distance simultaneously while masking material social inequalities that determine the basis on which people either have motivation, or the means to conform to lockdown restrictions (Reicher, 2020; Foster & Feldman, 2021).

The pub represents an iconic site of working-class community life, sociability and leisure activity (Hey, 1986). The political and media discourse that seemingly targeted pubs as a primary 'risk' to easing of lockdown restrictions, highlights 'risk' as embedded in class dynamics and the 'dangerous', pathological working class other. The representation and tone adopted in much media reporting on pub 'covidiots' (while down-playing the role of other institutions and consumer spaces in causing surges in coronavirus transmission rates) reveals the asymmetric power relations in the lockdown consumer context. The fascination, anxiety and moralising discourse involved here connect with earlier debates surrounding 'chav scum' (Tyler, 2008; Nayak & Keehily, 2014) and 'poverty porn' in the 2010s (Jensen, 2014, Allen et al, 2017). This can be extended elsewhere within consumer markets during the UK pandemic context if we focus upon fashion retailer Primark.

3.3   *Primark and the 'Hordes'*

Away from the 'hospitality' sector, other sites of consumption and goods were also lauded as examples of working-class excess, cited as routinely problematic and the source of clustered cases that risked imposition of local lockdowns. Once restrictions were eased for non-essential retail, the media used budget fashion store Primark to secure 'poverty-porn' style 'money-shots' of shoppers queueing in meandering lines along high streets and shopping malls. In fact, after the second UK lockdown was lifted, Primark provided the basis of a series of concerns in the media as the next 'ground zero' for another wave of infection (Gamp, 2020). These representations highlight the 'imagined connections' between lower social class groups and 'moral laxity, greed and even criminality'

(Jensen, 2014: para 1:1). Connections that, according to Jensen provide a source of fascination, anxiety and voyeuristic pleasure as part of a broader 'politics of disgust' emanating from neoliberal 'commonsense' doxa – 'making the social world appear as self-evident and requiring no interpretation' (2014, para 1:2).

However, such excess was rarely attached to retailers favoured by the middle-classes such as M&S or John Lewis (the former who implemented their 'book to shop' service mentioned earlier to avoid the 'chaos' of overcrowding and queues). Instead, the media focused upon the 'hordes' of the dangerous working-class consumer-other, forming 'enormous' queues from 5am and the constant threat that their simultaneous excessive desperation and lack of self-regulation poses. We are routinely reminded by the UK media of the 'undisciplined' Primark shopper-mob – often described in terms of excess – 'hungry', 'frenzied', 'storming' and 'flooding'. (Rice, & Rodger, 2020; Pugh & Lynch, 2020). The latter here not entirely unlike the same negative representation and antagonistic othering of immigrants and racialised groups documented elsewhere (KhosraviNik, 2009; Strom & Alcock, 2017; Bates, 2023). The condemnation of the Primark shopper is explicit and relentless on social media with UK tabloid newspaper *The Mirror* highlighting twitter users' exasperation and disgust once the low-cost retailer reopened following lockdown:

> People are queueing up outside Primark in Oxford Street since early morning hours!! We might find a cure for the Covid but will we ever find a cure for people's stupidity?

> So, you've been in your house for three months and you risk catching coronavirus to go to Primark, I mean, is it worth it?
> POCHIN, 2020

The language and emotive tone here are citational devices that reinforce the stupidity, unworthiness and excess frequently attached to notions of the underclass (Murray, 1990), 'underserving poor' (Romano, 2017), or 'white trash' (Kohlemainen, 2017). We are thus confronted with how the characterisation of the Primark shopper reflects the reproduction of class stigma and struggles over the 'classification' of subjects in consumer culture (Bourdieu, 1986; Kohlemainen, 2017).

If we look beyond the individual consumer to the organisation itself, the business model of Primark does not show the same 'flexibility' or 'mobility' as other fashion brands aimed at middle-class shoppers. Despite the pandemic lockdowns, Primark did not develop an online strategy or digital platformisation. Refusing to adapt, the organisation can be seen as institutionally stagnant, as 'inflexible' as their target demographic. This also 'fixes' those who do not have the means to shop online as somehow 'stuck' in the past. Being able to shop online presupposes access to digital resources such as credit/debit cards and online banking. However, many of the least privileged tend to manage finances through 'hard' cash. UK website Moneyexpert reported in 2018 that a survey by consumer watchdog Which?, revealed that 75% of low income households relied heavily on cash with 41% of those surveyed 'concerned' over the shift towards cashless transactions (moneyexpert.com, 2018). As such, we again see the 'immobility' of the less privileged, forced to queue and 'flood' the 'bricks and mortar' outlets of Primark or Aldi as they lack the resources and opportunity to shop by any other means. As a fast-fashion retailer, Primark is also subject to the increasing disdain targeted towards organisations deemed as contributing to the climate crisis, damaging the environment, worker abuse through modern slave labour and exploiting labour forces in developing countries. From this standpoint those who are not forward-looking, stuck in the past, damaging the environment (immobile and inflexible) are constructed as 'lacking'. A lack in awareness, a lack in ability, a lack in morality. Citizen-consumers and ethical-consumers have some level of overlap here and we can see the intersections of how they are constructed through the inevitable 'othering' that relational forms of identity rely upon (Said, 1978; Foucault, 1978) through the condemnation of the twitter users above – that the Primark shoppers show 'stupidity' that can never be 'cured', or that their activity and choices lack worth/reason. As if queuing for a more 'worthy' establishment would somehow be excusable or acceptable. Here we can see the 'moral economy' (Sayer, 2003) in full flow as overcrowding, irresponsibility and consumerism collide into a heady mix – the selfish, 'covidiot' and 'unethical consumer' all bundled into a single target demographic. However, within this economy exist sites, spaces and facilitators of consumer activity that are equally farmed within the neoliberal logic of consumer culture and the lockdown context.

4   Conclusion

Although a more comprehensive examination of social factors and discourses surrounding the coronavirus pandemic is beyond the scope of this single chapter, we can perhaps, from the above discussion, begin to unpack how social class and consumption behaviour intersect with notions of value, danger/risk and morality in this context. A new terrain emerged with associated lifestyle practices and behaviours that were quickly integrated into a landscape of pre-existing 'exchange-value' mechanisms that both categorise and order human subjects. Through consumption we were encouraged to 'manage' the pandemic as contained, self-regulating and flexible 'citizen-subjects'.

If we acknowledge the points made by theorists (e.g. Strathern, 1992a, 1992b; Taylor, 1994; Cronin, 2000; Skeggs, 2005) that our selves are formed and produced through acts of choice-making and consumption, then in respect of the present volume, perhaps the pandemic did not only 'disrupt' knowledge in the sense of academia but in fact, disrupted the very source of subjectification in consumer culture – the ability to choose between shopping options, consumer goods and ultimately to conspicuously consume. Of course, this was never completely 'closed off'. As mentioned earlier, commerce adapted quickly to provide online services and e-tailers experienced increased volume in consumer traffic and sales. Such strategies are emblematic of the ideal 'enterprising' subject in consumer capitalism, whether that be the adaptable business-owner or the 'flexible/mobile' middle-class consumer-subject. However, for those groups excluded from these strategies, this may help to account for some of the clamour amidst the early stages of lifting restrictions to go shopping and eventually get back into the pubs and clubs despite potential risk to physical well-being posed by the coronavirus. However, the above discussion indicates that some consumers and industries were more 'disrupted' and 'disruptive' than others, and that the ability to navigate consumption throughout various lockdown contexts remains heavily politicised in terms of the logic of neoliberal selfhood, the choices that individual subjects have capacity to make, and the ways in which they may be interpreted and represented.

It may be the case that categorisations like the 'covidiot' and 'at-home-Barista' serve to mask social inequalities while also providing sites and mechanisms through which they are actually reinforced. As Goldthorpe (1996) and Skeggs (2004) point out – the ability to make rational choices is determined by class, whereby the 'middle-class utilize their choices most effectively, assuming that the working-classes have choices which they utilize less adequately (Skeggs, 2004, p. 139)'. What individuals consume, and their practices of consumption, are heavily enmeshed within the cultural politics of value and worth in neoliberal societies where the self is shrouded in the logic of capitalism and enterprise (du Gay, 1996). Power is exercised here through the attribution of morality to specific consumer lifestyles, behaviours and subjectivities and through pathologizing others (Bourdieu, 1986; Skeggs, 1997, 2004; Waquant, 2000; Haylett, 2001; Sayer, 2005, Jensen, 2012). Linking this back to the lockdown and the 'risky' consumer habits of 'covidiots', we can draw connections between social class and cultural value attached to privileged subject positions. Living in privatised spacious dwellings, with disposable income, enjoying access to gardens/outside areas and digital technology which facilitates online consumption, lockdowns reinforced class-based stratification within the UK pandemic context. Restrictions, associated policy directives and the examples from the discussion above highlight the material and ideological inequities framed through the construction of consumer practice as either 'heroic' or pathological. As shown, such definitions remain heavily determined through neoliberal social relations that oversimplify and condense wider social inequalities into 'good' or 'bad' choices and individual worth under the logic of capitalism.

References

Adkins, L. (2002) *Revisions: Gender and Sexuality in Late Modernity*. Buckingham, UK: Open University Press.

Allen, K., Tyler, I., and De Benedictis, S. (2017) "Thinking with 'White Dee': The Gender Politics of 'Austerity Porn'". *Sociological Research Online* 19(3), pp. 1–7.

Alpers, S.E., Skogen, J.C., Mæland, S., Pallesen, S., Kjetland Rabben, A., Lunde, L.H., and Fadnes, L.T. (2021) "Alcohol Consumption during a Pandemic Lockdown Period and Change in Alcohol Consumption Related to Worries and Pandemic Measures". *International Journal of Environmental Research and Public Health* 18(3), p. 1220.

Bates, D. (2023) "'This is Britain, Get a Grip": Race and Racism in Britain Today'. In G. Longstaff, T. Sikka and S. Walls (eds.) *Disrupted Knowledge: Scholarship in a Time of Change*. Leiden: Haymarket/Brill.

BBC NEWS (2020) 'Coronavirus: Pub cluster cases rise to 32 after FM warning', BBC News, 4 August, available at: https://www.bbc.co.uk/news/uk-scotland-53650214 (Accessed 10 August 2020).

Binkley, S. (2003) "The Seers of Menlo Park". *Journal of Consumer Culture*, 3(3), pp. 283–313.

Bjørnskov, C., and K.M. Sønderskov. (2013) "Is Social Capital a Good Concept?" *Social Indicators Research* 114(3), pp. 1225–242.

Bourdieu, P. (1986) *Distinction: A Social Critique of the Judgement of Taste*. London: Routledge.

Brown, K.M. (2009) *Foul Bodies: Cleanliness in Early America*. New Haven: Yale University Press.

Butler, S. (2021) 'Aldi and Lidl lose out as UK online grocery sales hit new heights', *The Guardian*, (2nd March, 2021), available at: https://www.theguardian.com/business/2021/mar/02/aldi-and-lidl-lose-out-as-uk-online-grocery-sales-hit-new-heights (Accessed 18 June 2022).

Callinan, S., Mojica-Perez, Y., Wright, C.J.C., Livingston, M., Kuntsche, S., Laslett, A., Room, R., and Kuntsche, E. (2021) "Purchasing, Consumption, Demographic and

Socioeconomic Variables Associated with Shifts in Alcohol Consumption during the COVID-19 Pandemic". *Drug and Alcohol Review* 40(2), pp. 183–91.

Clark, J. (2020) 'Lockdown: M&S rolls out shopping slot booking service to stop queuing chaos', CityAM, (Tuesday 3rd November, 2020) available at: https://www.cityam .com/marks-spencer-rolls-out-shopping-slot-booking-service-in-preparation-for -lockdown/ (Accessed 18 June 2022).

Cohen, S. (1972) *Folk Devils and Moral Panics: The Creation of the Mods and Rockers.* London: Routledge.

Cronin, A.M. (2000) 'Consumerism and "Compulsory Individuality": Women, Will & Potential' in S. Ahmed, J. Kilby, C. Lury, M. McNeil and B. Skeggs (eds.) *Transformations: Thinking Through Feminism.* London: Routledge.

Davies, I.G. (2020) 'Covitiot Pub: Council to shut Cwmbran's Castell-y-Bwch', *South Wales Argus*, 11th September, 2020, available at: https://www.southwalesargus .co.uk/news/18712887.cwmbran-pub-castell-y-bwch-shut-coronavirus-breaches/ (Accessed 18 June 2022).

Du Gay, P. (1996) *Consumption and Identity at Work.* London: Sage.

Felici M. (2020) *'Social capital and the response to Covid-19,' Bennett Institute for Public Policy.* University of Cambridge. Available at: https://www.bennettinstitute.cam .ac.uk/blog/social-capital-and-response-covid-19/ (Accessed 18 March 2020).

Fetzer, T. (2020) 'Subsidizing the spread of Covid19: Evidence from the UK's Eat-Out-to-Help-Out scheme', CAGE working paper no.517, Oct 29, 2020. University of Warwick.

Foster, R., and Feldman, M. (2021) "From 'Brexhaustion' to 'Covidiots': The UK United Kingdom and the Populist Future". *Journal of Contemporary European Research* 17(2), pp. 116–127.

Foucault, M. (1977) *Discipline and Punish: The Birth of the Modern Prison.* Trans. Alan Sheridan. Harmondsworth: Penguin.

Foucault, M. (1978) *The History of Sexuality Volume I: The Will to Knowledge.* Harmondsworth: Penguin.

Gamp, J. (2020) 'Here Comes Another Lockdown. Fears Primark Shoppers could Spark Third Covid wave as Bargain Hunters Flock to 24/7 stores and Queue for HOURS', *The Scottish Sun.* 5th December, 2020 available at https://www.thescottishsun .co.uk/news/6365901/coronavirus-primark-shoppers-queue-third-wave/ (Accessed 21 November 2021).

Goldthorpe, J.H. (1996) 'Class analysis and the re-orientation of class theory: the case of persisting differentials in educational attainment'. *British Journal of Sociology* 61, pp. 311–35.

Hancock, A.M. (2004) *The Politics of Disgust: The Public Identity of the Welfare Queen.* New York: New York University Press.

Haraway, D.J. (1991) *Simians, Cyborgs and Women: The Reinvention of Nature.* London: Free Association Press.

Haylett, C. (2001) 'Illegitimate Subjects?: Abject Whites, Neo-Liberal Modernisation and Middle Class Multiculturalism'. *Environment and Planning D: Society and Space.* 19(3), pp. 351–70.

Hey, V. (1986) *Patriarchy and Pub Culture.* London: Tavistock.

Hutton, G. (2020) 'Eat Out to Help Out Scheme', Briefing Paper No. CBP 8978, House of Commons Library. 22 December, 2020.

Jayne, M., Valentine, G., and Hollowway, S.J. (2011) *Alcohol, Drinking, Drunkeness: (Dis) ordely Spaces.* Farnham: Ashgate.

Jensen, T. (2012) 'Tough Love in Tough Times' *Studies in the Maternal,* 4(2), pp. 1–26.

Jensen, T. (2014) "Welfare Commonsense, Poverty Porn and Doxosophy". *Sociological Research Online* 19(3), pp. 1–7.

KhosraviNik, M. (2009) "The Representation of Refugees, Asylum Seekers and Immigrants in British Newspapers, during the Balkan Conflict (1999) and the British General Election (2005)". *Discourse & Society* 20(4), pp. 477–98.

Kolehmainen, M. (2017) "The Material Politics of Stereotyping White Trash: Flexible Class-making". *The Sociological Review* 65(2), pp. 251–66.

Lawler, S. (2005) "Disgusted Subjects: The Making of Middle-class Identities". *The Sociological Review* 53(3), pp. 429–46.

Le Grand, E. (2020) "Representing the Middle-class 'hipster': Emerging Modes of Distinction, Generational Oppositions and Gentrification". *European Journal of Cultural Studies* 23(2), pp. 184–200.

Mann, S., Nolan, J., and Wellman, B. (2003) 'Sousveillance: Inventing and Using Wearable Computing Devices for Data Collection in Surveillance Environments' *Surveillance & Society* Vol.1(3), pp. 331–35.

Merrick, J. (2021) 'Fears over 19 July have triggered a marked shift in tone from ministers on face masks', inews (11th July, 2021) available at: https://inews.co.uk/news /politics/fears-over-19–july-triggered-shift-ministers-face-masks-1097815 (Accessed 18 June 2022).

Moneyexpert (2018), available at: https://www.moneyexpert.com/news/move-cashl ess-society-will-disproportionately-affect-pensioners-poorest-uk/ (Accessed 20 June 2022).

Murray, C. (1990) "The British Underclass". *The Public Interest* 99.99, pp. 4–28.

Nayak, A., and Keehily, M.J. (2014) "'Chavs, Chavettes and Pramface Girls": Teenage Mothers, Marginalised Young Men and the Management of Stigma', *Journal of Youth Studies* 17(10), pp. 1330–45.

Pochin, C. (2020) 'Primark shoppers shamed for queueing urge others to "be kind" instead of judging'., *The Mirror,* (16th June 2020), available at: https://www.mirror .co.uk/news/uk-news/primark-shoppers-shamed-queuing-urge-22194173 (Accessed 20 June 2022).

Poutler, S. (2020) 'From work-out gear to tequila, John Lewis's lockdown must-haves as middle-class consumers settle into leisurely spending habits', MailOnline (6th May, 2020) available at: https://www.dailymail.co.uk/news/article-8294737/John-Lewiss -lockdown-haves-middle-class-consumers-settle-leisurely-spending-habits.html (Accessed 18 June 2022).

Pugh, R., and Lynch, T. (2020) 'Primark shoppers in a frenzy over new "designer" £30 winter coat', *Leicestershire Live*, (8th October, 2020), available at: https://www.leice stermercury.co.uk/whats-on/shopping/primark-shoppers-frenzy-over-new-4588 377 (Accessed 20 June 2022).

Putnam, R.D., Leonardi, R., and Nanetti, R.Y. (1993), *Making democracy work: Civic Traditions in Modern Italy*. Princeton, New Jersey: Princeton University Press.

Raisbrorough, J., Frith, H., and Klein, O. (2013) 'Media and Class-Making: What Lessons are Learnt when a Celebrity Chav Dies?', *Sociology* 47(2), pp. 251–66.

Reicher, S. (2020) "Don't Blame 'selfish Covidiots'. Blame the British Government". *The Guardian* (Online) (2nd September, 2020) available at: https://www.theguardian .com/commentisfree/2020/sep/02/selfish-covidiots-blame-british-government- greek (Accessed 18 June 2022).

Rice, E.M., and Rodger, J. (2020) 'Primark shoppers sent into a frenzy over £9 product as stores reopen', *Birmingham Live*, (1st July, 2020) available at: https://www.birming hammail.co.uk/motoring/primark-shoppers-sent-frenzy-over-18523721 (Accessed 20 June 2022).

Romano, S. (2017) *Moralising Poverty: The 'Undeserving Poor' in the Public Gaze*. London: Routledge.

Rossow, I., Bye, E.K., Synnøve Moan, I., Kilian, C. and Bramness, J.G. (2021) "Changes in Alcohol Consumption during the COVID-19 Pandemic-Small Change in Total Consumption, but Increase in Proportion of Heavy Drinkers". *International Journal of Environmental Research and Public Health* 18(8), p. 4231.

Rowbotham, S. (1973) *Women's Consciousness, Man's World*. London: Pelican books.

Said, E. (1978) *Orientalism*. New York: Vintage Books.

Sayer, A. (2003) '(De)commodification, consumer culture, and moral economy', *Environment and Planning D: Society and Space* 21(3), pp. 341–57.

Sayer, A. (2005) *The Moral Significance of Class*. Cambridge: Cambridge University Press.

Sennett, R., and Cobb, J. (1993) *The Hidden Injuries of Class*. New York: Norton.

Sharman, L. (2020) 'Preston deploys "don't kill Granny slogan" after new local lock- down imposed', *The Mirror*, 8 Aug. available at: https://www.mirror.co.uk/news/uk -news/preston-dont-kill-granny-slogan-22488913 (Accessed 8 August 2020).

Siena, K.P. (2019) *Rotten Bodies: Class and Contagion in Eighteenth Century Britain*. New Haven: yale University Press.

Skeggs, B. (1997) *Formations of Class and Gender: Becoming Respectable*. London: Sage.

Skeggs, B. (2004) *Class, Self, Culture*. London: Routledge.

Skeggs, B. (2005) 'The Making of Class and Gender through Visualizing Moral Subject Formation', *Sociology* 39(5), pp. 965–82.

Speare-Cole, R. (2020) 'Coronavirus Cluster Linked to Staffordshire Pub after 19 People test Positive', *Evening Standard*, 2nd August, 2020. Available at: https://www.stand ard.co.uk/news/uk/coronavirus-cluster-staffordshire-put-a4514726.html (Accessed 10 August 2020).

Speirs, K. (2021) 'Cops bust Covidiot party at Scots pub as revellers fined', *Daily Record*, 20th March 2021, available at: https://www.dailyrecord.co.uk/news/scottish-news/cops-bust-covidiot-party-scots-23765664 (Accessed 18 June 2022).

Stafford, I. (2020) 'Bus passenger slams lager-drinking 'covidiots' gathering outside Edinburgh pub in worst-hit area', *Edinburgh Live*, (12th November, 2020), available at: https://www.edinburghlive.co.uk/news/edinburgh-news/bus-passenger-slams-lager-drinking-19271713 (Accessed 18 June 2022).

Strathern, M. (1992a) *After Nature: English Kinship in the Late Twentieth Century*. Cambridge: Cambridge University Press.

Strathern, M. (1992b) 'Qualified Value: The Perspective of Gift Exchange' in C. Humphrey, and S.C. Jones (eds.) *Barter, Exchange & Value: An Anthropological Approach*. Cambridge: Cambridge University Press.

Strom, M and Alcock, E. (2017). "Floods, Waves, and Surges: The Representation of Latin Immigrant Children in the United States Mainstream Media". *Critical Discourse Studies* 14(4), pp. 440–57.

Taylor, C. (1994) 'The Politics of Recognition' in D.T. Goldberg (ed.) *Multiculturalism: A Critical Reader*. Oxford: Blackwell.

Thompson, S.J. (2020) "Lockdown sees Coffee Machine sales soar as Scots become a nation of 'at-home-Baristas'", *Daily Record*, 17th November, 2020, available at: https://www.dailyrecord.co.uk/lifestyle/food-drink/best-coffee-machine-black -friday-23025741 (Accessed 18 June 2022).

Thurnell-Read, T. (2013) '"Yobs" and "Snobs": Embodying Drink and the Problematic Male Body', *Sociological Research Online* 18(2), pp. 1–10.

Trottier, D., Huang, Q., and Gabdulhakov, R. (2021) "Covidiots as Global Acceleration of Local Surveillance Practices". *Surveillance & Society* 19(1), pp. 109–13.

Tyler, I. (2008) '"Chav Mum Chav Scum": Class Disgust in Contemporary Britain', *Feminist Media Studies* 8(1), pp. 17–34.

Tyler, I., and Bennett, B. (2010) '"Celebrity Chav": Fame, Femininity & Social Class', *European Journal of Cultural Studies* 13(3), pp. 375–93.

Walls, S. (2012) *Examining Male Service Work: Gendered and Sexualised Aesthetics*. Saarbrucken: Lambert Academic Publishing.

Waquant, L. (2000) 'Durkheim and Bourdieu: the common plinth and its cracks' in B. Fowler (ed.) *Reading Bourdieu on Society and Culture*. Oxford: Blackwell.

CHAPTER 2

'A Huge Social Experiment': Postdigital Social Connectivity under Lockdown Conditions

Deborah Chambers

1   Introduction

During government-imposed lockdowns in response to the Covid 19 pandemic, stay-at-home restrictions mounted barriers against physically present informal socializing. This led to isolation and loneliness for many. In response, online householders relied on the internet as a lifeline to sustain social connections with loved ones, family, and friends (Ofcom, 2021). Remarkably, social connections increased during lockdown periods, albeit digitally enabled. With dramatic speed, multiple digital technologies including video communications apps such as Zoom were vitalized to support remote connections from home whether work-based, learning-based or for socializing. This intensified domestic engagement with digital devices during lockdowns raises questions about the social implications of a shift from mobile sociality to immobile trans-domestic sociality. As Jandrić states "The Covid-19 pandemic has brought a huge social experiment into our homes, streets, cities, countries, and globally" (Jandrić, 2020, p. 236). How peoples' hyper-dependence on home-based digital technology reconfigured social connectivity is the theme of this chapter.

During the March 2020 lockdown, the number of people in the UK reporting high levels of anxiety escalated. Nearly half (49.6%) of people were suffering high anxiety – a significant increase from the last quarter of 2019 (WHO, 2020a). The term 'social distancing' was widely used by governments and news media during the pandemic. But some weeks into the crisis, experts called for a change of terminology, arguing that 'social distancing' was ambiguous and unproductive (Abel and McQueen, 2020; Sørensen et al., 2021; van den Broucke, 2020). By March 2020, when the virus was declared a pandemic, the World Health Organization (WHO) advised citizens to practice 'physical distancing', not 'social distancing' in response to lockdown measures (WHO, 2020b). The organization argued that the issue was about 'distant socialization' rather than 'social distancing'. A change in terminology was requested by WHO to urge people to find new ways to sustain social ties while geographically separated, by staying in touch with older friends and family using digital technology (Sørensen 2020; Hart 2020). Yet the term 'social distancing' was lodged in public consciousness and continued to be used by governments and the media.

To gauge how online householders managed and adapted to distant socialization during lockdowns in 2020 and 2021, this chapter offers an analysis of householders' engagement with digital technologies with a focus on video communication such as Zoom. Data from the UK communications regulator Ofcom, the Office of National Statistics (ONS) and sources such as the World Health Organisation (WHO) are utilised to identify patterns of internet use among UK adults during these periods. Qualitative studies of online social connectivity during lockdowns in the UK, Canada, and Australia are also drawn on to provide further insights. The concepts of 'domestic mediatization' and the 'postdigital' are employed as heuristic tools to assess the implications of changes in trans-domestic social connectivity during these episodes.

This chapter shows that reliance on digital media to maintain contact with family and friends rose and intensified during lockdown, albeit unevenly. Yet the amplified use of digital technologies by householders was less dramatic than expected. Data on levels of use confirm that most UK homes were already well resourced, enabling householders to migrate swiftly to full online communication. Nevertheless, the chapter argues that lockdown conditions triggered new communicative norms and protocols resulting from a surge in the domestic use of relatively new video call communication software. By activating visually oriented screen-based communication, described here as a form of scopic mediation, video call technology enabled online householders to 'get a visual' on remote family, friends and community members. Video call technology became a highly cherished resource that fostered a sense of *shared time*. Forcing householders to renegotiate relations between public and private space, these domestic adjustments reconfigured meanings of 'home' as an immobile yet dynamic timespace (see Barad, 2007). This now pervasive, trans-domestic social connectivity marks a new phase of domestic mediatization, one that can be called 'postdigital'. This phase heralds a new mode of *sociality*.

2 The Postdigital Phase of Domestic Mediatization

A heightened household dependence on digital communication technologies during lockdowns evokes the concept of mediatization. From a social-constructionist perspective, mediatization theory foregrounds the social dynamics that underpin the interconnections between media and wider social cultural transformations. The term describes how media and communication technologies mediate the construction of daily social life (Couldry and Hepp, 2013). The emphasis, here, is not on the impact of media and communication technologies over other domains, as a one-way effect. Rather, by taking mediatization as a broad approach, the term guides a conceptual analysis of forms, velocities, and intensities of digital media proliferation in particular social contexts (Couldry and Hepp, 2013). Mediatization can also take account of the role of outside actors in driving mediatizing trends and tendencies such as corporate capitalism and government led Covid 19 lockdown measures. The concept of *domestic mediatization* is introduced to examine how domestic and mobile media and communication technologies are entangled in home life as spatially and temporally organized social practices (Chambers, 2016: 2023).

Domestic mediatization addresses how householders negotiate and mediate macro-scale mediatizing processes within their daily habits and routines (Chambers, 2016; 2023). These processes comprise a sequence of distinctive temporal phases during which the integration of media and communication into home life changes pace. For example, from the early twentieth century, the *analogue phase* of radio, television and landline phones was followed by a *hybrid phase* which marked the coexistence of analogue and digital equipment and co-located media-oriented activities. This phase was followed by a *digital phase* characterized by escalating media convergences. Each phase steered discernable modes of adoption, use, affective registers and domestic encounters. And as key feature of this domestic mediatization process, each phase was surpassed at an accelerated pace. Each pinpointed householders' changing navigation of media and communication technologies and how these technologies fundamentally reshaped domestic space, household dynamics and affective relations. However, the lockdown measures introduced in 2020 and 2021 by governments in response to the pandemic can be approached as a new and distinctive *postdigital phase* of domestic mediatization.

Centering on the augmented potential of digitally enabled interpersonal communication, the 'postdigital' condition refers to the mutable quality of human interchanges with digital devices and software. The postdigital paradigm has been advanced in the digital humanities (Berry and Dieter, 2015), the social sciences (Taffel, 2016), technology studies (Pepperell & Punt, 2000), and education (Jandrić et al., 2018). The breach between the digital and the postdigital condition is "neither absolute nor synchronous, but an asynchronous process, occurring at different speeds and over different periods and being culturally diverse in each affected area" (Cramer, 2013, p. 1). This shift has evolved from a unique interruption or interlude to an ongoing condition (Abblitt, 2019; Cramer, 2015). The postdigital condition comprises, then, a sequence of subtle changes that nonetheless constitutes an epoch: a period after which the digital has become the hegemonic paradigm (Abblitt, 2019). As such, the term 'postdigital' describes the current state of technology yet denies that this shift represents a 'digital revolution' (Jandrić 2020).

The dawn of the current postdigital phase was when mundane yet vital social interactions were *driven* online. However, March 2020 – when the WHO declared Covid 19 a pandemic – can be taken as a defining moment. That is to say, the postdigital phase is characterised by the heightened and pervasive reliance on digital technologies resulting from lockdown measures. Now filled with devices and software, internet connected homes which form the main focus of this chapter, transform digitally literate householders' social networks and modify their social relationships and identities. As such, the term 'postdigital' signifies an incongruity. It comprises gradual, almost undetectable yet accelerated and intensified engagement with media and communication technologies. During pandemic-led lockdowns, these subtle changes surfaced. They were encountered as an albeit predictable *rupture* in the sense that they were viewed by online householders as abrupt and disrupting but also as inevitable. Yet they were almost immediately rendered routine. Triggered by the suddenness of lockdown measures, this new domestically steered but immobile social connectivity comprises a postdigital 'rupture and continuation event' (Jandrić et al., 2018, p. 895), one that has transformed human communication in a manner likely to change our future lives. Online householders coped with this rupture precisely because a digital phase had *preceded* lockdown. The following analysis explores how they did so.

3   Household Internet Use during Lockdown Conditions

To assess how internet connected householders engaged with digital technologies to manage lockdown conditions, this section draws on Ofcom and related data. Stay-at-home conditions disrupted daily life in varied ways depending on the demands of telework, online schooling and householders' needs for social connectedness. The unsettling effects of incorporeal digital exchanges during lockdowns were exacerbated by low levels of digital literacy among the unemployed and also socially disadvantaged and low-income groups (Ofcom, 2021). Those with disabilities struggled to maintain social connections or receive support (Goggin and Ellis, 2020) as did many older people (Burke, 2020; Wilson et al., 2020). Less tech savvy older populations and rural dwellers with inadequate or no internet connectivity were also rendered vulnerable by the shift of interpersonal communication online.

For those deprived of digital resources and digital literacy – among older citizens and low-income or unemployed households – the postdigital is as ongoing calamity that makes everyday life precarious. Survey evidence from the UK, US and Germany also showed that during March and April 2020, working women in all three countries disproportionately carried the burden of combining work online from home with primary responsibility for home schooling of children and most of the housework (Craig, 2020; Nash and Churchill, 2020). While the drivers of postdigital communication technologies claim to overcome issues of access, equity, inclusion, and participation in 'digital cultures', they perpetuate stark social asymmetries. These social disparities and vulnerabilities form a reprehensible backdrop to the following analysis of how *online* householders used digital media and communications technologies to negotiate distant socialization during lockdowns.

The number of physical contacts among adults in the UK decreased over time across all ages during lockdowns, generating an acute need for online entertainment, news, and social connectedness (ONS 2021). The indispensability of internet access for UK householders during these conditions is confirmed by Ofcom (2021). By the end of 2020, the vast majority of households were already digitally mediatized spaces with around 94% of UK homes having internet access, rising from about 89% in 2019. Most people who accessed the internet in the UK were proficient users with almost three-quarters of adults having ten or more years' experience online. Internet use was lower among those in low socio-economic groups and among older people. In March 2020, 6% of households had no access to the internet. Older people, less likely to have home internet access, comprised 18% of people over the age of 64. Among those in low socio-economic groups, 11% had no internet access (Ofcom 2021). Consequently, the digitally excluded were the most negatively affected by lockdown measures. Inequalities of race within low-socioeconomic status households, not addressed in Ofcom's data, are also significant dimensions of digital exclusion that require further research attention (see Nguyen et al., 2021).

Obstacles also confronted internet users who either lacked the skills or confidence to benefit from internet services or had no access to suitable devices. Five per cent of UK adults admitted to a lack of confidence in using the mobile phone. At 9%, this comprised people over the age of 64 and at 10%, those in lower socio-economic households. Ofcom confirms that the smartphone seems to be the 'base layer' of connectivity. Among those in lower socio-economic groups for example, 42% of users depended on this device to access the internet because they lacked a computer. This posed enormous difficulties in completing online forms or conducting work online from home.

In March and November 2020 lockdowns and the first quarter of 2021, UK online citizens spent an average of just over three and a half hours a day on smartphones, tablets, and computers. These devices were used not only for home-based working and education but also for watching films, gaming, shopping, and information about the pandemic as well as for video calling to socialize with friends and family. Yet the increased amount of time spent online was modest: only 9 minutes more than in 2019. For example, UK internet users spent 03.37 hours online. This was less online time than those in the US at 04.38 hours but significantly more than householders in France 02.20 hours, Germany 02.06 hours and Spain 03.06 hours (Ofcom, 2021). Despite online householders' heavy dependence on digital services during lockdowns, then, this modest increase reveals an already pervasive use of the internet before lockdown measures were introduced.

3.1   *Types of Platforms Accessed by Householders*

OfCom found that the five US-based tech giants – Google, Apple, Facebook[1], Amazon, and Microsoft (known as GAFAM) – strengthened their already omnipotent property ranking during lockdown. In the Spring 2020 lockdown, UK adult internet users spent an average 52 minutes a day on Google- and Facebook-owned sites and apps, an increase of only around half an hour compared to September 2019. In September 2020, almost all UK adult internet users were using Google- and Facebook-owned sites and apps as the two most favoured online properties. They were accessed by 99% and 97% of online adults respectively. UK internet users devoted an average of 52 minutes a day on Google-owned sites and 29 minutes on Facebook-owned sites. Across its e-commerce sites Amazon was used by 92% of online adults. Microsoft sites also extended their reach to 90%. Adult users in the UK also spent 20 minutes per day on TikTok, owned by Bytedance Inc. Although Netflix and Spotify were not in the top ten properties in terms of reach per visitor, they came fourth and fifth, respectively in 2020, with people using Netflix on connected TV sets. In other countries, the most visited properties in 2020 were Google sites. GAFAM further consolidated their dominance during lockdown periods by adding new services or affordances. For instance, within the Apple app suite, Apple Music gained the widest reach since September 2019, when Apple released a web version27 of its Music service. Facebook introduced cross-app messaging and

---

1   During Covid 19 lockdown conditions in 2021, Facebook changed its corporate name to 'Meta' while retaining the name 'Facebook' for its social media platform. However, the term 'Facebook' is used here to reflect the company name both during the lockdown periods referred to, and the time of writing.

calling across Instagram and Messenger in September 2020, enabling users to use either app to send messages and join video calls. Instagram added new features to Instagram Live in April 2021 to enable hosts to create an audio-only stream.

Regarding social media use, Facebook and Instagram continued to be the most widely used platforms during lockdown. Older online adults tended to have a Facebook profile, at 82% of those aged 16 and over (Ofcom, 2021). For younger social media users, aged 16–24, Instagram, Snapchat and Tiktok were favoured. In the US, women were 1.58 times more likely than men to access social media during lockdowns to share information about the pandemic (Campos-Castillo and Laestadius, 2020). Similarly, in the US, women were 2.17 times more likely to rate the perceived importance of social connectedness more highly than men. This pattern corresponds with women's' higher rates of sharing information on social media (Lee et al, 2021). Within circuits of caregiving, it reflects the gendered obligations of keeping contact with relatives and friends as demanding and time-consuming forms of emotional and affective labour assumed mainly by women (Oksala, 2016; Strazdins and Broom, 2004). Research confirms that women's care burdens and health care inequalities have been exacerbated during the pandemic (Power, 2020; Ryan and Ayadi, 2020). And, although not the central focus here, intersectional studies of care ethics confirm that racialized difference shapes care practices (Hankivsky, 2014: Raghuram, 2019).

In terms of social video use, TikTok grew rapidly in popularity in 2020 but YouTube, owned by Google, continued to be used by nearly all UK internet users. Ofcom found that social video services offered significant benefits as a medium of entertainment and education for 97% of adult internet users during lockdown periods. By September 2020, YouTube and Facebook were the leading social video platforms in the UK, with both accessed by 95% of internet users. Together, these two platforms occupied most of users' time spent on social video (Ofcom, 2021, p. 6). Lockdown also affected types of social videos accessed. Not only was the unfolding crisis mediated by online news. Firmly tied to digital media and communications, householders witnessed comfy or energized visions of home on their screens: home makeovers, home gyms and fitness regimes, home baking, DIY and home crafts (Ofcom, 2021, p. 6). The most watched video in the UK in 2020 was a home fitness YouTube video. At the start of lockdown, 'self-care' titled videos rose by 215% and daily views of 'home workout' titled videos increased by 515%, highlighting concerns about weight (see Pausé and Taylor, 2021). Conversely, viewed videos about 'sourdough bread' also rose by 458%, signifying revitalizations of traditional middle-class domesticities.

Framed by cultural, historical, economic, and social preconceptions about 'home', these venerated images invoked middle class ideals of home as a safe and comfortable retreat rather than a space of confinement and oppression (Chambers, 2020). However, social video was also accessed in 2020 for sharing content on key social and political concerns, with an emphasis on the #BlackLivesMatter movement, climate change and anti-lockdown protests. By facilitating user-generated content, this medium was also a site for self-expression with 31% of adults and 40% of 13 to 17 year olds posting video content.

While social video services offered benefits, these platforms also carried insensitive and harmful content. Video-sharing was used during lockdowns to sanction violence or hate crime. When surveyed, 70% of users said they had viewed or encountered harmful content in the last three months. This was followed closely by fake or misleading images or videos during a period when householders relied heavily on accurate information about the coronavirus. YouTube deleted 34.8 million videos in 2020 of which 1% were uploaded in the UK. Likewise, TikTok deleted 194 million videos. On both platforms, child safety was the main reason for these removals (Ofcom, 2021). For householders, contending with harmful and misleading content is now a *normalized* dimension of this new, postdigital encounter. Moreover, an intensive reliance on 'Big Five' tech giants corresponds with a narrowing of knowledge, decision-making, and reasoning as facets of the postdigital condition (Jandrić 2020). Designed to maximize time spent online, these platforms' algorithms function by displaying excessive and misleading content.

4   The Upsurge in Video Calling during Lockdowns

From the start of the pandemic, householders showed a willingness to try new screen-based technologies. Video calling technology such as Zoom, Skype, MS Teams, WhatsApp, House Party, and Facebook Messenger acquired enormous significance for sustaining remote social connections. Video call technology was increasingly favoured, not only for business purposes and education but also for creating a sense of belonging and closeness with significant others. These platforms sustained embodied modes of *trans-domestic* digital communication (Chambers, 2019). They enabled householders to overcome the lack of physical closeness during lockdowns and to cope with isolation by keeping in touch, remotely, with friends and family.

In the UK, video calls accelerated as a key means of connecting with family and friends as well as for work purposes, exemplified by the rise in Zoom calls from a few thousand in early 2020 to more than 13 million by May of that year (Ofcom, 2021, p. 3). Platforms such as Microsoft Teams, used mainly for work and education, also increased in use. Noted for their uncomplicated interfaces, the apparent simplicity and intuitiveness of these software platforms ensured their speedy absorption into domestic media habits. This technology enables people to essentially *see and hear* one another on the screen. Nevertheless, the crisis-driven context of adoption meant that this new trans-domestic communication was encountered as a dramatic 'techno-social' rupture (see Chayko, 2019).

Taking Zoom as an example, the service was used during lockdowns by schools, universities, banks, government agencies, the UK Parliament and healthcare professionals for telemedicine. As one of the fastest growing apps, Zoom expanded its reach in the UK in the Spring 2020 lockdown but dropped after an early peak in April 2020 and then stabilized into steady growth during the rest of the year (Zoom Company Data 2021). The visual and audio features of Zoom were valued qualities that ensured its appeal. Initially designed for work purposes, informal use among family and friends was then tagged on to Zoom, as a design after-thought. Its power to reproduce a sense of community online was then realized. While the mobile phone is an intrinsically *personalised* tool for curating and sharing individualized material and sustaining interpersonal contact, Zoom is a *social* tool for collective connectivity. The technology enabled householders to sustain familial, friendship and community ties, and convey affection, care and emotional support to vulnerable individuals.

Although adoption of video call technology was a new skill for many householders during lockdown, it was used in multiple ways (Greenwood-Hickman et al., 2021). For example, Zoom not only supported digitally enabled coffee mornings, dinner parties, choirs, religious services, dance parties, happy hours, pub quizzes, virtual craft nights, cooking classes, fitness classes and workouts, virtual karaoke, musical jam sessions, plays and music gigs. With social gatherings banned during lockdown, this technology served to capture emotionally charged celebratory or commemorate events. Weddings, birthday parties, Bar and Bat Mitzvah services and, tragically, funerals were events conducted virtually, as were protesting organizations such as Black Lives Matter (Li, 2020).

5   The Visual Qualities of Video Calling

Qualitative studies of distant socializing among family and friend communication during lockdowns confirms the significance of video call software's visual features. In Canada, Heshmat and Neustaedter (2021) found that participants' mediated communication with close family and friends increased, particularly with vulnerable elderly parents. Significantly, some contacts became closer with more frequent communication. Highlighting the importance of atmosphere and physicality, Heshmat and Neustaedter confirm video call users' strong desire to feel as if they were in the same physical space as their remote relatives or friends. This sense of *shared space* and *shared atmospheres* was facilitated by activities such as game playing and shared meals or drinks. Likewise, qualitative research in Australia by Watson et al. (2021) underlines the value of 'getting a visual' on someone during lockdowns when compared to other technologies. Users valued the multisensory and affective mode of engagement afforded by video call apps' visual features. However, this technology fell short of creating the atmosphere gained when people are co-present.

With a rise in frequency of contact and length of time spent during contact, Watson and colleagues (2021) found that their participants made more effort to connect with distant family and friends during lockdown by phone or video calls. Compared to other devices or apps, the visual features of video call technology enabled users to achieve a greater sense of closeness and connection for both daily routines and special events. As Watson et al. (2021) explain, "This was not only a matter of 'checking up' on the well-being of friends and relatives deemed more or less vulnerable, but of a sort of extended conversation or exchange that is more like 'checking in'" (2021, p. 146). Participants checked in with people they had been close to previously such as parents or children and with those they were concerned about in relation to the pandemic such as relatives working abroad or in essential services.

Video calling technology also supported intergenerational ties during lockdown. For example, the frequency of grandchild-initiated contact with grandparents increased due to concerns with Covid-19 (McDarby et al., 2020). In a study of older adults in the UK, Wilson et al (2020) found that the use of online visual communication tools such as Skype, Zoom, and Facetime were viewed positively by those aged 65+ who considered these platforms to be the closest to a face-to-face communication encounter. For a significant minority, these virtual connections were easier to tailor to their lives than co-present meetings. Grandparents helping with grandchildren's remote learning provided unique occasions for shared time. Age UK, a leading charity dedicated to helping people in later life, stressed the importance of video calling: " Keeping in touch with family, friends and other loved ones makes us feel connected and helps with feelings of loneliness".[2] The charity now provides computer

---

2   Age UK: 'Keeping in Touch Using a Video Call' https://www.ageuk.org.uk/information-adv ice/work-learning/technology-internet/video-calling/ (accessed 03/10/2021).

training and instructions for older people on how to download and use video call technology. During lockdown, 28,000 people in the UK signed up to "adopt a grandparent" by holding video calls with care home residents in a scheme run by CHD Living.[3]

However, older people who felt lonely or isolated during lockdowns were less likely to use video call technology (Wilson et al., 2020). Even among regular users, older individuals encountered difficulties with physical functioning, self-efficacy, fear, and those values and attitudes toward communication and networking shaped by social capital (Bourdieu, 1986). These negative attitudes and aversions lowered older people's uses of video calling and social media, whether they suffered from social isolation or not. Similarly, a qualitative study of coping strategies among older people during the pandemic by Greenwood-Hickman et al. (2021) found that while virtual media enabled older people to stay connected to friends and family, they were thought to be less rewarding than in-person interactions.

Examples of Zoom's ability to bring community members together have been documented in the news as well academic studies. For instance, Wired. co.uk recounted a women's committee at East London Mosque that relied on video calls during lockdown (Turk, 2020). To relieve the social isolation felt by women in their community, particularly in relation to Ramadan, the group hosted monthly Zoom events in Bengali and English. The number who joined the first event, from across the UK as well as London, surpassed the limit of a hundred participants. The hosts had to upgrade their plan. Initial challenges in using Zoom highlight the scopic properties of this medium: the risk of men attempting to join these women-only sessions or being caught on camera in the background of a woman's video. The hosts alerted participants who wear headscarves to keep them on during calls. Indicating the success of these Zoom meetings, organizers planned to continue such events after lockdown. Likewise, Zoom events made online church services accessible to those unable to attend weekly including those with disabilities and even overseas missionaries.

Such examples of how householders navigated home-based communication technologies resonate with pre-pandemic studies of digital connections between distant family and friends, as Watson et al. (2021) point out (see Madianou, 2016; Baldassar, 2016; Cabalquinto, 2017; Zhao, 2019). Filipino migrant workers in Australia favour video calls over audio calls to capture a

---

3 CHD Living, digitises 'adopt a grandparent' campaign and calls for 'virtual volunteers' amidst coronavirus crisis, https://www.chdliving.co.uk/journal/m-care-at-home/chd-living-digitises-adopt-a-grandparent-campaign/ (accessed 03/10/2021).

sense of ambient proximity with family members and conjure a sense of 'home' (Cabalquinto, 2017). Video calls are used for conversations and family rituals such as playing instruments together, helping with children's homework or cooking and eating a meal together in real time. Likewise, Madianou (2016) refers to the 'ambient co-presence' achieved by transnational families to cement intergenerational ties. Capable of fostering and sustaining embodied modes of trans-domestic communication, video calling then also flourished during lockdown circumstances.

6   The Frictions of Video Calling as a Scopic Medium

While video call software such as Zoom facilitates remote social connectedness and sustains affective qualities by imitating co-presence, research during lockdowns confirmed that this technology is invariably judged as a supplement to co-present communication. Heshmat and Neustaedter (2021) found that online householders in Canada favoured large group video calls of four people or more, rather than paired connections, to feel connected with wider groups of friends and family. When coordinating large group video calls, householders tried to reproduce a *sense* of being together in-person, but this demanding online interaction waned after a while. Large group video calls can become raucous and difficult to negotiate, making participants feel disconnected and depersonalized. And the software was not thought to be 'mobile device friendly'. Some found it difficult to see participants' video feed on their phone's screen. Since those using tablets or laptops could see everyone more easily, this generated inequities. For transnational contacts, it was also a challenge to synchronize call times across time zones. Some of Heshmat and Neustaedter's participants experienced a sense of digital overload or media saturation and eventually 'cleansed' themselves of the technology, in a manner reminiscent of the 'demediatization' described by Kopecka-Piech (2019).

Since large group video calls are relatively new digital encounters, the procedures and protocols about turn-taking and the types of activities to engage in during a call have not yet been settled. Video calls often felt 'confusing' and 'chaotic' (Heshmat and Neustaedter, 2021). Householders often struggled with distractions, conversational challenges, and unpredictable device competencies. Transmission delay in video calls also affects users' perceptions during conversations. The higher the digital delays, the more that talkers are perceived to be inattentive or unfocused. A related challenge is the uncomfortableness of silences in video calls (Schoenenberg et al., 2014). Householders often found it difficult to turn-take during conversations and either exaggerated or missed social cues. Processing non-verbal cues such as tone and pitch of voice, facial expressions, and body language requires concerted attention. These complications lowered users' concentration and control over exchanges. Erica Dhawan (2021) employs the term 'digital body language' to foreground the elusiveness of cues that, in co-present communication, convey mood, level of engagement and meaning.

These negative encounters draw attention to the frictions embedded in the interface, reminding us that video calling ruptures the apparent simplicity and spontaneity of co-present interpersonal communication. Further examples of this postdigital dissonance include temporary screen freezing, voice echoes, partial views of faces, temporary loss of audio connection and repeated 'you're on mute' prompts. For instance, Hardley and Richardson's participants in Australia experienced video sessions as "really intensive and draining" (2020, p. 1). During periods of stress and crisis, this visual mode of online communication can generate feelings of information overload and fatigue (Farooq et al 2020) Among those using video calling for both work and personal connections, the technology can cause context slippage. Heshmat and Neustaedter (2021) found that swift changes between work and personal time, in the home, are often distracting. Their participants complained that they missed the mental transition from work to personal life enabled by commute times. Mobile phone connectivity can generate a sense of being permanently 'on call' for work (Duxbury and Smart, 2011). Likewise, video calling can generate feelings of being permanently 'on duty'. This can cause tensions between work and family time, leading to stress and burnout. These challenges highlight relations of power and the ethical dimensions of these new digital communication systems. Unsurprisingly, many users of video calling apps have reported greater depression, loneliness, and stress resulting from increased screen time and reduced physical activity (Meyer et al., 2020).

What becomes apparent is that the communication technologies most widely used by householders during lockdowns depended predominantly on screen-based interfaces. From video sharing platforms such as Instagram to video communication apps such as Zoom, these technologies rely on scopic mediation involving the visual attentiveness of observing, staring, or viewing. Scopic media are screen-based tools that enable users to observe and project images and sounds including representations of users and other content to bring the physically distant into virtual proximity (Tschaepe, 2020). In a study of the use of video conferencing technology for educational purposes during lockdown periods, Tschaepe (2020) offers a critical postdigital evaluation of the swift transition to this scopic media by differentiating between 'viewing' and 'seeing'. Given that most exchanges during lockdowns occurred on screen, the term 'scopic mediation' becomes relevant. 'Seeing' is the experience of being in the same physical space as another person whereas 'viewing' is a scopic projection via screen-based technology. This differentiation provides clues about the implications of using this visual technology to support trans-domestic affiliations.

With family, loved ones, friends or community members appearing to be in the same physical space, the visual mode of video call exchanges generates a powerful sense of an embodied encounter. Merging home, technology and sociality, this habitual dependence on scopic mediation by householders during lockdown gave rise to new domestic encounters and new modes of distant socialization that fostered sociability, intimacy, and a sense of sharing time. The corporeal senses involved in video calls foregrounds the feeling of physicality and embodiment offered by technology's visual affordances, enabling users to generate a shared atmosphere and space. But the sense of 'viewing' in a video call requires much more effort than the 'seeing' encounter of a co-present chat. When a Zoom meeting is used for socializing and bonding, it is not simply a form of passive spectatorship implied by Tschaepe's notion of 'viewing'. This digitally steered 'viewing' involves a dynamic screen performance. Yet the scopic interaction necessitated by the technology renders the encounter more stressful. During lockdowns, remote family members often felt like an observer than a participant (Heshmat and Neustaedter 2021).

With the acute awareness of being watched as if on a stage, pressure is placed on video callers to engage performatively to overcome the numerous disruptions involved. The visual element of seeing one's own face while communicating, as if in a mirror and sometimes as a ghostly apparition, can be an unsettling experience as can the multiple boxes of faces we observe during calls with more than two people. Users are blasted with images of faces and nonverbal cues. Feeling under constant scrutiny when eyeballed by others or watching ourselves can generate a hyper-vigilance, 'zoom fatigue' and 'nonverbal overload' (Bailenson, 2021). More women than men tend to be concerned about their appearances and how they will be judged during video calls (Wang and Roubidoux, 2020). Modes of self-presentation such as how we are dressed, what the food and drink we consume while 'on screen', whether and how we use the blurring facility, where we place the screen device, the topic of conversation and upper bodily movement all become vital issues, exemplified by the adoption of a ring light to cast an even glow over the video caller. A Twitter account called 'Room Rater' for "Rating bookcases, backsplashes and hostage videos since April, 2020" posts and ranks the home backdrops of broadcast video callers, making snap judgments about each one.[4]

Such performative challenges involved in this scopic encounter highlight not only the digital (dis)functionalities of visual technology but also what Petriglieri (2020) calls the 'double deprivation' of sensing *too little* during the encounter while having to process *too much* information:

> Our minds are tricked into the idea of being together when our bodies feel we're not. Dissonance is exhausting. It's easier being in each other's presence, or in each other's absence, than in the constant presence of each other's absence.
>
> PETRIGLIERI, 2020, p. 641

This double deprivation harbours habituated dissonances that characterize the postdigital condition – a condition that reconfigures relations between home, technology and sociality.

When video calling, conscious decisions must also be made about camera orientation, the positioning of the self and home surroundings to either preserve a sense of personal privacy or enact a home-specific mode of networked corporeality (Brubaker et al., 2012; Hardley and Richardson 2020). These vital decisions gradually become habitual and normalized but they are not unconscious. The connotations of domestic space and background settings in video calls, and how these spatial signals frame enactments of intimacy and sociality at a distance require further study (Watson et al., 2021). Although earlier research on the use of video call technology focused on connections made between paired homes or individuals, it revealed that video calls can be privacy intrusive, causing family and friends to feel uncomfortable when having to share background events occurring in their home while online (Kirk et al., 2010). This is illustrated by the example of the East London Mosque Zoom meetings above, when men intruded on women-only sessions or were caught on screen in a woman's video.

This postdigital encounter accentuates further social disparities. With group video calls favoured over one-to-one calls during lockdowns, the marginalization of women's voices becomes an issue. We know that the length of a person's speaking time generally determines who has the most influence and approval. When women are outnumbered in a group meeting, men are inclined to occupy the longest floor time: women speak about two-thirds of

---

4   See Room Rater at https://twitter.com/ratemyskyperoom (accessed 03/10/2021).

the time that men do. And men tend to communicate with a power dynamic while women tend towards a rapport dynamic (Mendelberg et al., 2014). In the context of video calling and audio lag, which leads to overlapping speech during a meeting, the negative effects of these gendered communicative styles are likely to be amplified and inhibit women's conversational exchanges (Wang and Roubidoux, 2020). Moreover, women are socialized to rely more heavily than men on nonverbal cues such as smiling, nodding in agreement, using facial expressions, and gesticulating to gauge when to speak and judge feedback. The visual cues required to sense others' expressions about whether the speaker's idea is valued can be confusing in video calls and can hamper an individual's contribution to dialogue. Exactly how these dynamics play out as gendered restraints in the context of socializing or care giving via video calls from home, is not yet known.

Attention has also been drawn to Zoom's face-detection algorithm which manifests as a racial bias. Zoom allegedly erases faces with dark pigmentation when a virtual background is applied on the app. One user noticed that Zoom appeared to be removing the head of Black people when using a virtual background. This does not happen to people with a lighter skin pigmentation (Hern, 2020; see Noble, 2018). Coupled with the burden placed on women during lockdowns to take responsibility for maintaining social contacts as part of affective kin-work, emerging evidence suggests that this non-proximate scopic encounter may exacerbate *socially* and *algorithmically* coded racial and gender disparities. However, whether the voices of racialized individuals are drowned out or ignored in video calls has yet to be studied.

While 'getting a visual' on remote family, friends and community networks is highly valued, the discordant qualities of this video call encounter involve obstacles that characterize the postdigital condition. Yet this scopic mediation has been rendered routine. It is now tolerated as the 'new normal'. When compared to the 'seeing' of physically proximate interactions, this trans-domestic screen-based encounter alters our sense of self embodiment. It involves a renegotiation of domestic space as *digital space*. Overall, the intensified scopic mediation enfolded in video calls engenders new post digital practices and routines that comprise a radical social and cultural shift, one that has spawned a domestically mediatized postdigital culture.

7   Conclusion

This chapter has shown that although dependence on digital media intensified during lockdown, the increased use of digital technologies was not as dramatic as anticipated. Despite the hurdles of physical distancing, informal social contact between friends and family surged during lockdown periods. However, Ofcom data on use levels of digital technology by householders to maintain distant socialization during lockdown confirms the pre-pandemic pervasiveness of digital technology. Already equipped to tackle the transition to digital connectivity from home, most online householders coped resourcefully during the crisis – by means that strengthened the dominance of the tech giants. It also boosted the video-conferencing platform, Zoom Video Communications Inc. which rapidly gained a market share in the category. A widespread use of video calling technology for work and educational purposes during lockdowns emboldened householders to try out this relatively novel technology in order to maintain social connections.

The analysis pinpoints, then, four defining components of the postdigital phase of domestic mediatization. The first is the *preceding* but strengthened velocity, intensification and habituation of digitally sustained social relations woven into the fabric of home life. As such, the postdigital transition represents not so much a 'revolution' but a "thickening intensity and complexity of the digital in our personal, social and professional lives" (Abblitt, 2019, p. 98). Given the preceding digital mediatization of home, the digitally enabled navigation of lockdown conditions entailed a surprisingly smooth transition yet was encountered as a techno-social fracture.

Second, screen-based solutions to domestic immobility offered by video calling technology fostered newly embodied trans-domestic connectivity among householders. This visual medium enabled geographically separated families, friends and communities to reconnect and foster new ambiances of *shared screen time* with distant others. These new encounters transformed home into a dynamic timespace. Heralding a new, postdigital mode of interpersonal communication that extends and alters modes of social connectivity, this digital transition changed our perceptions of space and altered the bounded nature of home and households.

Third, a surge in the domestic adoption of video call software during lockdown significantly altered the codes of behaviour that conventionally guide sociable communication. As a visually oriented screen-based communication mode, video calling can be described as a form of scopic mediation that reconfigures sociality. Although we now assume that our interpersonal interactions will be sustained predominantly via digital screens, the gendered, generational and racial power dynamics and social disparities involved are, as yet, undetermined.

The postdigital phase concerns, then, a fourth dimension: the profoundly disruptive features of lockdown-driven sociality. Despite claims that digital solutions are inevitably beneficial, emerging evidence suggests that this intensified dependence on digital communication has amplified existing gendered, racial, and generational digital inequalities. The digital divide, algorithmic coding biases, digital literacy asymmetries and gender disparities in conversational dynamics highlight the precarities embodied in the postdigital condition. While GAFAM companies such as Facebook and Microsoft's pledge to remove bias from their technologies (see Thilmany, 2021), their extraordinary proprietary power and lack of accountability have unknown consequences. This 'huge social experiment' in the heart of our homes is not just a crisis-driven interlude. The signs suggest that this new digital mode of social connectivity, triggered by lockdown conditions, is the prelude to a more permanent reconfiguration of relations between 'home', technology, and everyday life.

References

Abblitt, S. (2019) 'A postdigital paradigm in literary studies', *Higher Education Research and Development*. 38:1, pp. 97–109.

Abel T., and McQueen D. (2020) 'The COVID-19 pandemic calls for spatial distancing and social closeness: not for social distancing!', *International Journal of Public Health* DOI: 10.1007/s00038-020-01366-7.

Bailenson, J. (2021) 'Non-verbal overload: A theoretical argument for the causes of Zoom fatigue', *Technology, Mind and Behavior*, 2(1) DOI: 10.1037/tmb0000030.

Baldassar L. (2016) 'De-demonizing distance in mobile family lives: co-presence, care circulation and polymedia as vibrant matter', *Global Networks* 16(2), pp. 145–163.

Barad, K. (2007) *Meeting the Universe Halfway: Quantum Physics and the Entanglement of Matter and Meaning*. Durham, NC: Duke University Press.

Berry, D., and Dieter, M. (2015). *Postdigital Aesthetics: Art, Computation and Design.* London: Palgrave.

Bourdieu, P. (1986) 'The Forms of Capital', in Richardson, John G., ed., *Handbook of Theory and Research for the Sociology of Education*. New York: Greenwood, pp. 241–258.

Brubaker, J.R.,Venolia, G., and Tang, J.C. (2012) 'Focusing on shared experiences: moving beyond the camera in video communication', In *Proceedings of the Designing Interactive Systems Conference*. DIS '12, ACM Press, 96.

Burke, S. (2020), 'Stronger together? Intergenerational connection and Covid-19', *Quality in Ageing and Older Adults*. 21(4) pp. 253–259.

Cabalquinto E.C. (2017) Home on the move: negotiating differential domesticity in family life at a distance. *Media, Culture & Society* 40(6), pp. 795–816.

Campos-Castillo C, Laestadius L. (2020) 'Racial and Ethnic Digital Divides in Posting COVID-19 Content on Social Media Among US Adults: Secondary Survey Analysis', *Journal of Medical Internet Research*, 22(7): e20472 doi: 10.2196/20472.

Chambers, D. (2016) *Changing Media, Homes and Households*. London: Routledge.

Chambers, D. (2019) 'Emerging temporalities in the multiscreen home', *Media, Culture & Society*, 1–19 doi.org/10.1177/0163443719867851.

Chambers, D. (2020) *Cultural Ideals of Home: The Social Dynamics of Domestic Space*. London: Routledge.

Chambers, D. (2023 forthcoming) 'Mediatization's Tensions and Tendencies: The Context of Homes, Householders and Emerging Screen Interactions' in K. Kopecka-Piech and G. Bolin (eds) *Contemporary Challenges in Mediatisation Research*, London: Routledge.

Chayko, M. (2019) Digital Technology, Social Media, and Techno-Social Life, in Ritzer, G., and Murphy, W.W. (eds.) *The Wiley Blackwell Companion to Sociology*. Second Edition, London: John Wiley, pp. 377–397.

Couldry, N., and Hepp, A. (2013) 'Conceptualizing Mediatization: Contexts, Traditions, Arguments'. *Communication Theory*, 23(3), 191–202.

Craig, L. (2020) 'Coronavirus, domestic labour and care: Gendered roles locked down', *Journal of Sociology,* 56(4) pp. 684–692.

Cramer, F. (2013) 'Post-digital aesthetics. Lemagazine', May 1. available at: http://lem agazine.jeudepaume.org/2013/05/florian-cramer-post-digital-aesthetics/ (accessed 6/10/2020).

Cramer F. (2015) 'What Is 'Post-digital'?', in: Berry D.M., and Dieter M. (eds.) *Postdigital Aesthetics*. Palgrave Macmillan, London, pp. 12–26.

Dhawan, E. (2021) *Digital Body Language: How to Build Trust and Connection, No Matter the Distance*. London: HarperCollins.

Duxbury, L., and Smart, R. (2011) The "Myth of Separate Worlds": An Exploration of How Mobile Technology Has Redefined Work-Life Balance. In Kaiser, S. Ringlstetter, M.J., and Eikhof D.R. et al. (eds.) *Creating Balance?* Berlin: Springer, pp. 269–284.

Farooq, A., Laato, S., Islam, A.K.M.N. (2020) 'Impact of online information on self-isolation intention during the COVID-19 Pandemic: Cross-Sectional Study', *Journal of Medical Internet Research*, 22, e19128.

Goggin, G. and Ellis, K. (2020) 'Disability, communication, and life itself in the COVID-19 pandemic', *Health Sociology Review*, 29:2, pp. 168–176.

Greenwood-Hickman M.A, Dahlquist J, Cooper J, et al. (2021) '"They're going to Zoom it": A qualitative investigation of impacts and coping strategies during the COVID-19 pandemic among older adults', *Front Public Health*. DOI: 10.3389/fpubh.2021.679976.

Hankivsky, O. (2014) 'Rethinking Care Ethics: On the Promise and Potential of an Intersectional Analysis', *American Political Science Review,* 108(2), pp. 252–264.

Hardley, J., and Richardson, I. (2020) 'Digital placemaking and networked corporeality: Embodied mobile media practices in domestic space during Covid-19', *Convergence* 27(3), pp. 625–636.

Hart, M. (2020) WHO Changes 'Social Distancing' to 'Physical Distancing' [Internet]. *Nerdist*; 2020, available at: https://nerdist.com/article/socialdistancing-changed -physical-distancing/ (accessed 28/07/2021).

Hern, A. (2020) 'Twitter apologises for 'racist' image-cropping algorithm', September 2020, available at: https://www.theguardian.com/technology/2020/sep/21/twitter -apologises-for-racist-image-cropping-algorithm. (accessed 28/07/2021).

Heshmat, Y., and Neustaedter, C. (2021) 'Family and Friend Communication over Distance in Canada During the COVID-19 Pandemic', *Designing Interactive Systems Conference*, DIS '21m, pp. 1–14, https://doi.org/10.1145/3461778.3462022.

Jandrić, P., Knox, J., Besley, T., Ryberg, Y., Suoranta, J., and Hayes, S. (2018) 'Postdigital science and education', *Educational Philosophy and Theory*, 50(10) pp. 893–899.

Jandrić, P. (2020) 'Postdigital Research in the Time of Covid-19', *Postdigital Science and Education*, 2, pp. 233–238 https://doi.org/10.1007/s42438-020-00113-8.

Kirk, D.S., Sellen, A., and Cao, X. (2010) 'Home video communication: mediating "closeness"', In Proceedings of the 2010 ACM conference on Computer supported cooperative work – CSCW '10, Savannah, Georgia: ACM Press, 135. doi.org/10.1145 /1718918.1718945.

Kopecka-Piech, K. (2019) *Mediatization of Physical Activity: Media Saturation and Technologies*. London: Lexington books.

Lee, Y.-C., Malcein, L.A., Kim, S.C. (2021) 'Information and Communications Technology (ICT) Usage during COVID-19: Motivating Factors and Implications', *International Journal of Environmental. Research on Public Health* 18(7), 3571, DOI: 10.3390/ijerph18073571. PMID: 33808218; PMCID: PMC8036312.

Li, S. (May 7, 2020). 'Zoom funerals are a new reality in quarantine. This is what they're like', *Insider*, available at: https://www.insider.com/zoom-funerals-are-a-new-real ity-during-the-coronavirus-pandemic-2020-5 (accessed 18/07/2020).

Madianou, M. (2016) 'Ambient co-presence: transnational family practices in polymedia environments', *Global Networks* 16(2), pp. 183–201.

McDarby, M., J. C. H., and Carpenter, B.C. (2020) 'Frequency of contact and explanations for increased contact between grandchildren and their grandparents during the COVID-19 pandemic', *Journal of Intergenerational Relationships*, 19(2), pp. 163–178, https://doi.org/10.1080/15350770.2020.1852995.

Mendelberg T., Karpowitz C.F., Oliphant J.B. (2014) 'Gender inequality in deliberation: unpacking the black box of interaction', *Perspectives on Politics*, 12, pp. 18–44.

Meyer, J., McDowell, C., Lansing, J., Brower, C., Smith, L., Tully, M., Herring, M. (2020) Changes in physical activity and sedentary behavior in response to COVID-19 and their associations with mental health in 3052 US adults, *International Journal of*

Environmental Research on Public Health, 17, 6469. https://doi.org/10.3390/ijerph1
7186469.

Nash, M. and Churchill, B. (2020) 'Caring during COVID-19: A gendered analysis of
Australian university responses to managing remote working and caring responsibilities', *Feminist Frontiers,* 27(5) pp. 833–846.

Nguyen, M.H., Hargittai, E., and Marler, W. (2021) Digital inequality in communication
during a time of physical distancing: The case of COVID-19, *Computers in Human
Behaviour 120,* 106717, pp. 1–10.

Noble, S.U. (2018) *Algorithms of Oppression.* New York: New York University Press.

Ofcom (2021) *Online Nation,* available at: https://www.ofcom.org.uk/__data/assets
/pdf_file/0013/220414/online-nation-2021-report.pdf. (accessed 02/08/2021).

Oksala, J. (2016) 'Affective Labor and Feminist Politics', *Signs,* 41(2), pp. 281–303.

ONS (2021) 'A "new normal"? How people spent their time after the March 2020 coronavirus lockdown', Data and Analysis from Census 2021, *Online Time Use Survey,*
available at: https://www.ons.gov.uk/peoplepopulationandcommunity/healthan
dsocialcare/conditionsanddiseases/articles/anewnormalhowpeoplespenttheir
timeafterthemarch2020coronaviruslockdown/2 020-12-09 (accessed 27/07/2022).

Pausé, C., and Taylor S.R. (eds.) (2021) *The Routledge International Handbook of Fat
Studies.* London: Routledge.

Pepperell, P., and Punt, M. (2000) *The postdigital membrane: Imagination, technology
and desire.* Bristol, OR: Intellect Books.

Petriglieri, G. (2020) 'Musings on Zoom Fatigue', *Psychoanalytic Dialogues,* 30:5, pp.
641–641.

Power, K. (2020) 'The COVID-19 pandemic has increased the care burden of women
and families', *Sustainability: Science, Practice and Policy,* 16(1), pp. 67–73. https://doi
.org/10.1080/15487733.2020.1776561.

Raghuram, P. (2019) 'Race and feminist care ethics: intersectionality as method',
Gender, Place and Culture: A Journal of Feminist Geography, 26(5) pp. 613–637.

Ryan, N.E., and El Ayadi, A., M (2020) 'A call for a gender-responsive, intersectional
approach to address COVID-19', *Global Public Health,* 15:9, pp. 1404–1412.

Schoenenberg, K., Raake, A., Koeppe, J. (2014) 'Why are you so slow? – Misattribution
of transmission delay to attributes of the conversation partner at the far-end',
International Journal of Human-Computer Studies, 72(5), pp. 477–487.

Sørensen, K., Okan, O., Kondilis, B., and Levin-Zamir, D. (2021) 'Rebranding social distancing to physical distancing: calling for a change in the health promotion vocabulary to enhance clear communication during a pandemic', *Global Health Promotion*
1757–9759, 28(1), pp. 5–14.

Strazdins, L., and Broom, D.H. (2004) 'Acts of love (and work): gender imbalances in
emotional work and women's psychological distress', *Journal of Family Issues,* 25(3),
pp. 356–378.

Taffel, S. (2016) 'Perspectives on the postdigital: Beyond rhetorics of progress and novelty', *Convergence*, 22(3), pp. 324–338.

Thilmany, C. (2021) 'Diversity, inclusion, and Responsible AI are now the bedrock of bias prevention', available at: https://cloudblogs.microsoft.com/industry-blog/micros oft-in-business/ai/2020/09/10/diversity-inclusion-and-responsible-ai-are-now-the -bedrock-of-bias-prevention/ (accessed 27/07/22).

Tschaepe, M. (2020) 'Seeing and Viewing Through a Postdigital Pandemic: Shifting from Physical Proximity to Scopic Mediation', *Postdigital Science and Education*, 2, pp. 757–771 https://doi.org/10.1007/s42438-020-00156-x.

Turk, V. (2020) 'Zoom took over the world. This is what will happen next', *WIRED*, available at: https://www.wired.co.uk/article/future-of-zoom, (accessed 27/07/2022).

van den Broucke, S. (2020) 'Why health promotion matters to the COVID-19 pandemic, and vice versa', *Health Promotion International*, 35(2) pp. 181–186.

Watson, A., Lupton, D., and Michael, M. (2021) 'Enacting intimacy and sociality at a distance in the COVID-19 crisis: the sociomaterialities of home-based communication technologies', *Media International Australia*, 178(1), pp. 136–150.

Wang S.S., and Roubidoux M.A. (2020) 'Coronavirus Disease 2019 (COVID-19), Videoconferencing, and Gender', *Journal of American College of Radiology*, 17(7) pp. 918–920.

WHO (2020a) *Coronavirus and the social impacts on behaviours during different lockdown periods, Great Britain*, available at: https://www.ons.gov.uk/peoplepopulat ionandcommunity/healthandsocialcare/healthandwellbeing/articles/coronavirus andthesocialimpactsonbehavioursduringdifferentlockdownperiodsgreatbritain /uptofebruary2021#staying-at-home. (accessed 27/07/2022).

WHO (2020b) *Mental Health and Psychosocial Considerations during the COVID-19 Outbreak*. Available at: https://www.who.int/publications-detail-redirect/WHO -2019-nCoV-MentalHealth-2020.1. (accessed 27/07/2022).

Wilson, G., Gates, J., Vijaykumar, S., Morgan, D. (2020) *Understanding the experiences of older adults using technology to stay connected: A facilitator or creator of new vulnerabilities?* Available at: https://researchportal.northumbria.ac.uk/ws/portalfiles /portal/33081065/Final_project_report_Wilson_Gates_Vijaykumar_Morgan_2020_ 002_.pdf (accessed 27/07/2022).

Zhao X (2019) 'Disconnective intimacies through social media: practices of transnational family among overseas Chinese students in Australia' *Media International Australia* 173(1), pp. 36–52.

Zoom Company data (2021) *Zoom Reports Second Quarter Results for Fiscal Year 2021*, available at: https://investors.zoom.us/node/7996/pdf. (accessed 27/07/2022).

CHAPTER 3

The Colour of Technology: Covid-19, Race, and the Pulse Oximeter

Tina Sikka

Throughout this pandemic, one of the things that has struck me most is the transformation in the ways in which the intersection between race and health has been taken up and discussed both in academic circles as well as in media (inclusive of social media). These conversations have become considerably more nuanced wherein such terms as social determinants of health, environmental racism, racial weathering, structural racism, and implicit (and explicit) medical bias have become normalised. In light of this, my research has shifted to studying how race and racialisation has and is becoming manifest and felt vis-à-vis medical technologies – particularly those devices that are programmed to assume racial difference. The relationship between racial embodiment, phenotype versus genotype, skin, structural racism, racialised technoscience, and health disparities, when examined within the context of Covid-19, has pushed me to ask new questions. Two of the most pressing include: what do we do with technologies that (re)inscribe *biologized* race through phenotypical difference (i.e. skin colour)? And how does this biologization intersect with efforts to de-geneticise race, and discourage potentially harmful practices that seek to re-embed racial sorting for profit (e.g., via race-based medicine and ancestry testing)?

In this chapter, I examine a particularly troubling disjuncture made evident by the unique pressures exerted by Covid-19 as it relates to race and life-saving technologies. Specifically, I draw on a case study of the pulse oximeter (P.O.), a device that measures oxygen saturation levels through the skin, to demonstrate how this technology materialises race via perceived phenotypical difference. The biocultural enactments made evident by Covid-19 has revealed that this device has been providing biased findings by failing to account for how darker skin alters its results. In addition to the requisite harm caused by the structural default to whiteness, I contend that the exposure of bias (wherein the P.O. fails to attend to a difference of the most obvious sort, skin colour), paves the way for a re-evaluation of how we think about race, technology, embodiment, and health. It also brings to the fore the fact that while adjusting for skin colour might be necessary in this case, it does not have to be a racialising act.

The P.O. case illustrates the following:

- First, the widespread use of yet another technology in which racialised difference is built into its design;
- Second, the potential for unanticipated consequences including inaccurate readings that impede access to equitable and life-saving care; and,
- Third, the biocultural instantiation of an understanding of race that collapses phenotype into genotype in ways that reinscribes it (race) as biological fact (which it is not).

In response, I contend that it is possible for the pulse oximeter to be recontextualised as a technology that reflects phenotypical difference in ways that encourages us to take a closer look at other socio-material artefacts that also exert racialising forms of power.

Thus, my objective is to demonstrate how technologies that are adjusted for biological 'race' perpetuate essentialist racial thinking and, as Troy Duster puts it, reintroduces eugenics through the backdoor (Duster 2003). The P.O. represents a unique site of racial disjuncture reflecting our desire to deny biological racial difference, work within socio-scientific realities, and avoid embedding race into our machines. After diagnosing this problem using a case study and other contextualising examples, I examine how we might move beyond the status quo by retaining a materialist and embodied conception of race while also pushing back against its geneticization. This approach allows for the *experience* of racialisation to be respected while also detaching phenotypical difference from practices of hierarchical racial sorting that has been part of white Western heteropatriarchy for centuries.

I begin with an overview of racialisation vis-à-vis the history of medicalisation followed by a discussion of critical scholarship on race and technology. I then draw on two similar technologies with embedded racial biases in order to demonstrate how race is concretised in everyday artefacts. Next, I offer an analysis of race as it relates to technology and Covid-19 in particular through the pulse oximeter. In order to do so, I draw on new materialism to demonstrate how the pulse oximeter acts a technology of racialisation because of the way in which it molecularises phenotypical difference. I conclude by offering a way forward – one that ameliorates the kinds of co-constructed inequalities discussed throughout this chapter by placing race in context (via embodied materialism) and proposing modes of research practice and technological design that pushes back against initiatives that perpetuate medical inequality.

1   Racialisation and Medicalisation

It has been well-established that race is a biologically irrelevant category when it comes to differentiating between populations and that there is more genetic diversity *within* so-called 'races' than *between* them. In fact, as established by the Human Genome Project (HGP) decades ago, 99.9% of humanity's genes are identical while the .1% remaining, after much searching, has not identi-fied genes indicative of racial difference. And yet, when it comes to much of medical science and technologies, race remains the default way in which pop-ulations are categorised such that even the alternative, geographical markers, act as proxies for race (e.g., West African = Black, European = white). My own research, as well as a significant body of work in STS (science and technology studies), challenges the use of racial categories in science by arguing that their use, as Omi and Winant contend, ends up "reproduce[ing] ... structures of domination based on [these] essentialist categories of race" (Omi and Winant 1994, p. 71).

Traditionally, technologies that embody racial biases tend to directly assume or reflect a belief in essential race-based genetic difference (which I discuss below). There is a surfeit of research challenging these racialised assumptions that draws on scientific and anthropological evidence (Perez-Rodriguez and de la Fuente 2017; Fields and Fields 2014). However, race is also materially expe-rienced by racialised groups and this is something that cannot be overlooked. By establishing how race can be both socially constructed *and* materially felt, scholars have worked to challenge the belief that phenotypical difference is anything more than a function of biochemical activations that are environ-mental in origin (Guthman and Mansfield 2013). To be clear, this means that superficial differences in skin colour are a result of natural selection that offers protection to those living in areas with high UV irradiation by selecting for more melanin (Barsh 2003; Roche 2020). Importantly, these assemblages of genes are in no way related to what we have come to call race and thus are not indicative of essentialised behaviours, disposition, or capabilities.

Yet, despite this, there exists a host of technologies and medicines that have been 'adjusted' to accommodate a belief in biological racial difference includ-ing that of BiDil, the first race-targeted medication for heart failure marketed to Black patients exclusively (despite evidence it works just as well in white patients and evidence that it was labelled a race-targeted drug in order to extend its patent), and racial adjustments made to risk scores for osteoporo-sis, breast cancer, organ procurement, and heart surgery (Ellison et al 2008; Vyas, Eisenstein Jones, 2021). Yet, in none of these cases is there dispositive evi-dence that these adjustments are necessary or that biological racial difference requires it. Rather, what extensive research does suggest is that any population level differences in health outcomes amongst racialised patients is a result not of genetic difference but of social inequities resulting from racism (Turner, Brown and Beardall Hall 2017). Fundamentally, it is discriminatory policies and structures based on decision-making that insists on 'making race real' that make inequalities manifest (Williams and Braboy Jackson 2005).

Before moving on to the P.O., it is helpful to consider a couple of other examples in more detail, namely the spirometer which scholar Lundy Braun (2014) examines in her book, *Breathing Race into the Machine: The Surprising Career of the Spirometer from Plantation to Genetics.* In it, Braun traces how this particular device, which measures lung capacity, came to be adjusted for race and how this adjustment reflects racist assumptions and biases. Braun shows how the belief that Black lungs had a lower lung function (10–15%), due to deficient biology rather than social and environmental factors, served political ends wherein Blackness was framed as inferior and even immoral. This served to justify slavery, racial hierarchy, and economic rationales, such that a higher level of lung damage would have to be demonstrated for Black mine workers, for example, to be compensated for diseases related to mine work (e.g., silica poisoning). This history is laid out in excruciating detail by Braun who demonstrates precisely how the "racialization of spirometric measurement (that is, the process by which concepts of race as innate difference) got attached to and embedded in the instrument and the entity it purports to measure" (Braun 2014, xx). Post facto research revealing that any differences in aggregate could be explained by social and economic factors inclusive of poverty, differential access to health care, allergen exposure, living conditions, and generalised environmental racism were ignored.

While illuminating in demonstrating how racialisation rooted in such weighty histories of slavery, insurance, phrenology, and racial superiority are structured into the design of contemporary technologies, it is notable that skin, in a direct sense, is not a relevant factor in the spirometer case. Lung capacity and other assumptions about medical health vis-à-vis internalised racial difference are internal and thus epistemologically flexible in that their invisibility can be used to gloss over socio-cultural beliefs about geneticized racial difference (i.e., we are all the same on the inside). However, it is also this very connection between lung capacity, its measurement, and population level distribution that can be used to re-examine and challenge racial ideologies. Namely, by deconstructing this assemblage, or what Karen Barad calls enacting a 'strategic agential cut' (Barad 2007).

The P.O. is different since it relies on visible difference. It is part of a network of medical technologies in which skin colour *is* a salient factor (I return to this further on). The principle that racial difference and racial ideologies are informed and perpetuated by seemingly neutral technologies is called co-construction or co-production defined by the process through "which analysts seek to show, first, how the social meaning of an emerging technology is shaped by prevailing gender [and raced/classed] conceptions, and, second, how that evolving technology in turn shapes and reshapes cultural understandings of gender and individual forms of gender consciousness" (Leach and Turner 2015, p. 2; Wajcman 2004). This approach, also cultivated by technofeminist scholars, is helpful in conceptualising how technologies are co-constituted by race in which both exert a shaping force.

Importantly, it is the algorithms embedded in 'superficial' medical devices that make visual appearance *the* relevant factor such that skin colour ends up acting as an obstacle to challenging imposed racial difference (since these visible markers demand that race be factored in). Put another way, it is these technologies of bodily difference that brings race back and reinscribes it as genetically extant – i.e., as real. This 'real reality', however, is one that does not shrink from conversations about relations of power and sites of injustice, and thus is a lot more complicated. In what follows, I discuss the second of the two existing racializing technologies that help inform the analysis of the P.O. further on, namely facial recognition.

2   Facial Recognition

A technology that comes close to approximating the problems with the P.O., particularly with respect to biologized visual differences that are then mapped onto socio-cultural difference, is that of facial recognition technologies. Ruha Benjamin (2019a) examines these technologies in her book, *Race After Technology: Abolitionist Tools and the New Jim Code.* In it, Benjamin details how racial hierarchies are inscribed into surveillant technologies such that their algorithms and settings work on a default 'white setting' in which particular facial features become the norm. As a result, according to Benjamin, police departments now rely on technologies that compare individuals in real time to ""hot lists" that are filled disproportionately with Black people – and these also happen to be the least recognizable figures in the world of facial recognition software" (Benjamin 2019a, p. 224). The number of academic studies and media stories examining the biased findings of surveillance technologies is extensive (Garcia 2016; Garvey and Frankle 2016; Ferguson 2019). Similarly important work by Jacob Hood connects the inadequacy of predominantly white male photographs used to "teach" the algorithm to recognize faces to its wider impact. According to Hood, this bias has led to life changing errors, the use of "data points ... [to] reproduce ... oppression", and the consolidation of "political power in being able to identify, track, and authorize the subjects captured in footage" into a few hands (Hood 2020, p. 163–164). Importantly, it is this consolidation of power that amplifies racial difference through surveillant technologies in which skin colour is made dispositive.

It is important to underscore that it is the act of distinguishing groups by phenotypical difference, which is then used to infer psychological states and behavioural predispositions, that is the problem (Hanna, Denton, Smart, and Smith-Loud 2020). This act most often comes at the expense of racialised groups – particularly when more refined and diverse algorithms are used to proclaim diversity, i.e., 'we are working to make said algorithms more representative/accurate', not police the already marginalised and stigmatised. However, it is this initial manifestation of default whiteness 'rectified' through the building of these diverse algorithms then which ends up strengthening biased policing practices.

What unites technologies like that of facial recognition to the pulse oximeter is its focus on skin as a salient factor. Thus, skin colour re-emerges as a site of social sorting in ways that perpetuate racialisation by marking some bodies as Other. As Patricia Williams writes, "[t]he simple matter of the colour of one's skin so profoundly affects the way one is treated, so radically shapes what one is allowed to think and feel about this society, that the decision to generalize from such a division is [seen as] valid" (Williams 1991, p. 256). This, to be clear, occurs in spite of moves by science to debunk notions of genetic racial difference and a push by social scientists to emphasise that observable phenotypic differences are reflections of environmental adaptation, not distinct races. Scholars have consistently warned against using phenotypical difference as a proxy for race and thus a means by which to read "race in the DNA ... and, in turn ..." classify DNA, and racialised groups, "ethnoracially" (El Haj 2007;, p. 287; Duster 2003).

In light of this and other realities introduced by Covid-19, I contend that it is the perfect time to re-evaluate the meaning of phenotypical difference, to reconsider how Blackness and brownness signify difference only insofar as our adaptive phenotypical coding has made it thus, *and still retain a conception of produced race as materially felt and socio-culturally significant*. In the domain of human-driven technoscience, however, race needs to be approached carefully such that population level disparities are attended to but not understood as a product of essential group (read: raced) pathologies. As I demonstrate below, the pulse oximeter functions as an inciting technology which, much like surveillant technologies, assert their own form of productive non-human agency since, as Jane Bennett argues, "agentic capacity is distributed along a continuum of ontological types" (Bennett 2005, p. 452). For Bennett, a prominent scholar of feminist new materialism, it is through mutual and entangled constitution of variegated actants, inclusive of technologies, people, artefacts structures, and animals, that we come to certain conclusions about the world. By placing everything on a level playing field, new materialism is able to foster a kind of seeing such that we can better understand how race, the pulse oximeter, and human skin intra-act in ways that reveal how "agency itself is located in the complex interinvolvement of humans and multiple nonhuman actants" (Bennett 2015, p. 88). In the next section, and using new materialism, I delve more fully into the P.O. case by tracing this assemblage, disentangling the forces at play, and providing avenues for ways forward.

3 The Pulse Oximeter

As stated, the pulse oximeter is a non-invasive medical device used to measure one's pulse and arterial oxygen levels. The probe is most often placed on the finger or ear, although some are now contactless. Functionally, the P.O. uses the principle of photoplethysmography to estimate the oxygen saturation levels of arterial blood which is returned in the form of a number (Verkruysse et al 2017). Operationally, it works by shining a light at specific wavelengths through the skin (i.e., the fingernail bed) and since haemoglobin that is oxygenated or deoxygenated absorbs light at different wavelengths, a number is produced to represent a saturation value (Tsiakaka, Gosselin, and Ferugio 2020; Klaus, Modi Simon 2020). P.O.s are most often used for patients undergoing anaesthesia, those in intensive care, and individuals suffering from cardiac arrest or respiratory distress.

While primarily used in a hospital setting, there are now a suite of new wearable commercial pulse oximeters now available for purchase that also use light sensors to measure oxygen. These devices, found on Fitbits, Apple Watches, Versa 2, and as standalone devices, have been used by high altitude athletes and individuals with sleep apnoea to monitor oxygen levels for reasons of health and performance (Sawh 2020). In late October 2020, the *British Medical Journal* called for Covid-19 patients to be given pulse oximeters in the UK to monitor oxygen levels which would have to reach a certain level before coming to hospital thereby forestalling bed shortages *and* silent hypoxia "where[in] desaturation occur[s] ... [with] ... no obvious symptoms" (Torjesen 2020). In hospitals, pulse oximeters are also relied upon to gauge whether and when patients need to be put on a ventilator. This is particularly salient vis-à-vis

Covid-19 since ventilators are often in short supply, unequally distributed (nationally and internationally), and available only in well-funded institutions (Badgujar et al 2020).

As stated, the problem with pulse oximeters with respect to race rests on the fact that most models overestimate arterial oxygen saturation levels in individuals with darker skin.

Recent research at the University of Michigan of 10789 patients (in two cohort studies), for example, concluded that Black patients were three times more likely to suffer from silent hypoxia and this was not registered by the pulse oximeter (Sjoding et al 2020). Likewise, a controlled lab study of 36 patients by researchers at the University of California, San Francisco (UCSF) found significant variations between P.O. results due to differences in skin pigmentation (Bickler, Feiner, and Severinghaus 2005). It is notable that while these studies point out the clinical problem of racial bias, they do not consider its source, cause, or consequences beyond immediate concerns related to health. The lead author of the former article, for example, stated in an interview for *New York Times* that, "If we cannot ensure that its definition of low oxygen in people, especially Black people, is accurate, there is a concern that it is increasing or driving disparities" (Rabin, 2020). While this is accurate, I would argue that it does not address the core problem of systemic racism, structural bias, differences in power relations, marginalisation, and oppression that this technology enacts and reproduces (Feiner, Severinghaus and Bickler 2007; Nakamura and Chow-White 2012).

One of the most comprehensive and compelling articles on the P.O. I have come across was published in August 2020 by Amy Moran-Thomas for *The Boston Review* in which she details the evolution of the pulse oximeter and precisely how it became a device that came to give inaccurate results for darker skinned patients. Thomas connects this bias to that of photographic film which was standardised to white skin reflecting what Benjamin refers to as 'flesh toned imperialism', a form of sociotechnical injustice that formalised how even the "the chemistry of film emulsions could ... be developed or modified on the basis of cultural choices" (Benjamin 2019b, p. 283).

The lead doctor and baseline research on which Moran-Thomas' article draws most of its evidence is the UCSF study which concluded that amongst the devices tested, "skin pigment introduces a consistent positive bias at low Sao2". These researchers also established that "the bias error does not arise simply from inadequate signal intensity and confirms the problem as a real pigment-related difference in pulse oximeter optical factors, which deserves attention and possible provision of correction factors, tables, or even built-in user-optional adjustments" (Bickler, Feiner and Severinghaus 2005). A follow up study by the same researchers came to similar conclusions. It found that this bias was particularly acute for patients with saturations below 80% which impacted Latinx, Indigenous, and other non-white patients (Bickler, Feiner and Severinghaus 2007).

Importantly, vis-à-vis Covid-19, these readings determine when patients are put on oxygen, if/when they are placed on a ventilator, and whether or not (in the US) they are covered by insurance. From these findings, what becomes clear is that, on average, pulse oximeters are likely to undershoot the blood oxygen levels of Black and some brown patients meaning that they could be placed on oxygen and/or a ventilator too late. While it might be argued that perceived and communicated distress could mitigate this bias by adding additional information to the diagnosis, it is also the case that, for many racialised individuals, the medical establishment has not served them well on this front. Medical racial and gender biases in perceived pain perception, decision making, and diagnosis is well established (FitzGerald and Hurst 2017; Pereda and Montoya 2018). A recent meta-analysis of 40 experimental studies, for instance, found a strong tendency to register the pain on Black faces as less acute while another study, run by scholars from NYU and the University of Delaware, found that racial biases in perception facilitated biases in pain treatment decisions and that this relationship existed "over and above biased judgments of status and strength, explicit racial bias, and endorsement of false beliefs regarding biological differences" (Lin, Drain, Goharzad and Mende-Sieldlecki 2020; Mende-Siedlecki, Qu-Lee, Backer, and Van Bavel 2019, p. 863). As such, these implicit forms of bias would likely obviate the mitigating potential of perceived distress. They are also indicative of a long history of racial dehumanisation and subjugation scholars like Orlando Patterson (2018) and Kenneth Addison (2009) detail in their own work.

4   Race, the Pulse Oximeter, and Covid-19

The imbrication of race and Covid-19 as it relates to pulse oximeter is significant in that it speaks directly to a unique socio-technical tension. Namely that it is a technology encoded by racial biases and demands a kind of racial sorting that forces us to calibrate for skin colour in ways that discursively and materially reaffirms racial difference. This ontological move thus concretises racial difference not because adjusting for skin colour is itself racialising but because of the *meaning we give skin colour*. In these final sections, I underscore and reaffirm the argument that the use of *biological* race in medical practice is unnecessary and unsubstantiated but relied upon at least in part because it is historically concordant with centuries of discrimination and marginalisation. The pulse oximeter thus acts as a paradigmatic technology whose use has brought this argument to the surface while also raising a tension I have been grappling with for the past year: namely, that while it might be possible to de-ontologise race on a socio-biological level, it becomes much harder to do so when that technology is one of embodiment and involves our largest organ, the skin. In the next section, I unpack the intricacies of this tension before examining how we might move forward.

5   Adjusting for Race

As a first step, it is important to emphasise that the very act of 'adjusting' a technology to accommodate 'race' (or simply phenotypical difference) amplifies and concretises racial hierarchies by rendering it necessary to identify an individual, patient, or consumer as different. It is not, however, the act of accommodation on its own that is of concern, but the meanings we attach to acts of differentiation – in this case to the skin we are in. Making adjustments for patients who require it is important – but what is also important is where those requirements come from. The tendency to biologize, racialise, and personalise health, rather than attending to larger socioeconomic inequalities or determinants inclusive of poverty, education, housing, employment, and environmental resiliency, has become par for the course (Baum and Fisher 2014). The reasons for this are manifold but, for the purposes of this chapter, can be understood as: one, the result of the confluence of neoliberal social and economic policies that have promoted "market-make-over of more collective health systems with a new emphasis on [an] individualizing and consumerist ideal" (Sparke 2017, p. 290), and two, the outcome of a socio-political project of racialisation going back generations which pathologises Black and brown bodies as unruly and requiring biopolitical management in order to function or, in this case, 'test' properly. As Rana Hogarth argues, this practice can be traced to colonial medicine in which it was believed "that black and white people had distinct constitutions, required different kinds of sustenance, and adapted to new environments differently" thereby setting the stage for differential treatment (Hogarth 2017, p. 75).

This logic is not limited to the P.O. but is part of a constellation of adjustments to tests and procedures inclusive of kidney function for which results are recalibrated up (rendering the score higher) based on the unsubstantiated but widespread belief that Black people have more muscle mass and thus produce more creatine. Many medical institutions over the last few years, and in light of being challenged, have dropped race from their base equation given the danger that accurate diagnosis and life-saving procedures were being denied to Black patients (Eneanya, Yang, Philip Reese 2019). Another example of race correction is the score given to women during birth with respect to whether or not to recommend a C-section such that Black and Hispanic patients are given a higher vaginal birth risk score because of their ascribed race (and thus undergo higher rates of the procedure despite the heightened overall risk) (Amanishakete 2015). Changing this in addition to encouraging patient-centred care, as Currie and MacLeod argue, "would reduce overall C-section rates without depriving high risk women of necessary care" (Currie and MacLeod 2017, p. 27). It would also establish that risk should be clinically decoupled from race but also leave space for consideration of the ways that racial marginalisation and negative health outcomes are experienced in everyday life.

Differences in outcomes that are health specific and congeal around certain populations, whether in the case of kidney function, cardiac surgery, caesarean section, or lung function are finally being re-evaluated as a function not of race but of socio-economics (Vyas, Eisenstein and Jones 2020). As stated, this includes such indicators as poverty, education, access to health care, housing, environmental racism, stress, pollution, and sexism, rather than biological race. It is thus important to interrogate the mechanisms through which our continuing history of racism, segregation, wealth dispossession, redlining, and structural discrimination have produced worse health outcomes for racialised groups. To double down on the fact that this is not a result of genetic distinctions but because of the lived experiences of marginalisation is to make differential outcomes tangible (Williams, Priest and Anderson 2016; Richardson and Norris 2010). As Zuberi states, we need to challenge, "The population perspective in both demography and statistics corresponds to the tendencies of group objectification in social statistics. ... This perspective views groups as entities with collective traits that can be statistically described" (Zuberi 2001, p. 29–30).

6   P.O. and the Materiality of Race

New materialism, as a methodology and field of research practice, has a lot to offer on this subject. While I have drawn on feminist materialism in my own research for years, it was Covid-19 that drew my attention to the distinct ways in which race has become materialised vis-à-vis technology and health. Karen Barad (2007), and other materialist scholars of technology like Rosi

Braidotti (2013) and Donna Haraway (2016), make a persuasive case for the study of technologies through the lens of 'natureculture matterings' (Pitts-Tayler 2016). Overall, new materialism is a plural and relational theoretical framework that aims to reconcile the discursive turn in social theory, in which technologies, institutions, and identities are the products of discursive formations, and materialism in which material things are seen as having a "positive, productive [force] of their own" – ones that reflects the 'active role [played by] ... *nonhuman* materials in public life' (Bennett 2010, p. 1–2; Foucault 1970). Embodiment, affect, vibrancy, agency, agential realism, and natureculture are just a few of the terms used to extend the analysis of language to the material world. For Karen Barad, materiality and language or nature and culture, traditionally binarised, are reconceived of as entangled:

> The relationship between the material and the discursive is one of mutual entailment. Neither is articulated/articulable in the absence of the other; matter and meaning are mutually articulated. Neither discursive practices nor material phenomena are ontologically or epistemologically prior. Neither can be explained in terms of the other. Neither has privileged status in determining the other.
>
> BARAD 2003, p. 822

Scholars like Emily S. Lee (2014), Linda Martin Alcoff (1999) have taken this framework and extended it to the study of race in which race is seen simultaneously as materially felt *and* as a product of discursive formations that serve the interests of those in power. This relation of co-constitution exemplifies what Elisabeth Grosz (2010) refers to when she discusses how the phenomenology of everyday life (or culture) impinges on the living such that race itself becomes a bodily practice.

Applied to the study of the P.O. and race, wherein both are seen as sociomaterial forces that exert a vitalism and power within the assemblages of which they are a part, this approach allows for an understanding of race as discursively constructed by the machine, which is itself understood as a neutral technology of health (but whose material impacts are anything but), and race as made tangible by the visible marker of one's skin. The question then becomes: how do we challenge the socially constituted structures of racial difference that are embedded in the P.O. while accounting for felt bodily difference?

New materialism brings us closer to answering this question by revealing how race manifests as a mechanism of power, a visual technology, and a site of resistance that, while continuing to be expressed theoretically and institutionally, is also experienced as an embodied reality made real *by being diffracted through this particular technology*. As such, it is the P.O., enacted by Covid-19, that has (re)marked Black skin as a problem to be fixed or "corrected". This folds back on individuals receiving treatment for Covid-19 in which their ascribed race precedes their individual lived experience. As such, the P.O. reinscribes racial difference by designating white skin as the norm (and everything else 'Other' by default), and reflecting a failure to consider how skin functions as an embodied organ steeped in a history of taxonomic and scientific injustice (wherein darker skin is devalued). And yet, in a practical sense, it remains the case that in order to test for low oxygen, we must adjust for ... something. The solution I propose requires an ontological shift from the purportedly justified biologization of race, as made manifest by skin colour, to environmental and population-based forms of medical categorisation. I discuss this below.

Before doing so, we need to expand upon what we have learned about the P.O. and what makes this particular technology so illuminating vis-à-vis the deep inter-connection between race, health, and technology. Namely, that the raced biases embedded in the P.O. need to be seen in the context of wider health inequalities wherein racialised groups have lower life expectancies and higher rates of diabetes, heart attack, stroke, asthma, and miscarriage not because of individual failings but, as critical race scholar Chandra Ford puts it in an essay on Covid-19 and race, "unequal conditions that render some populations more susceptible to the virus than others and that render mainstream interventions less accessible to them; therefore, they represent missed opportunities to promote "optimal health for all"" (Ford 2020, p. 185; Gilbert, Walsemann and Brontolo 2012; Williams, Lawrence and Davis 2019).

One of the tools of new materialism that can help push this forward is that of the agential cut which Barad uses to refer to the act of temporarily stabilising an assemblage of forces, actants, discourses, and artefacts for the purpose of analysis. I argue that the field or agential cut for the purposes of this research entails several motivated acts of discursive closure, material adjustments, and embodied effects. The flow of this cut also reflects stages and intra-actions that move between bodies and objects working together to stabilise indeterminacy – something that is particularly necessary in light of the flux introduced by Covid-19 and the new forces and flows that have shifted existing assemblages. The cut itself thus consists of a chain of demarcated stages that are applicable to other sociotechnical assemblages, but which have kicked into high gear in light of this particular virus.

7   Covid-19 Cut

Assemblage: Racialisation of those with phenotypical differences as distinct peoples (*historical*) – marginalisation of said group (*material and social*) resulting in negative health outcomes (*historical and current*) – requiring companies to adjust algorithms and diagnostic technologies to account for lower baseline health or skin colour because said technologies are calibrated for deracialized 'healthy' white men (*pulse oximeter*) – realisation that this action has reinscribed racial difference as natural or genetic, even though it is a difference that is produced rather than being extant (while also being materially felt) (*current and future – and this time made all the more complicated because of the way in which phenotype has collapsed into genotype*).

This complicated assemblage draws attention to the way in which the P.O. is just one in a long line of racialising technologies, several of which I have discussed in this piece, and yet is distinctive because of the role played by skin colour. It is skin colour, I contend, that enacts concerns about re-racialisation (i.e., the inadvertent reinscription of race as real), but also encourages a wider conversation about embodiment and race. In the remainder of this section, I unpack both of these axes before engaging in a discussion of what can be done going forward.

In the context of Covid-19 and the P.O., it is important to attend to race first and foremost. According to new materialism, both race and technology function as agential and co-constituting material-discursive artefacts that are also active containers of norms, values, and ideologies. What distinguishes them from one another is that race is visually and materially inscribed onto the surfaces of our bodies. Rooting difference *in and on* the body risks "overlook[ing] how the body itself is an effect of practices of genetic 'corporealization', that is made manifest by socio-cultural and economic forces" (Haraway 1997, p. 141). Ignoring these risks overlooking the function of race and the role played by skin and skin colour therein. On a more personal, socio-cultural level, as Patricia Williams puts it, the "simple matter of the color of one's skin so profoundly affects the way one is treated, so radically shapes what one is allowed to think and feel about this society" (Williams 1991, p. 256). Race can thus be seen as not natural but as ontological (i.e., lived). Being raced affects one's life experience wherein one's skin colour functions as a visible signifier of difference linked to perceived racial traits. This, in turn, risks being recreated and reified through the use of technologies like the P.O. wherein, skin, and in particular Blackness, is both representational and materially productive (Ashley and Billies 2019, p. 190).

Thus, the pulse oximeter can be seen as just one more in a host of forces, technologies, and institutions that reinscribe racial difference. What differentiates the P.O. from other 'adjustment' technologies and algorithms however is the partiality toward visual sight. Because of this, the pulse oximeter acts as a technology through which racial difference is reaffirmed by necessity. Put another way, if you have to adjust the P.O. to accommodate for what we have socially defined as *the* signifier of race (namely skin), then it becomes easy to reach the conclusion that biological race is real. Epistemologically, this fits with a long history of racial logics in which *visual* Othering is used to consolidate the boundaries of group identity (Nunnally 2010; Kastoryano 2010).

This focus on sight is important and something that scholars have written about in philosophy and postcolonial theory for decades. For both, Enlightenment philosophy and western notions of progress are understood as supported by and through the development of rational thinking, the scientific method, empiricism, and the elevation of sight as the preeminent sense through which truth is discerned (Jenks 1995; Levin 1993). The form of ocularcentrism can be traced to Plato, the Enlightenment, and the Renaissance through which "the invention of perspectival representation made the eye the centre point of the perceptual world as well as of the concept of the self" (Pallasmaa 2012, p. 14). Feminist scholars point out how this mode of reasoning is juxtaposed with inferior, feminine coded capabilities including emotions, irrationality, recalcitrance, and the body (over the mind) (Harding 1991). Those who are racialised also bear the weight of colonialism and slavery which, as discussed above, function as socio-material transcendental signifiers of oppression and dehumanisation. Afropessimist scholars see the founding act of slavery as a form of social death in which the future of those racialised as Black is forever compromised. Wacquant, for example, locates this primordial anti-Blackness in the unequal way in which markets function, in the penal system (mass incarceration), in institutions, in laws, and, for the purposes of this chapter, in medical technologies (Wacquant 2002).

As a result, prescribed characteristics emerging out of historical oppressions like that of irrationality, violence, difference, and unruliness are incarnated into material bodies through visual interpellation and racial ontologicalisation (Tallbear 2013). There is, of course, a gendered component to all of this with women, particularly Black women, being constructed as Other through the lens of hypersexualization and licentiousness that can be traced to slave laws but continues to be perpetuated by media stereotypes and deep-seated cultural biases (Gammage 2015).

If we think of the P.O. as a sociotechnical object in this way, i.e., as a social artefact reflective of norms, values, practices, actors, and materialities, what become clear is that in order to understand how this device came to "be patterned to generate effects like organisations, inequality and power" (Law 1992, p. 381), (including that of race), we need to disentangle racial ideology from artefact as I have done here using new materialism and explore ways to reconstitute it prosocially.

8   Conclusion

In this chapter, I have attempted to distil and characterise the trajectory of my research around Covid-19, technology, and race using new materialism and the critical study of race. Its focus has been on the pulse oximeter and how to think about it as an inciting artefact that reveals how racialisation operates such that phenotypical difference risks being used to reify racial difference. Also discussed is how technologies like that of the P.O. but also facial recognition, algorithms, and the spirometer, reflects and perpetuates racialisation through the co-constitution of discursive and material enactments. For Barad and other new materialists, this means thinking about how bodies and technologies emerge out of material-discursive contexts but also imagining how they could look going forward.

With respect to the P.O., my focus has been on how it functions as a source of agential diffraction or amplification that reveals how whiteness is normalised and how race operates as a source of differential ordering. Also revealed by this agential cut is the agency of skin colour (and all of the historical baggage it brings with it), and how, when enmeshed with this technology, it risks solidifying race as biological and genetic rather than phenotypical (because of its inscribed visibility). Skin colour will have to be considered when producing technologies that rely on light projected through the skin to function. This is something that creators of the P.O. did not do thus revealing how racial bias can be built into the infrastructural algorithms of technologies. The P.O. thus identifies and thematises the significance of skin colour forcing us to think about its role in racialisation more carefully. With technologies that use racial adjustments, a persuasive argument can be made about how these 'adjustments' are either relics of perceived biological inferiority or reflective of structures that make these modifications necessary (e.g., correcting for kidney function not because of race, but because a population who happens to have darker skin have been historically marginalised in ways that have negatively impacted their health). For the pulse oximeter, racial bias comes in the form of neglect and disregard and, in contradistinction to other racialised and racialising technologies, is not as easily corrected since skin colour, which we have relied upon for centuries to hierarchically sort populations, is a factor one cannot ignore. Thus, race, as expressed through one's skin, becomes sticky, agential, culturally embedded, and thus more than either biological or cultural (Saldanha 2006). At the very least, it is something we have to consider when testing for oxygen levels because failing to do so will result is negative health outcomes for those who contract Covid-19.

This, however, should not occur in ways that reinscribe and perpetuate the kind of racial ordering other technologies have been used to justify. Which is to say that we must resist collapsing phenotype into genotype and think carefully about what skin colour signifies as a scientific artefact, but also as a robust and diverse marker of belonging wherein racialised communities share experiences of marginalisation, build ties, and construct identities (Best 2019). This community element is often thought of as ethnic rather than racial, however, I argue that the two cannot be disaggregated since "one's sense of belonging ... and the emotional tie(s) one has with the group" are a function of one's lived bodily experience, shared traditions, cultural expressions (e.g., food and music), and co-produced knowledges and histories (Neville et al 2014; Austin 2006)

What Covid-19 has also made me consider as a scholar working with racial-ised groups and being racialised myself, is how race as expressed by one's physi-cal appearance (inclusive of skin colour) can persist as a joyful identity, cultural affiliation, embodied reality, and spatial practice (Bonnett and Nayak 2003). Something new materialism makes clear is that race as imposed and discur-sive, what Fanon (1970) calls a 'racial epidermal scheme', is also embodied and expressed by a shared sense of community in which phenotype matters. This notion of race as a hybrid or as a culturally embedded phenotype is important and something that needs to be considered going forward (Saldhana, 2006).

Thus, the solution to my basic quandary – namely, how to prevent technol-ogies that require the factoring in of one's skin from becoming a biologized signifier of race that works to naturalise racial difference – is somewhat open. Any resolution must leave space for race to function as a form of embodied cultural belonging – one that exists in a particular space-time and recognises that "the past that is not past reappears, always to rupture the present" (Sharpe 2016, p. 9). Solutions emerging from the medical community tend to be limited to addressing the first part – e.g., ensuring that medical professions work with technology companies to remove such biases, dispensing with the current skin tone scale (and finding a more objective way to reflect its impact), lobbying for companies to improve their products (e.g., by using multiple wavelengths), and ensuring that testing populations are diverse (Colvonen et al 2020).

While these are good first steps, how to go about challenging essentialised racial hierarchies and raced technologies, when those hierarchies rely on socially significant and embodied phenotypical signifiers, while also allowing for racial-ethnic communities to grow and flourish remains an open question. My own research is bringing me back to the foundational work of Patricia Hill Collins (1990), Kimberly Crenshaw (2018), and Black Lives Matter (#BLM) whose work on embodied racial identity as it is experienced with and through other positionalities is critical, as is other work examining the brown experience as it relates to darker skin. #BLM in particular has been able to hold the experience of marginalisation, technological bias, and community organising together and thus strikes me as an ideal place to start. I end this piece with a three-pronged approach that reflects this ethos. I argue we should:

1.   Deconstruct technologies like the P.O. and de-geneticises race with respect to phenotype while allowing it to be used as a non-racial adjustment factor (i.e., in the same way that one would adjust for height or eye colour);

2.   Deal with the material-discursive outcome of racialisation in which some groups are ignored and seen as less than (and thus not included in technological design), thereby reiterating that these inequalities are imposed, inscribed, but also lived; and

3.   Attend to the fact that race is experienced by people in multiple ways and that this socio-cultural iteration of race must be part of our understanding of racialisation, health, and technology going forward.

Overall, what Covid-19 has brought to the fore for me is that culture, race, and technology are and will likely continue to intersect in assemblages that are complex, but which open up new ways to engage, rearticulate, and challenge existing formations. We must harness these opportunities to push things towards a more just social order.

References

Addison, K.N. (2009) *'We hold these truths to be self-evident ...': An interdisciplinary analysis of the roots of racism and slavery in America.* Lanham: University Press of America.

Alcoff, L.M. (1999) "Towards a phenomenology of racial embodiment". *Radical Philosophy* 95: pp. 15–26.

Ani, A. (2015) "Droppin' science for the struggle: A purposeful profile of Professor Sylvester James Gates, Jr. in the era of the" New Jim Crow". *Journal of Pan African Studies* 8(6): pp. 64–84.

Ashley, C.P., and Billies, M. (2019) 'Affect & race/(Blackness)'. *Athenea Digital: revista de pensamiento e investigación social* 20(2): pp. 16–17.

Austin, A. (2006) *Achieving Blackness: Race, Black nationalism, and Afrocentrism in the twentieth century*. New York: NYU Press.

Badgujar, Kirtikumar C., Ashish B. Badgujar, Dipak V. Dhangar, and Vivek C. Badgujar. (2020) 'Importance and use of pulse oximeter in COVID-19 pandemic: general factors affecting the sensitivity of pulse oximeter', *Indian Chemical Engineer* 62(4): pp. 374–384.

Barad, K. (2003) 'Posthumanist performativity: Toward an understanding of how matter comes to matter', *Signs: Journal of women in culture and society* 28(3): pp. 801–831.

Barad, K. (2007) *Meeting the universe halfway: Quantum physics and the entanglement of matter and meaning*. Durham, NC: Duke University Press.

Barsh, G.S. (2003) 'What controls variation in human skin color?', *PLoS Biol* 1(1): https://doi.org/10.1186/s41065-017-0036-2.

Baum, F., and Fisher, M. (2014) 'Why behavioural health promotion endures despite its failure to reduce health inequities', *Sociology of Health & Illness* 36(2): pp. 213–225.

Benjamin, R. (2019a) *Race after technology: Abolitionist tools for the new Jim Code*. Hoboken, NJ: John Wiley & Sons.

Benjamin, R. (2019b) *Captivating technology: Race, carceral technoscience, and liberatory imagination in everyday life*. Durham, NC: Duke University Press,

Bennett, J. (2005) 'The agency of assemblages and the North American blackout', *Public Culture* 17(3): pp. 445–65.

Bennett, J. (2010) *Vibrant matter: A political ecology of things*. Durham, NC: Duke University Press.

Bennett, J. (2015) 'Ontology, sensibility and action', *Contemporary Political Theory* 14: pp. 82–89.

Best, S. (2019) *None like us: Blackness, belonging, aesthetic life*. Durham, NC: Duke University Press.

Bickler, P.E., Feiner, J.R., and Severinghaus, J.W. (2005), 'Effects of skin pigmentation on pulse oximeter accuracy at low saturation', *Anesthesiology: The Journal of the American Society of Anesthesiologists* 102(4): pp. 715–719 https://pubs.asahq.org/anesthesiology/article/102/4/715/7364/Effects-of-Skin-Pigmentation-on-Pulse-Oximeter.

Bonnett, A., and Nayak, A. (2003) 'Cultural geographies of racialization: The territory of race', in K. Anderson, M. Domosh, S. Pile, and N. Thrift (eds.) *Handbook of Cultural Geography*. Newbury Park: Sage: pp. 300–312.

Braidotti, R. (2013) *The posthuman*. Hoboken, NJ: John Wiley & Sons.

Braun, L. (2014) *Breathing race into the machine: The surprising career of the spirometer from plantation to genetics*. Minneapolis: University of Minnesota Press.

Collins, P.H., 1990. Black feminist thought in the matrix of domination. *Black feminist thought: Knowledge, consciousness, and the politics of empowerment, 138*(1990), pp. 221–238.

Colvonen, P.J., DeYoung, P.N., Bosompra, N.O.A., and Owens, R.L. (2020) 'Limiting racial disparities and bias for wearable devices in health science research', *Sleep*, 43(10), https://doi.org/10.1093/sleep/zsaa159.

Crenshaw, K., 2018. Demarginalizing the intersection of race and sex: A Black feminist critique of antidiscrimination doctrine, feminist theory, and antiracist politics [1989]. In *Feminist legal theory* (pp. 57–80). Routledge.

Currie, J. and MacLeod, W.B. (2017) Diagnosis and unnecessary procedure use: Evidence from C-sections. Columbia Academic Commons: https://doi.org /10.7916/D87M05W4.

Currie, J., and MacLeod, W. Bentley (2013) 'Diagnosis and unnecessary procedure use: Evidence from c-section'. *National Bureau of Economic Research*, https://www .nber.org/system/files/working_papers/w18977/revisions/w18977.rev1.pdf.

Duster, T. (2003) *Backdoor to eugenics*. Abingdon, UK: Routledge.

El-Haj, N.A. (2007) The genetic reinscription of race. *Annual Review of Anthropology., 36*, pp. 283–300.

Ellison, G.T.H., Kaufman, J.S., Head, R.F., Martin, P.A., and Khan, J.D. (2008) 'Flaws in the US Food and Drug Administration's rationale for supporting the development and approval of BiDil as a treatment for heart failure only in black patients', *The Journal of Law, Medicine & Ethics* 36(3), pp. 449–457.

Eneanya, N.D., Yang, W., and Reese, P.P. (2019) 'Reconsidering the consequences of using race to estimate kidney function', *JAMA* 322(2), pp. 113–114.

Fanon, F. (1970) *Black skin, white masks*. London: Paladin.

Feiner, J.R., Severinghaus, J.W. and Bickler, P.E. (2007) Dark skin decreases the accuracy of pulse oximeters at low oxygen saturation: the effects of oximeter probe type and gender. *Anesthesia & Analgesia, 105*(6), pp. S18–S23.

Ferguson, A.G. (2019) *The rise of big data policing: Surveillance, race, and the future of law enforcement*. New York: NYU Press.

Fields, K.E., and Fields, B.J. (2014) *Racecraft: The soul of inequality in American life*. London: Verso Trade.

FitzGerald, C., and Hurst, S. (2017) 'Implicit bias in healthcare professionals: a systematic review', *BMC Medical Ethics*, 18(1), p. 19. https://bmcmedethics.biomedcentral .com/articles/10.1186/s12910-017-0179-8.

Ford, C.L. (2020) 'Commentary: addressing inequities in the era of COVID-19: the pandemic and the urgent need for critical race theory', *Family & Community Health* 43(3), pp. 184–186.

Foucault, Ml. (1970) 'The archaeology of knowledge', *Social Science Information* 9(1), pp. 175–185.

Gammage, M.M. (2015) *Representations of black women in the media: The damnation of black womanhood*. London: Routledge.

Garcia, M. (2016) 'Racist in the machine: The disturbing implications of algorithmic bias', *World Policy Journal* 33(4): pp. 111–117.

Garvie, C., and Frankle, J. (2016) "Facial-recognition software might have a racial bias problem", *The Atlantic* 7, June, https://www.theatlantic.com/technology/archive/2016/04/the-underlying-bias-of-facial-recognition-systems/476991/ (Accessed 12 June 2021).

Gee, G.C., Walsemann, K.M., and Brondolo, E. (2012) 'A life course perspective on how racism may be related to health inequities', *American Journal of Public Health*, 102(5), pp. 967–974.

Grosz, E. (2010) 'Feminism, materialism, and freedom', in D. Coole, and S. Frost (eds.) *New Materialisms: Ontology, Agency, and Politics*. Durham, NC, and London: Duke University Press, 2010, pp. 139–158.

Guthman, J., and Mansfield, B. (2013) 'The implications of environmental epigenetics: A new direction for geographic inquiry on health, space, and nature-society relations', *Progress in Human Geography* 37(4), pp. 486–504.

Hanna, A., Denton, E., Smart, A., and Smith-Loud, J. (2020) 'Towards a critical race methodology in algorithmic fairness', *Proceedings of the 2020 Conference on Fairness, Accountability, and Transparency*, pp. 501–512. 2020.

Haraway, D. (1997) *Modest Witness@SecondMillennium* [etc.] New York: Routledge.

Haraway, D.J. (2016) *Manifestly Haraway*. Vol. 37. Minneapolis: University of Minnesota Press.

Harding, S. (1991) *Whose science? Whose knowledge?: Thinking from women's lives*. Ithaca: Cornell University Press.

Hogarth, R.A. (2017) *Medicalizing Blackness: making racial difference in the Atlantic world, 1780–1840*. Durham, NC: UNC Press Books.

Hood, J. (2020) 'Making the body electric: The politics of body-worn cameras and facial recognition in the United States', *Surveillance & Society* 18(2), pp. 157–169.

Jenks, C. (1995) *Visual culture*. New York: Routledge.

Karl, R. (2020) '23andDiverseMe: Using genetic ancestry tests to establish minority status', *Health Matrix* 30, pp. 475–510.

Kastoryano, R. (2010) 'Codes of otherness', *Social Research: An International Quarterly* 77, 1, pp. 79–100.

Law, J. (1992) 'Notes on the theory of the actor-network: Ordering, strategy, and heterogeneity', *Systems Practice* 5(4), pp. 379–393.

Leach, L, and Turner, S. (2015) 'Computer users do gender: The co-production of gender and communications technology', *Sage Open* 5(4), https://doi.org/10.1177/2158244015604693.

Lee, E.S. (ed.) (2014) *Living alterities: Phenomenology, embodiment, and race.* New York: SUNY Press.

Levin, D.M. (ed.) (1993) *Modernity and the hegemony of vision.* California: University of California Press.

Lin, J., Drain, A., Goharzad, A., and Mende-Siedlecki, P. (2020) 'What factors fuel racial bias in pain perception and treatment. A meta-analysis across', *PsyArXiv Preprints* 40, pp. 1–40.

Mende-Siedlecki, P., Qu-Lee, J., Backer, R., and Van Bavel, J.J. (2019) 'Perceptual contributions to racial bias in pain recognition', *Journal of Experimental Psychology. General*, 148(5), pp. 863–889.

Nakamura, L., & Chow-White, P. A. (2012) Race and digital technology: Code, the color line, and the information society. In L. Nakamura & P. A. Chow-White (Eds.), *Race after the Internet* (pp. 1–18). New York: Routledge.

Nunnally, S.C. (2010) 'Linking Blackness or ethnic othering?', *Du Bois Review* 7(2), pp. 335–355.

Omi, M., and Winant, H. (1994) *Racial formation in the United States: From the 1960s to the 1990s.* New York: Routledge.

Pallasmaa, J. (2012) *The eyes of the skin: Architecture and the senses.* Hoboken, NJ: John Wiley & Sons.

Patterson, O. (2018) *Slavery and social death: A comparative study, with a new preface.* Cambridge: Harvard University Press.

Pereda, B., and Montoya, M. (2018) 'Addressing implicit bias to improve cross-cultural care', *Clinical Obstetrics and Gynecology* 61(1): pp. 2–9.

Perez-Rodriguez, J. and de la Fuente, A. (2017) 'Now is the time for a postracial medicine: Biomedical research, the National Institutes of Health, and the perpetuation of scientific racism', *The American Journal of Bioethics* 17(9), pp. 36–47.

Pitts-Taylor, V. ed. (2016) *Mattering: Feminism, science, and materialism.* Vol. 1. New York: NYU Press.

Rabin, R.C. (2020) 'Pulse oximeter devices have higher error rate in patients with dark skin', *New York Times*, 22 December, https://www.nytimes.com/2020/12/22/health/oximeters-covid-black-patients.html/ (Accessed 13 January 2021).

Richardson, L.D., and Norris, M. (2010) 'Access to health and health care: how race and ethnicity matter', *Mount Sinai Journal of Medicine: A Journal of Translational and Personalized Medicine,* 77(2), pp. 166–177.

Rocha, J. (2020) 'The evolutionary history of human skin pigmentation', *Journal of Molecular Evolution* 88(1), pp. 77–87.

Saldanha, A. (2006) "Reontologising race: the machinic geography of phenotype", *Environment and Planning D: Society and Space* 24, no. 1: 9–24.

Sawh, M. (2010) "SpO2 and pulse ox wearables: Why blood oxygen is the big new health metric", *Wareable*. 17 September, https://www.wareable.com/wearable-tech/pulse -oximeter-explained-fitbit-garmin-wearables-340 (Accessed 12 January 2021).

Sharpe, C. (2016) *In the wake: On blackness and being*. Durham, NC: Duke University.

Sjoding, M.W., Dickson, R.P., Iwashyna, T.J., Gay, S.E., and Valley, T.S. (2020) 'Racial bias in pulse oximetry measurement', *New England Journal of Medicine*, 383(25), pp. 2477–2478.

Sparke, M. (2017) 'Austerity and the embodiment of neoliberalism as ill-health: Towards a theory of biological sub-citizenship', *Social Science & Medicine* 186, pp. 287–295.

TallBear, K. (2013) *Native American DNA: Tribal belonging and the false promise of genetic science*. Minneapolis: University of Minnesota Press.

Torjesen, I. (2020) 'Covid-19: Patients to use pulse oximetry at home to spot deterioration', *BMJ: British Medical Journal (Online)* 371, https://www.bmj.com/content/371 /bmj.m4151/rr-5.

Tsiakaka, O., Gosselin, B. and Feruglio, S. (2020) Source–detector spectral pairing-related inaccuracies in pulse oximetry: Evaluation of the wavelength shift. *Sensors*, 20(11): https://doi.org/10.3390/s20113302.

Turner, R.J., Brown, T.N., and Hale, W.B. (2017) 'Race, socioeconomic position, and physical health: A descriptive analysis', *Journal of Health and Social Behavior*, 58(1), 23–36.

Verkruysse, W., Bartula, M., Bresch, E., Rocque, M., Meftah, M., and Kirenko, I. (2017) 'Calibration of contactless pulse oximetry', *Anesthesia and Analgesia*, 124(1), pp. 136–145.

Vyas, D.A., Eisenstein, L.G., and Jones, D.S. (2020) 'Hidden in plain sight—reconsidering the use of race correction in clinical algorithms', *New England Journal of Medicine*, 383(9), pp. 874–882.

Wacquant, L. (2002) 'From slavery to mass incarceration'. *New Left Review* 13, pp. 41–60.

Wajcman, J. (2004) *Technoscience*. Cambridge: Polity Press.

Williams, D.R., and Jackson, P.B. (2005) 'Social sources of racial disparities in health', *Health Affairs* 24(2), pp. 325–334.

Williams, D.R., Lawrence, J., and Davis, B. (2019) 'Racism and health: evidence and needed research', *Annual Review of Public Health*, 40, 105–125.

Williams, D.R., Priest, N., and Anderson, N.B. (2016) 'Understanding associations among race, socioeconomic status, and health: Patterns and prospects', *Health Psychology*, 35(4), 407–411.

Williams, P.J. (1991) *The alchemy of race and rights*. Cambridge: Harvard University Press.

Zuberi, T. (2001) *Thicker than blood: How racial statistics lie*. Minneapolis: University of Minnesota Press.

CHAPTER 4

The Pedagogy of the Distressed: Truth-Twisters and Toxification of Higher Education

Joss Hands

1   The Rise of Truth-Twisting

The UK Civil Service Twitter feed famously had a rogue moment when its anonymous operator Tweeted a general reflection on the UK Conservative government under Prime Minister Boris Johnson, presumably right before they were fired, musing: "Arrogant and offensive. Can you imagine having to work with these truth twisters?". Having been deleted on the official account the tweet has been repeated twice a day ever since by the 'That Civil Service tweet twice a day (fan account)'. This, by now notorious tweet, clearly resonated with many people fatigued by a string of corrupt practices, dubious claims, campaigns of misinformation, deception and outright lies.

The truth-twisters of the world have experienced a notable increase in political prominence, associated with the rise of right wing and populist movements in the first decades of the 21st Century. These movements are characterised as existing across a spectrum of rightward moving tendencies. Historically their common enemies are intellectuals, the educated, and the educators. Populist rulers project such 'elites' as the enemy of the mass of 'ordinary people'. This division is a common theme of authoritarian populism, and indeed in its more extreme versions has characterised totalitarianism, which manifests a "desire to subjugate, and where possible exterminate, the groups, associations, statuses, and roles that are the building blocks of civil society" (Nisbet, 1992, p. 88).

The role of the 'masses' in this has been a recurrent theme in the progress towards fascism, as quoted from the political theorist Hannah Arendt, "no matter what the specifically national tradition with a particular spiritual source of its ideology, totalitarian government always transformed classes into masses, supplanted the party system not by one party dictatorship but by a mass movement" (Nisbet, 1992, p. 90). Despite the attack on 'elites' the totalitarian logic still necessitates the authority of rulers to "run the system" (Nisbet, 1992, p. 91). Arendt argues that the elite have little capacity for, or tolerance of, truth, "its members whole education is aimed at abolishing their capacity

for distinguishing between truth and falsehood, between reality and fiction"
(Nisbet, 1992, p. 91).

Arendt's understanding of the capacity to move at will between reality and
fiction, and to act on grounds of pure expedience, is the absence of the capacity for thought and is very much aligned with this logic. Such politics has historically come under the banner of fascism, though the definition of 'fascist'
has been especially slippery. It is no longer the case that fascism means the
kind of politics represented by the uniformed and jackbooted collective adhering to the authority of a dominant leader and an attendant elite cadre. Many of
the family resemblances of fascism are now more subtly distributed amongst a
range of more seemingly innocuous political philosophies, but which still offer
significant dangers and challenges.

At its root fascism's core characteristic is division. As Jason Stanley argues,
"The most telling symptom of fascist politics is division. It aims to separate a
population into an 'us' and a 'them'" (2018, p. xxx). This aligns with a broad
principle that states "The dangers of fascist politics come from the particular
way in which it dehumanizes segments of the population. By excluding these
groups, it limits the capacity for empathy among other citizens, leading to the
justification of inhumane treatment" (2018, p.xxiv).

Aside from provoking divisions the use of lies is a central tool of fascist
power, this is historically true – as Federico Finchelstein points out, "Fascist
political power was significantly derived from the co-optation of truth and the
widespread promulgation of lies" and what was true of historical fascism is
true now, with the new wave of populists, for whom "much like fascist leaders
of the past, a great deal of their political power is derived from questioning
reality; endorsing myth, rage, and paranoia; and promoting lies" (2020, p. 2).
Lies manifest in many forms, and this aligns with Stanley's broader claim that

> Fascist politicians justify their ideas by breaking down a common sense
> of history in creating a *mythic past* to support their vision for the pres-
> ent. They rewrite the population's shared understanding of reality by
> twisting the language of ideals through *propaganda* and promoting
> *anti-intellectualism*, attacking universities and educational systems that
> might challenge their ideas. Eventually, with these techniques, fascist
> politics creates a state of *unreality*, in which conspiracy theories and fake
> news replace reasoned debate.
>
> STANLEY, 2018, p. xxx

This view of an updated fascism manifesting in multiple new and dispersed
ways is shared by Mikkel Bolt Rasmussen (2022), who theorises the development

of a 'late capitalist fascism' in his book of the same name. Fascism in this renewed and contemporary mode is no longer reliant on unequivocal totalitarian political rule but functions "perfectly within the framework of national democracy addressing the 'real' population, animating a hollowed-out political system" and "wishes to return to a simpler time, most often the post-war era, and it does not have the swagger of inter-war fascism; it is less about colonial expansion than about returning to an imagined previous order" (Rasmussen, 2022, p. 7).

At the same time this renewal of fascism works on a much broader spectrum than formal politics, or via the direct imposition of spectacle and propaganda, rather, "late capitalist fascism is a much broader phenomena that manifests itself not just in right-wing nationalist politicians but also, and especially, in the field of culture, everyday life and online" (Rasmussen, 2022, p. 9) and as such "fascism is not merely a question of political parties and fascist leaders but also something broader – a lived reality and an unfolding process" (2022, p. 11). This lived reality includes growing intolerance and hostility, often running parallel with ever widening economic divisions, fuelled by the various capitalist crises that have unfolded since the banking crisis of 2008, and the subsequent transfer of this crisis to the public sector and the imposition of austerity legitimised by that entirely political manoeuvre.

At least three further contextual elements have acted as an accelerant to this situation, firstly the colonisation of online networks and platforms by the extreme right, secondly the creeping of that discourse into mainstream politics and media and thirdly the global Covid-19 pandemic. In the first instance the Internet offers a well-established capacity for otherwise disparate groups and individuals to network and cluster together in ways that were previously impossible. This was an affordance that was initially more utilised by the left and contributed towards the global justice movement of the early 2000s, as well as numerous activism and pro-democracy movements (Hands, 2011). The kind of mutually run and distributed open fora that were created and operated by these movements, for example Indymedia, Alternet, People's Global Action, The World Social Forum and others encouraged mutual respect and inclusivity as well as advocating for social and economic justice. The platforms built and run for these purposes were designed to reflect movement ideals as much as possible. Open source, open access, distributed across multiple servers for robust security and reliability and to ensure the wisest dissemination of information and contribution. Subsequently there has been a well-documented process of centralisation and colonisation of the Internet (Dahlberg, 2004) in which more and more of the publicly funded commons has been enclosed with a 'platformisation' of the Internet (Hands, 2013).

Platformisation intensified the process of monetising Internet traffic, directing what had previously moved through the open web though enclosed proprietorial systems. The gathering of massive amounts of data paired with pinpoint advertising provided the model that has persisted since. There are both structural and managed processes involved in the process of platformisation that have contributed towards the increasing prominence of the extreme right, though the two are linked. In terms of structural processes all the major social media platforms operate through concision – either in a spatial or temporal form. Spatially, while there is in principle unlimited space online, attention is the primary monetary resource and has a finite supply. This creates a temporal pressure to minimise time spent reading, processing and responding to messages – thus we see most social media feeds encouraging, or forcing, posts to be kept to a maximum length. Concision means that complex ideas, claims that deviate from received ideas or 'common sense' are far more difficult to express. This is further emphasised by the difficulty in supplying significant evidence to support, and or debunk, claims (Herman and Chomsky, 1994).

This is manifest in the invention of 'wokeness' as an empty signifier. To be 'woke' is framed by the right as a pejorative term that indicates a person sympathetic to minority identities, but twisted as if to appear ridiculous or extreme. 'Wokeness' as a term of attack enables the right, and conservatives more generally, to undermine the legitimacy of complaints of exclusion, oppression and demands for recognition of minority identities of anyone identifying as LGBTQ+, persons of colour, religious minorities and generally persons on the left in solidarity. Attempts by progressives to defend the ideas deemed 'woke' are then characterised as attacks on free speech. Similarly building spaces of mutual respect and recognition are deemed 'cancel culture'. These are derivations of the debates over 'political correctness' and 'political correctness gone mad' that came to prominence in the 1980s and gained traction in the culture around, for example, alternative comedy and its anti-racist and anti-sexist tendencies. It is a short journey for this notion of 'the woke' to be recast as an elitist group, a group of overeducated and privileged 'snowflakes' fermented in the universities, an elite against the 'common sense' of the masses.

Such right-wing and conservative prejudices become embedded through repetition and reinforcement amongst groups of networked sympathisers, they identify with each other, and their beliefs are underpinned by mutual reinforcement. These conditions are conducive to an ontological, as opposed to an epistemological, understanding of the world. That is a world in which understanding is led by conviction alone. This is not to decry the power and value of commitment and conviction, but there is a level of commitment that becomes attached to an identity at an ontological level, wherein only experience and evidence that supports and reinforces the ground of that identity is accepted. This is something like conformation bias, but at an even more fundamental level. The logic of the conspiracy theory or the cult applies here.

This is a phenomenon that Neal Curtis refers to as 'idiotism' (Curtis, 2012), that is 'idiot' taken from the original Greek referring to a person whose life is undertaken as separate or dislocated from the interests of society – a private person, opposed to a citizen of the polis. I have argued elsewhere that, to an extent counter-intuitively, this conceptualisation can be applied to collective behaviour. Such a grouping I referred to as an 'idiotic collective' (Hands, 2019). This is an association of individuals who form an affiliation through a set of shared beliefs that are gathered, not through any deliberative process or application of public reason, but through a process of aggregation of private beliefs and interests. These are not tested against competing arguments or evidence but reinforce each other to the extent that they 'feel right', they 'make sense' or they 'stand to reason'.

This resonates with the second accelerant of creeping discourse: many structural features of social media are shared across mainstream platforms. For example, the need for concision and direct emotional or affective impact – eyes on screens means revenue. Where we have sets of ontologically rooted 'idiotic' beliefs that circulate on social media there is a strong benefit for mainstream outlets to repeat and amplify these points of view, even if notionally as part of a 'debate'. An absurd and paranoid idea becomes a discussion about the merits of that idea, before too long it is merely a talking point, before its repetition as a claim means it needs to be seriously debunked and now there are 'two-sides' to the argument – and from there it becomes embedded in the common sense of many. The merging together of disparate grievances into an 'anti-woke' position is a dangerous form of joined up truth-twisting, resonant with the divisive tendencies of fascism mentioned above, and have become increasingly dangerous as they have been picked up and been widely publicised in mainstream UK press.

Such dynamics have been abundant in reaction to the Covid-19 pandemic, the third accelerant. We have witnessed the emergence of movements around 'anti-vax' positions, mingling with discourses of the far and 'alt' right and legitimated by a profoundly divisive politics. The common trope that passes between these tendencies is that of 'anti-woke' sentiment. Conservative figureheads gain notoriety on social media by amplifying these views, then their ideas are spread and legitimated through the press and broadcasters and often also then reproduced in the discourse of populist politics – creating an emergent structure of feeling that can readily become a gateway to more extreme ideas.

For example, the Canadian psychologist and commentator Jordan Peterson has presented himself as a victim of cancel culture when a scheduled fellowship and talk at the Cambridge Union was abandoned after complaints and protests by students. Peterson claimed this represented an example of 'cancel culture' and as such an attack on the ability to think, given that, "if you can't say what you think soon you won't be able to think" and that this represents "a battle for the heart of universities" (Chakravarty, 2021). This created a flurry of consternation and concern amongst the commentariat, for example we see Allison Pearson in the Daily Telegraph opining that "Winter is coming for free speech" and that "The abominable blizzard of snowflakes has universities frozen with fear" and that she, a nationally syndicated newspaper columnist, is "sick of being silenced by social justice warriors" (Pearson, 2019). Such views are then propagated as just a part of a debate amongst an ecosystem of sympathetic websites such as 'Rebel Wisdom' that advocate for the 'common sense' positions of Peterson and others.

Yet, as it turns out, Peterson did complete a subsequent visit to Cambridge, after being invited back in November 2021 to "attend a variety of engagements and seminars" (Moss, 2021). This return was met with significantly less commentary. Such a hyperbolic response to a 'controversy' suggests a mode of division that seeks to portray a reasoned objection to someone's presence on a particular platform as a hysterical blanket attack on free speech. While such exchanges may be perceived as minor 'culture war' skirmishes the broader implications are concerning. For example, the 'anti-woke' agenda has been picked up and shared by UK Government ministers and authoritarian political leaders around the world. I am not suggesting that the Conservative government of the UK, or other populist governments, are fascist as such, but there are several contemporary developments in the understanding of fascism as described that are resonant with the techniques of these governments, the UK being of especial interest here with practice of 'truth-twisting' as an early warning sign.

The chairman of the UK's ruling Conservative Party has made speeches denouncing 'woke' agendas, to both his own party conference and to the right-wing US thinktank The Heritage Foundation. He claimed to The Heritage Foundation that the 'woke ideology' is "a dangerous form of decadence" and that we "should be focused on external foes" and we cannot accept that "freedom is reactionary or that somehow it's kind or virtuous to submit to these self-righteous dogmas" (Mason, 2022). At the 2021 Conservative Party conference Dowden offered invective against, in this instance, "So called cancel culture". He claimed that "we've all seen this simplistic narrative in action. Divisions are heightened, statues torn down, and history rewritten. But, Conference, I'm afraid it's even worse than that. Anyone who dares resist this argument – anyone who objects to this woke aggression – is branded as instigating culture wars!" (Dowden, 2021).

A politician at the centre of the governing party expressing such views suggests that the divisive approach to shoring up power, is indeed evidence of a "hollowed out political system" that wants to return to an "imagined previous order" (Rasmussen, 2022, p. 7). Again, one of the highlighted culprits in this narrative – now that the EU can no longer be blamed – is the education system, "It's in our universities, but also in our schools" (Mason, 2022). This line of attack has been evolving at least since the UK general election of 2010 and is worth addressing as a precursor to understanding both the current situation in UK education, but also as wider indication of the dangers of truth-twisting as a flirtation with some of the fascist tendencies discussed above.

2   Truth-Twisters and the 'Blob'

When the Conservative MP Michael Gove became the UK education secretary in 2010, under the then Conservative led coalition with the Liberal Democrats, he set about attacking and undermining what he referred to as 'the Blob'. Nick Robinson, the BBC political editor at the time, wrote that "Gove sees himself as a revolutionary fighting the Blob's "progressive" grip over teacher training, classroom standards and qualifications". (Robinson, 2014). By using the term 'the Blob' Gove was undertaking a rhetorical stance designed to appeal to a populist logic in which the enemy were seen to be raising a generation in their own image, as liberal left-wing troublemakers.

The populist and purposefully divisive approach was instigated early on in the education reforms. In his analysis of the Conservative reforms James Craske argues that "Conservative politicians readily drew on an 'elite/popular antagonism', situating the reforms within a populist frame, which constituted their attempt to reorganise the social imaginary of educational thinking" (Craske, 2021, p. 280). This agenda was predicated on a view of a previous golden era that had somehow been ruined by progressives and that the reforms were designed "to restore and rectify grievances and disgruntlements that Tory politicians share about perceived 'cultural decay', declining rigour in the school system and so-called 'progressivism'" (ibid, p. 280). The Blob was subject to the paranoid treatment with Gove attesting a "conspiratorial alignment between progressives sitting on LEA committees, university departments and the quangos that they control" (ibid, p. 288). The development of an enemy block allowed the Conservatives to present themselves as the radical underdogs fighting against an out of touch elite – which is an approach honed here and revisited across several issues in subsequent years. The use of the term 'Blob' enabled the reduction of a professional and qualified group of experts to be de-legitimated at a stroke.

At the centre of the Blob were the local authorities, with their democratically accountable local representatives, and the universities, with their experienced and research driven teaching training education departments. In the first case Gove pushed through a large expansion of the academy programme that took away control from local education authorities (LEAs) switching to a direct funding model that also allowed for the introduction of academy chains sponsored by private businesses, often with strong connections to, and a shared ideology with, the Conservative Party. For example, one of the largest is the Harris Academy chain, with 51 primary and secondary schools around London, it is sponsored and 'inspired' by the Conservative peer Philip Harris (Harris Federation n.d.).

In the second case teacher training was removed from universities and handed to educational charities such as Teach First, who oversaw the shift of teacher training from universities to schools. This shift was a considered and overt political move, in which "the 'common sense' of teachers and schools is freed from 'ideologues'" (Craske 2021, p. 289). The emergence of Covid-19 afforded an opportunity to revive the trope of 'the Blob'. In a byline in the Daily Telegraph on 9 June 2020 Ross Clark blames Matt Hancock's decision not to fully reopen primary schools on 'the Blob'. Clark proclaims that was "a shameful capitulation to militant teaching unions and the naysayers who run our councils" (Clark 2020). Clark then claims that it is the education 'establishment' that is holding back schools and contributing to increasing educational inequality, as if this was anything but prudence about the spread of Covid-19. This is indeed impressive truth-twisting. Clark asks, "Why can't the government take on the Educational Blob as it has done in the past?" He associates 'the Blob' with "many on the left who have opposed schools reopening" and goes on to suggest that "schools were nevertheless happy to take part in mass protests at the weekend", those being Black Lives Matter protests – the implication being that there is a political motivation at work in maintaining school closures by the 'establishment'.

It would be worth considering that if the government and those on the right were really so keen to return schools to normal then they would have provided the funding to do so, instead school leaders "described desperately shuffling budgets, sidelining projects and plans and making do with a fraction of what was required" (Quinn 2020). The longer-term picture in education is no better. In the time since 2010 when the Conservative Party came to power the shortfall in funding of state schools, compared to private schools, has more than doubled (Sibieta 2021). Clark (2020) finishes his article by associating the failure of the government's 'levelling up' policy with "appeasing unions and councillors" which resulted in "condemning a generation of children to a lifetime of educational inequality". Again, this is quite an accusation in the context of a Conservative government who have cut at least 50% of funding from local government budgets since coming to power in 2010 (Centre for Cities, 2019). The Mail on Sunday offers a similar framing of the story. They offer the insight that "The Blob – an army made up of political opponents and union barons – is colluding to politicise the coronavirus outbreak, The Mail on Sunday has learned" (Cole, Carlin and Powell, 2020). Despite the interesting use of term 'has learned' the Mail claims that there is "outrage over a threat by unions to block schools reopening unless their demands for extra money are met by Whitehall". The outrageous demands, as reported, were "extra money for deep cleaning and personal protective equipment, and local powers to close schools if clusters of Covid-19 infections broke out". In other words, basic evidence-based public health measures. Such demands meant "Tory MPs also reacted in fury to suspicions of a Left-wing stitch-up" and castigated "irresponsible teachers". The article then offers a distinction between the education Blob and "education experts", the distinction between the Blob and experts being that the "experts" agree with the Mail and the government's political line that the teaching unions are "sacrificing children's education to make political gain". The 'expert' cited being Sir Anthony Seldon, the vice-chancellor of the University of Buckingham – the UK's only private University and often cited in defence of market based educational drives.

Such attacks are replicated across the British press with the same phrases and the same logic twisting, "Doubtless the 'Blob' is even now readying itself to exploit the disruption to exams to try and roll back hard-won reforms to standards", claims Henry Hill (2021). 'The Blob' is also 'woke', as is argued by Glen Owen, (Owen, 2021) managing to crowbar in a supposed 'woke' ban on using the phrase 'home for Christmas' – referring to civil service advice being drawn up for students travelling for the festive period. The advice was to exclude the word Christmas for the purposes of inclusivity. This was interpreted by Owen to mean that the Blob is now "waging war on Christmas" in the name of preventing the spread of Covid-19. Incredibly The 'Blob' was also blamed for the more general failures of the government's response to Covid-19. Camilla Tominey claimed that the 'managerialist' culture in Whitehall was to blame, citing a study by the think tank Civitas, she tells us "The Blob led Downing Street down the wrong path over its handling of the global pandemic" (2020). It is unclear which failures Tominey is referring to, one presumes more likely the economic one of locking down too extensively. This line of argument is resonant with Tominey's extraordinary claim that "the Blob" is "blinded by the science". The fact that the Civitas think tank is closely associated with Michael Gove, the previous Conservative education secretary and Brexit campaigner, is an offshoot of the right-wing libertarian Institute of Economic Affairs, as well as the Leave campaign, is not mentioned. Neither is the IoE's problematic relationship with representing research mentioned, with their long-standing track record of manipulating statistics for political effect (Islam, 2004).

Such conflations of 'the Blob', 'the left', 'wokeness' and Covid-19 mitigation are a clear propaganda technique across the spectrum of government and their associated supporters in the press. Theodor Adorno argues that the association of logically unconnected elements by repetition and affective interconnection are a mechanism well used in fascist propaganda, "It does not employ discursive logic but is rather, particularly in oratorical exhibitions, what might be called an organized flight of ideas. The relation between premises and inferences is replaced by a linking-up of ideas resting on mere similarity, often through association by employing the same characteristic word in two propositions which are logically quite unrelated" (1994, p. 222). Adorno also notes that "constant reiteration and scarcity of ideas are indispensable ingredients of the entire technique" (1991, p. 133) and that the purpose of such propaganda is "to win the support of millions of people for aims largely incompatible with their own rational self-interest" (1991, p. 134). Key to this for Adorno is the creation of a bond through a process of identification – to a leader or a group. In the fascism of the 1930s this was primarily to the leader, but as we've seen in relation to more contemporary forms of fascism this can be to an ideal-type identity under threat from the 'other'. Today this still draws on the "rigid distinction between the beloved in-group and the rejected out-group" (1991, p. 143). In the articles mentioned and in the general political attitude shown by the governing Conservative Party and their network of supporters and clients, the combination of mythologised past, a demonised and dehumanised group alongside an alignment between a populist elite and a 'common sense' driven segment of the population has this distinctly dangerous resonance.

3   The Toxification of Higher Education

This long-developed narrative framing is easily transferred from schools to universities and back, and whatever convenient enemy of the day can be slotted into place. When we look more closely at the place of higher education in the current cultural and political climate we can draw these threads together. At the same time that this radical reorganisation of schools and teaching training was taking place in 2010/11 there was a wholesale shift in the funding arrangement for universities from grants supported by a small top up fee towards full fees supported by a loans system, and the abolition of other grants supporting disadvantaged students – for example the abolition of the EMA (educational maintenance allowance) which supported disadvantaged students while gaining entry qualifications to university.

Given the independent nature of universities it is much harder to impose formal control on the curriculum, however the logic of turning tertiary education into a consumer product, alongside the introduction of sets of metrics around employability, 'value for money', and customer satisfaction does much of the work here. The changes were clearly designed to impose a market logic on the university system that would push non-business and training-oriented courses out of the market. The UK Universities minister Michelle Donelan makes this logic explicit in her claim to want to tackle 'mickey-mouse' courses, which for her are judged entirely on completion rates and job outcome, regardless of any other context. She makes an overt analogy between shopping and education, explaining that, "When consumers buy a product in a shop, they expect two things when it comes to quality: first, that the product has satisfied minimum standards and second, that the product has proper labelling to inform them of the quality of what goes into it" and as such can be judged "like the food in their fridge or the car on their driveway". This logic will then be used as a mechanism to sanction universities as 'requiring improvement' – yet in practice what this means is that the regulatory 'Office for Students' "will now be setting stringent minimum requirements for completion rates and graduate outcomes for every course" (Donelan, 2022).

Following Donelan's own logic this is the equivalent of arguing that we can deem food as low quality if the person eating it isn't able to run a 5k in under five minutes after eating the food, or indeed that a car could be deemed below par because the driver got caught in traffic and was late for work. A logic that is not only purely consumer oriented but doesn't even work properly in that regard. This is a version of truth-twisting as policy development and echoes the slow drum beat of the right-wing press and establishment that has been underway since at least the introduction of higher fees in 2011.

This same logic is then used by Donelan to gain political points against universities in the context of Covid-19. Universities have been under severe challenge since the outbreak of Covid-19. Donelan decided that the way to address this complex situation was by "Demanding that universities "offer students good value for money", Michelle Donelan encouraged disgruntled students to apply for their money back through the Office of the Independent

Adjudicator". The imperative then is that to 'give value for money', "universities need to get back to face-to-face teaching fully, not just a token amount" (Tominey, 2022). Not only was such an instruction offered but also universities "should not force students to wear masks because they have "sacrificed enough"" (Somerville, 2022). Though when universities were told to switch over to online only teaching, almost overnight in March 2020, no government support was offered. There was no furlough for academics or support staff, and no support for students forced to abandon their pre-paid accommodation, no support for fees reductions when leaving the house more than once a day for anything other than exercise was illegal – yet teaching went on, assignments set, completed, and assessed, students graduated – with no government support. In character with this the instruction to return to maskless face-to-face teaching in the name of good value offered no account of the risk to the health of numerous university staff in the workplace, no consultation was done – just admonition when individual universities decided to keep mask mandates in place.

This is a view in lockstep with the narrative of the populist right-wing press, who were happy to report that universities were a ""Stasi-like environment" where students police their maskless peers" (Somerville, 2022). This Covid-19 response is indicative of the more general chorus of hostility towards universities from this quarter. Such a narrative in this constantly rightward moving constellation of journalists and politicians reflects the need for an 'other', an enemy. In the absence of a now vanquished pro-European left and centre, other representatives of the 'liberal elite' are needed to take their place. Universities and their 'expert' academics fulfil this role as enemies very nicely. This approach, framing universities as havens for radical dangerous intellectuals to stifle common sense, reflects the right's general discourse about universities attacking freedom of expression. In university seminar rooms and student unions, supposedly "the subjective feelings of the most sensitive member of such a group, or of an activist claiming to represent them, override the freedom of academics and students to research, teach and express their thoughts" (Kaufman, 2021). This kind of claim is one that is made repeatedly, for example, "students attempting to hold debates on supposedly contentious topics such as feminism, abortion or Israel, may find their speakers intimidated away" (Lilico, 2021) and "Free speech campaigners last night likened some campuses to Maoist re-education camps" (Aitchison, 2020).

Such claims are nonsense, there is no evidence of any systemic silencing, there is no such common cause. A BBC Reality Check report investigated instances of free speech restrictions in universities and concluded that "of the 136 universities and more than two million higher education students in the UK, the numbers of incidents uncovered is small" (Butcher and Schraer, 2018) and "research by the government's Office for Students found that of more than 62,000 requests by students for external speaker events in English universities in 2017–18, only 53 were rejected by the student union or university" (Fazackerley, 2021).

Despite the lack of evidence, the UK government is pressing ahead with a law that is presented as protecting free speech in universities, but only serves to limit it. Freedom of expression campaigners, including Index on Censorship have explained that the planned legislation "may have the inverse effect of further limiting what is deemed 'acceptable' speech on campus and introducing a chilling effect" (Adams, 2021). Meanwhile, as Priyamvada Gopal has pointed out "scores of staff have been made redundant at Goldsmiths University, eliminating entire humanities subjects. That is real cancellation on a scale which deserves our attention" (Gopal, 2021). The defunding of large segments of higher education, crucially the critical and humanities-oriented elements, makes no sense either in immediate terms, or in terms of economic benefit – but certainly does act to contain universities as a source of opposition and free speech. Simultaneously in English schools "the Department for Education (DfE) issued guidance deeming anti-capitalism an "extremist" stance that should not be included in teaching materials". As Gopal observes, "appreciation for truth, critical thinking and facts is therefore deemed "indoctrination" of students by the left" (2021). This interpretation is attested by the reporting of this DfE advice in the Daily Mail, who observed that "Teachers will be banned from indoctrinating pupils on politically charged topics such as Black Lives Matter, the British Empire and the Israel-Palestine conflict under new guidance out today" (Harding 2022), as if this were some commonly understood and evidenced problem.

In reality, what threatens and creates systemic misery and undermines institutional autonomy and academic freedom in universities is marketisation and an attendant mental health epidemic, both intensified during the Covid-19 pandemic. A survey undertaken in October 2021 revealed that over half of the academics surveyed "show probable signs of depression" and "almost eight in 10 (79%) respondents said they need to work very intensively, often or always" and a third of respondents were in danger of burnout as they "reported feeling emotionally drained from work every day" (UCU, 2021). Another study undertaken by Durham University revealed similar findings, for example that "one in two university staff reported experiencing chronic emotional exhaustion", and that "half of the staff surveyed (47%) described their mental health as poor" (Dougall, Weick and Vasiljevic, 2021). They also crucially note, citing Kinman (2014), that even pre-Covid "overarching all these factors is the increased pressure to be "doing more with less" in the wake of the marketisation of the higher education sector". There are also shockingly high levels of casualisation and precarity in the sector which make it very hard for academics to speak out. As the general secretary of the University and Colleges Union has argued, "the biggest threats to academic freedom and free speech come not from staff and students, or from so-called "cancel culture" but from ministers' own attempts to police what can and cannot be said on campus, and a failure to get to grips with the endemic job insecurity" (Grady, 2021).

Yet, despite all this, the university sector retains relatively high unionisation levels, pension rights and autonomy. It remains one of the few industries with national pay scales, recognised collective bargaining, incremental pay advancement. Students also continue to apply in record numbers for university places. So naturally these remaining aspects of security are under concerted attack to level down the sector. As of spring 2022 there is a series of ongoing disputes and industrial action. This entails resistance to the severe downgrading of the USS pension (Universities Superannuation Scheme) that applies to the 'pre-1992' sector, which includes the Russell Group and the older red brick Universities. There is also a 'Four Fights' campaign. The Four fights include struggles for equality, against casualisation, for higher pay and manageable workloads. All these issues are direct factors in the negative experiences and exhaustion university employees face. The downward pressures these exert on security and freedom of research and expression are real and measurable impacts – the place of 'wokeism' presents nothing but a foil for the truth-twisters in the continuing war of attrition against their convenient enemy.

Covid-19 brought the best out of universities. Adaptability, resilience and cooperation allowed higher education in the UK to continue and for students to learn and graduate. Yet this achievement came at a cost of untold hours of unpaid labour, pushing an already overstretched workforce close to burn-out – and the consequence of this was for it to be weaponised in the intensified toxification and demonisation of higher education, of academics and indeed teachers too. The material reward for all this was a 40% pension cut and to be told by the minster in charge of universities that "Quite frankly, our young people have been taken advantage of" (Adams, 2020).

4   Conclusion – Defending Critical Pedagogy

The classical liberal conceptualisation of the university, as a force for the pursuit of truth, necessarily entails training in critique, it also entails freedom of expression and the security of tenure – and of course the fundamental right to be wrong. These ideals contribute towards the ideal that Wilhelm von Humboldt frames as "well-informed human beings and citizens" a higher education providing "a certain cultivation of the mind and character that nobody can afford to be without" (Günther, 1988). A somewhat more radical modern version of this sentiment comes from Paulo Freire, who argues that humans "relate to their world in a critical way. They apprehend the objective data of their reality [...] through reflection – not by reflex" (2008, p. 3). It is this understanding of our place in time, in relation to temporalities in multiple dimensions, that creates agency and consequence. Enriching and developing critical faculties through education, and the encouragement of an awareness of agency and consequence, is of fundamental importance to human freedom and flourishing.

There is a crucial difference between such a vision of critical consciousness and the kind of attitudes offered by the current 'anti-woke' mindset. The cluster of viewpoints which tend to be associated with the 'anti-woke' attitude – be they Covid-19 denial and minimisation, climate change denial, hostility towards transgender persons –are often presented as critical or independent thinking but are very far from this. In fact, invariably anti-woke sentiments are in defence of existing power structures. Power structures are being challenged because of generational shifts, but also significantly the direct result of research, of truth seeking in the areas of gender and race research, of climate change science, of epidemiology and virology and so on. The result is that 'anti-woke' and associated discredited positions become increasingly ideological, in which discredited 'truths' become myths, and beliefs become rooted in desires based on nostalgia.

We can see clear examples of this dynamic in media representation and public discourse over balance and bias. The notion of balance is a long-held principle of public broadcasting in democracies, but it very easily misunderstood or applied with disingenuous intentions. The fallacious notion that one strong idea must be balanced by a directly opposing position proves deeply flawed when we recognise that evidence matters. For example, the many years when climate change deniers were given equal footing and the right of reply based on myth alone, even when the evidence for climate change was utterly overwhelming, has proved very damaging. The BBC gave a platform to climate change deniers such as Nigel Lawson on the basis that balance was necessary, but instead this just reinforced the common-sense notion that there are 'two sides' to every argument, and reflects a further simplistic Aristotelian instinct that the truth will lie somewhere in the middle. With climate change the BBC was finally forced to concede given the massive imbalance of evidence, admitting in 2018 that "To achieve impartiality, you do not need to include outright deniers of climate change in BBC coverage" (Charrington 2018). Yet still here the notion that there should be impartiality towards climate change remains. When a truth is so fundamentally established the debate then becomes what to do about it. In this circumstance to refuse a platform that legitimates climate denial is not an infringement of freedom of speech, rather it is a defence of it because it clears the way for a meaningful discussion about the appropriate response. Yet still in many powerful quarters this denial continues, for example when key members of government committees share rogue non-peer reviewed articles – as influential Conservative MP Steve Baker did in April 2022 (Horton, 2022).

This logical fallacy is seeded widely and it allows the truth-twisters to scream about being 'cancelled' and 'silenced' across any number of issues, such as 'wokeness', Covid-19, racism and so on. Insisting on the right to a platform to spread lies, misinformation or hate is not a defence of freedom of speech but a limitation of the recognition of others, of other people's right to exist, as Freire tells us, "To be human is to engage in relationships with others and with the world" (2008, p. 3). To be a fully formed human means not simply to accept and adapt to the world as a natural given, but to integrate with it, and others, and in so doing alter and change it and each other. If the notion of a search for truth is to mean anything it is to recognise that some arguments and positions get more and more wrong over the years, and it becomes more and more difficult to defend them – knowledge moves forward, and we need to integrate our politics, practice, and sense of self with that. To engage in critical pedagogy in this context means at the very least offering an education in basic thinking to enable such capacities of judgement. This should be an essential component of any higher education and is what brings it into conflict with the truth-twisters and their dangerous dallying with fascist techniques and tendencies. What this means for educators is teaching a healthy scepticism – not cynicism. It means equipping students with an understanding of media power, economic structures and the rhetorical techniques that distort and manipulate – that is a thorough grounding in critical theory and practice. In short, pedagogy in this time of distress should be an act of bolstering intellectual and emotional defences against truth-twisting, and as such to transform distress into reflection and critical practice.

References

Adams, R. (2021) *The Guardian*, May 12. https://www.theguardian.com/education/2021/may/12/campus-free-speech-law-england-likely-opposite-effect (Accessed April 13, 2022).

Adams, R. (2020) *The Guardian*, July 1. https://www.theguardian.com/education/2020/jul/01/minister-lambasts-uk-universities-policy-for-letting-down-students (Accessed April 13, 2022).

Adorno, T. (1994) "Anti-Semitism and Fascist Propaganda". in *The Stars Down to Earth and Other Essays on the Irrational in Culture*, London: Routledge.

Adorno, T. (1991) "Freudian Theory and the Pattern of Fascist Propaganda". in *The Cultural Industries*, London: Routledge.

Aitchison, M. (2020) "Quarter of Students Self Censor in Fear of Cancel Culture at Woke Universities". *Mail on Sunday*, November 22.

Butcher, B., and Schraer, R. (2018) *BBC News*. October 28. https://www.bbc.co.uk/news/education-45447938 (Accessed April 12, 2021).

Centre for Cities. (2019) *Cities Outlook 2019*. January 28. https://www.centreforcities.org/reader/cities-outlook-2019/a-decade-of-austerity/#figure-4-change-in-total-spending-on-a-per-capita-basis-200910-201718-201718-prices (Accessed May 2, 2022).

Chakravarty, D. (2021) "Interview Jordan Peterson". December 13.

Charrington, D. (2018) *The Guardian*. September 7, https://www.theguardian.com/environment/2018/sep/07/bbc-we-get-climate-change-coverage-wrong-too-often (Accessed April 15, 2022).

Clark, R. (2020) "How can ministers 'level up' Britain if schools remain shut for months on end?; By capitulating to the Blob over the reopening of schools, children have been condemned to a lifetime of educational inequality". *The Daily Telegraph*, June 9.

Cole, Ha., Carlin, B., and Powell, M. (2020) "The Blob is Back – To Sabotage the Return to School". *Mail on Sunday*, May 10.

Craske, J. (2021) "Logics, Rhetoric and 'the blob': Populist logic in the Conservative Reforms to English Schooling". *British Educational Research Journal* 47(2): 279–298.

Curtis, N. (2012) *Idiotism*. London: Pluto Press.

Dahlberg, L. (2004) "Cyber-Publics and The Corporate Control of Online Communication". *Javnost – The Public* 11(3): 77–92.

Donelan, M. (2022) *Conservative Home*. January 21, https://www.conservativehome.com/platform/2022/01/michelle-donelan-how-the-government-will-crack-down-on-low-quality-higher-education.html (Accessed April 8, 2022).

Dowden, O. (2021) *UKPOL*. October 5, https://www.ukpol.co.uk/oliver-dowden-2021-speech-to-conservative-party-conference/ (Accessed March 31, 2022).

Fazackerley, A. (2021) *Gavin Williamson using 'misleading' research to justify campus free-speech law.* February 27, https://www.theguardian.com/education/2021/feb /27/gavin-williamson-using-misleading-research-to-justify-campus-free-speech -law (Accessed April 12, 2022).

Finchelstein, F. (2020) *A Brief History of Fascist Lies.* Oakland: University of California Press.

Freire, P. (2008) *Education For Critical Consciousness.* London: Continuum.

Günther, K.H. (1988) "Profiles of educators: Wilhelm von Humboldt (1767–1835)". *Prospects* 8: 127–136.

Gopal, P. (2021) *Aljazeera.* December 15, https://www.aljazeera.com/opinions/2021 /12/15/no-the-uk-government-is-not-defending-freedom-of-speech (Accessed April 13, 2022).

Grady, J. (2021) *UCU response to government 'free speech' proposals.* February 16. https:// www.ucu.org.uk/article/11407/UCU-response-to-government-free-speech-propos als (Accessed April 12, 2022).

Hands, J. (2011) *@ is For Activism: Dissent, Resistance and Rebellion in a Digital Culture.* London: Pluto Press.

Hands, J. (2019) *Gadget Consciousness: Collective Thought, Will and Action the age of Social Media.* London: Pluto Press.

Hands, J. (2013) "Introduction: Politics, Power and Platformativity". *Culture Machine* 14.

Harding, E. (2022) "New Rules Ban Woke Teachers from Left-Wing Brain Washing". *Daily Mail*, February 17: 71.

Harris Federation (n.d) https://www.harrisfederation.org.uk/80/welcome-from-the -chief-executive (Accessed April 29, 2022).

Herman, E, and Chomsky, N. (1994) *Manufacturing Consent.* London: Vintage.

Hill, H. (2021) "Ministers cannot afford to keep letting their domestic agenda keep get- ting blown off course by events". *The Telegraph*, April 23.

Horton, H. (2022) *The Guardian.* April 15, https://www.theguardian.com/politics/2022 /apr/15/tory-mp-steve-baker-shares-paper-denying-climate-crisis (Accessed April 15, 2022).

Islam, F. (2004) *Foreign Workers: Fact and Fiction.* April 11, https://www.theguardian. com/business/2004/apr/11/pressandpublishing.politics (Accessed April 6, 2022).

Kaufman, E. (2021) "Britain needs a university of dangerous ideas too; But new US anti- woke institution doesn't mean we should give up on fixing the existing bodies". *The Daily Telegraph*, November 10: 19.

Kinman, G. (2014) "Doing more with less? Work and wellbeing in academics". *Somatechnics* 219–235.

Lilico, A. (2021) "Some have proposed new rules enshrining universities' obligation to protect free expression on campus- another path would be competition". *The Telegraph*, November 28.

Mason, R. (2022) *The Guardian.* February 14. https://www.theguardian.com/politics/2022/feb/14/oliver-dowden-says-painful-woke-psychodrama-weakening-the-west (Accessed March 31, 2022).

Moss, B. (2021) *Controversial professor Jordan Peterson to return to Cambridge after being disinvited in 2019.* October, https://www.varsity.co.uk/news/22119 (Accessed March 30, 2022).

Nisbet, R. (1992) "Arendt on Totalitarianism". *The National Interest,* Vol. 27, Spring 1992, 85–91.

Owen, G. (2021) "Now the Woke Blob Tries to Ban Christmas". *Mail On Sunday,* November 28: 20.

Pearson, A. (2019) "Thanks to snowflake students, winter is coming for free speech". *Daily Telegraph,* March 27: 25.

Quinn, B. (2020) *The Guardian.* August 30, https://www.theguardian.com/world/2020/aug/30/covid-19-forcing-schools-in-england-to-juggle-pupil-and-financial-safety (Accessed April 29, 2022).

Rasmussen, M.B. (2022) *Late Capitalist Fascism.* Cambridge: Polity.

Robinson, N. (2014) BBC *News.* February 3. https://www.bbc.co.uk/news/uk-politics-26008962 (Accessed December 10, 2021).

Sibieta, L. (2021) *Institute of Fiscal Studies.* October 8. https://ifs.org.uk/publications/15672 (Accessed April 29, 2022).

Somerville, E. (2022) "Dozens of universities ignore easing of Covid mask rules". *The Telegraph,* March 22.

Stanley, J. (2018) *How Fascism Works.* New York: Random House.

Tominey, C. (2022) "Teach in person or give refunds, universities told". *The Daily Telegraph,* January 22: 1.

Tominey, C. (2020) "Civitas think tank accuses ministers of being 'blinded by the science' and says experts 'made many mistakes'". *The Telegraph,* June 25.

UCU. (2021) *Half of UK university staff showing signs of depression, report shows.* October 2021,https://www.ucu.org.uk/article/11839/Half-of-UK-University-staff-showing-signs-of-depression-report-shows (Accessed April 10, 2022).

Weick, D.I.M., and Vasiljevic, M. (2021) "Inside UK Universities: Staff mental health and wellbeing during the coronavirus pandemic". *Durham Research Online.* August 11, https://doi.org/10.31234/osf.io/23axu (Accessed April 11, 2022).

CHAPTER 5

'This Is Britain, Get a Grip': Race and Racism in Britain Today

David Bates

In May 2020, viral video footage of American security guard George Floyd being suffocated to death by a Minneapolis Police Officer triggered global protests under the banner of the Black Lives Matter (BLM) movement. Having initially emerged in the United States in 2013 in response to longstanding police brutality against African Americans (Taylor, 2019), in 2020 BLM protests spread rapidly across the world, shifting the focus of public debate in many countries onto racism, state violence and legacies of slavery, colonialism and imperialism. In the UK, building on earlier activism around deaths in police custody, the Windrush scandal and the Grenfell Tower tragedy, BLM protests took place in scores of towns and cities throughout the summer, in what commentators noted as some of the largest demonstrations in the country's history (Mohdin, Swann and Bannock, 2020). As UK-based film-maker and scholar Patricia Francis observed, 'in the hush created by the pandemic, there appeared to be sufficient quiet for the injustice of George Floyd's killing to reverberate unimpeded around the world' (Francis, 2021). In the midst of the BLM protests, sales of books about racism soared, while governments and multinational corporations clamoured to be seen to be publicly opposing racism in all its forms (Flood, 2020).

Even at the height of the BLM protests, however, the political right sought to reassert control of the narrative on race, racism and national history. In Britain, far-right and conservative activists mobilised on the streets to defend statues of historical figures, after BLM activists in Bristol toppled a statue of slave-trader Edward Coulson (Branscome, 2021). On social media, the hashtag 'All Lives Matter' attracted widespread support. Later in the summer, as the number of refugees crossing the English Channel increased, far-right groups mobilised to 'patrol' the English coast, while others organised protests outside hotels rumoured to accommodate refugees. Opinion polls indicated that almost half of the British public had little or no sympathy with the refugees (YouGov, 2020), while more than two thirds thought it was acceptable for the Royal Air Force or Navy to be deployed to prevent refugees from arriving in England (Ibbetson, 2020).

The British government's response to BLM, meanwhile, was to establish a Commission on Race and Ethnic Disparities (CRED) to investigate the persistence of racism in Britain. Established in July 2020, the Commission's controversial report, published in March 2021, concluded that Britain was not institutionally racist, and argued, among other things, that the education system should cover the positive legacy of 'the slave period' as well as its negative aspects (CRED, 2021, p. 8). In a House of Commons debate on Black History Month during October 2020, Equalities Minister Kemi Badenoch condemned the BLM movement, announced that the government was 'unequivocally against Critical Race Theory' and told MPs: 'We do not want teachers to teach their white pupils about white privilege and inherited racial guilt' (Badenoch, 2021).

All the while, deaths from Covid-19 soared, particularly among Black Asian Minority Ethnic communities (HM Government, 2021), yet the governing Conservative Party retained widespread support in opinion polls, at times surpassing fifty per cent. The Police, Crime, Sentencing and Courts Bill, published in March 2021, proposed that criminal damage to statues be punishable by up to ten years in prison, and created a new offence of 'intentionally or recklessly causing public nuisance' which included causing 'serious annoyance' and 'serious inconvenience'. As Liz Fekete of the Institute of Race Relations commented, taken alongside the government's New Plan for Immigration, 'the Police Bill sets the seal on a new era of state power where marginalised groups and political dissenters will be governed less as citizens than as subjects' (Fekete, 2021).

The focus of this chapter is on the role of critical scholarship in the age of authoritarian right-wing populism, particularly in the context of Covid-19 and the 'pressure cooker' atmosphere in which the aforementioned developments have taken place. It considers new resonances for theoretical and methodological approaches associated with Media, Culture and Heritage, and contends that concepts, theories and methods drawn from these academic fields are well suited to critical analysis in the age of right-wing 'culture wars'. In particular, Cultural Studies' interest in culture and popular culture as a terrain of ideological conflict is especially useful for understanding the rise of the right in the early twenty-first century, with methodological approaches drawn from Critical Discourse Studies also proving useful for understanding how racist discourses operate at the level of popular cultural practices. The chapter draws on cultural theories of race and racism to sketch out a conjunctural analysis of racism in early twenty-first century Britain, followed by a case study which examines discourses of race, national identity and heritage on Facebook. In doing so, it considers the key importance of self-reflexivity and critical political engagement for scholarship which attends to such issues. As Joseph-Salsbury

(2018, p. 45) asks: 'Should these times of explicit racist violence not be the wakeup call that urges us to do more?' With this in mind, the chapter concludes with a brief autobiographical discussion in which the author reflects on learning and teaching on 'race' as a student and educator in the early twenty-first century.

1   Racism, Whiteness and the State

Debates around race have become central to mainstream political debate in recent times. But how are race and racism conceptualised in these discussions, and how can we make sense of these concepts drawing on theories and methods from Cultural Studies? Many commentators have observed that race has become another front in an ongoing set of 'culture wars' being waged by a resurgent populist right (Chaddah, 2021). In Britain, right-wing politicians have sought to manage and defuse the radical energies unleashed by BLM by defining racism in such a way as to absolve government (and in a wider sense, the British state) from responsibility in sustaining racist structures of power. The CRED, for example, complained of a 'linguistic inflation on racism' and instead focused its attention on 'racial bias' and 'racial disparities'. In doing so, it disavowed the terms 'white privilege', 'white fragility' and 'structural racism', arguing that the latter had 'roots in a critique of capitalism, which states that racism is inextricably linked to capitalism' (2021, p. 36). This reflects broader moves among some politicians, academics and commentators to emphasise individualised attitudinal aspects of racism and to deny the racialised power relations which structure whole societies. Journalist and writer David Goodhart, for example, is cited throughout the CRED report and listed as a Commission stakeholder; in a 2014 article for the *Political Quarterly*, Goodhart argued that racism should be defined as

> irrational hostility based on race, usually accompanied by a belief in the superiority or inferiority of certain races. Today, the most common form of racism is based around the idea of stereotyping: as I have argued, we all operate with more or less conscious stereotypes much of the time, but a racist stereotype is a distinctive type premised on the assumption of fixed, and usually negative, racial characteristics.
>
> GOODHART 2014

This tendency to downplay racism's structural and institutional dimensions is certainly nothing new: as Bourne (2001) observes, racism has traditionally been considered a matter of psychology, with distrust between different groups seen as natural. Contrary to Goodhart's claim that commonly used definitions of racism are expansive and all-encompassing, racism continues to be associated with extremism in the popular imagination (Bates, 2017). Indeed, rarely has racism been popularly understood as a structural by-product of 'race' itself. Drawing on the work of Hesse (2013) and Reynaud-Paligot (2009), Lentin (2020, p. 68) has argued that the concept of 'racism' was Eurocentric from its inception: the late nineteenth and early twentieth century anthropologists who sought to demonstrate that there were no 'races' were nevertheless 'untroubled by either antiblackness or the colonial constitution of race'. Yet the links between race, racism, colonialism and capitalism are well established: as documented over a long period by scholars such as WEB du Bois, Oliver Cox, Eric Williams and Walter Rodney, the idea of race was not only used to justify slavery and colonial exploitation from the fifteenth century onwards, but also came to permeate capitalist modernity in a system Cedric Robinson (1983/2021) famously referred to as 'racial capitalism'. Hence Chun (2009, p. 7) argues that race can be seen as a 'technology of power' – a 'carefully crafted, historically inflected system of tools, mediation, or enframing that builds history and identity'. Building on Chun's work, Lentin urges race-critical scholarship to consider not what race 'is' but what race 'does'. 'Our focus', she argues, 'should be on the function performed by the idea of race and how it continues to underpin institutions, laws, policies and consequent attitudes' (Lentin, 2018, p. 44).

Such insights are central to the body of knowledge known as Critical Race Theory (CRT) (Delgado and Stefancic, 2001; Rollock and Gilborn, 2011). Despite having its own distinct history, CRT has much in common with, and almost certainly draws inspiration from, Cultural Studies work on race and racism, such as that found in classic studies like Hall et al.'s (1978) *Policing the Crisis: Mugging, the State, and Law and Order*. As Perry (2005) points out, Cultural Studies meets CRT in its focus on how popular cultural texts and practices (such as film, television and social media) play a role in the reproduction of power relations, including the operation of white supremacy through law, policing and media. In this context, the right's current preoccupation with Critical Race Theory and 'woke academics' can be seen as an attempt to shore up white supremacy through the neutering of critical anti-racist scholarship.

The concerted pushback against CRT and similar race-critical perspectives has included moves to relativise race in a bid to contend that political mobilisations around whiteness are a legitimate exercise of democratic rights. The

CRED report reflects favourably on the argument that 'even in a relatively open society like today's UK a psychological comfort can be derived from looking like the majority of people around you'. Thus, the term 'affinity bias', the report argues, 'usefully captures the tendency for groups to favour their own' (CRED 2021, p. 36). An influential figure in this regard is academic Eric Kaufmann, whose work for the Policy Exchange think-tank was cited extensively in the UK government's white paper on free speech and academic freedom in Higher Education (Department for Education, 2021). In an earlier Policy Exchange paper published in 2017, provocatively titled 'Racial Self-Interest is Not Racism', Kaufmann argued that the term racism should be reserved for 'irrational feelings about other racial groups: fear, hatred, disgust, lazy stereotypes or a perception of the other as less intelligent. In addition, a belief that one's own group must be kept "pure" is irrational because, genetically, there are no pure races' (Kaufmann, 2017, p. 10). In a blog for the London School of Economics in 2016, Kaufmann argued:

> Politicians from Gordon Brown to David Cameron have articulated a centralised Britishness based on common values and institutions. But the question politicians need to keep asking is not 'What does it mean to be British' but rather 'What does it mean to be white British' in an age of migration. This is not racist, but reflects the fact that all ethnic groups – including the majority – want their community to have a future.
>
> KAUFMANN, 2016

Such sentiments would later be echoed by Kaufmann's Policy Exchange colleague David Goodhart, who argued in the *Financial Times* that 'white self-interest is not the same thing as racism' (Goodhart, 2017). In November 2020, Goodhart, a supporter of the previous government's 'hostile environment' agenda, was appointed as a commissioner on the statutory Equality and Human Rights Commission. That such thinking finds influence in the UK government's approach to race and racism arguably reveals a great deal about the current political climate described in the introduction to this chapter, as here it is possible to discern the face of British racism in the early twenty-first century: fiercely defensive of Britain's past and sufficiently emboldened to claim the mantle of 'anti-racism' in the name of protecting 'white self-interest'. The next section of the chapter explores suitable methods for examining these discourses as they circulate in popular culture.

2   Methods for Studying Race and Racism

Racism is not a natural response to human diversity, but rather a cultural phenomenon which can be studied, challenged and collectively dismantled. Anti-racist scholarship has sought to emphasise that while race may be socially constructed, it is nevertheless materially constituted, born out in systems of oppression, domination, exploitation and discrimination. As Carter (2000, p. 4) argues, ideas about race 'have a social reality, embodied in texts of various kinds and in the practices of social life', which give race a 'definite ontological status'. The boundaries of categories such as 'white' are mutable, as seen in the contingent whiteness of the Jewish, Irish, Italian and even England's so-called 'undeserving' poor throughout modern history (Bonnett 2000; Allen 2012). As Stuart Hall memorably described it, race is a 'floating signifier', always bound up with power relations, drawing on language and myth to structure the world socially, culturally, politically and economically. Hall's work calls attention to how race involves 'specific and elaborate ideological work' to justify and reproduce societies structured in (racial) dominance. Addressing similar claims to those advanced by Kaufmann and Goodhart, Hall argued: 'The question is not whether men-in-general make perceptual distinctions between groups with different racial or ethnic characteristics, but rather what are the specific conditions which make this form of distinction socially pertinent, historically active. What gives this abstract human potentiality its effectivity as a concrete material force?' (1980/2018, p. 212).

Given the importance of language and representation in maintaining racist structures of power, what concepts and methods are appropriate for studying how race is made and re-made in different ways and at different moments? This chapter argues that Critical Discourse Analysis (CDA) provides a fruitful approach to such questions, particularly when transplanted into the realm of social media in the form of Social-Media Critical Discourse Studies (SM-CDS). Secondly, and relatedly, it is contended that the concept of 'affect' offers a useful point of departure for studying the operations of white supremacy on social media. Thirdly, it is acknowledged that the study of race on social media is fraught with ethical dilemmas, particularly issues of privacy, consent and harm. Finally, the chapter calls for a combination of academic rigour and critical self-reflexivity, in which the researcher acknowledges the role of their own biography in the research process, a factor which is crucial when discussing issues of power, inequality and ideology.

In analysing British racism in the context of austerity, Brexit and the Covid-19 pandemic, Bhattacharyya et al. (2021) make a plea for scholars to understand how racist state practices address the everyday problems and experiences of ordinary people. 'We need to think', they argue, 'about the relationship between state racism and the making of political subjectivities' (2021, p. 4). One way of pursuing this aim is through the study of discourse. Discourse Analysis has long been a staple of Media and Cultural Studies (Barker and Galasinski, 2001) and although models of analysis and terms of reference vary wildly, a great deal of work on media and popular culture has drawn upon notions of discourse associated with social theorists such as Michel Foucault, Ernesto Laclau and Chantal Mouffe. Indeed, Hall drew on such influences to suggest that race itself could be understood as the 'organising category of those ways of speaking, systems of representation, and social practices (discourses)' which differentiate some groups of people from others (1992, p. 298).

This chapter draws on the approach of Fairclough (2001) wherein discourse is understood as all communicative practices in context, including their relations with non-signifying practices: as Richardson (2004, p. 3) puts it, 'such an approach views discourse as practice, not separate from it, and therefore regards racist discourse as constitutive of racist practice'. This understanding of discourse is useful in the sense that it allows researchers to examine, in detail, how people discursively construct the world around them, how perceptions are shaped by and constitutive of language, and how language helps to reproduce social inequalities and injustices. Fairclough (2017, p. 35) argues: 'CDA is a form of critical social analysis. Critical social analysis shows how forms of social life can damage people unnecessarily, but also how they can be changed'. Drawing on an extensive repertoire of linguistic concepts, CDA pays close attention to the content of cultural texts – be they political speeches, newspaper articles or social media posts – to examine how meaning is constructed, how actions are justified, how power is enacted and how ideologies are naturalised or challenged through language. This makes it particularly well suited to the analysis of racism, where the task of the analyst is to understand where and how race is produced and reproduced, how racial logics inform and underpin social practices, and how racial rule is maintained (Lentin, 2020).

In recent years, CDA scholars have paid increasing attention to online discourse, particularly with the proliferation of user-generated content on global social media platforms such as Facebook, Twitter, YouTube and Instagram. This has led to the emergence of Social-Media Critical Discourse Studies (SM-CDS), in which the methods and perspectives of CDA are applied to social media content (KhosraviNik, 2017). Since the onset of Covid-19, the critical study of social media has arguably become even more pressing, with early data suggesting that social media usage rocketed from 2020 onwards (Ofcom, 2020). KhosraviNik and Unger (2016) note some of the characteristics of this new media ecology: a mixing and blurring of genres; access to unprecedentedly large amounts of raw data; brevity and ephemerality (as social media posts are edited or deleted); and a flow of texts which is multi-directional, as institutions jostle with individuals for attention. In their literature review of research on internet racism, Matamoros-Fernández and Farkas (2021) observe an abundance of research on social media racism in the latter half of the 2010s, and call for greater attention to be paid to how 'race is baked into social media technologies' design and governance'. In the context of the analysis below, this includes a consideration not just of Facebook's status as a multinational commercial operation, and its commercial-technological imperative for generating 'scrolls', 'clicks' and 'likes' to generate advertising revenue (Fuchs, 2017), but also the political economy of Britain's local and regional newspaper industry, whose paper sales have seen long-term decline (Ramsay et al., 2017).

Another relevant concept in the study of racism on social media is 'affect'. Drawing on Wetherell (2012), KhosraviNik (2018) observes that while the social sciences have increasingly seen an 'affective turn' in recent decades, this has arguably led to a depoliticization of media analysis, with critical theory nudged out and concepts such as power and ideology marginalised. Nevertheless, KhosraviNik argues that 'affect' remains a potentially useful means of understanding how discourses evoke and incorporate affective and emotional responses including rage, fear, disgust and excitement. While social media platforms can certainly be recognised as networks of affect, they are nevertheless discursive: they involve signifying practices which construct meaning. The interplay between these elements is an important aspect of SM-CDS.

Finally, critical analysis of racism and social media requires that very close attention be paid to the ethical implications of research. On this note, it should be made clear that the following research focuses on an online discussion which took place on the Facebook page of the researcher's local newspaper. Many of the contributions are, from an anti-racist perspective, highly problematic. Is it ethical to analyse social media content without social media users' consent? The Facebook page examined below is an open, public forum. Nevertheless, to safeguard the privacy of Facebook users, I have taken the decision not to directly identify the Facebook page in question, nor to provide any details which make its users identifiable. This includes the use of lengthy verbatim quotations: though challenging for a Critical Discourse Analysis, no lengthy excerpts are provided here, and presentation of the analysis relies on the use of brief phrases and words (Linabary and Corple, 2019; Matamoros-Fernández and Farkas, 2021).

Feminist researchers have long argued that total critical disengagement from the 'object' of research is neither possible nor necessarily desirable, and that researchers should always be 'aware of the ways in which their own biography is a fundamental part of the research process' (May 2001, p. 21). Indeed, Roseneil (1993, pp. 180–7) favours an approach that utilises a full declaration of the researcher's 'intellectual autobiography' as a means of 'locating the researcher on the same critical plane as the researched'. As she comments of her own personal and intellectual development and its bearing on her research: 'This intellectual biography is uniquely mine, mediated by my pre-existing subjectivity and prior life experiences, and it is this that has shaped my research project' (1993, p. 187). Appeals to objectivity, it is argued, mask more than they reveal and are often informed by theoretical and methodological approaches which reinforce and reproduce existing inequalities of race, class and gender. As Green states: 'Research is a political exercise – what we choose to investigate is determined by the way in which we perceive the world – that is, by what and who we see as important, unjust or repressive' (1993, p. 116).

Although not directly involved in this particular Facebook discussion, its content was highly familiar to me: in the days and weeks after Coulson was toppled, I participated in many conversations and debates with family members, friends and colleagues over the politics of race, memory, commemoration and heritage. The implications of this proximity for anti-racist scholarship and practice, particularly from the perspective of a privileged white scholar, are considered in greater depth in the conclusion.

3   'This Is Great Britain': Racism and National Identity on Facebook

The following analysis takes the form of a case study in which the concepts and methods outlined above are applied to a Facebook discussion on BLM which took place in June 2020. In early June, BLM protesters in Bristol forcibly toppled a statue of slave trader Edward Coulson. This prompted counter-mobilisations by right-wing activists who sought to defend statues and monuments against actual and perceived threats from anti-racist campaigners. In the North East of England, this resulted in a heated public debate about the legacy of historical figures celebrated in statues and monuments across the region. Several politicians in the region, mostly belonging to the Conservative Party, promptly took to social media to call on their political opponents to defend the legacy of figures depicted in statues across the North East, including the eighteenth century explorer, Captain James Cook. The legacy of Cook subsequently became the focus of numerous reports in several of the region's newspapers. One of the first of these reports, when posted on the newspaper's Facebook page, elicited over 600 comments, 277 'thumbs up' and 224 'angry' emoticon responses. The vast majority of the comments were from people who were angry at the suggestion that monuments to Captain Cook should be removed, with only a small handful arguing that Cook was complicit in Britain's history of colonial conquest.

In line with KhosraviNik's call for a focus on the affective resonances and affordances of social media, the following analysis is focused on the 10 most 'liked' comments which appear under the aforementioned Facebook post. Employing an approach inspired by SM-CDS, it is possible to explore the following questions: what might the comments in this social media debate tell us about how race and racism are understood and discussed in Britain today? What discourses are at work and how are they articulated? What kinds of rhetorical strategies are drawn upon by social media users in making their argument about Captain Cook and BLM? And how are the politics of affect implicated in these processes? The analysis proceeds in two stages: the first examines the discursive construction of Britishness in social media discourse; and the second looks at how race and racism are understood in these debates. At each stage, the analysis draws on linguistic concepts such as transitivity, presupposition and use of pronouns to examine how social media users assemble their arguments.

3.1   *Britishness*

Perhaps the most striking feature of the Facebook debate on monuments and BLM is the extent to which posters identify Captain Cook as a national hero. Perceived criticism of Cook elicits a strong affective response: 'angry face' emoticons and exclamation marks are frequent, and it is notable that the comment with the most 'likes', pushed to the top of the comments thread by virtue of its popularity, articulates barely concealed disgust with BLM protesters who criticise Cook. The comments are also permeated with 'banal nationalism': Billig (1995) observes how the regular use of pronouns can signal national belonging, naturalising a process of cultural identification which is highly ideological, and drawing people into a logic of inclusion and exclusion which seems barely conscious. This can be seen throughout the ten most popular comments, with numerous references to pride in 'our past' and 'our history'. In the single most popular comment, 'liked' by 152 people, one poster identifies very strongly with the British state: in talking about 'our past' and 'our achievements', the history of the British colonial elite becomes synonymous with the history of British people *per se*. Divisions of class, race, gender and region are overridden, and any notion that the British state represents only a segment of the wider population is foreclosed. Hall (1992) notes that British nationalism constructs a pole of identification which cuts across class and gender; an opposing argument, for example, might argue on class lines that monuments to historical figures such as Captain Cook represent 'their history' (i.e., the history of the ruling class) rather than 'our history' (the history of working class people). The extent to which nationalist ideology is normalised is also signalled in the same poster's use of idioms and euphemisms such as 'getting sick of us apologising' and 'people need to get a grip' – language which is conversational, appealing to other readers on an affective level.

Presupposition is also key: the sense of wounded national pride is predicated on an assumption that the British state and its representatives regularly apologise for their past actions; on this basis, calls for debate and discussion over Britain's past are dismissed as tiresome and unnecessary. A sense of national pride even pervades the poster's views on how BLM activists should engage in debate: it is argued that the British way is to 'argue your point' and not resort to violence. Clearly this draws on a myth of Britishness as entailing a civilising mission, with the British state's history of violent repression (at home) and conquest (abroad) expunged.

Elsewhere in the comments, one poster claims that Britain (or 'England') is being singled out and asks why other nations are not also called to account for their past actions, while many other posters complain that history is being 're-written' in a way that is unfair to Britain. In terms of the 'transitivity' of these claims – namely, who does what, to whom, and how – it is notable that it is rarely specified who or what is doing the 're-writing'. In many of the comments, BLM becomes an amorphous mass: one of the most 'liked' comments, for example, links BLM campaigners with immigration and blames them for lenient policing of criminals and poor discipline among children, while another comment likens them to terrorists. Indeed, many of the Facebook comments recall Gilroy's (1987) account of those moments of hegemonic crisis when the law itself becomes synonymous with the nation, with law-breakers constructed as a threat to a national way of life. The overall picture which emerges from these Facebook comments is one of Britain under siege from internal enemies, and anti-racists as an unlawful and unruly mob threatening the nation and its history. Furthermore, there is little in the way of dialogue: rather than engage with each other, the comments merely re-articulate the same anger repeatedly. As KhosraviNik (2018) suggests, such politics is not based on rational deliberation in the Habermasian sense but on affective communication which foregrounds feeling and reaction.

3.2   *Racism and Anti-racism*

How were race and racism discussed by posters in Facebook comments? Outbursts of overt racism were rare: one person expressed pride in their white identity but few if any posters used explicitly racialised language. More common was what Song (2014) refers to as 'racial equivalence' where even the drawing of attention to whiteness or blackness is seen to be racist. Here the currency of Goodhart and Kaufmann's 'racial self-interest' can be seen: the response of predominantly white Facebook users to BLM was one of defensiveness, articulated in an anti-racist language which relativised whiteness and Blackness.

A number of comments drew on this 'colour-blind' approach to anti-racism which essentially argued that BLM is racist because 'All Lives Matter' (though only one person actually used this specific phrase). One of the most popular comments argued that racism and accusations of racism were both 'awful'. Another argued that police brutality was bad regardless of 'skin colour'. Posters adopting this stance often drew on what van Dijk (1993) refers to as positive self-presentation and negative other-presentation: posters emphasised their reasonableness with disavowals of racism and prejudice, or by acknowledging that we must (as a nation) 'learn from our mistakes'. This was followed by condemnation of BLM for their violence or extremism. Another one of the most popular comments, liked by 93 people, accused BLM of amplifying 'racial tensions'. Above all, BLM and anti-racist campaigners were constructed as extremists, who make 'race' into an issue when it is supposedly irrelevant. As Lentin (2020, p. 54) comments, 'naming racism is heard as an outrageous accusation' and this stems from the white, Eurocentric definition of racism which prevails in the popular imagination, associating racism with the long-forgotten past, or with political extremism

In another popular comment, 'liked' by 59 people, a poster sarcastically asks whether Captain Cook statues might be replaced with statues of Martin Luther King, Nelson Mandela or the 'violent criminal' George Floyd. In a rare example of direct engagement between different posters, a debate ensues in which a number of posters denounce Nelson Mandela as a 'terrorist'. Through the repeated emphasis on this point – BLM as violent, George Floyd as criminal, Nelson Mandela as terrorist – Blackness is linked with violence and criminality, whiteness remains an invisible, civilised, non-violent norm, and Britain's history of imperial violence is expurgated from national history.

4   Conclusion

The brief analysis above suggests that British racism in the early twenty-first century has seen a renewed preoccupation with nation, empire and 'white self-interest', and frequently draws on the language of equality and anti-racism. This can be seen at both an elite and popular level, from the UK government's official report on racism to the Facebook comments of a local newspaper report on BLM. The structuring power of race is disavowed, with whiteness and Blackness relativised, and the label of 'racism' consigned either to history or the political margins. In this perverse culture of racial equivalence, white English people are as much the victims of racism as people of colour (Lentin, 2020; Song, 2014).

CDA is useful for closely examining how such claims are made, and on what grounds they are justified, while SM-CDS accounts for the particular affordances and affective resonances of these discourses on social media. But once this analysis is undertaken, and the operations of racist discourse are understood, with findings published in books and journals, what comes next? Speaking in 1990, Stuart Hall reflected on the status of Cultural Studies in the midst of the AIDS epidemic. His words are arguably as relevant in the age of George Floyd and Covid-19 as they were three decades ago:

> Against the urgency of people dying in the streets, what in God's name is the point of Cultural Studies? [...] At that point, I think anybody who is into Cultural Studies seriously as an intellectual practice, must feel, on their pulse, its ephemerality, its insubstantiality, how little it registers, how little we've been able to change anything or get anybody to do anything. If you don't feel that as one tension in the work that you are doing, theory has let you off the hook.
>
> HALL, 1992/2018, p. 83

Teaching students to understand and recognise racist discourse can be a worthy and rewarding endeavour, but is it enough? For white scholars, even to ask the question can seem like a righteous self-indulgence. The recent prominence of BLM has at least put the notion of white allyship on the public agenda, perhaps to a greater degree than ever before. Apart from listening to, and boosting, the voices of people of colour, anti-racist scholarship in the early twenty-first century requires engagement well beyond the confines of academia: in homes, health care settings, workplaces, community centres and on the streets as well as online. Addressing academics of colour, Joseph-Salsbury (2018) offers five points of praxis which form a useful guide for anti-racist academics: be aware of the historical and contemporary role of the university in maintaining white supremacy; speak truth to power, using expertise and specialist knowledge to put forward anti-racist counter-narratives wherever possible; support academics of colour in their work and career trajectory; know and connect with local communities; and consider who benefits from the research being undertaken. 'To be anti-racist', writes artist-activist Joshua Virasami (2020, p. 114), 'means to involve yourself directly in the movement to end racism: to take action'. This is, without doubt, the very least that can be done by any scholar whose work involves learning, teaching or writing about racism.

References

Allen, T.W. (2012) *The Invention of the White Race, Volume 1: Racial Oppression and Social Control.* London: Verso.

Badenoch, K. (2021) 'Black History Month' *Hansard: House of Commons Debates,* 20 October, 682, c1012. https://hansard.parliament.uk/commons/2020-10-20/debates/5B0E393E-8778-4973-B318-C17797DFBB22/BlackHistoryMonth.

Barker, C., and Galasinski, D. (2001) *Cultural Studies and Discourse Analysis: A Dialogue on Language and Identity.* London: Sage.

Bates, D. (2017) The 'red door' controversy: Middlesbrough's asylum seekers and the discursive politics of racism. *Journal of Community and Applied Social Psychology,* 27, pp. 126–136. DOI: https://doi.org/10.1002/casp.2300.

Bhattacharyya, G., Elliott-Cooper, A. Balani, S. Nişancıoğlu, K., Koram, K., Gebrial, D., El-Enany, N., and de Noronha, L. (2021) *Empire's Endgame Racism and the British State.* London: Pluto.

Billig, M. (1995) *Banal Nationalism.* London: Sage.

Bonnett, A. (2000) *White identities: historical and international perspectives.* Harlow: Prentice Hall.

Bourne J. (2001) 'The Life and Times of Institutional Racism', *Race & Class,* 43(2), pp. 7–22. DOI: https://doi.org/10.1177/0306396801432002.

Branscome, E. (2021) 'Colston's Travels, or Should We Talk About Statues?', *ARENA Journal of Architectural Research,* 6(1), pp. 1–29: DOI: http://doi.org/10.5334/ajar.261.

Carter, B. (2000) *Realism and racism: concepts of race in sociological research.* London: Routledge.

Chaddah, K. (2021) 'The Tories Are on a Mission to Destroy Black Lives Matter', *Novara Media,* 26 July. https://novaramedia.com/2021/07/26/the-tories-are-on-a-mission-to-destroy-black-lives-matter/.

Chun, W.H.K. (2009) 'Introduction: Race and/as Technology; or, How to Do Things to Race', *Camera Obscura,* 24, 1(70), pp. 7–35. DOI: https://doi.org/10.1215/02705346-2008-013.

Commission on Race and Ethnic Disparities (2021) *Commission on Race and Ethnic Disparities: The Report.* https://assets.publishing.service.gov.uk/government/uploads/system/uploads/attachment_data/file/974507/20210331_-_CRED_Report_-_FINAL_-_Web_Accessible.pdf.

Delgado, R., and Stefancic, J. (2001) *Critical Race Theory: An Introduction*. New York & London: New York University Press.

Department for Education (2021) *Higher education: free speech and academic freedom*. https://www.gov.uk/government/publications/higher-education-free-speech-and -academic-freedom.

Fairclough, N. (2001) *Language and Power*. 2nd ed. Harlow: Longman.

Fairclough, N. (2017) 'CDA as dialectical reasoning' in J. Flowerdue, and J.E. Richardson, (eds.). *The Routledge Handbook of Critical Discourse Studies*. London: Routledge, pp. 35–52.

Fekete, L. (2021) 'Policing in the Brexit State – Back to the 1980s', *Institute of Race Relations*, 26 March. https://irr.org.uk/article/policing-in-the-brexit-state-back-to -the-1980s/.

Flood, A. (2020) 'Anti-racist book sales surge in US and Britain after George Floyd kill-ing', *Guardian*, 3 June. https://www.theguardian.com/books/2020/jun/03/anti-rac ist-book-sales-surge-us-uk-george-floyd-killing-robin-diangelo-white-fragility.

Francis, P. (2021) 'Black Lives Matter: how the UK movement struggled to be heard in the 2010s', *The Conversation*, 7 June. https://theconversation.com/black-lives-mat ter-how-the-uk-movement-struggled-to-be-heard-in-the-2010s-161763.

Fuchs, C. (2017) *Social Media: A Critical Introduction*, 2nd Edition. London: Sage.

Gilroy, P. (1987) *There Ain't No Black in the Union Jack*. London: Routledge.

Goodhart, D. (2014) 'Racism: Less is More', *The Political Quarterly*, 85, pp. 251–258. DOI: https://doi.org/10.1111/1467-923X.12097.

Goodhart, D. (2017) 'White self-interest is not same thing as racism', *Financial Times*, 3 March. https://policyexchange.org.uk/white-self-interest-is-not-same-thing-as -racism/.

Green, P. (1993) 'Taking sides: Partisan research on the 1984–1985 miners' strike', in D. Hobbs, and T. May (eds.) (1993) *Interpreting the Field: Accounts of Ethnography*. Oxford: Oxford University Press, pp. 99–121.

Hall, S., Critcher, C. Jefferson, T., Clarke, J., and Roberts, B. (1978) *Policing the Crisis: Mugging, the State, and Law and Order*. London: Macmillan.

Hall, S. (1992) 'The question of cultural identity', in S. Hall, D. Held, and T McGrew (eds.) *Modernity and its Futures*. Cambridge: Polity Press, pp. 273–316.

Hall, S. (1980/2018) 'Race, Articulation, and Societies Structured in Dominance' in. S. Hall, and D. Morley (eds.) *Essential Essays, Volume 1: Foundations of Cultural Studies*. Durham: Duke University Press, pp. 172–221. DOI: https://doi.org/10.1215/978147 8002413-010.

Hall, S. (1992/2018) 'Cultural Studies and Its Theoretical Legacies', in S. Hall, and D. Morley (eds.) *Essential Essays, Volume 1: Foundations of Cultural Studies*. Durham: Duke University Press, pp. 71–100. DOI: https://doi.org/10.1215/9781478002 413-006.

Hesse, B. (2013) 'Raceocracy: How the racial exception proves the rule', *Irving K. Barber Learning Centre, University of British Columbia,* 7 March. DOI: https://dx.doi.org /10.14288/1.0076724.

HM Government (2021) *Third quarterly report on progress to address COVID-19 health inequalities.* https://assets.publishing.service.gov.uk/government/uploads/system /uploads/attachment_data/file/1015026/Third_Covid_Disparities_Report_correcti ons.pdf.

Ibbetson, C. (2020) 'Should the military patrol the English Channel?', *YouGov,* 13 August. https://yougov.co.uk/topics/politics/articles-reports/2020/08/13/support -RAF-Navy-English-Channel-migrant-crossing.

Joseph-Salisbury, R. (2018) 'Confronting my duty as an academic of colour in times of explicit racial violence', in. A. Johnson, R. Joseph Salsbury, and B. Kamunge (eds.) *The Fire Now: Anti-Racism in Times of Explicit Racial Violence.* London: Zed Books.

Kaufmann, E. (2016) 'Assimilation and the immigration debate: shifting people's attitudes', *British Politics and Policy at LSE.* https://blogs.lse.ac.uk/politicsandpolicy/ assimilation-and-the-immigration-debate-shifting-peoples-attitudes/.

Kaufmann, E. (2017) 'Racial self-interest is not racism: Ethno-demographic interests and the immigration debate', *Policy Exchange.* https://policyexchange.org.uk/wp -content/uploads/2017/03/Racial-Self-Interest-is-not-Racism-FINAL.pdf.

KhosraviNik, M. (2017) 'Social Media Critical Discourse Studies (SM-CDS)' in J. Flowerdew, and J.E. Richardson (eds.) *Routledge Handbook of Critical Discourse Studies.* London: Routledge, pp. 582–596.

KhosraviNik, M. (2018) 'Social Media Techno-Discursive Design, Affective Communication and Contemporary Politics', *Fundan: Journal of the Humanities and Social Sciences,* 11(4), pp. 427–442.

KhosraviNik, M., and Unger, J. (2016) 'Critical Discourse Studies and Social Media: Power, resistance and critique in changing media ecologies', in R. Wodak, and M. Meyer (eds.) *Methods of Critical Discourse Studies.* London: Sage, pp. 206–233.

Lentin, A. (2018) 'Beyond denial: 'not racism' as racist violence', *Continuum: Journal of Media & Cultural Studies,* 32(4), pp. 1–15. https://doi.org/10.1080/10304312.2018.1480309.

Lentin, A. (2020) *Why Race Still Matters.* Cambridge: Polity Press.

Linabary, J.R., and Corple, D.J. (2019) 'Privacy for Whom?: A Feminist Intervention in Online Research Practice', *Information Communication and Society,* 22(10), pp. 1447–63.

Matamoros-Fernández, A., and Farkas, J. (2021) 'Racism, Hate Speech, and Social Media: A Systematic Review and Critique', *Television & New Media,* 22(2), pp. 205– 224. DOI: https://doi.org/10.1177/1527476420982230.

May, T. (2001) *Social research methods: Issues, methods and process.* Buckingham: Open University Press.

Mohdin, A. Swann, G., and Bannock, C. (2020) 'How George Floyd's death sparked a wave of UK anti-racism protests', *Guardian,* 29 July. https://www.theguardian.com /uk-news/2020/jul/29/george-floyd-death-fuelled-anti-racism-protests-britain.

Ofcom (2020) 'UK's internet use surges to record levels', 24 June. https://www.ofcom .org.uk/about-ofcom/latest/media/media-releases/2020/uk-internet-use-surges.

Perry, I. (2005) 'Cultural Studies, Critical Race Theory and Some Reflections on Methods', *50 Vill. L. Rev,* 915. https://digitalcommons.law.villanova.edu/vlr/vol50 /iss4/14.

Ramsay, G.N., Freedman, D., Jackson, D., and Thorsen, E. (2017) *Mapping changes in local news 2015–2017: More bad news for democracy?* https://www.mediareform.org.uk/wp -content/uploads/2015/11/Mapping-changes-in-local-news-2015-2017-interactive .pdf.

Reynaud-Paligot, C. (2009) *La République raciale: Paradigme social et idéologie républicaine, 1860–1930.* Paris: Presses Universitaires de France.

Richardson, J. (2004) *(Mis)Representing Islam: The racism and rhetoric of British broadsheet newspapers.* Amsterdam: John Benjamins.

Robinson, C. (1983/2021) *Black Marxism: The Making of the Black Radical Tradition.* London: Penguin.

Rollock, N., and Gillborn, D. (2011) 'Critical Race Theory (CRT)', *British Educational Research Association,* https://www.bera.ac.uk/wp-content/uploads/2014/03/Criti cal-Race-Theory-CRT-.pdf.

Roseneil, S. (1993) 'Greenham revisited: Researching myself and my sisters', in D. Hobbs, and T. May (eds.) *Interpreting the Field: Accounts of Ethnography.* Oxford: Oxford University Press, pp. 177–208.

Song, M. (2014) 'Challenging a culture of racial equivalence', *The British Journal of Sociology,* 65, pp. 107–129. DOI: https://doi.org/10.1111/1468-4446.12054.

Taylor, K.Y. (2019) 'Five Years Later, Do Black Lives Matter?', *Jacobin,* 30 September. https: //jacobinmag.com/2019/09/black-lives-matter-laquan-mcdonald-mike-brown-eric -garner.

van Dijk, T.A. (1993) *Elite discourse and racism.* London: Sage.

Virasami, J. (2020) 'Anti-racism requires more than passive sympathy', in G. Blakeley. (ed.) *Futures of Socialism: The Pandemic and the Post-Corbyn Era.* London: Verso, pp. 113–116.

Wetherell, M. (2012) *Affect and emotion.* London: Sage.

YouGov (2020) *How much sympathy do you have, if any at all, for the migrants who have been crossing the channel from France to England?* 11 August. https://yougov.co.uk /topics/politics/survey-results/daily/2020/08/11/f4dc7/1.

CHAPTER 6

Traditional Chinese Medicine Is Fake: Politicised Medical Commentaries in China in the Covid-19 Pandemic

Altman Yuzhu Peng

1 Introduction

During the unprecedented Covid-19 pandemic, investing in medical science to combat the $SARS\text{-}CoV\text{-}2$ virus has become an administrative priority in almost every national government in the world. Under these circumstances, we have witnessed more and more political interference in the public health sector. High-profile incidents of this kind include Donald Trump's controversial support for hydroxychloroquine treatment for Covid-19 patients, which was heavily criticised by both scientists and the media (BBC, 2020a). In China, where the outbreak started, such political interference is most notably reflected in the Chinese government's advocacy of traditional Chinese medicine (TCM) treatment for Covid-19 patients (The Paper, 2020). This public health policy most recently prompted a wave of public debates on TCM in Chinese society. The influence of the current debate on TCM has gone far beyond the science community, which is evidenced by volumes of related commentaries posted on various social media platforms (Peng & Chen, 2021). The most recent wave of debates on TCM is indeed indicative of how public health-related topics are politicised in Chinese society during the Covid-19 pandemic.

The way in which the current TCM debate has unfolded on the Chinese Internet[1] is contextualised against the backdrop of the Chinese government's pandemic crisis management being assessed by Chinese people in relation to the escalation of the crisis in Europe and North America. Due to the Chinese authority's pro-TCM propaganda campaign, the use of TCM has become a symbolic dimension of its pandemic responses. Against this background, public criticisms of TCM have become associated with political challenges to the Party leadership, which undermines the legitimacy of the authoritarian political

---

1 Here the Chinese Internet refers to the Internet used by people living in China, where the state government's censorship system has effectively created a digital environment more or less disconnected from the outside world.

system. At a time when public opinions are constantly changing as the pandemic unfolds, such criticisms have become highly concerning to the Party leadership (Dyer, 2020). This, in part, explains why a controversial consultation draft was tabled by the Beijing local authority, which aims to criminalise 'slander or defamation of TCM' (The Paper, 2020). The attempt to legally penalise critics of TCM is of little relevance to the scientific debate itself. Instead, it is part of the holistic approach taken by the Chinese government to deal with public criticisms within an authoritarian polity. If this argument holds, it may also rationalise outside observers' questioning of why the World Health Organization (WHO) dropped its warnings against herbal medical treatment for Covid-19 patients, which reflects the Chinese government's political manipulation behind the scenes (BBC, 2020b).

This chapter makes no attempt to reassess the controversy surrounding TCM through a scientific or health communication lens. Instead, I explore the current TCM debate between Chinese Internet users by analysing the political motives behind their postings. Given the symbolism of TCM in Chinese culture and the framing of modern medicine as a Western concept in the Chinese language (Zheng, 2006), the current debate provides an opportunity to foreground how nationalist sentiments and dissenting opinions play out at the intersection of political and scientific discourses on the Chinese Internet. Such an account helps us to assess the politicisation of medical commentaries by Internet users inhabiting different ends of the political spectrum in order to rationalise their public opinions in the wake of the pandemic. It feeds into Fang and Repnikova (2018) and Schneider's (2018) conceptualisation of the rise of nationalism and political polarisation in Chinese society.

This research is based on a case study conducted on the most popular Chinese community question-answering (CQA) site – Zhihu. Similar to its English equivalent, Zhihu is branded as a social media platform for knowledge-sharing, and this branding has effectively encouraged middle-class intellectuals' participation (Peng & Chen, 2021). Marketing research reveals that "typical Zhihu users are university students and professionals living in [...] cities, with 80% possessing a bachelor's degree or above" (Zhang, 2020b, p. 96). Due to the user demographics, the posts circulated on Zhihu generally feature "quality, argumentative, and information-rich" content and often relate to trending topics on current socio-political affairs (Zhang, 2020b, p. 96). In the present research, I sampled a question, titled *"what role does Chinese medicine play in the Covid-19 pandemic"* (中医药在此次新冠肺炎疫情中起到了哪些作用), posted on Zhihu on 7th February 2020. The question invited Zhihu users to assess the effectiveness of TCM in the context of Covid-19 patient treatment and was the most answered question of this kind (URL:

https://www.zhihu.com/question/370162778; 1,906 posts, 3,416,869 views; 4,222 followers). Using the question as a data repository, I collected a total of 1,906 posts from Zhihu and analysed them by using thematic analysis. A thematic analysis method offers a qualitative account of the themes embedded in textual data (Guest et al., 2014). The implementation of this method allowed me to offer a snapshot of how the politicisation of TCM unfolds on the Chinese Internet from the perspective of textual analysis.

The remainder of this chapter proceeds with a review section, which provides a discussion of the context in which TCM debates take place in China today. This is followed by a detailed analysis of the empirical data, which captures how TCM debates have unfolded on Zhihu in the wake of the Covid-19 pandemic. The socio-political implications of the research findings are also discussed.

2   Background

2.1   *Overt Nationalist Sentiments and Subtle Dissenting Opinions*

Recent scholarship has noted the rise of nationalist sentiments in Chinese society (Fang & Repnikova, 2018; Schneider, 2018; Zeng & Sparks, 2020). Such nationalist sentiments are a construct of the modern narratives of Chinese history, which highlight both the ancient glories of the East Asian country and its defeats in military encounters with Western powers in the late 19th and the early 20th century (Ji & Bates, 2020; Peng, 2021b). Given this emphasis, such narratives have constructed a dual-face image of the West in the minds of the Chinese public. On the one hand, the defeats of China by Western powers are understood to have opened the country's once closed border, which has effectively facilitated its commercial and cultural exchanges with the outside world (Cong, 2009). On the other hand, these military defeats have also smashed the ancient glories of the country, creating a collective memory of national humiliation unique to Chinese national identity (Tang & Darr, 2012). As such, while acknowledging that the West has cultivated the world's highest level of industrialisation and material prosperity, many Chinese people also believe that Chinese civilisation is very unique, and it requires a political system different from Western-style democracy to uphold its modernisation (Cong, 2009). The dual-face image of the West characterises a notable aspect of Chinese nationalist ethos, enabling Chinese people to contextually "oscillate between identifying with the local and national [...] and aspiring to the Western and cosmopolitan" (Gao, 2016, p. 1,204).

The recent rise of nationalism in Chinese society both exploits and feeds into the changing political climate. Since the late 1970s, the CCP's reform of the economy has effectively addressed absolute poverty in China, providing people with a wide range of life choices (Peng, 2021a, 2021b). Yet, amid the widening gap between the rich and the poor, and growing cases of official corruption, there are also mounting domestic voices critical of the administration (Yu, 2014). With national pride representing an "important value shared by the regime and its domestic critics", nationalist propaganda campaigns have been adopted by the CCP to reaffirm its authority (Steele & Lynch, 2013, p. 443). A nationalist propaganda campaign requires an imaginary 'external enemy' to stimulate a centripetal hostility in the population. Being historically portrayed as both villains and enlighteners in China's modernisation, there is no better 'external enemy' than Western democracies, whose existence facilitates the CCP's propagation of nationalist rhetoric. This rhetoric, which paints Western democracies as hostile to the renaissance of China, is well-received by advocates of nationalism, as demonstrated by a series of recent pro-regime demonstrations in Sino-foreign political disputes (Fang & Repnikova, 2018; Schneider, 2018). In this process, a positive portrayal of the CCP's Party-State polity is simultaneously created, representing an alternative path to modernisation (Wu, 2020).

Certainly, the popularity of nationalist ethos in mainstream opinions by no means suggests that dissidents do not exist in China. Nationalist sentiments are evidently dismissed by many domestic critics of the CCP, who tend to embrace the ideas of Western democracy (Tang & Darr, 2012). However, given the authority's strict political censorship and technology-assisted propaganda campaigns, such dissenting voices do not resonate as much as their opponents on the Chinese Internet (Keane & Su, 2019). This is especially the case since Xi Jinping became president and government-paid commentators have been aggressively deployed on social media platforms to distort public attention (King et al., 2017). In this politically restrictive environment, the expression of dissenting opinions, therefore, often takes a subtle form which is reflective in how Internet users engage with seemingly apolitical affairs or political affairs occurring outside of China. This is done by sub-textually communicating their views – particularly those that are not in line with the CCP's policies (Fang, 2020; Pfafman et al., 2015). An understanding of the uniqueness of Chinese political engagement offers us scope to unpack how debates on TCM play out in Chinese society today.

2.2 The Politics of Debates on Traditional Chinese Medicine

The recent public debate on the efficacy of TCM provides an up-to-date case study to illustrate how nationalist and liberal-leaning Internet users clash on Chinese social media platforms. In China, discussions about the efficacy of TCM have always been intertwined with politics. Sun Yat-Sen, recognised by both the Chinese Communist Party (CCP) and the Chinese Nationalist Party (CNP) as the 'founding father' of modern China, was a high profile sceptic of TCM and was reported to have refused such treatment in the very last moments of his life (Schiffrin, 1970). Sun claimed that "some Chinese drugs might be effective, [but] knowledge of a [biomedical] diagnosis is lacking [in TCM]" (Lei, 2014, p. 1). However, his reported refusal of TCM treatment was not based on purely scientific reasoning. Rather, it amounted to a political statement, which fed into his revolutionist ideology of the early 20th century. It underscored how one's acceptance of Western democratic politics could be articulated through their support for modern medicine, which was considered a symbolic achievement of Western civilisation in the Chinese context (Lei, 2014).

The existence of high-profile sceptics does not change the fact that TCM is still supported by a large cohort of Chinese people today. Certainly, the development of TCM was inseparable from ancient medical practitioners' empirical observation and clinical experience. Many medical studies have also confirmed the efficacy of certain TCM herbs by using modern research methods (Scheid, 2002). However, the knowledge system of TCM is unique and sits uneasily in the paradigm of modern scientific inquiry (Wang & Farquhar, 2009). Under these circumstances, many Chinese patients are evidently taking a rather pragmatic approach to the use of TCM in their everyday lives. While acknowledging that the unique knowledge system of TCM emerges as an obstacle to modern science as a subject area (Wang & Farquhar, 2009), they accept the "empirical and time-tested value" of TCM treatment without questioning its scientific basis (Rogaski, 2014, p. 305).

Given the strong social basis for TCM treatment in China, it continues to play an important role in the country's public health sector. Unlike public health systems elsewhere, the Chinese equivalent is characterised by its dual-track, which provides both modern and traditional medical treatments for Chinese patients to choose from (Scheid, 2002). The establishment of this dual-track public health system is often considered as a result of the first-generation CCP leader – Mao Zedong's – 'concluding remarks' on the TCM debate, which ended the abolition of the TCM movement at an institutional level (Zheng, 2006). In this sense, the institutionalisation of TCM in China's public health system is part of the Party founder – Mao Zedong's – political legacy, which is constitutive of China's Party-State polity. This contingent political legitimacy, in part, explains the Chinese government's support for TCM treatment in its pandemic propaganda campaign.

The CCP's political endorsement for TCM treatment has been highly visible in public discourses around the Covid-19 pandemic. Since early 2020, when the outbreak was still mainly within the Chinese territory, one of the leading experts in China's Covid-19 medical task force, Zhong Nanshan, began calling for scholarly attention to the value of TCM treatment for patients infected with Covid-19 (Peng & Chen, 2021). His positive note on TCM is, in part, supported by many scientific reports, in which non-double-blind clinical trials seem to have proved the usefulness of TCM treatment (Li et al., 2020; Ren et al., 2020). Both expert opinions and scientific evidence are used, as in other CCP propaganda campaigns, to endorse its long-standing official position of support in the TCM debate (National Administration of Traditional Chinese Medicine, 2020). As a consequence of this, TCM is no longer viewed as an alternative medical treatment. Instead, it has been repacked as a political symbol, with notable indigenous features, which aligns with the definition of the CCP's Party-State system coined by Deng Xiaoping as 'socialism with Chinese characteristics'. TCM has also been promoted through official media channels as a way to reinforce the CCP's public health policies and help to contain the spread of Covid-19.

Nonetheless, the CCP's support for TCM treatment in its Covid-19 pandemic response sparked some controversy. In the early stages of the outbreak, a research team based in the Chinese Academy of Sciences claimed that their testing results confirmed the efficacy of the Shuanghuanglian Oral Liquid, a patent drug extracted from Chinese herbs, for Covid-19 patient treatment (Peng & Chen, 2021). After the announcement was broadcast, the Shuanghuanglian Oral Liquid was quickly sold out on almost all major Chinese e-shopping websites. However, this announcement was widely criticised by medical experts because the scientific basis of the testing results was considered unreliable due to the absence of strictly designed clinic trials. This provoked a wave of public anger, which encouraged a fresh debate on TCM treatment online. This most recent TCM debate unfolding on Chinese social media platforms has evidently captured the CCP's attention, which explains why the Beijing local authority attempted to censor the debate in mid-2020 by criminalising 'defamation or slander of TCM' (The Paper, 2020).

With the current TCM debate in mind, we can see how the government's pandemic crisis management (i.e. its broad political thought management and citizen expression of their political) views intersect on the Chinese Internet. Compared with many major Western democracies, the CCP's pandemic crisis management can be seen as 'successful' after it abandoned the cover-up strategy at the very beginning of the outbreak (Zhang, 2020a). This successful handling of the crisis is sustained by the CCP's use of unprecedented lockdown measures, alongside its control of people's access to information as well as physical mobility through the launch of strict contact-tracking policies and broader digital surveillance systems (Rodrigues & Xu, 2020; Yang et al., 2021). The implementation of such measures has ensured China's nationwide collectivist response to the Covid-19 crisis (de Kloet et al., 2020). As the pandemic sweeps across the world outside of the Chinese territory, the 'success' of the CCP's pandemic crisis management has fuelled Chinese people's support for the regime, with many self-motivated pro-CCP Internet users being mobilised to express their nationalist sentiments on various popular social media platforms (Zhang, 2020a). Yet, because of the intersecting forces that make up China's political spectrum, affairs concerning the pandemic have opened up opportunities for Internet users to engage in wider social debates (Peng et al., 2022a; Peng et al. 2022b). This raises the question of how the CCP's advocacy of TCM is received by the general public beyond the context of public health. This reception can be traced by analysing how medical commentaries are appropriated by people with differing political views to reassess the CCP's legitimacy in a politically restrictive Chinese digital environment.

3   Analytical Discussion

As previously mentioned, the present research is based on a case study collecting Zhihu users' postings in comment threads below a question entitled "*what role does Chinese medicine play in the Covid-19 pandemic*" (中医药在此次新冠肺炎疫情中起到了哪些作用) asked on 7th February 2020. Utilising the volume of posts collected (N = 1,906), I first calculated the frequency of content words used in the postings (Table 6.1) to sketch out the key themes addressed by Zhihu users.

As represented in the word list, different expressions concerning TCM constitute a cluster of the most frequently used content words (7,572 hits). This phenomenon emerges alongside medical science-related terms, such as Covid-19 (2,671 hits), Western medicine (2,671 hits), pneumonia (1,480 hits), patient (1,460 hits), and clinic (681 hits), which are used repeatedly throughout. The linguistic features show that aspects of Zhihu users' postings indeed occur in a way that shows relevance to the long-existing debate on the scientisation of TCM in Chinese society. In contrast to scientific publications, however, Zhihu users' frequently reference first-person pronouns (I: 2,644 hits) which reveals

TABLE 6.1   Content-word list by hits[a]

Word	In Chinese	Hits
(traditional) Chinese medicine	中医, 中药, 中医药	7,572
Covid-19	Covid, 新冠, 冠状病毒	2,671
I	我	2,644
Western medicine	西医, 西药	1,644
treatment	治疗	1,544
pneumonia	肺炎	1,480
People	人	1,471
Patient	患者, 病人, 病患	1,460
You	你	1,389
Research	研究	1,062
We	我们	980
Function	作用	905
(modern) medical science	(现代) 医学	875
Clinic	临床	681
black (hater)	黑	666
Science	科学	638
Virus	病毒	584
Self	自己	581
problem, question	问题	553
epidemic, pandemic	疫情	505
China	中国	422
Effect	效果	408

a   All function words are excluded, as they are frequently used in composing sentences but contain little or no meaningful content at all.

that seemingly scientific discussions are likely to be based on personal framing (which is associated with one's personal experience of, or perspective on, the issue). This trend becomes more apparent when the detailed postings are scrutinised through a qualitative lens. The section below details my further, qualitative scrutiny of the sampled postings.

3.1   *Expressing Medical Expert Opinions*

Zhihu is a social media platform branded as a knowledge-sharing hub. As such, it is not surprising to see many medical experts posting their opinions in response to the sampled question. The personal framing involved in these medical experts' postings is dramatically different from that of most other Zhihu users, given that their standpoints in the TCM are very much informed by their relevant academic training.

> *A-8*: Those who say that Chinese medicine is a soup randomly mixing different ingredients are fxxxing nuts [...]. Today, all the bioinformatics research teams in [China's] medical schools are all using AD and DS molecular simulation technologies [to find out what Chinese herbs are effective in treating Covid patients ...]. We not only send practitioners to the frontline but also work hard in our research.

The above extract from A-8, who self-identifies as a lecturer working at a Chinese university specialising in medical science on their Zhihu profile, is typical of the medical experts' commentaries encountered beneath the sampled question. While the post comprises the use of informal, or even offensive wordings, such as 'fxxxing nuts', it stands out because of the highly specialised medical terms also cited. Michel Foucault's (1972) observation shows that the emergence of modern clinic experience is inseparable from the development of medical discourse, which uses specialized terms to explain "[how] disease and illness were formulated" and "how they were then treated" (Rendell, 2004, p. 35). The employment of specialized medical terms in communicative practice forms a discursive pattern, which allows doctors to exercise asymmetric power over the general public (Foucault, 1972). In the post, the use of specialised medical terms underscores the professional identity being evoked in the user's commenting practice. While using highly emotive language to make their argument stand out, the user's support for TCM is not based on their personal belief but findings of scientific research, including those projects in which they participated in personally. In this way, a scientific argumentation strategy is evoked in the textual production showcasing the user's attempt to engage in the debate following evidence-based reasoning.

> *A-2*: Chinese medicine [...] is something you cannot explain in a nutshell [...]. How it was used in clinical trials, we do not know. Without a randomised double-blind placebo control method being used, the results of the case studies were not convincing at all. They cannot confirm whether it was Chinese medicine or the patient's immune response took effect.

Despite taking a very different stand on the debate, A-2's post shows similar linguistic features to that of A-8, which includes the use of both highly expressive language and specialised medical terms in the posting. The two users are typical of a small but salient group of Zhihu users, namely medical experts, participating in the current TCM debate. During the Covid-19 pandemic, we have witnessed large numbers of well-trained medical experts being involved in the fight against the virus, with many of them actively using non-academic channels to communicate their professional opinions. In China, Zhihu has become a popular platform to further this end. In this process, the long-existing controversy surrounding TCM has once again come under scrutiny, due to its extensive use in Covid-19 patient treatment in China (Li et al., 2020; Ren et al., 2020). It is undeniable that a series of recent research findings by Chinese scientists seem to have confirmed the efficacy of TCM treatment (Li et al., 2020; Ren et al., 2020). However, owing to the incompatibility between TCM and the modern scientific research paradigms (Wang & Farquhar, 2009), such findings are doubted by many scientists who are sceptical of both the efficacy and the testing protocols of TCM. Against this backdrop, a few medical experts' support for, or rejection of TCM marks how the scientific debate on TCM leaks into medical experts' public engagement on the Chinese Internet.

3.2   *Influenced by Nationalist Sentiments*

As a topic of significant socio-political relevance, the TCM debate not only occurs within the context of medical science but also attracts the attention of ordinary Internet users, many of whom have received no medical training. Under these circumstances, large numbers of Internet users' participation in the debate turns it into a personal-opinion expression exercise, which does not sufficiently align with the scientific nature of the question.

> *A-177*: The 'no body' Chinese scientist – Tu Youyou discovered artemisinin, which is a cure for paludism. The discovery was inspired by classic literature in Chinese medicine and led to the award of her Nobel Prize in [Psychology and] Medicine. The award is indeed a recognition of Chinese medicine by the whole world. As a Chinese person, [I] do not want to see the heritage our ancestors left for us being treated like a treasure not by ourselves but by other nations. I hope the pandemic could become a revelation, which reminds more Chinese people of the value [of TCM]. [I] do not want to see that our next generation would have to travel abroad for TCM treatment.

A-177's posting is representative of the commentaries shared beneath the sampled question by Zhihu users who are supportive of TCM treatment. As can be seen in the above extract, A-177 does not justify their belief in TCM on the basis of scientific evidence. Instead, emotionally expressive language is used to voice their advocacy of TCM treatment. To a certain extent, A-177's argument holds in the sense that there are threads supporting the scientific grounding of certain TCM treatment, with the Chinese scientist Tu Youyou's award of the Nobel Prize in 2015 being hailed by many as the international scientific community's recognition of TCM's contributions to modern medical research (The Nobel Prize, 2015). However, without any critical assessment, the post fails to account for the fact that Tu Youyou's research does, in fact, adhere to the paradigm of modern medical science, despite aspects of it being inspired by some medications documented in classic TCM literature. This omission, either intentionally or unintentionally, is illustrative of the user's attempt to ground their argument to national pride. In particular, by deploying phrases, such as "our ancestors' heritage" and associating said ancestors with TCM such that attitudes towards TCM are reconstructed as the criteria of an ideological test, which then determine one's loyalty to Chinese national identity. Nationalist rhetoric has surfaced from the user's discursive practice, pointing towards the intersection of the TCM debate and nationalist politics in the Chinese context.

As discussed previously, the construction of Chinese national identity is often based on the narratives of China's ancient history, which highlight the once world-leading position the country had in scientific innovation (Tang & Darr, 2012). In such narratives, TCM is framed as a localised academic discipline symbolic of China's historical achievement (Scheid, 2002). However, supported by ancient practitioners' empirical research, TCM has a unique knowledge system, which relies on speculative philosophical interpretations of human bodies, and this hampers the modern scientisation of this subject area (Wang & Farquhar, 2009). However, while exploiting the historical achievement rhetoric, many pro-TCM commentaries have completely ignored the scientific relevance of TCM, turning the debating forum into a platform for pledging their loyalty to the nation, despite the seemingly apolitical veneer of the issue.

> *A-404:* You can compare the mortality rate before and after Chinese medicine was used [for Covid-19 patients]. Why the outbreak was quickly under control [in China ...]. Those who say Covid-19 patents are cured by themselves, you can go abroad and show us how you heal yourselves!

With the state politics becoming mainstream in Zhihu users' postings, the TCM debate has become intertwined with a performance-based assessment of China and major Western democracies' pandemic response. As demonstrated in the above extract, postings involving a note reflecting a positive valence on TCM tend to portray China's pandemic response as an exemplar of good practice in which the use of Chinese medicine for Covid-19 patients plays a prominent role in achieving its outcomes. Yet, this kind of post is largely ideologically driven and tends to conflate the assessment of public health policies with that of political systems. By encouraging supporters of modern medicine to go abroad and get infected there, the post once again discursively links an individual's support for TCM to their faith in their home nation's strong political leadership.

> *A-1,048*: Alas, our ancestors' medical books are just a fraud. I am going to burn them all [because] they are useless anyway. Western medicine and foreign lords (洋大人) are your second parents!

In line with the trending nationalistic framing of the TCM debate, A-1,048's posting exploits the opportunity to voice their support for TCM, not by making positive remarks on TCM per se, but by attacking supporters of modern medicine. This is accomplished through the use of highly sarcastic language, which creates an association between the behaviours of supporting modern medicine and worshipping Western powers. On a textual level, the reference to a seemingly out-of-context concept – "foreign" (洋) is key to this discursive practice. In the Chinese language, the word – 'foreign' takes many different forms. User A-1,048 intentionally chooses to use the outdated form, which is more often used in a historical context, in an attempt to evoke Chinese people's collective memory of national humiliations brought by Western powers to their home nation during the late 19th and early 20th centuries (Y. Liu & Self, 2019). Furthermore, the word – 'foreign' is co-located with the word – 'lord' to imitate the way supporters of modern medicine address Western powers, thereby creating a submissive image of these modern medicine supporters. In this way, the post completely detaches the TCM debate from its scientific basis, turning it into an ideological battleground that tests an individual's loyalty to their national identity. In particular, user A-1,048's lexical choice is in line with the referential strategy in everyday Chinese-language communication which refers to modern medical treatment as "Western medicine". This referential strategy creates a natural association between modern medical science and Western democratic systems. It becomes the foundation leading to the further politicisation of the TCM debate by encouraging the use of Western-Chinese dualistic rhetoric in Internet users' postings.

In China's quest for superpower status on the world stage, there has been a consistent rise in nationalist sentiments in Chinese society, manifested as an attempt to challenge the current order of international politics (Cong, 2009). With world governments' responses to the Covid-19 pandemic being placed under the spotlight, public health has become a site of critique, which is used by the Chinese population to reassess their understandings of China's Party-State system and vis-à-vis Western democratic politics (de Kloet et al., 2020).

> *A-571*: While the epidemic has been largely under control in China, Covid-19 has become a scourge of the world, with the rocketing numbers of people infected in Italy, Spain, Germany, and the US every day. Foreign haters cannot criticise China's performance in the pandemic. As such, they start attacking the [Chinese government's public health] policy, which involves a combined use of Western and Chinese medicine, provided that many young Chinese people are haters of TCM.

A-571's posting is indicative of how a Western-Chinese dualistic worldview unfolds in the TCM debate. By listing Western democratic nations worst hit by the pandemic, the extract deploys a performance-based assessment of China's pandemic response. However, without scrutinising the CCP's public health policy per se, the user creates an imaginary foreign enemy that attempts to smear China by baselessly criticising the CCP's public health policies. In this sense, the discourse promoted by the user is twofold, pointing not only towards a positive assessment of the CCP's pandemic response, but also to a negative assessment of Western democracies' political agendas.

In Chinese society, Chinese people's perceptions of their national government's pandemic response reflects the changing situations of the crisis both within and outside of Chinese territory (de Kloet et al., 2020). In early 2020, when the outbreak was contained within their own country, the crisis disproportionately impacted Chinese people's everyday lives. At that stage, many Chinese people were highly critical of the government's cover-up of the outbreak. This is most tellingly revealed by the memorial events for the whistleblowers who first warned the general public of the discovery of Covid-19 and were subsequently silenced by the government. These events were self-organised by ordinary Chinese citizens on social media platforms (Zhang, 2020a). However, this political momentum gradually disappeared in March 2020 after the CPP started using drastic measures, such as severe national lockdowns, systematic contact tracking and intensive health care for infected patients leading to outbreak came under control (Zhang, 2020a). At the same time, as the pandemic was escalating outside of China, Covid-19 became politicised in major Western democracies by right-wing populist politicians such as Donald Trump (the US) and Scott Morrison (Australia) (Fuchs, 2020). This trend, alongside the poor handling of the crisis by many Western democracies', has provided the CCP with the opportunity to organise propaganda campaigns so as to fuel its domestic support (de Kloet et al., 2020). Against this backdrop, the discursive grounding for rebranding critics of TCM as submissive to Western powers is established, facilitating the alignment between supporters of the CCP and believers of TCM in an ideological battleground within the Zhihu community.

3.3   *Driven by Different Ideologies*

With the participation of politically motivated Internet users, the TCM debate that is taking place on Zhihu has become a hub for the propagation of polarised views. Although notes of discord do exist, an alignment between pro-CCP activists and TCM supporters, as well as an overlapping of political dissidents and TCM critics form a trend in Zhihu users' postings. Interestingly, the pro-CCP voices are often found to be vocal and blunt, but their opponents tend to express their opinions in an understated way on the CQA site.

> *A-343*: It is so pathetic that Chinese medicine did not find a chance to show how awesome it is. It is more pathetic that our guojia (郭嘉) [...] makes a fuss about it.

As shown in the extract, A-343's posting is critical of TCM, predicting that it never played a pivotal role in China's combat against Covid-19. This assertion is dramatically different from the Chinese government's narrative, in which the party leader – President Xi Jinping – personally acted as a spokesperson endorsing the effectiveness of TCM in Covid-19 patient treatment (National Administration of Traditional Chinese Medicine, 2020). By rejecting this narrative, the user's commentary, by extension, contains a challenge to the CCP's pandemic propaganda campaign. Interestingly, A-343's challenge to the narrative takes a rather subtle form, referring to the state government not by the correct characters, but by using characters with similar pronunciations in their textual production. As Liu (2011) notes, this kind of textual production practice is a strategy commonly adopted by Internet users to bypass the CCP's censorship when discussing topics deemed 'politically sensitive' in Chinese society. In this sense, A-343's posting shows a level of consistency with the general trend on the Chinese Internet which manifests as a cautious yet creative way of communicating dissenting opinions which facilitates a kind of freedom of speech in a politically restrictive digital environment (Fang, 2020; Meng, 2011; Wallis, 2015).

As the association between political dissidents and critics of TCM has become recognised in the current debate, posts containing criticisms of TCM treatment are swiftly targeted by a large number of Zhihu users inhabiting the opposite end of the political spectrum, irrespective of the intention of the users who shared these posts.

> *B-15*: Zhihu [users] now only pay attention to one's standpoint and have no interest in right or wrong. It seems hating Chinese medicine is now politically correct.

> *C-15*: Do you know what is politics at all? Do you think the Central Committee [of the CCP] announcing that both Chinese medicine and Western medicine should be used [for treating Covid-19 patients] is politically incorrect?

> [...]

> *D-15*: I have seen enough of those people who talk about national integrity all day and accusing others of betraying China all the time.

> *E-15*: Anyone is good and can be their daddy as long as his surname is 'foreign' (洋).

The above commentaries are posted beneath the post by user A-15, who quotes WHO's warning against using traditional herbal treatments for Covid-19 patients to argue against TCM. The post is largely an evidence-based statement that does not invite political commentary. Yet, the follow-up commentaries clearly show the tendency towards overt politicisation, evidenced by the concept of 'political correctness' being assessed in the commenting circle. As can be seen in the above extracts, the follow-up comments start with B-15 suggesting that polarised views are found on Zhihu concerning the current TCM debate and that critics of TCM seem to have gained the upper hand. The comment is a statement based on B-15's personal observation, and it is very critical of TCM critics. Interestingly, user B-15's use of the notion of politics is attacked by user C-15, who, paradoxically, happens to be on the same side of the argument as B-15. It seems that C-15 has misread their peer's commentary. By referencing the pro-TCM public health policy issued by the CCP, C-15 accuses

TCM critics of challenging the Party Central Committee's position. It provides a good illustration of how politically accepted behaviours are defined in the eyes of pro-CCP nationalists online. Challenging user C-15's accusation, user D-15 presents their dissenting opinion by making clear their disapproval of nationalist supporters of TCM. Unsurprisingly, this commentary is challenged by a nationalist supporter of TCM, E-15, who suggests that users like D-15 are representative of people who blindly worship Western democracies. With few contributions on the scientific debate on the efficacy of TCM, the follow-up comments have indeed become an exchange of words. Their existence in the Zhihu community has turned the TCM debate into a messy political argument, where a person's understanding of science becomes inextricably linked to their political standpoints.

In this study, there are more posts approving of TCM circulated beneath the sampled question on Zhihu – a phenomenon in line with the strong support for TCM treatment in wider Chinese society. Given the interweaving of the TCM debate and state politics (Zheng, 2006), it was not surprising to see a small number of anti-TCM users in the Zhihu community being verbally assaulted by members of the larger pro-TCM camp, who often happened to be supporters of the CCP as well. This, in part, explains the CA results in terms of the heightened interactions underneath posts critical of TCM. In such interactions, multiple layers of the imaginary of TCM were constructed in relation to Zhihu users' political standpoints. They provide a glimpse into how, during the pandemic, both pro-regime nationalists and anti-establishment dissidents use medical commentaries to argue for their political opinions on Chinese social media platforms.

4   Conclusion

This chapter has discussed how the debate on the efficacy of TCM has become politicised in the midst of the Covid-19 pandemic. In particular, I have identified a general alignment between self-mobilised nationalists and supporters of TCM, as well as one between CCP critics and sceptics of TCM treatment, in Internet users' postings on the Chinese community question-answering (CQA) site – Zhihu. Building upon the interactive design of the CQA site, these two camps of Zhihu users have turned Zhihu into an ideological battlefield, where an individual's approval or disapproval of TCM might be used to pledge their loyalty to the nation or express their dissenting political opinions. Such a discursive practice is unique to the politically restrictive digital environment established on the Chinese Internet.

An emerging body of literature has noted the rise in pandemic nationalism in the midst of the current global crisis, which has engineered how different narratives of the CCP and major Western democracies' crisis management strategies are received by the Chinese public (de Kloet et al., 2020; Zhang, 2020a). Building on their observations, this chapter reveals an overlapping of pro-regime nationalists and TCM supporters. To a certain extent, this phenomenon has been exploited by the Chinese government who seeks to justify both its active, official promotion of TCM treatment and attempt to censor voices critical of such an initiative. Speaking to this global trend, it also confirms the politicisation of medical discourses in the unprecedented public health crisis we are facing today (de Kloet et al., 2020).

References

BBC (2020a) *Trump drug hydroxychloroquine raises death risk in Covid patients, study says.* Available at: https://www.bbc.co.uk/news/world-52779309 (Accessed: 16 August 2022).

BBC (2020b) *WHO removes suggestions against the use of "traditional medicine", provoking public debates in China* [肺炎疫情: 世卫删除"传统医药可能有害"建议引爆中国公众争议]. Available at: https://www.bbc.com/zhongwen/simp/world-51797178 (Accessed: 16 August 2022).

Cong, R. (2009) 'Nationalism and democratisation in contemporary China', *Journal of Contemporary China*, 18(62), pp. 831–848.

Dyer, O. (2020) 'Beijing proposes law to ban criticism of traditional Chinese medicine', *British Medical Journal*, 369, p. 2,285.

Fang, K. (2020) 'Turning a communist party leader into an Internet meme: The political and apolitical aspects of China's toad worship culture', *Information Communication and Society*, 23(1), pp. 38–58.

Fang, K., and Repnikova, M. (2018) 'Demystifying "little pink": The creation and evolution of a gendered label for nationalistic activists in China', *New Media and Society*, 20(6), pp. 2,162–2,185.

Foucault, M. (1972) *The Birth of the Clinic*. London: Tavistock.

Fuchs, C. (2020) 'Everyday life and everyday communication in coronavirus capitalism', *TripleC*, 18(1), pp. 375–398.

Gao, Y. (2016) 'Inventing the "authentic" self: American television and Chinese audiences in global Beijing', *Media Culture and Society*, 38(8), pp. 1,201–1,217.

Guest, G., MacQueen, K., and Namey, E. (2014) *Applied Thematic Analysis*. Thousand Oaks, CA: Sage.

Ji, Y., and Bates, B.R. (2020) 'Measuring intercultural/international outgroup favouritism: Comparing two measures of cultural cringe', *Asian Journal of Communication*, 30(2), pp. 141–154.

Keane, M., and Su, G. (2019) 'When push comes to nudge: A Chinese digital civilisation in-the-making', *Media International Australia*, 173(1), pp. 3–16.

King, G., Pan, J., and Roberts, M.E. (2017) 'How the Chinese government fabricates social media posts for strategic distraction, not engaged argument', *American Political Science Review*, 111(3), pp. 484–501.

de Kloet, J., Lin, J., and Chow, Y.F. (2020) '"We are doing better": Biopolitical nationalism and the COVID-19 virus in East Asia', *European Journal of Cultural Studies*, 23(4), pp. 635–640.

Lei, S.H. (2014) *Neither Donkey nor Horse: Medicine in the Struggle over China's Modernity*. Chicago, IL: University of Chicago Press.

Li, T., Lu, H., and Zhang, W. (2020) 'Clinical observation and management of COVID-19 patients', *Emerging Microbes and Infections*, 9(1), pp. 687–690.

Liu, F. (2011) *Urban Youth in China: Modernity, the Internet, and the Self*. Hoboken: Routledge.

Liu, Y., and Self, C.C. (2019) 'Laowai as a discourse of othering: Unnoticed stereotyping of American expatriates in mainland China', *Identities*, pp. 1–19.

Meng, B. (2011) 'From steamed bun to grass mud horse: E'gao as alternative political discourse on the Chinese Internet', *Global Media and Communication*, 7(1), pp. 33–51.

National Administration of Traditional Chinese Medicine (2020) *Today, let us review General Secretary Xi Jinping's important comments on Chinese medicine* [今天，让我们一起回顾习近平总书记关于中医药的重要论述]. Available at: http://www.satcm.gov.cn/xinxifabu/shizhengyaowen/2020-03-08/13704.html (Accessed: 16 August 2022).

Peng, A.Y. (2021a) 'A techno-feminist analysis of beauty app development in China's high-tech industry', *Journal of Gender Studies*, 30(5), pp. 596–608.

Peng, A.Y. (2021b) Amplification of regional discrimination on Chinese News Portals: An affective critical discourse analysis, *Convergence*, 27(5), pp. 1,343–1,359.

Peng, A.Y., and Chen, S. (2021) 'Traditional Chinese medicine works: A politicised scientific debate in the COVID-19 pandemic', *Asian Journal of Communication*, 31(5), pp. 421–435.

Peng, A.Y., Kuang, X., and Hou, J.Z. (2022a) 'Love NBA, hate BLM: Racism in China's sports fandom', *International Journal of Communication*, 16, pp. 3,133–3,153.

Peng, A.Y., Wu, C., and Chen, M. (2022b) 'Sportswomen under the Chinese male gaze: A feminist critical discourse analysis', *Critical Discourse Studies*, pp. 1–18.

Pfafman, T.M., Carpenter, C.J., and Tang, Y. (2015) 'The politics of racism: Constructions of African immigrants in China on ChinaSMACK', *Communication Culture and Critique*, 8(4), pp. 540–556.

Ren, J., Zhang, A.-H., and Wang, X.-J. (2020) 'Traditional Chinese medicine for COVID-19 treatment', *Pharmacological Research*, 155, p. 104, 743.

Rendell, J. (2004) 'A testimony to Muzil: Herve Guibert, Foucault, and the medical gaze', *Journal of Medical Humanities*, 25(1), pp. 33–45.

Rodrigues, U.M., and Xu, J. (2020) 'Regulation of COVID-19 fake news infodemic in China and India', *Media International Australia*, 177(1), pp. 125–131.

Rogaski, R. (2014) *Hygienic Modernity: Meanings of Health and Disease in Treaty-Port China*. Berkeley, CA: University of California Press.

Scheid, V. (2002) *Chinese Medicine in Contemporary China: Plurality and Synthesis*. Durham, NC: Duke University Press.

Schiffrin, H. (1970) *Sun Yat-Sen and the Origins of the Chinese Revolution*. Berkeley, CA: University of California Press.

Schneider, F. (2018) *China's Digital Nationalism*. New York, NY: Oxford University Press.

Steele, L.G., and Lynch, S.M. (2013) 'The pursuit of happiness in China: Individualism, collectivism, and subjective well-being during China's economic and social transformation', *Social Indicators Research*, 114(2), pp. 441–451.

Tang, W., and Darr, B. (2012) 'Chinese nationalism and its political and social origins', *Journal of Contemporary China*, 21(77), pp. 811–826.

The Nobel Prize (2015) *Tu Youyou: Facts*. Available at: https://www.nobelprize.org/prizes/medicine/2015/tu/facts/ (Access: 16 August 2022).

The Paper (2020) *The Beijing consultation draft of Chinese medicine: Criminalising defamation or slander of Chinese medicine* [北京中医药条例草案：诋毁、污蔑中医药将依法追究责任]. Available at: https://www.thepaper.cn/newsDetail_forward_7668829 (Access: 16 August 2022).

Wallis, C. (2015) 'Gender and China's online censorship protest culture', *Feminist Media Studies*, 15(2), pp. 223–238.

Wang, J., and Farquhar, J. (2009) '"Knowing the why but not the how": A dilemma in contemporary Chinese medicine', *Asian Medicine*, 5(1), pp. 57–79.

Wu, A.X. (2020) 'The evolution of regime imaginaries on the Chinese Internet', *Journal of Political Ideologies*, 25(2), pp. 139–161.

Yang, F., Heemsbergen, L., and Fordyce, R. (2021) 'Comparative analysis of China's Health Code, Australia's COVID Safe, and New Zealand's COVID Tracer Surveillance Apps: a new corona of public health governmentality?', *Media International Australia*, 178(1), pp. 182–197.

Yu, H. (2014) 'Glorious memories of imperial China and the rise of Chinese populist nationalism', *Journal of Contemporary China*, 23(90), pp. 1,174–1,187.

Zeng, W., and Sparks, C. (2020) 'Popular nationalism: Global Times and the US-China trade war', *International Communication Gazette*, 82(1), pp. 26–41.

Zhang, C. (2020a) *Covid-19 in China: From 'Chernobyl moment' to impetus for nationalism.* [Online] [online]. Available from: https://madeinchinajournal.com/2020/05/04/covid-19-in-china-from-chernobyl-moment-to-impetus-for-nationalism/ (Accessed: 11 May 2020).

Zhang, C. (2020b) 'Right-wing populism with Chinese characteristics? Identity, otherness, and global imaginaries in debating world politics online', *European Journal of International Relations*, 26(1), pp. 88–115.

Zheng, D. (2006) 'The ideological burden in the debate on whether to abolish Chinese medicine [意识形态负荷的中医存废之争]', *The Twenty-First Century* [二十一世纪], 122 pp. 56–64.

CHAPTER 7

Representing the Stasi: Archives, Knowledge, and Citizenship in the Former German Democratic Republic

Alexander D. Brown and Joanne Sayner

1   Introduction: the Stasi as a Site of Institutionalised Memory and Knowledge

In March 2021, towards the end of another Covid-19 lockdown in the UK, amid discussions of 'roadmaps', vaccine passports, and the ability and desirability of the state to interfere in the lives of its citizens, *Deutschland 89* premiered on More4, a British free-to-air TV channel. The final film in a trilogy, it followed *Deutschland 83* and *Deutschland 86*, which all depict the (mis-)adventures of an agent belonging to the former Ministry for State Security (MfS), or *Stasi*, of the former German Democratic Republic (GDR). The earlier two instalments led the programme to be named as the most successful foreign television programme of all time (Rodgers, 2018). Their success followed that of another internationally renowned film focussing on the GDR, *The Lives of Others*, which won Oscar and BAFTA awards for best foreign film. Its fictional story of omnipresent surveillance by the Stasi was considered educationally significant enough for inclusion in the UK's national school curriculum (Film Education, 2021). It is axiomatic that such representations matter, that they can provide points of understanding and identification. Schoolchildren and viewers of More4 come to 'know' the histories of the GDR through the narratives and images contained within them, whether seen in isolation or as part of a panoply of different voices, contexts and memories. Such representations matter even more so in Germany where, since the fall of the Berlin Wall in 1989 and the beginning of the German unification process, there has been a seemingly unceasing public and intellectual discussion centred more or less on one question– how to remember the GDR? At the heart of this discussion is what is, and what should be, known about the Stasi? What we can know about the former Stasi in the present is of course interlinked with sources of knowledge about the Stasi in the past. Investigating these within a German

context necessitates a focus on some key institutions – gatekeepers of knowledge – which, given their political power and impact, have been surprisingly
under-researched.

As part of the dissolution of the Stasi following formal German unification
in 1990, the holdings of the former Ministry for State Security were placed
under the control of a federally-appointed commissioner, known in English
as the Stasi Records Agency, but commonly referred to by their German acro-
nym BStU. The German government, led by the centre-right CDU party, made
the unprecedented decision to allow public access to these holdings of the
former Ministry (Deutscher Bundestag, 1991). As the modern gatekeepers of
the Stasi's knowledge, the BStU was responsible for securing, evaluating and
controlling access to the files of the Ministry. The institution is also strongly
involved in memorial practice concerning the GDR. Until June 2021, when it
was absorbed into the Federal Archives of Germany, the BStU maintained two
outward facing press and research departments which published books, leaf-
lets and other pedagogical materials as well as sponsoring memorial events and
academic research projects that align with their own aims. It remains to be seen
how this public educational mission will be affected by the recent institutional
overhaul but initial indications are that it will remain largely unchanged (Das
Stasi Unterlagen Archiv, 2021). However, the role which these institutions play
in communicating normative narratives – and the multiplier effect their treatments of the GDR have had within popular discourse – are relatively unexplored
(Brown, 2019). This is all the more surprising given that, over the past thirty
years, the Stasi Archive in Berlin has repeatedly yielded scandal, revelation and
political intrigue.

Journalists, scholars, artists and cultural practitioners have used the myriad
materials from the BStU across a variety of media. An impression of a behe-
mothic all-knowing secret police unrivalled in capricious malevolence or size
has subsequently become encoded within the public discourse of Germany
and indeed the wider global community, with the *Deutschland* 83–89 series
and *The Lives of Others* being just two of the most prominent examples. Such
expressions of *Stasi* discourse demonstrate how the Stasi has become inextricably linked to the wider image of the GDR. Indeed, the historical Stasi has
become a 'site of memory' in popular and academic discourse.[1] While it is

---

1   'The Stasi' was included in a dedicated section of a three-volume collection of German
    Erinnerungsorte, sites of memory, by editors Étienne François und Hagen Schulze, following
    the now canonised model of Pierre Nora's 'lieux de mémoire'. Schulze and François define
    sites of memory as: "long-lasting, generation-spanning crystallisation points of collective
    memory and identity, which are embedded in social, cultural and political conventions, and

clear that processes of remembering the past are inherently selective, subjective and constructed, the significance of such collective sites of memory, and the foundations upon which they are built, demand academic investigation. Indeed, an integral aspect of the *Stasi* phenomenon is linked to the notion that the information emanating from the Stasi Archive represents objective truth. The lack of scholarly attention to the accompanying narratives used to frame the information and the effects they have had on the political and social life of Germany is therefore problematic.

This is particularly noticeable when it comes to the phenomenon of what is known as 'state-mandated memory', defined as the materials and discourse emanating from institutions that are financially sponsored, managed or otherwise explicitly endorsed by the government (Beattie, 2011, pp. 24–25). German state-mandated memory is a wide field and arguably constitutes the largest state-sponsored intervention into representations of, and knowledge about, the past in the Western world (Brown, 2019). To those unfamiliar with the details of the German political context, and perhaps more used to debates about top-down memory politics in authoritarian states, it might be surprising to learn that two German parliamentary investigations, the 'Enquete Commissions', produced some twenty-six volumes of materials which sought to define parameters and paradigms for future study of the GDR and its legacy, resulting in what they themselves describe as "politically directed historiography".[2] On the recommendation of these Enquete Commissions, a central institution, the *Bundesstiftung zur Aufarbeitung der SED-Diktatur* (Federal Foundation for the Study of Communist Dictatorship in East Germany), was formed. Their stated mission is to influence the unification process and promote the comprehensive study of the causes, history and consequences of the system of the Soviet Zone of Occupation (1945–49) and GDR (1949–1990) (Bundesstiftung Aufarbeitung, 2021). They do so by funding and promoting exhibitions, events and publications, including those of third parties, on a national and regional level.

It is within this highly institutionalised, and politicised, context that this chapter seeks to exemplify how knowledge of the Stasi, as well as the Stasi's

---

which change in accordance with the manner in which their perception, appropriation, implementation and communication changes" (François and Schulze, 2001, p. 18). All translations from the German are our own.

2   These were the Bundestag's Enquete Commissions: "Aufarbeitung von Geschichte und Folgen der SED-Diktatur" (Study of the History and Consequences of the SED Dictatorship) in 1992–1994 and "Überwindung der Folgen der SED-Diktatur im Prozeß der deutschen Einheit" (Overcoming the Consequences of the SED Dictatorship in the Process of German Unification) 1995–1998.

knowledge, have been communicated and 'disrupted'. It draws out and interrogates for the first time how medial constructions like the *Deutschland* trilogy and *The Lives of Others* are framed and how they feed into ongoing transformational processes and debates about citizenship in contemporary Germany. In doing so, this chapter scrutinises the primary source foundations of these re-constructions in order to highlight the continued, though often neglected, importance of source analysis in these debates. Ultimately, this is important because one impact of a particular and persistent focus on the Stasi has arguably been to overshadow legitimate criticism of the troubled unification process, which has seen economic and social problems to this day, and to disrupt the socialisation of East Germans within the unified state. In short, it has played a pivotal role in transformations of identity and the ongoing construction of nationality and citizenship in the former East.

   The following discussion approaches this contentious topic by looking at its intersection with another historical period of unparalleled public interest: Nazism. The chapter investigates how the theme of the Nazis and the Stasi has been reconstructed in popular memory since 1990 with a particular emphasis on the the Stasi's own collection of National Socialist era materials, often referred to as the Stasi "NS Archive". As such, these archival files are different to many others in the BStU. While still containing details about "secret lives", many of them originated not during the lifetime of the GDR state but instead during the Nazi period (1933–45) (Lewis et al, 2017, p. 9). These materials were used by the Stasi to research and investigate the crimes of Nazism – and the antifascist resistance to the Nazi regime during the 1930s and 40s – and were then accompanied by files relating to the way the Stasi itself processed these sources. Since 1990, the historic gathering of such materials in the GDR has brought prominent accusations of hoarding and perverting the course of justice, academic historiography and public scholarship (e.g. Unverhau, 1998; Leide, 2005). This has even led to contemporary German state-financed publications accusing the Stasi of protecting Auschwitz perpetrators (Leide, 2020). Given that antifascist self-identity was a cornerstone of the East German state and many of its citizens (Sayner, 2013, pp. 1–24), these accusations assume great political significance due to their use in dismantling this source of legitimacy. The contemporary significance of this discourse is highlighted in recent attempts to link the GDR's alleged failure to come to terms with the Nazi past and the recent electoral successes of the populist right wing party, Alternative für Deutschland (AfD), prevalent in both popular medial and state-mandated forums (Heitzer et al, 2018; Booß, 2019; Kraus, 2021).

2   The Stasi and the Nazis: before 1989

Prior to German unification in 1990, interpretations of the GDR (and indeed
the wider Eastern Bloc) were conditioned primarily by the context of the
Cold War. During the early phase, the paradigm of totalitarianism was instru-
mentalised to cast the former antifascist allies in the East as essentially the
same as their erstwhile fascist combatants, as a counterfoil to West Germany's
"anti-totalitarian consensus" (Arendt, 1958; Wippermann, 1997; Ross, 2002,
p. 8). While this paradigm dissipated somewhat and had been replaced by
more system-immanent and less antagonistic approaches in the 70s and 80s,
the post-unification era would see a resurgence in totalitarian theory and a
renewed emphasis on contemporary Germany's anti-totalitarian consensus
against all forms of communism as well as Nazism (Ross, 2002, p. 12; Carrier,
2011, pp. 27–34). Given the centrality of the Stasi to post-1990 memory of the
GDR, it is therefore easy to understand why interfaces between the *topoi* of
Stasi and Nazi take on such significance in the German memorial landscape.
Indeed, the BStU has consistently sought to flesh out the narrative of totalitarianism by claiming the communist Stasi frequently worked with former Nazis
(Das Stasi Unterlagen Archiv, 2020a; 2020b).

    During the course of 1991, the BStU made the public officially aware of the
Stasi's Nazi Archive. This archive, formally founded in 1968 and known offi-
cially as the *Hauptabteilung IX/11* (*HA IX/11*) (*Primary Department IX/11*), formed
a distinct unit within the wider *Untersuchungsabteilung* (department of investigation) of the Stasi. By mandate HA IX/11 were required to create "criminal
investigation files against persons who have committed war crimes or crimes
against humanity". Furthermore, they were required by their founding statute
to support any international mutual judicial assistance requests made to the
GDR's state prosecutor's office, from both their socialist allies and their capitalist opponents (including West Germany).[3] The history of its holdings stretches
back much further, however, to the earliest days of the post-war era.

    Antifascists returning from exile, imprisonment and hiding in 1945, many
of them members of the Communist Party of Germany (KPD) and its former
clandestine intelligence network, set about gathering any Nazi files they could
get their hands on – but particularly Gestapo and other such security related
information (Ministerium für Staatssicherheit, 1988, pp. 58–65). Their motivation combined the personal and the political: firstly, they sought to determine
who had been involved in betraying the KPD's members to the Gestapo; all

---

3 BStU, MfS BdL Dok 1172 Befehl Nr. 39/67 23.12.1967.

of those involved in the early stages had been denounced and survived prisons and concentration camps during the Second World War. Secondly, these antifascists were tasked by the authorities of the Soviet Zone of Occupation to provide evidence for the forthcoming de-Nazification trials and processes (Meyer-Seitz, 1998, pp. 62–65). Bruno Haid, a Jewish German Communist who had fought with the French Resistance during the War and was now a leading figure in the emerging Party security apparatus became involved and oversaw the transition of this secret gathering of files into a more official framework headed-up by the criminal police commisariat, K 5. Established in accordance with, and in order to implement, the Soviet Military Administration's de-Nazification law No. 201,[4] the K 5 was responsible for gathering evidence in order to prosecute former Nazis. Heinrich Fomferra, who fought alongside Slovakian partisans against the Nazis, headed-up the so-called "excavation department" responsible for gathering any and all Nazi files, whether legally or otherwise. This K 5 police unit was then the primary investigator, alongside the Soviet Military Administration, of Nazi and War criminals within the fledgling state of the GDR until the end of the aforementioned Soviet directive's legal power in 1955. This work of gathering sources highlights the emerging importance of knowing who was who, an imperative which would come to define the work of the file gatherers and interpreters in East and West for the rest of the Cold War era.

By the early 1950s, the mere membership of a proscribed fascist organisation, such as the SS or Gestapo between the years of 1933–1945, which had been punishable under the statute of the Allied Powers, was no longer grounds for legal punishment (an analogous development occurred in the West around the same time). However, murder and importantly *Völkermord* (genocide) along with other related "Nazi and War crimes" remained punishable for the rest of the existence of the GDR. For both, individual actions and guilt had to be proven. This came to a head when, in 1965, West Germany prepared to allow murder and genocide to fall under the statute of limitations, meaning that, even if incontrovertible evidence of individual guilt arose, the case could not be prosecuted. International uproar from the socialist bloc but also from some of West Germany's allies, such as France, eventually caused the West German government to re-consider and, after a longwinded process, the statute of limitations was eventually rejected by the West German *Bundestag* in 1979 (Weinke, 2002, pp. 197–235). However, in the GDR, Nazi and War crimes were

---

4 German Federal Archives, *BArch* DR 2/871 Befehl Nr. 201 des Obersten Chefs der SMAD vom 16. Aug. 1947 "Richtlinien zur Anwendung der Direktive Nr. 24 und Nr. 38 des Kontrollrates über die Entnazifizierung".

never subject to such a debate and indeed the commitment to prosecute any and all perpetrators of such crimes was enshrined in the state's first post-War constitution in 1949 and then strengthened in a new constitution in 1968 (The Constitution of the German Democratic Republic, 1968, art. 91). This constitutional antifascist commitment helped the GDR to profile itself as dealing with the Nazi past more consistently in comparison to their Western rivals.

During a period of heightened tensions in the mid-1960s, the GDR went on a large-scale propaganda offensive, using the files that had been gathered and researched since 1945. Perhaps the most famous example of this was the *Braunbuch* (Brown Book) which was edited by Albert Norden, the communist son of a Rabbi murdered in Theresienstadt concentration camp and member of the Politburo (Nationalrat der Nationalen Front der DDR and Dokumentationszentrum der Staatlichen Archivverwaltung der DDR, 1965). The *Braunbuch* named and shamed some 1,800 West German politicians, civil servants, judges and business people and was published in 1965. It is often held that this campaign was in response to the international furore caused by the kidnapping and trial in Israel in 1961 of Adolf Eichmann, a key figure in the systematic persecution and murder of European Jews, what the Nazi's labelled 'the Final Solution' (Cesarani, 2004; Lipstadt, 2011). However, the GDR's efforts to publicly shame and compel prosecutions of West German elites with fascist backgrounds goes back to at least 1955 and the first GDR publication titled *Braunbuch* was actually published in 1960 about the newly appointed West German Federal Minister Theodor Oberländer. In April 1961 (before Eichmann's kidnapping in Argentina), Oberländer was tried and convicted in absentia by the GDR's Supreme Court for war crimes (Oberstes Gericht der DDR, 1960).[5]

It is within this context that we find the first attempts by the West German state to undermine the moral authority of the GDR's Nazi hunters and their efforts. In 1962, the Western Bundesministerium für Gesamtdeutsche Fragen (Federal Ministry for All-German Questions) published a document which sought to substantiate their claims of totalitarianism by painting the Stasi as having employed former Nazis (Bundesministerium für Gesamtdeutsche

---

5 Oberländer had played a commanding role during the massacre of Lemberg and penned influential essays calling for the "Ausschaltung des Judentums" (elimination of Judeaism) in the run up to the Holocaust. These papers were so influential they led two Holocaust experts to refer to Oberländer as one of the masterminds of the Judeocide. See: Oberländer's *Der Osten und die deutsche Wehrmacht. Sechs Denkschriften aus den Jahren 1941–43 gegen die NS-Kolonialthese* (1987) and Aly and Heim's *Vordenker der Vernichtung: Auschwitz und die deutschen Pläne für eine neue europäische Ordnung* (1991, p. 446).

Fragen, 1962, p. 216). The echo of these allegations lasted a long time and they re-surfaced prominently in the 1990s until the BStU quietly announced in 1996 that they had found no evidence of former Nazis working for the Stasi as direct full-time employees.[6] Attention then turned to a different phenomenon in order to demonstrate the alleged inauthenticity of the antifascist work of the HA IX/11 and to reiterate totalitarian theory: the question of how the Stasi utilised their so-called "NS Archive" and who had access to it – a focus on which highlights the convergences between the media, public academic work, and the politics of memory practice.

2.1 *The Stasi and the Nazis: a Contemporary Debate on the 'NS-Archive'*

There are three key elements which bear closer inspection in relation to how public and academic knowledge about how this archive has been constructed and represented: the allegedly closed nature of the archive; the purported purpose of the archive; and the role it still has to play in understanding the horrors of Nazism. The writing of these histories played-out in the transformative years of German unification. Our research into these narratives has occurred during the much-restricted circumstances of the Covid-19 pandemic of 2020 and 2021, bringing into even sharper focus the gate-keeping functions of key institutions and the layering of media and cultural texts in the writing of what is publically known about the work of HA IX/11.

One of the earliest publicistic treatments which announced the existence of the 'NS-Archive' to the wider world came from the renowned West German historian of the Holocaust, Götz Aly, in late 1991. Under the title *Stasi hortete Nazi-Akten* (Stasi hoarded Nazi Files), Aly proclaimed: "The Document Center of the East was located here, an up-to-now completely unknown but deeply unsettling collection of files from the Nazi era". (1991)[7] He continues to characterise this file gathering activity as little more than the deliberate obfuscation of civilian and academic research in order to instrumentalise the files in a base power struggle over their own population and to support the GDR's concept of fascism and antifascism (Aly, 1991).

---

6 "The ban on hiring former National Socialists was evidently fundamentally adhered to". (Gieseke, 1996, p. 13). A narrative of the alleged role of former high ranking Nazis as 'Unofficial Collaborators' (IMs) has similarly continued but can also be unequivocally refuted on the basis of detailed archival work. See below and forthcoming: Alexander Brown, *"Diener zweier Herren"?: The Stasi and the Nazis*.

7 The Document Center of the West which Aly implicitly references here was the collection of Nazi files confiscated by the Americans after the Second World War and held under their strict control in West Berlin and Virginia until the 1990s when they were returned to the control of the German federal government.

Aly's statement inspired a flurry of sensational media articles which all proclaimed that the *Stasi* had squirrelled away fascist era documentation and therefore had inhibited international research, distorted commemoration of non-communist victims, and even allowed Nazi criminals to walk free (Der Spiegel, 1991; Gunkel, 1992; Renz, 1992; Deckwerth, 1992). In short: that its distortion of historical knowledge had far-reaching legal and ethical consequences. Given the unequivocal tone of these accusations, and their continued impact, it is surprising that none of these articles are the result of detailed research into the files. Based on his own account, Aly had visited the former MfS archive once and viewed information on just three people at the time of writing his article (1991). It is, in hindsight, possible to say that Aly, and those journalists inspired by his narrative – all of whom reference only his work as the source of their claims, fell victim to the heightened tension and furore of the early 1990s. Nevertheless, it is precisely these journalistic texts which we found were proffered as references in an official BStU account of the Stasi's "NS Archive" written by Henry Leide some fourteen years later (2005, pp. 13–14; pp. 143–186). It seems to us problematic that a state-mandated agency dedicated to investigating and educating the public relies largely on sensationalised and unevidenced narratives when presenting what is seen to be an original investigation. Even more problematic is that, in turn, it is precisely Leide's work which is subsequently adopted in texts by a key representative of the German Federal Archives.

Leide is cited in an article written by Sabine Dumschat, one of the employees of the Federal Archives, who has been responsible for evaluating and incorporating the holdings of the "NS Archive" into the collections of Germany's main national archive. Dumschat's article is hosted on the official website of the Federal Archives and acts as an introductory and explanatory piece about the files. It is marked by a caustic tone, asking whether the "NS Archive" was in fact more of a "Mülleimer" (rubbish bin) than an archive per se. Despite Dumschat's position within the team evaluating the files for the Federal Archives and the presentation of her article as the results of this work, it is in fact Leide's work for the BStU which is being presented as evidence of the MfS's distorted Cold War priorities in dealing with both the files and consequently with Nazi perpetrators:

> This has been proven by the research by Henry Leide, an employee of the Stasi Records Agency. Whether Nazi criminals were to be publicly tried or their prosecution foiled or even motivated or blackmailed to work with the secret service, whether requests for legal assistance from the Federal Republic were to be answered seriously or remain unprocessed was

essentially dependent on what appeared opportune during the respective political situation.

DUMSCHAT, 2007, pp. 3–4

Leide's portrayals are marked by a clear agenda, and a somewhat tenuous relationship to the actual files of the BStU in order to create his picture.[8] Yet here
we see Dumschat, another state employee, citing Leide uncritically as having proven this problematic interpretation. It is on the basis of his work that
the legitimacy of the MfS's work against former Nazis is undermined and, as
a result, a key element of antifascism in the GDR. This is certainly what the
Federal Archive's Dumschat takes from his work: "It is self-evident that [Leide's]
findings do not coincide with the antifascist state doctrine of the GDR".

Dumschat's report also relies upon a third party source for one of its allegedly key revelations about the "NS Archive", namely its "Mülleimerfunktion"
(rubbish bin function). Dumschat's article claims that the Archive was aimed
primarily at locking away collections such as papers on forced labour, foreign
labourers or the de-nazification files gathered as part of SMAD Order 201 in
order to keep them away from prying eyes which might undermine the GDR's
preferred version of antifascism. Intriguingly, under closer inspection, this
rubbish bin ascription is taken directly from Matthias Wagner, the expert for
archival affairs in the post-Wall GDR government, founding member of the
state-mandated BStU, and subsequently deputy head of the entire GDR section of the Federal Archives. Even more intriguing is that the cited *rubbish bin*
ascription from Wagner is not a summarial epithet nor does it form part of an
evidenced narrative but, rather, it is a throwaway comment which does not
read in the same accusatory tone in its original context (Wagner, 2001, p. 45).

---

8 Leide is the main proponent of the theory, subsequently adopted across a range of media,
that the Stasi sought-out former Nazis and blackmailed them into collaboration by threatening prosecution or public revelation of their fascist backgrounds unless they agreed to work
with them as 'Unofficial Collaborators' (IMs). Across three different publications spanning
sixteen years, Leide has largely repeated the same few cases, expressly presented as indicative or representative of a larger phenomenon. Detailed archival work shows however that
none of these IMs were senior Nazis or war criminals. It has revealed only that a forerunner
organisation of the Stasi ran one war criminal based in West Germany until the extent of his
Nazi past became known. See: BStU, MfS, HA II/6 Nr. 1158, 118–120. Summary Report on the
investigation of the Party's former intelligence network and its liquidation. 18. 09. 1952. For
further details see also Alexander Brown, forthcoming *"Diener zweier Herren"?: The Stasi and
the Nazis.* (For Leide's claims to the contrary see: 1999; 2005: 2020).

Its inclusion as focal point creates the impression that Dumschat sought only to supply an ostentatiously negative summation.

Indeed, this appears to reflect a wider tendency to accept the sensationalist narratives of the early 1990s and recycle their contents. It is precisely because of this lack of in-depth research into the "NS Archive" that the *Knowing the Secret Police* project[9] decided to order and access the pertinent files in the holdings of the BStU over the last two years and to interview as many surviving eye-witnesses as possible. These efforts have been severely hampered by the Covid-19 Pandemic,[10] nevertheless, it was possible to gain access to materials which have never been seen by academic researchers before[11] and which nuance one of the most significant claims regarding this "NS Archive".

This claim, as so often when it comes to this subject, originates in Aly's aforementioned newspaper article. Firstly, that the Archive came into being with the exclusive aim of politically instrumentalising original documents both as a means of ruling, and of stabilising the dominant view on fascism in the GDR. Aly here takes aim at the GDR's allegedly over-simplified portrayal of fascism as being the result of monopoly capitalists seizing power in order to stave off social revolution. He argues that

> [the HA IX/11] researchers could happily occupy themselves with the fascist system and monopoly capitalism and did not need to face that part of the human support structure which carried the Nazi Reich and would have exploded any one-dimensional fascism theory – that despicable and terrifying mix of denunciation, narrow-mindedness and state surveillance, of xenophobes and know-it-alls, of German manual and intellectual workers who wanted to conquer and "improve" the world. In keeping these materials secret, the MfS was also able to avoid awkward questions about possible continuities.
>
> ALY, 1991

---

9   The AHRC funded project: "Knowing the Secret Police: Secrecy and Knowledge in East German Society" is a collaboration between the Universities of Newcastle and Birmingham. This chapter is the result of research conducted under its auspices.

10   This has restricted the access of individual researchers to an average of one or two days a fortnight during non-lockdown periods. The archives of Germany were understandably entirely shut during the lockdowns themselves and interview settings with older interlocutors were severely hampered by social-distancing regulations.

11   As stated to the authors by the BStU's administrator.

This narrative also alleges that the GDR, and therefore in this instance the MfS, deliberately omitted other victims of fascism such as Jews, the disabled and Sinti and Roma from their memorial culture in order to secure their own legitimacy and power.[12] Furthermore, this account proposes that files pertaining to these subjects were confiscated and held in the "NS Archive" and access was denied to researchers for the same reason. This narrative has been widely communicated by the German institutions of state-mandated memory (Haury, 2006; Kahane, 2010, pp. 6–10; Antonio Amadeu Stiftung, 2011; Heitzer et al, 2018).

However, the files reveal that the reality is far more complex and important context is missing from this portrayal. Firstly, the majority of the files which came to be in the "NS Archive" had been seized by the Soviets along with a great deal of other official documentation during the end phase of the war and were only returned to the GDR in the mid-1960s, alongside a whole host of other unrelated materials. A triumvirate of the Institute for Marxism-Leninism Central Party Archive, the Stasi and the GDR's civilian Central State Archive in Potsdam convened to divide-up the files into relevant sections. On the insistence of the Soviets, all materials deemed significant to the study of the Nazis' security apparatus, repression and crimes against humanity should be given to the Stasi. The logic appeared to be that they would then be able to use the materials to pursue Nazi criminals and uncover prominent Nazis in the West in order to publicly embarrass their Cold War rivals. As previously stated, the Stasi unit which ran the "NS Archive", the HA IX/11, was formally established in 1968 to professionalise this activity. However, they did not have a monopoly on such files, many were housed in the other archives of the GDR and only available in copy in the "NS Archive" and indeed the same situation occurred in reverse.[13]

The BStU's holdings reveal that the officers of the HA IX/11 would frequently research in the civilian Central Archive. However, what is perhaps most interesting is the revelation that academic and private researchers were far from discouraged to research into the very topics that Aly et al allege they were. Repeatedly, research applications for materials on the Holocaust were supported by the HA IX/11 and in some cases its officers performed initial research in their own collections and the wider GDR's in order to present the material to them.[14] Eminent Western historians of the Holocaust such as Raul Hilberg and

---

12   For a critical response to such allegations in relation to memories of persecution of Jews
      see Niven (2009, pp. 205–213).
13   BStU, MfS AV 21/75, vols 1–29.
14   Ibid. vol. 2 p. 481, vol. 3 p. 56; p. 268, vol. 5 p. 618, vol. 6 pp. 329–342.

Adolf Diamant as well as American Nazi hunter Charles R. Allen Jr. all received
the go-ahead from the HA IX/11 alongside many other lesser known academics.[15] Intriguingly, even Aly himself had research applications on Holocaust
thematics expressly approved by the MfS several times, including a large project on Auschwitz in 1988.[16] Indeed, it is one of his applications which gives
us insight into the intricate interconnectedness of the GDR's archival system.

On the 10th of March, 1989, Aly wrote to the Central Archive complaining
that he was not being presented with a copy of a key document he had accessed
in their reading room and believed was integral to demonstrate the industrialisation and economic logic of the Holocaust.[17] From Aly's letter it is obvious
that he considered this to be an act of censorship. However, the files of the HA
IX/11 reveal that, in reality, the issue was that the document was due to be published in a collection of original documents by GDR researchers.[18] Indeed, the
HA IX/11 interceded on behalf of Aly and sought advice from renowned GDR
Holocaust historian Kurt Pätzold as to when the document could be handed
over to Aly.[19] The issue was therefore not whether the document should be
published but whether the West German historian should be allowed to steal a
march on the GDR's own historians.

This indicates just how fraught the politics of memory were during the Cold
War and that potential embarrassment for one's own side was to be avoided at
all costs. This was also the case in the West where GDR researchers, let alone
Stasi officers, were generally not allowed to research in the archives of the
West. This was especially true of the Berlin Document Center which housed all
the documents confiscated by the Americans after the war and to which access
was strictly controlled for Westerners and entirely impossible for Easterners.[20]
Due to these difficult circumstances, the GDR's archives, both civilian and Stasi
were compelled to gain copies of Western-held materials in quite unusual

---

15   Raul Hilberg is often considered to have been the pre-eminent historian of the Holocaust,
      see: Joffe (2007), Adolf Diamant is one of the most prolific Jewish West German Holocaust
      researchers, often referred to as the 'Lord of the files', see: Riebsamen (2004). Charles
      R. Allen Jr. was an internationally renowned Nazi hunter and Holocaust researcher,
      see: YIVO Institute for Jewish Research (2010).
16   BstU, MfS AV 21/75, vol. 1, 103.
17   The document in question is a thirty-five page fascist record entitled "Niederschrift der
      Beauftragten des Rechnungshofs des Deutschen Reichs über die örtliche Prüfung der
      Ernährungs- und Wirtschaftsstelle Getto des Oberbürgermeisters der Stadt Litzmannstadt
      in Litzmannstadt, Hermann Göringstraße Nr. 21". See: AV 21/75, vol. 1., 58–59.
18   BStU, MfS AV 21/75, vol. 1., 54.
19   Ibid.
20   BStU, MfS AV 21/75, vol. 1, 102. See: Heusterberg (2000).

ways. Frequently, the records speak of Western visitors to GDR archives being asked to acquire copies of coveted materials from these forbidden Western archives in return for copies from GDR archives.[21] In one remarkable episode, Erwin Geschonneck, a Jewish victim of fascism turned successful actor in the GDR, was tasked with secretly copying files in the concentration camp Neuengamme near Hamburg, West Germany, where he had been interned during Nazism (Der Spiegel, 2000). Access to materials on both sides was generally weighed-up against respective security considerations, as neither side wished to be embarrassed by awkward revelations or be accused of covering anything up. The following episode regarding files on the victims of the Nazis' murderous euthanasia campaign captures this Cold War context.

In 1982, two West German doctors, Herwig Lange and Günther Elsässer, contacted the GDR's State Archival Administration with a request for the files of patients who had been investigated at a so-called nerve clinic in the western Rheinland during Nazism, where many had ultimately been sterilised or euthanised. In consultation with the Ministry for Health, the HA IX/11 decided to support the application: The files suggest that they believed it to be about medical research, family history and honouring the victims of fascism.[22] However, the support of the GDR in these matters was subsequently used against them. In an article from 1987 in the West German magazine *Stern*, Lange claims that the files were obtained through some sort of subterfuge whereby he tricked the GDR authorities (Erbsommer and Müller, 1987, pp. 96–99). Furthermore, the article reveals that Lange's co-researcher, Elsässer, had himself been involved in the sterilisation of some of the patients. The article presents the story as though the GDR were covering up Nazi crimes and a heroic doctor uncovered both the crimes and a Nazi perpetrator. The files show that this was particularly irksome for the HA IX/11 as Lange and his employers kept insisting that Elsässer be involved in the research and praised him during the application process.[23] While magazine articles such as that in *Stern* may seem less significant in the modern era, they were at the forefront of the Cold War's soft power politics and the narratives established during this zero-sum game have reverberated to the present day.

Indeed, euthanasia victims were one of the key *topoi* to accompany the post-1990 narrativisation of the Stasi's "NS Archive". Aly announced to the world that:

---

21   Ibid., vols 1–29.
22   BStU, MfS AV 21/75, vol. 3, 612–667.
23   BStU, MfS AV 21/75, vol. 3, 612–667.

Even patient and deportation reports from the 'Euthanasia Action' which were believed to have been destroyed are emerging from the archive cellar. This collection is – even though not yet accessible as the previous landlords showed no interest in evaluating them and the files need to be organised and restored – a macabre sensation.

ALY, 1991

As previously mentioned, Aly suggested these files were hidden for political expediency and in order to ensure that the GDR's central focus on the victims of the communist resistance would not be watered down. The BStU's Leide makes the same claims, referring to a "Lack of will to pursue 'Euthanasia' perpetrators" (Leide, 2005, pp. 332–333).[24] It is worth reiterating that the HA IX/11 unit's primary task was not archival, but rather the everyday activity of the unit involved preparing investigation files on suspected Nazi war criminals, fulfilling international judicial assistance requests and "special research assignments" which came either from other units of the Stasi, the SED Party or the State Prosecutor's office. Internal Stasi requests for information amounted to some 15–20,000 individual reports being processed a year by the unit of fifty officers. Furthermore, it was decided largely by the Soviets and a triumvirate of State Archive, Party *and* the Stasi as to which files landed where. It therefore bears consideration that the files fell victim to the constraints of time and manpower rather than that they were confiscated and deliberately not evaluated.[25]

Such an interpretation is tentatively confirmed by the post-1990 history of the "NS Archive". In 1993, the first highly preliminary academic assessment of the euthanasia files contained within the "NS Archive" of the Stasi was conducted by two German specialists. Their summary was telling:

The initial and incredibly necessary archival work cannot be reckoned with due to the current lack of staff at the intermediate archive. The Federal Archive should provide additional funding for this objective, whereby funding from third parties might also be a good idea. It is the task of both academia and the wider public to advocate for the full indexing of these files.

ROELCKE AND HOHENDORF, 1993, pp. 479–481

---

24 In fact, the GDR brought more cases against euthanasia perpertrators than the much larger by population West Germany. See: C. F. Rüter (2000–2009; 2013).

25 A claim which is backed up by the testimony of the former head of the HA IX/11, Dieter Skiba.
     Interview conducted with Dieter Skiba, 18 February 2020.

Funding for the initial indexing would not be granted until 2001 and this first stage would not be completed at the Federal Archive until 2006. However, in many cases the files were not made researchable and therefore usable until as recently as 2018 even with the resources at the disposal of this specialist research archive, including advances in digital technology (Brandenburgische Landeshauptarchiv, 2018). Furthermore, it is evident from the actual content of the files, which consisted primarily of patient histories, that although undoubtedly historically significant, the Stasi had not been sitting on any sort of sensational revelations, let alone information which would undermine the GDR's antifascism. As Dumschat of the Federal Archive concedes, tersely: "Decidedly sensational finds have however not been found". Even more intriguing is that, as we have seen in the episode described above, the euthanasia files held by the HA IX/11 in the "NS Archive" were indeed accessed by international academic researchers. A collection of user applications held in the BStU reveals that the subject was far from taboo.[26] The evaluation by HA IX/11 of an application from one West German academic from the University of Frankfurt am Main wishing to research euthanasia includes the following statement: "The corresponding groups of files have already been used by numerous citizens of the West and partially published. There are no objections on our part to this application".[27]

It can be deduced that the Stasi's role in policing Nazi euthanasia records does not correspond to the reductive portrayals of Aly or Leide. Indeed, throughout the research conducted so far it has become clear that the MfS' role in the archival landscape of the GDR was more complex than has been portrayed in the media and state-mandated memorial representations produced since 1990. Which raises the question as to why these narratives were able to become so well-established and why they seem resistant to critical re-writing. Matthias Wagner, the originator of the *rubbish bin* epithet for the Stasi's' "NS Archive" and former senior BStU and Federal Archives employee eventually came to be very critical of the German state-mandated reconstructions of the Stasi, a process he refers to as:

> a mix of prejudice, calculation, stupidity, cunning, blaming, excuse-making and grandstanding, a miserable battleground of opportunism and narrow-mindedness. Under the guise of uncovering the structures and mechanisms of an apparatus of oppression it was really about something quite different. In the first instance [the intention seems to have been

---

26   BStU, MfS AV 21/75 vols. 1–29.
27   Ibid., vol. 3, 206.

that], the entire [GDR] state which had produced such things and those who worked for it should be criminalised. It made their liquidation easier.

WAGNER, 2001, p. 7

Whether one agrees with Wagner about the motivation for, and track record of, state-mandated memory of the *Stasi* and GDR or not, it is clear, based on the research presented in this chapter that, despite a range of discourses on the subject, there has been insufficient investigation into the archive. Instead, there has been a clear tendency to rely upon the established media narratives of the 1990s, constructed out of particular priorities of that time, which fit into the totalitarian model of understanding both the *Stasi* and the wider GDR. The resulting tropes lend themselves to narratives of delegitimation aimed at the historical German socialist state and concurrently serve to affirm West Germany and now united Germany's own narratives of self-legitimation.

The research and archive materials presented in this chapter, which nuance or even contradict established narratives, have been brought to light during the challenging research environment of the Covid-19 pandemic. Given the continuing interest in the subjects of antifascism in the GDR and the *Stasi* generally – and the MfS' "NS Archive" particularly – this begs the question as to why these materials have not been evaluated and publicised during times not marked by such restrictions on researchers. The fact that they have not been points potentially to other inhibiting factors beyond the physical factors which affect us in non-pandemic periods; namely ideology and the politics of memory. While aware of the many challenges ahead, as a project we look forward to navigating them and delving further into these questions in a (hopefully) post-pandemic world.

References

Aly, G., and Heim, S. (1991) *Vordenker der Vernichtung: Auschwitz und die deutschen Pläne für eine neue europäische Ordnung.* Hamburg: Fischer.

Aly, G. (1991) 'Stasi hortete Nazi-Akten', *taz*, 13 April. Available at: https://taz.de/Stasi-hortete-Nazi-Akten/!1722673/ (Accessed: 30 November 2021).

Amadeu Antonio Stiftung. (2011) *Ausgeblendet? Der Holocaust in Film und Literatur der DDR.* Berlin: Amadeu Antonio Stiftung.

Arendt, H. (1958) *The Origins of Totalitarianism.* Cleveland: World Publishing.

Beattie, A.H. (2011) 'The Politics of Remembering the GDR: Official and State-mandated Memory since 1990', in Clarke, D., and Wölfel, U. (eds.) *Remembering the German*

Democratic Republic: Divided Memory in a United Germany. Basingstoke: Palgrave Macmillan, pp. 23–35.

Booß, C. (2019) 'Braune Wurzeln?: Thesen zu den Erfolgen des Rechtspopulismus im Osten', *Deutschland Archiv*, 4 September. Available at: https://www.bpb.de/ges chichte/zeitgeschichte/deutschlandarchiv/296068/braune-wurzeln (Accessed: 30 November 2021).

Brandenburgische Landeshauptarchiv. (2018) 'Potsdam beendet Erschließung des NS-Archivs der Stasi', *Aktuelles*, 9 May. Available at: https://www.augias.net/2018/05/10 /8843/ (Accessed: November 30, 2021).

Brown, A.D. (2019) *Rethinking the GDR opposition: reform, resistance and revolution in the other Germany*. PhD thesis. University of Birmingham.

Bundesministerium für Gesamtdeutsche Fragen. (1962) *Der Staatssicherheitsdienst. Ein Instrument der politischen Verfolgung in der Sowjetischen Besatzungszone Deutschlands*. Bonn: Bundesministerium für Gesamtdeutsche Fragen.

Bundesstiftung Aufarbeitung. (2021) 'Stiftungsauftrag', Available at: https://www .bundesstiftung-aufarbeitung.de/de/stiftung/stiftungsauftrag (Accessed: 30 November 2021).

Carrier, P. (2011) 'Anti-totalitarian rhetoric in contemporary German politics (its ambivalent objects and consistent metaphors)', *Human Affairs*, 21(1), pp. 27–34.

Cesarani, D. (2004) *Eichmann: His Life and Crimes*. London: W. Heinemann.

Constitution of the German Democratic Republic (1968) Dresden: Staatsverlag der DDR.

Das Stasi Unterlagen Archiv. (2021) *Das Archiv in Zukunft*. Available at: https://www.stasi -unterlagen-archiv.de/ueber-uns/bstu-in-zukunft/ (Accessed: 30 November 2021).

Das Stasi Unterlagen Archiv. (2020a) *Staatssicherheit und Auschwitz*. Available at:https://www.stasi-unterlagen-archiv.de/informationen-zur-stasi/themen/beitrag /staatssicherheit-und-auschwitz/ (Accessed: 30 November 2021).

Das Stasi Unterlagen Archiv. (2020b) *Vom V-Mann der SS zum Stasi*. Available at:https:// www.stasi-unterlagen-archiv.de/informationen-zur-stasi/themen/beitrag/vom-v -mann-des-sd-zum-stasi-spitzel/ (Accessed: 30 November 2021).

Deckwerth, S. (1992) 'NS-Verbrecher als Waffe im Klassenkampf', *Berliner Zeitung*, 4 August.

Der Spiegel. (1991) 'NS Verbrechen: Hälfte hinter Efeu' 19 May. Available at: https:// www.spiegel.de/politik/haelfte-hinter-efeu-a-d98f502f-0002-0001-0000-000013489 060 (Accessed: 30 November 2021).

Der Spiegel. (2000) 'Rollen-Spiele eines DDR-Stars', 6 February. Available at: https:// www.spiegel.de/kultur/rollen-spiele-eines-ddr-stars-a-3ba48a6f-0002-0001-0000 -000015613912 (Accessed: 30 November 2021).

Deutscher Bundestag. (1991) *Gesetz über die Unterlagen des Staatssicherheitsdienstes der ehemaligen Deutschen Demokratischen Republik* (Stasi Unterlagen-Gesetz- StUG)

Available at: http://www.gesetze-im-internet.de/stug/StUG.pdf. (Accessed: 30 November 2021).

Dumschat, S. (2007) '"Archiv oder "Mülleimer"? Das "NS-Archiv" des Ministeriums für Staatssicherheit der DDR und seine Aufarbeitung im Bundesarchiv', *Archivalische Zeitschrift*, 89, pp. 3–4.

Erbsommer, M., and Müller, L.A. (1987) 'Erfasst, erforscht, ermordet', *Stern*, 26 November.

Film Education. (2021) *The Lives of Others: Teacher's Notes*. Available at: http://www .filmeducation.org/livesofothers/teachers.html (Accessed: 30 November 2021).

François, E., and Schulze, H. (eds.) (2001) *Deutsche Erinnerungsorte*. Vol. I. Munich: C. H. Beck.

Gieseke, J. (1996) *Die hauptamtlichen Mitarbeiter des Ministeriums für Staatssicherheit* Berlin, BStU.

Gunkel, G. (1992) 'Nazi Verbrecher waren für Stasi tätig', *Mitteldeutsche Zeitung*, 17 February.

Haury, T. (2006) *Antisemitismus in der DDR*. Available at: http://www.bpb.de/politik /extremismus/antisemitismus/37957/antisemitismus-in-derddr?p=all (Accessed: 30 November 2021).

Heitzer, E., Jander, M., Kahane, A., and Poutrus, P. (eds.) (2018) *Nach Auschwitz: Schwieriges Erbe DDR*. Schwalbach: Wochenschau Verlag.

Heusterberg, B. (2000) 'Personenbezogene Unterlagen aus der Zeit des Nationalsozialismus: Das Bundesarchiv und seine Bestände, insbesondere des ehemaligen amerikanischen Berlin Document Center (BDC)'. Available at: https://www.bunde sarchiv.de/DE/Content/Publikationen/Aufsaetze/aufsatz-heusterberg-persbez-unt erlagen-ns-zeit.pdf?__blob=publicationFile. (Accessed: 29 May 2021).

Joffe, L. (2007) 'Obituary: Raul Hilberg', *The Guardian*, 25 September. Available at:https://www.theguardian.com/news/2007/sep/25/guardianobituaries.obituaries (Accessed: 30 November 2021).

Kahane, A. (2010) 'Mit Stumpf und Stiel ausgerottet? Antisemitismus in der DDR', in Amadeu Antonio Stiftung (ed.) *'Das hat bei uns nicht gegeben!' Antisemitismus in der DDR Das Buch zur Ausstellung der Amadeu Antonio Stiftung*. Berlin: AAS.

Kraus, R. (2021) 'Wie hängen AfD-Wählen und DDR-Vergangenheit zusammen?', *MDR Aktuell*, 1 June. Available at: https://www.mdr.de/nachrichten/deutschland/politik /faktencheck-demokratie-ostdeutschland-100.html. (Accessed: 30 November 2021).

Leide, H. (1999) 'Die verschlossene Vergangenheit Sammlung und selektive Nutzung von NS-Materialien durch die Staatssicherheit zu justiellen, operativen und propagandistischen Zwecken' in Engelmann, R., and Volhals, C. (eds.) *Justiz im Dienste der Parteiherrschaft*. Berlin: Ch. Links Verlag.

Leide, H. (2005) *NS-Verbrecher und Staatssicherheit: die geheime Vergangenheitspolitik der DDR*. Göttingen: Vandenhoeck & Ruprecht.

Leide, H. (2020) *Auschwitz und Staatssicherheit: Strafverfolgung, Propaganda und Geheimhaltung in der DDR*. Berlin: BStU.

Lewis, A., Glajar, V., and Petrescu, C. (2017) 'Introduction', in Petrescu, C., Lewis, A., and Glajar, V. (eds.) *Secret Police Files from the Eastern Bloc Between Surveillance and Life Writing*. Cambridge, Cambridge University Press, pp. 1–26.

Lipstadt, D. (2011) *The Eichmann Trial*. New York: Nextbook/Schocken.

Meyer-Seitz, C. (1998) *Die Verfolgung von NS-Straftaten in der Sowjetischen Besatzungszone*. Berlin: Arno Spitz.

Ministerium für Staatssicherheit. (1988) *Deckname Stabil. Stationen aus dem Leben und Wirken des Kommunisten und Tschekisten Paul Laufer*. Leipzig: Offizin Andersen Nexö.

Nationalrat der Nationalen Front der DDR and Dokumentationszentrum der Staatlichen Archivverwaltung der DDR. (1965) *Braunbuch: Kriegs- und Naziverbrecher in der Bundesrepublik*. Berlin: Staatsverlag der DDR.

Niven, B. (2009) 'Remembering Nazi Anti-Semitism in the GDR', in Niven, B. and Paver, C. (eds.) *Memorialization in Germany since 1945*. Basingstoke: Palgrave, pp. 205–213.

Oberstes Gericht der DDR. (1960) *Der Oberländerprozess. Gekürztes Protokoll der Verhandlung vor dem Obersten Gericht der Deutschen Demokratischen Republik vom 20.-27. und 29.4.1960*. Berlin, Self-published.

Oberländer, T. (1987) *Der Osten und die deutsche Wehrmacht. Sechs Denkschriften aus den Jahren 1941–43 gegen die NS-Kolonialthese*. Asendorf: Mut Verlag.

Renz, U. (1992) 'Staatssicherheit hat mutmaßliche Verbrecher zur Mitarbeit erpreßt', *Mitteldeutsche Zeitung*, 29 May.

Riebsamen, H. (2004) 'Adolf Diamant – der Herr der Akten', *Frankfurter Allgemeine Zeitung*, 10 September.

Rodgers, T. (2018) '"Deutschland 83" Was a Hit Abroad but a Flop at Home. What About "Deutschland 86"?', *New York Times*, 11 October.

Roelcke, V., and Hohendorf, G. (1993) 'Akten der "Euthanasie"-Aktion T4 gefunden', *VfZ*, 41, pp. 479–481,

Ross, C. (2002) *The East German Dictatorship: Problems and Perspectives in the Interpretation of the GDR*. London: Hodder Arnold.

Rüter, C.F. (2000–2009) *DDR-Justiz und NS Verbrechen*, vols. 1–9. Amsterdam: Amsterdam University Press.

Rüter, C.F. (2013) *Justiz und NS-Verbrechen*, vols. 1–47. Amsterdam: Amsterdam University Press.

Sayner, J. (2013) *Reframing Antifascism: Memory, Genre and the Life Writings of Greta Kuckhoff*. London: Palgrave Macmillan.

Unverhau, D. (1998) *Das "NS-Archiv" des Ministeriums für Staatssicherheit*. Münster: LIT.

Wagner, M. (2001) *Das Stasi-Syndrom: Über den Umgang mit dem Akten des MfS in den 90ern*. Berlin: edition ost.

Weinke, A. (2002) *Die Verfolgung von NS-Tätern im geteilten Deutschland: Vergangenheitsbewältigungen 1949–1969.* Paderborn: Ferdinand Schöningh.

Wippermann, W. (1997) *Totalitarismustheorien: Die Entwicklung der Diskussion von den Anfängen bis heute.* Darmstadt: Wissenschaftliche Buchgesellschaft.

YIVO Institute for Jewish Research. (2010) 'Charles R. Allen, Jr'. Available at: http://yivoarchives.org/index.php?p=collections/controlcard&id=34373 (Accessed: 30 November 2021).

CHAPTER 8

(Not) Being the 'Cool Disabled Person': Queering / Cripping Postfeminist Girlhood on Social Media

Sarah Hill

1   Disabled Girls and Social Media

This chapter draws on research findings from a project that took place during the Covid-19 pandemic, which aims to explore how disabled young women mediate their intersectional disabled and gendered identities through their online self-representation practices. Young women's use of social media is typically situated within a postfeminist cultural context (Sheilds-Dobson, 2015), which addresses girls[1] as confident 'can-do' girls who are expected to 'make their private selves and "authentic" voices highly visible in public' (Harris, 2004, p. 125). As Rosalind Gill argues, postfeminism has intensified and tightened its hold on contemporary cultural life over the past decade or so, becoming more hegemonic and operating 'more like a form of gendered neoliberalism' (2017, p. 606), requiring women to not only undertake bodily regulation but also psychic regulation through the cultivation of a positive mindset in order to navigate the contemporary moment (Gill, 2017). This intensification of post-feminism means that its 'regulatory spotlight' (McRobbie, 2009) has expanded to incorporate those who are not just the typical postfeminist subject, that is, the white, middle class, able-bodied girl. As such, there have been attempts to 'open up [postfeminism] to intersectional interrogation' – although, disability has been mostly absent within this work (Gill, 2017, p. 612; Hill, 2017; Hill, 2022).

Contemporary neoliberal postfeminist society produces a system of 'compulsory heterosexuality/ compulsory able-bodiedness' (McRuer, 2006) while making marginalised groups newly visible on the basis of 'neoliberal inclusionism' (Mitchell and Snyder, 2015). Here, disabled people are granted visibility on the condition that they can adopt culturally specific ideals of normalcy and 'pass' as non-disabled or, 'at the very least, not too disabled' (Ibid, p. 15). This

---

1   'I use 'girls' and 'young women' interchangeably throughout this chapter in keeping with the tradition within girls' studies to view girlhood as a cultural construct, where the categories of 'girl' and 'young woman' are slippery and overlapping, rather than a fixed, essential biological state.

means that disabled girls on social media are expected to largely 'fit in' by per-petuating neoliberal postfeminist ideals. As Anastasia Todd argues in her study of disabled girls on YouTube, disabled girls are called on to 'narrate their bod-ies, their experiences and their feelings in ways that render disability intelligi-ble, palatable and sexy' (Todd 2018, p. 45). In the context of disabled content creators, disability becomes another way to present a flexible entrepreneurial self that capitalises on a disabled identity as a commodity or brand (Maria Bee Christensen-Strynø and Camilla Bruun Eriksen, 2020). As I have argued elsewhere, young women who present themselves as disabled girl bloggers are 'motivated and motivational' disabled girl subjects who work to educate a primarily non-disabled audience, all the while conforming to social media conventions which work to make disability less visible or visible in a way that is more palatable to non-disabled people (Hill, 2017).

The existing research on disabled girlhood and social media discussed above primarily involves textual analyses of social media whereas my explo-ration of disabled young women's self-representation practices combines textual analysis of social media with semi-structured interviews in order to elevate the voices of disabled young women and discern how their social media practices inform and are informed by their everyday lived experience of being a disabled young women in the contemporary moment. Significantly, in contrast to previous research, the young women did not position themselves as disabled content creators. This study took place during summer 2021 and spring 2022, and as such, is firmly located within the context of the Covid-19 pandemic. As this research emerged during the pandemic, the interviews pro-vided the young women with the space to reflect on how their use of social media may have changed during lockdown, as well as how they experienced the pandemic as disabled young women. Young people live their lives with and through social media (boyd, 2014) and this has no doubt intensified during the Covid-19 pandemic, particularly for young disabled people. Many disabled people were required to 'shield' at home with little support from the govern-ment or a clear sense of when they could safely resume their usual activities. The UK government's response to the pandemic laid bare the extent to which disabled lives are devalued through the continued reinforcement of certain 'pandemic discourses', which were perpetuated by both government min-isters and the media. These pandemic discourses sought to uphold ideals of normalcy by reassuring 'healthy' people that the majority of people who died from Covid-19 had 'underlying health conditions', and this was presented as a tragic but inevitable consequence of the pandemic (Ryan, 2021). This meant that disabled young people were largely ignored in the government's response to the pandemic, with social media providing one of the primary ways that they could share their experiences. For the disabled young women in this study, the Covid-19 pandemic has undoubtedly impacted their use of social media, and their experience of being a disabled young woman more broadly. For some, this has involved increased activism and awareness raising, while others have chosen to reduce or reconsider their use of social media (see Hill, forthcoming).

In this chapter I use a case study of one participant, Ali, who is 23 years old and lives in England. Ali is nonbinary and uses she/they pronouns. Ali's mediation of their gendered and disabled identity is, in many ways, in keeping with the other young women who participated in the study, particularly regarding how they navigate visibility online (Hill, forthcoming). At the same time, Ali also occupies a unique position in this research in that the Instagram account that I follow and analyse in this study is dedicated to Ali's performance of political drag and presented under the name of their drag queen persona. This chapter draws on crip theory (McRuer, 2006) and work on disability performance art to explore how drag is used to mediate an intersecting gender and disabled identity, specifically how drag can be used to make 'invisible' disability visible, and how it can be used to queer/ crip or 'speak back' to discourses of postfeminist girlhood. After exploring the relationship between crip theory and disabled performance art, I further examine how neoliberal postfeminist discourses structure disabled young women's self-representation practices by drawing on Ali's reflections to explore how these discourses are 'felt' by disabled young women. I then go on to examine how drag performance on social media can be used to queer/crip or resist ideals of postfeminist girlhood.

2 Methods

This study uses a qualitative mixed methods approach of textual analysis of social media posts and semi-structured interviews to explore how gender and disability intersect within young disabled women's use of social media as part of their everyday practices. Participants were recruited via an advert on my personal Twitter and Instagram accounts and selected through self-identification. They were invited to take part if they were a) aged between 16 and 25; b) identified as a disabled girl or young woman; c) lived in the UK. Participants had to give informed consent to take part in an interview and allow me to follow them on social media for the duration of the project. They were informed that I would only follow them on social media accounts that they provided me with the usernames of, and they were free to delete or hide any posts that they did not want me to view or include in the research. The social media posts used for analysis were all posted after the participants had consented to take part in the study. I also informed the participants that they were welcome to follow me in return in order to see how I also mediate my online identity as a disabled woman in an effort to reduce researcher-participant hierarchies in line with feminist approaches to research. Participants were given a £20 gift voucher as a token of appreciation.

This analysis of social media accounts was combined with semi-structured interviews in order to get a sense of how these practices are situated and understood by the participants as part of their lived experience. Participants were invited to choose an interview method that was most accessible for them, which resulted in four interviews taking place over a video call platform, while one participant chose to answer questions via email. Interviews typically lasted for an hour and I used the transcripts provided by the online platforms – with some editing for clarity – for the analysis. The interviews were coded to capture recurring themes. Semi-structured interviews are often used to privilege and promote the voices of those who are marginalised and typically missing from research, such as disabled young people. As Jessica Taft argues, ethnography provides more 'detailed, textured, and complicated data that is lively and engaging [and] incorporates the voices of a group whose words and ideas are not quite what most readers expect, giving space for their own understandings and interpretations' (2011, p. 193). While a study involving five participants is undoubtedly small, the combination of social media analysis and semi-structured interviews means that the data is rich and illuminating. Furthermore, this approach positions this research in line with those who 'argue the need to conceive of digital spaces as *real* spaces and built environments, in which the "disadvantaging of particular groups is not incidental but the logical product of designing our online spaces for certain publics at the exclusion of others" (Mendes, Ringrose and Keller, 2019, p. 38; Harvey 2016, p. 1; Penney 2013). It is aligned with work that views online spaces as 'embodied ' as opposed to distinct from other ways of being in the world (Hine, 2015) and contributes to work that seeks to problematise the simplistic binaries of 'online' or 'offline' and 'showcases the slippage of experience and affect between them' (Mendes, Ringrose and Keller, 2019, p. 38).[2] Indeed, it was clear throughout the study that certain affects 'stick' to the disabled young women, moving with them through 'online' and 'offline' spaces, and their experiences offline informed their activities online and vice-versa (see Hill, forthcoming).

---

2   See also Clark-Parsons, 2017; Jensen, 2012; Rentschler, 2017; Ringrose and Harvey, 2017.

3   'Defining' Disability

The young women who took part in this study all identified as disabled and situated their disabled identities within the 'social model' of disability, which views people as being disabled by societal barriers and attitudes rather than the individualistic 'medical model' approach to disability, which views people with impairments as having something 'wrong' with them that needs fixing (Oliver, 1983). Their understanding and approach to disability was politicised rather than individualistic, while at the same time they experienced certain affects of disability such as stigma, shame and internalised ableism. With this in mind, I draw on Alison Kafer's (2013) 'political/ relational' model of disability, which, builds on the social/ minority models of disability 'but reads them through feminist and queer critiques of identity' (p. 4). Under such a model, 'the problem of disability is located in inaccessible buildings, discriminatory attitudes, and ideological systems that attribute normalcy and deviance to particular minds and bodies' (Ibid, p. 6). A political/ relational framework views terms such as 'disability', 'disabled' and 'non-disabled' not as discrete categories (as per the social model) but as 'political, and therefore contested and contestable' (p. 10). A political/ relational framework 'recognizes the difficulty in determining who is included in the term "disabled", refusing any assumption that it refers to a discrete group of people with certain similar essential qualities' (Ibid). At the same time, a political/ relational framework leaves space for 'disability identification' (Ibid, p. 13). Kafer is therefore concerned with disability as 'collective affinity'. Drawing on historian Joan W. Scott, who in turn draws on the cyborgian theory of Donna Haraway, Kafer highlights how:

> Collective affinities in terms of disability could encompass everyone from people with learning disabilities to those with chronic illness, from people with mobility impairments ... to people with sensory impairments to those with mental illness. People within each of these categories can all be discussed within disability politics, not because of any essential similarities among them but because they have all been labelled as disabled or sick and have faced discrimination as a result.
>
> KAFER, 2013, p. 11

A political/relational framework that views disability as a collective affinity, then, helps to avoid a reductive focus on impairment; viewing disability as political while allowing for disability identification. A political/ relational framework helps us to move away from 'categories' of disability and the implicit ideas around deservedness or undeservingness inherent within them, making disability more expansive while attending to the intersections of gender, sexuality, race and class. This can help us to better understand the experiences of the disabled young women in this study, who all spoke of the various 'labels' they had received while also experiencing difficulties or even 'failing' in attempts to get a diagnosis from medical professionals. They were often aware of how this is more broadly indicative of how young women, queer people and people of colour are frequently disbelieved and dismissed by medical professionals (Olkin et al, 2019; Pollard and Hyatt, 1999), and how this, in turn, affected their ability and willingness to identify as disabled. Indeed, their relationship to their disabled identities had changed over time. As Ali explained, struggling to access healthcare and receive diagnoses means that using 'disabled' as more encompassing term is useful:

> It's not got a name but, like, in the same way [the term disabled] kind of helps me with it because it's like whatever it is I'm not able bodied … I think, in that sense, I identify more with the label disabled because, like, you don't have to have had a doctor tell you're disabled, you can just kind of recognise it in yourself.

The ability to identify as disabled within a political/ relational model, therefore, allows disabled young women who have a fractious relationship with the medical establishment to assert their feelings and experiences and gain a stronger sense of their identities.

4   Queer-Crip Identities, and Disabled Performance Artists

In exploring disabled girls' self-representation practices, this chapter also draws on Robert McRuer's (2006) crip theory. McRuer draws on queer theory, specifically Butler's (1990) idea of performativity, to argue that neoliberal capitalism has produced a system of 'compulsory able-bodiedness' that is interwoven with 'compulsory heterosexuality' in which disability, like gender, is performative. McRuer notes how 'like compulsory heterosexuality, then, compulsory able-bodiedness functions by covering over, with the appearance of choice, a system in which there actually is no choice' (2006, p. 8), adding that the 'emphasis on identities that are constituted through repetitive performances is even more central to compulsory able-bodiedness' (Ibid, p. 9). Compulsory able-bodiedness is both impossible in the way that ideals are impossible to achieve, and also temporary, as everyone will become disabled at some point in their lives if they live long enough (Ibid, p. 30). In this chapter I, in line with

Kafer (2013), refer to compulsory able-bodiedness in conjunction with compulsory able-mindedness. I do so in an effort to refute the mind/body dualism and acknowledge criticisms levelled at crip theory, and disability studies more broadly, for focusing on the physical in a way that upholds certain hierarchies and assumptions about disability (Kafer, 2013, p. 16).

As with gender and sexuality, disabled people are expected to 'perform' their disabled identities in everyday life as part of what Rosemarie Garland-Thomson (1997), drawing on Goffman, terms 'stigma management'. Stigma management is aimed at putting non-disabled people at ease by attempting to minimise the appearance and impact of impairment and can be considered 'an everyday performance of passing' (Sandahl, 2003, p. 40). Stigma management is triggered by non-disabled people as part of the social relations between disabled and non-disabled people, which includes staring. Garland-Thomson notes how disabled identities are constituted by the stare (as opposed to 'the gaze'), as 'staring is the visual practice that materializes the disabled in social relations' (2005, p. 32). Work within feminist disability studies has drawn on queer theory to explore how disabled performance artists invite staring on their own terms in order to refute the diagnostic gaze and reimagine disability. In exploring queer-crip performances, Carrie Sandahl argues, 'for queer performers, visibility often means proclaiming an otherwise invisible sexuality onstage; the task is different for disabled performers, whose visible impairments often lead to social invisibility' (2003, p. 30). This points to a tendency within this work on disabled performance artists to focus on the process of navigating the visibility of physical impairment, even though 'invisible' disabilities always 'threaten to disclose some inexplicable stigma' by challenging assumed able-bodiedness/ able-mindedness (Garland-Thomson, 2005, p. 31). Here, I am interested in how drag performance might function as queer-crip performance aimed at making 'invisible' disabilities more visible, facilitated by social media. In doing so, this chapter is positioned alongside Tamar Tembeck's (2016) work on 'selfies of ill health', in which Tembeck draws on the language of queer theory to argue that 'selfies of ill health', such as Karolyn Gehrig's #HospitalGlam series, enable individuals 'to "come out" as being invisibly ill'.[3] I view such practices as situated within the lineage of disabled performance art and solo autobiographical performance, while going beyond this to explore how the affordances of social media, specifically Instagram, can work to make 'invisible' disability visible while also queering/ cripping postfeminist girlhood.

---

3 To this I would also add 'disabled' given the politicised nature of such projects, and the fact that in the case of #HospitalGlam, Gehrig explicitly identifies as queer and disabled on her Instagram profile.

5   'It's Difficult': the Affects of Postfeminist Girlhood

The disabled young women who took part in this study were highly attuned
to the expectations and perceptions of non-disabled people in particular, and
the impact this had on how they presented themselves on social media. Their
accounts also highlighted how these experiences are situated within the intersections of gender and race. In our interview, Ali drew on the language of postfeminist 'can-do' (Harris, 2004) girlhood in order to reflect on their experiences:

> It's kind of like, yeah we can do whatever we want, we're so strong and
> we can do all these things, it's kind of, it's difficult in that regard because
> I am not strong. I am so tired … I have to take several naps a day … I'm in
> pain constantly.

This 'system of compulsory able-bodiedness'/ able-mindedness (McRuer,
2006, p. 9), as it intersects with postfeminist girlhood, demands that young
women be strong, capable and productive. This in turn affects whether and
how disabled young women feel able to discuss their experiences with others.
Ali discussed how this has affected them, explaining that they have found it
difficult to accept help in case this was perceived as being a 'sad little disabled
person' who is 'frail' and relies on others for help.

As discussed in the introduction, young women's self-representation
practices are constructed around postfeminist ideals of visibility, 'can-do'
confidence and authenticity (Shields Dobson, 2015.). While more recent postfeminist culture has made space for 'affective dissonance' with its positive 'feeling rules' through young women's expressions of anger, anxiety and insecurity,
this is only available to some young women, such as those who are white and
middle-class, rather than those who are less privileged, and only available in
certain ways (Dobson and Kanai, 2019). As such, this is not felt to be available
to disabled young women, as Ali articulated how they struggled with feeling
like they had to upload postfeminist can-do ideals when representing themself
on social media, which makes it difficult to talk about more 'negative' feelings,
such as being in pain or requiring disability accommodations:

> Particularly like on social media as well there's that kind of thing of not
> wanting to look like you're, like not wanting to be a disabled person that
> needs to have their access requirements met. Essentially, in like having to
> be, like, … a cool disabled person who's like 'oh I'm disabled but it doesn't
> stop me from doing anything', like the whole like superhuman thing. I feel
> like that's really been … made worse by social media in some aspects.

Being the 'cool disabled person' on social media means adhering to the self-representation practices of the disabled young women content creators discussed earlier in line with the demands for compulsory able-bodiedness/ able-mindedness. Here, neoliberal productivity and compulsory able-bodiedness/ able-mindedness coincide with the 'supercrip' disability stereotype. As Pullen, Jackson and Silk (2020) argue, when attached to the 'super' prefix – such as 'superhuman' or 'supercrip' – 'disability becomes positioned as a personal tragedy to be "overcome" by hard work and dedication to achieve success' (p. 720), qualities that are also key to neoliberal postfeminist girlhood. Therefore, while disabled people are granted visibility on social media, those who are most welcome are the folks who can demonstrate their flexibility and ability to 'overcome' disability by not demanding structural change, and, as per the logics of postfeminism, disabled young women are the ideal subjects in this regard. Moreover, the logics of social media self-branding are predicated on notions of authenticity, which includes being 'true to oneself' and being seen as open and transparent by allowing others to access one's inner self (Banet-Weiser, 2012). Such mediated authenticity means that disabled young women in particular are expected to give 'honest' insights into their lives and experiences of disability while at the same time making this palatable to non-disabled audiences without troubling the logics of social media self-representation (Hill, 2017). However, disabled young women consider being 'honest' about disability and allowing (non-disabled) people access to their inner selves too potentially risky due to feelings of shame and the possibility that they might be accused of 'faking' being disabled, which reinforces how authenticity, as understood within the context of social media self-branding, is based on able-bodied/ able-minded assumptions and norms, working to uphold compulsory able-bodiedness/ able-mindedness (Hill, forthcoming).

6   Queering/ Cripping Postfeminist Girlhood

The previous section demonstrated the rather narrow parameters for representing experiences of disabled young womanhood on social media within a postfeminist cultural context, and how the impossibility of this is affectively felt. In this section I examine how drag, as part of queer-crip performance on social media, can be used to queer/crip, or 'speak back to' discourses of postfeminist girlhood in order to make 'invisible' disabilities more visible and open up the possibilities for self-representations of disabled young womanhood. Drag makes the performativity of gender apparent as it 'implicitly reveals the imitative structure of gender itself' (Butler, 1990, p. 175). Although the performance of drag has traditionally 'play[ed] upon the distinction between the anatomy of the performer and the gender that is being performed' (Butler, 1990, p. 175; Newton, 1979), more recently it has diversified to include cis and trans women and nonbinary folks. Contemporary drag culture is indicative of how postfeminism and 'post-queer' culture intersect through a process of 'neoliberal normalisation' (Chen and Kanai, 2022, p. 102) whereby queer identities have become depoliticised as they have gained visibility and been co-opted by capitalism, as part of 'the "hollowing out" of politics in postfeminist culture' (Ibid; Gill, 2017). This is exemplified by the mainstream popularity of *RuPaul's Drag Race* (2009-present), a US reality TV competition where drag queens compete to the next drag superstar through giving performances and undertaking challenges such as costume-making and lip synching. The popularity of the show has led to a number of spin-offs, including *RuPaul's Drag Race UK* (2019). In line with broader developments within drag culture, the latest series of *RuPaul's Drag Race UK* features the series' first cisgender drag queen, Victoria Scone (Day, 2021). Indeed, Ali credits *RuPaul's Drag Race* with developing their interest in drag culture.

Ali's drag performance is primarily documented via a dedicated Instagram account. As Feldman and Hakim note, Instagram is the 'dominant platform for drag queens, arguably because its emphasis on imagery supports drag's long-standing connection to visual culture and is particularly well-suited to showcasing a queen's distinctive looks' (2020, p. 394). Ostensibly, Ali's Instagram account bears many of the hallmarks of the Instagram accounts belonging to the drag queens featured on *RuPaul's Drag Race*, such selfies showcasing drag looks, reflections on or promotion of performances and contact details for bookings, that are indicative of the contemporary 'celebrification' of drag that Feldman and Hakim (2020) argue shows like *RuPaul's Drag Race* have contributed to. However, Ali works to resist this broader depoliticisation of drag and queer culture by explicitly asserting that she specialises in 'political drag' in the profile. This is facilitated by Instagram's affordances and 'platform vernacular' (Gibbs et al, 2015) which not only places emphasis on visual images, which are key to drag performances as Feldman and Hakim (2020) note, but also gives users the ability to write lengthy captions, which, although limited, allow more characters than other platforms such as Twitter. Ali uses Instagram captions to contextualise her drag performances and situate them within a broader political context, marking them as explicitly political. As such, Ali's political drag performances include themes such as mental illness and the impact of mental health policy, drug legalisation, misogyny, and the UK government's response to Covid-19. A key way in which Ali expresses the theme of mental illness within drag performances is by wearing a hospital gown, which functions as a signifier of ill health and renders what is typically 'invisible' visible. Taking a selfie while wearing a hospital gown is reminiscent of Gehrig's #HospitalGlam series discussed earlier, which uses selfies to glamorise medical environments as a form of activism that draws attention to experiences of 'invisible' illness (Tembeck, 2016). Here, however, glamour becomes camp through drag. In one particular instance, Ali's drag performance evokes a type of camp body horror in order to visually represent the difficulties young people experiencing mental illness have when trying to access healthcare, often having to 'spill their guts', as it were, by having to repeatedly recount trauma, only to be turned away. Ali occasionally refers to their own experiences of disability in their Instagram posts, which is in keeping with the logics of social media self-representation that require disabled people to draw on their own experiences of disability in order to demonstrate their 'authenticity' while raising awareness of disability (Hill, 2017). However, Ali's experiences are consistently situated within the wider political context, which is always paramount. This is done through references to statistics and mental healthcare policies, for example. This queer-crip performance, then, works to de-individualise the presentation of the disabled identity by explicitly situating it within the realm of the political in order to resist the neoliberal depoliticisation that often structures social media self-representation practices.

Having a social media account dedicated to political drag with a selective following was very important to Ali, and it provides a space for her to express her opinions and experiences of disability and queerness away from the family and friends who may not be empathetic. Ali explained how they 'wanted to post about my political opinions, and raise awareness for things and be, like, kind of loud about things online that I want to be loud about'. The fact that Ali felt that they couldn't be 'loud' on social media outside of drag reiterates how girls' social media self-representation practices are expected to be 'authentic' but depoliticised. For Ali, being 'loud' is specifically linked to anger, as her political drag performances feature exaggerated expressions of anger, where rage is visible on her face. This is something Ali wanted to explore because 'there are lots of good reasons for people to be angry' and yet young women's anger is rendered a problem that should be managed and reformulated into something smaller that is more pleasing in accordance with the postfeminism's positive 'feeling rules' 'rather than acknowledge failure, loss, and frustration within a punishing neoliberal system' (Dobson and Kanai, 2019, p. 776). This is particularly the case for disabled girls who, in postfeminist culture, function as 'happiness objects' whose value is located in their ability to orientate neoliberal citizens in the 'right' ways (Todd, 2018). They must present a 'happy disabled identity' to reassure others by 'passing' and hiding signs of pain and fatigue

(Sheppard, 2020, p. 45). Anger must also be neutralised within girls' political activism. Previously associated with individualised success, postfeminist 'girl power' discourses have developed to invoke girls as political actors who are uniquely placed to solve structural problems, such as climate change. At the same time, girlhood's associations with harmlessness work to render (white) girls' activism as 'harmless', and explicitly not angry, curtailing any radical political potential (Taft, 2020). Performing political drag that is deliberately angry allows Ali to subvert dominant discourses of postfeminist 'girl power' and its emphasis on positive feelings, where the individual girl can solve problems through hard work and a positive attitude, and instead harness anger in a more radical way that draws attention to social justice issues and the damage being inflicted by neoliberal structures.

Performing 'high femme' drag also enables Ali to resist the pressure to conform to postfeminist hetero-femininity and provides a way to queer femininity:

> Since I've been doing the [drag] stuff I felt less pressure on myself to dress in a feminine way when I'm going out somewhere or like doing something big and important ... Now what I view a big occasion as is an occasion where I'm going out into drag ... I can do what I like ... If it's something else that's like a big event that's not drag related I don't have to look necessarily feminine for it, I can just kind of do what I want.

Ali described weddings as an example of a 'big occasion' that is not drag related, which reinforces the sense of freedom that drag provides as it implies a contrast between choosing to adopt 'high femme' queer femininity through drag and the kind of rigid hetero-femininity women and non-binary people are expected to adhere to when dressing for a wedding, even if this is seemingly freely-chosen in line with the broader logics of postfeminist culture (Boyce, Kay, Kennedy and Wood, 2020). The relationship between disability and femininity is complex, and disabled young women often feel compelled to embody heteronormative femininity in order to resist the typical view of them as genderless, desexualised and infantalised (Slater et al, 2018). For the most part, Ali is able to 'pass' as non-disabled – although I am not suggesting that this is easy – so is perhaps less likely to experience this kind of infantilisation. Nevertheless, it is important to note that being compelled to perform heteronormativity in order to resist ableism 'further marginalises – and even renders unintelligible – queer disabled people' (Ibid, p. 421). Therefore, the fact that drag lessens the 'pressure' of feeling the need perform heteronormative femininity in other aspects of life means that Ali's queer disabled identity can be more easily rendered visible as part of their everyday lived experience.

Drag also enables Ali to resist neoliberal postfeminist discourses of productivity and capacity. As Feldman and Hakim (2020) argue, the 'celebrification' of contemporary drag embraces neoliberal ideals of self-branding, entrepreneurship and hard work. Success as a drag queen is predicated on one's ability to work (or werk) hard and create fabulous looks and lip synchs, all of which involves effort and can be time-consuming as a form of creative labour. The time it takes to create hair and make-up for a drag performance is often a point of interest for those who do not participate in drag culture and Ali remarked that this is something that they get asked about 'a lot'. Significantly, drag is often viewed as a means of 'making feminine labour visible' (Brown, 2018, p. 65). As Alexis Brown notes, 'As RuPaul's famous catchphrase "You better work" implies, the sheer amount of labour necessary to embody normative feminine beauty can be enormous, for cisgender women and drag queens alike' (Ibid, p. 66). For Ali, however, this is not laborious. Although it can take 'up to two hours' to get ready for a drag performance, this is positioned as something fun rather than hard work, as the beauty practices are interspersed with other fun activities such as singing and dancing. While postfeminist culture works to present feminine beauty practices as fun, they are nevertheless a requirement for displaying heterosexual femininity (McRobbie, 2009). In contrast, Ali's account of using feminine beauty practices in the creation of drag performance is presented as a fun way to present a queer-crip identity. It is also implied that the beauty practices are not carried out consecutively in order to allow time for breaks. It is arguably possible to read this 'breaking' of the linear beauty routine through the addition of other activities, of making it flexible, as an example of crip time. Crip time refers to disabled bodyminds' failure to move through time in the 'right' ways. This can include, among other things, needing 'extra time' or having to use 'pacing' (Kafer, 2013). Pacing is a strategy typically used by disabled people as a means of conserving energy. Ali alluded to their own use of pacing when they referred to needing to take 'several naps a day'. Pacing can be read as both a 'practice of normalisation-rehabilitation' (Sheppard, 2020) and as a form of self-care. As a normalisation practice and as a form of self-care, crip time can work in the service of productivity; for example, resting in order to be able to work more. However, Kafer calls for us to consider how this practice of self-care might be read not as part of 'preserving one's body for productive work but as refusing such regimes in order to make room for pleasure' (2013, p. 39). Ali's non-linear drag beauty routine can be viewed as a refusal of the productivity discourses that inform contemporary drag culture by presenting drag's highly feminine beauty practices not as laborious or something to be considered work but as fun and energising. This challenge to productivity discourses was more broadly facilitated by the social and temporal conditions brought about by the pandemic, which, it has been suggested, caused more people to live their lives in crip time (Freeman, 2021; Arrow and Grant, 2021). The feeling of time slowing during lockdown, where days seemed indistinguishable from one another, as well as the changing sense of work and leisure time caused by working from home, provided many with a new sense of living crip (Samuels and Freeman, 2021).[4] It is significant, therefore, that Ali decided to start performing drag on social media during the first UK lockdown in 2020, something that they would not have had the time or space to develop had they still been doing their usual work. For young people like Ali, the pandemic has disrupted normative youth trajectories, such as going on to graduate roles and internships after university. This disrupts postfeminist ideals in particular, as success in work and education is paramount to postfeminist girlhood (Harris, 2004; McRobbie, 2009). However, this cripping of time and normative trajectories during lockdown provided Ali with the time to start performing drag on social media, and in doing so, enabled Ali to more fully explore and embrace their queer/ crip identity.

Young people's 'identity work' is largely facilitated by social media (boyd, 2014) and uploading selfies of drag performance has enabled Ali to mediate their queer/crip identity. Indeed, viewing the posts chronologically demonstrates this development of identity as Ali's drag performance becomes more confident. Instagram's affordances also enable this, as it allows users to have multiple accounts in order to manage varying self-presentations, so Ali can have an Instagram account dedicated to drag with a selective following as well as an account that is not related to drag. This is in contrast to Facebook's approach to identity, for example, which demands that users only have 'one identity' and use their real names (Duffy and Hund, 2019). Ali's Instagram account is structured in such a way that drag performance appears on the main grid, while Ali only appears out of drag on Instagram Stories, which appear fleetingly, lasting for 24 hours. Instagram Stories have been noted for allowing for a 'realness' of self-presentation akin to Goffman's (1990) 'backstage' identity as they allow users to present themselves in a way that may differ from their personal branding (Duffy and Hund, 2019: 4992). While we could see Ali's Instagram Stories as presenting 'herself' in a more mundane, everyday context so as to not disrupt the drag performance on the main grid, the question of

---

4   Any initial optimism that this experience of crip temporalities might prompt some kind of broader shift in accessibility and help us to reclaim some of our time under capitalism has since been lost through an emphasis on a 'return to normal' and the subsequent loss of the various accessible work practices that were introduced due to the pandemic in many areas.

'realness' and 'authenticity' is more complex when we consider how Ali views drag in relation to their identity:

> She's definitely, like, I see her as an exaggerated version of me basically. Like she's not a separate person in her own right, it's just kind of who I would be every day if, I don't know, if I could, and we were in a kind of more forthcoming society where you can just talk about things more openly.

Typically, the notion of an 'exaggerated version' of the self implies a degree of inauthenticity or artifice. However, there is a clear sense here that drag enables Ali to be what they consider to be their 'true self' by allowing Ali to 'talk about things more openly', which is suggestive of a degree of 'authenticity' and 'realness' that is unavailable to Ali when not in drag. For Ali, notions of openness and the ability to be forthcoming are also politicised, such as being able to openly situate their own gendered experiences of disability within a broader political context without fear of being criticised or attacked. This desire to live in a 'more forthcoming society where you can just talk about things more openly' points to the impossibility of living compulsory heterosexuality/ compulsory able-bodiedness/ able-mindedness, as neoliberal capitalism requires subjects to be flexible while maintaining a positive psychic disposition that produces and maintains positive affects, such as happiness and confidence (Gill, 2017). For Ali, it seems, drag performance offers a different kind of confidence and happiness, one that arises from the ability to queer/ crip postfeminist girlhood.

7   Conclusion

This chapter has examined disabled young women's self-representation practices on social media in an attempt to further intersectional interrogations of postfeminism through focusing on disability and how it intersects with gender. It has argued that neoliberal postfeminist discourses structure expectations and perceptions of gendered self-representations of disability in specific ways, as exemplified by disabled content creators (Hill, 2017; Todd, 2018). It has furthered this existing research by examining how this is affectively 'felt' by disabled young women as difficult and limiting, highlighting the impossibility of 'living' such discourses, both on- and offline. This chapter also explored how drag performance on social media, specifically, can work to make disability legible and how this is facilitated by Instagram's affordances. Moreover, this chapter has highlighted how drag performance functions to queer/ crip post-feminist girlhood by utilising expressions of anger that are typically pathologised under postfeminism's 'feeling rules' that emphasise positivity (Kanai, 2017), queering heteronormative beauty practices, and resisting 'can-do' productivity by living in crip time. It was also suggested that this was enabled, in part, by the disruption caused by the Covid-19 pandemic, as shifting temporalities provided the time and space to challenge ideas of productivity inherent within neoliberal postfeminist girlhood in favour of exploring queer/ crip identity. While this chapter has focused on one example of drag performance on social media, it nevertheless demonstrates a need to further explore ways in which contemporary self-representation practices are being or can be queered/ cripped in order to broaden the possibilities for disabled young women in terms of how they are able to represent themselves on social media. This would subsequently help us to gain a fuller sense of what it means to be a disabled young woman in the contemporary moment.

References

Arrow, K.M., and Grant, Z.S. (2021) 'Pandemic possibilities in crip time: Disrupting social work field education', *Intersectionalities: A Global Journal of Social Work Analysis,* Research, Polity, and Practice, 9(1), pp. 98–114.

Banet-Weiser, S. (2012) *Authentic™: The politics of ambivalence in a brand culture,* New York: New York University Press.

Boyce Kay, J., Kennedy, M., and Woods, H. (2020) *The wedding spectacle across contemporary media and culture: Something old, something new,* London: Routledge.

Boyd, d. (2014) *It's complicated: the social lives of networked teens.* Connecticut: Yale University Press.

Brown, A. (2018) 'Being and performance in RuPaul's Drag Race', *Critical Quarterly,* 60(4), pp. 62–73.

Butler, J. (1990) *Gender trouble Feminism and the subversion of identity,* Oxon Routledge.

Chen, S.X., and Kanai, A. (2022) 'Authenticity, uniqueness and talent: gay male beauty influencers in post-queer, postfeminist Instagram beauty culture', *European Journal of Cultural Studies,* 25(1), pp. 97–116, DOI: 10.1177/1367549421988966.

Christensen-Strynø, M.B., and Bruun Eriksen, C. (2020) 'Madeline Stuart as disability advocate and brand: exploring the affective economies of social media', in Garrisi, D., and Johanssen, J. (eds.) *Disability, Media, and Representations: Other Bodies.* Oxon: Routledge, pp. 35–50.

Clark-Parsons R. (2017) 'Building a digital girl army: The cultivation of feminist safe spaces online', *New Media & Society*, 20(6), pp. 2125–2144. DOI: 10.1177/1461444817731919.

Day, H. (2021) 'Drag Race UK's first female queen Victoria Scone: "I didn't know if drag was a possibility for me"', *BBC*, 19 August. Available at https://www.bbc.co.uk/bbcthree/article/f10ae11a-cf25-47b8-8757-e7d2b504d7f1 (Accessed 12 November 2021).

Dobson, A.S. (2015) *Postfeminist digital cultures: femininity, social media, and self-representation*. Basingstoke: Palgrave Macmillan.

Dobson, A.S., and Kanai, A. (2019) 'From "can-do" girls to insecure and angry: affective dissonances in young women's post-recessional media', *Feminist Media Studies*, 19(6), pp. 771–786, DOI: 10.1080/14680777.2018.1546206.

Duffy, B.E., and Hund, E. (2019) 'Gendered visibility on social media: navigating Instagram's authenticity bind', *International Journal of Communication*, 13, pp. 4983–5002.

Feldman, Z., and Hakim, J. (2020) 'From *Paris is Burning* to #dragrace: social media and the celebrification of drag culture', *Celebrity Studies*, 11(4), pp. 386–401, DOI: 10.1080/19392397.2020.1765080.

Freeman, E. (2021) 'Time', *Issues in Science and Technology*, March, https://issues.org/time-postpandemic/ (Accessed 28th April 2022).

Garland-Thomson, R. (1997) *Extraordinary bodies: figuring physical disability in American culture and literature*. New York: Columbia University Press.

Garland-Thomson, R. (2005) 'Dares to stares: disabled women performance artists & the dynamics of staring', in C. Sandahl, and P. Auslander (eds.) *Bodies in commotion: disability and performance*. Ann Arbor: The University of Michigan Press, pp. 30–41.

Gibbs, M., Meese, J., Arnold, M., Nansen, B., and Carter, M. (2015) '#Funeral and Instagram: death, social media, and platform vernacular', *Information, Communication & Society*, 18(3), pp. 255–268, DOI: 10.1080/1369118X.2014.987152.

Gill, R. (2017) 'The affective, cultural and psychic life of postfeminism: A postfeminist sensibility 10 years on', *European Journal of Cultural Studies*, 20(6), pp. 606–626, DOI: 10.1177/1367549417733003.

Goffman, E. (1990) *The presentation of self in everyday life*. London: Penguin.

Harris, A. (2004) *Future girls: young women in the twenty-first century*. London: Routledge.

Harvey, A. (2016) 'Dreams, design, and exclusion: the aggressive architecture of the utopian internet', from the *Film, Television and Media Studies Research Seminar Series*, University of East Anglia, 7 March.

Hill, S. (2017) 'Exploring disabled Girls' self-representational practices online', *Girlhood Studies*, 10(2), pp. 114–130, DOI: 10.3167/ghs.2017.100209.

Hill, S. (2022) 'Locating disability within online body positivity discourses: an analysis of #DisabledAndCute', *Feminist Media Studies*, DOI: 10.1080/14680777.2022.2032254.

Hine, C. (2015) *Ethnography for the internet: embedded, embodied and everyday.* London: Bloomsbury Academic.

Jensen, K.B. (2012) *Handbook of media and communication research,* 2nd ed. New York: Routledge.

Kafer, A. (2013) *Feminist, queer, crip.* Bloomington, IN: Indiana University Press.

Kanai A. (2017) 'On not taking the self seriously: resilience, relatability and humour in young women's Tumblr blogs', *European Journal of Cultural Studies,* 22(1), pp. 60–77. DOI: 10.1177/1367549417722092.

McRobbie, A. (2009) *The aftermath of feminism: gender, culture and social change.* London: Sage.

McRuer, R. (2006) *Crip theory: cultural signs of queerness and disability.* New York: New York University Press.

Mendes, K., Ringrose, J., and Keller, J. (2019) *Digital feminist activism: girls and women fight back against rape culture.* Oxford: Oxford University Press.

Mitchell, D.T., and Snyder, S. (2015) *The biopolitics of disability: neoliberalism, ablenationalism and peripheral embodiment.* Ann Arbor: University of Michigan Press.

Newton, E. (1979) *Mother camp: female impersonators in America.* Chicago: Chicago University Press.

Oliver, M. (1983) *Social work with disabled people.* Basingstoke: Macmillan.

Olkin, R., Hayward, H., Abbene, M.S., and VanHeel, G. (2019) 'The experiences of microaggressions against women with visible and invisible disabilities', *Journal of Social Issues,* 75, pp. 757–785. https://doi.org/10.1111/josi.12342.

Penny, L. (2013) *Cybersexism: sex, gender and power on the internet.* London: Bloomsbury.

Pollard, T.M., and Hyatt, S.B. (1999) *Sex, gender and health.* Cambridge: Cambridge University Press.

Pullen E., Jackson D., and Silk M. (2020) '(Re-)presenting the Paralympics: affective nationalism and the "able-disabled"', *Communication & Sport,* 8(6), pp. 715–737. DOI: 10.1177/2167479519837549.

Rentschler, C.A. (2017) 'Bystander intervention, feminist hashtag activism, and the anti-carceral politics of care', *Feminist Media Studies,* 17(4), pp. 565–584, DOI: 10.1080/14680777.2017.1326556.

Ringrose, J., and Harvey, L. (2017) 'Digital mediation, connectivity, and networked teens', in Silk, M.L, Andrews, D.L., and Thrope, H. (eds.) *Routledge Handbook of Physical Cultural Studies.* London: Routledge, pp. 451–464.

Ryan, F. (2021) 'During Covid, to be "vulnerable" is to be told your life doesn't matter', *The Guardian,* 24 June, https://www.theguardian.com/commentisfree/2021/jun/24/covid-vulnerable-life-death-toll-old-disabled (Accessed 5 May 2022).

Samuels, E., and Freeman, E. (2021) 'Introduction: Crip temporalities', *South Atlantic Quarterly,* 120(2), pp. 245–254. https://doi.org/10.1215/00382876-8915937.

Sandahl, C. (2003) 'Queering the crip or cripping the queer? Intersections of queer and crip identities in solo autobiographical performance', *GLQ: A Journal of Lesbian and Gay Studies*, 9(1–2), pp. 25–56.

Sheppard, E. (2020) 'Performing normal but becoming crip: living with chronic pain', *Scandinavian Journal of Disability Research*, 22(1), pp. 39–47. DOI: 10.16993/sjdr.619.

Slater, J., Ágústsdóttir, E., and Haraldsdóttir, F. (2018) 'Becoming intelligible woman: gender, disability and resistance at the border zone of youth', *Feminism and Psychology*, 28(3), pp. 409–426.

Taft, J.K. (2011) *Rebel girls: youth activism and social change across the Americas*. New York: New York University Press.

Taft, J.K. (2020) 'Hopeful, harmless, and heroic: figuring the girl activist as global savior', *Girlhood Studies*, 13(2), pp. 1–17, DOI: 10.3167/ghs.2020.1302xx.

Tembeck, T. (2016) 'Selfies of ill health: online autopathographic photography and the dramaturgy of the everyday', *Social Media + Society*, January-March, pp. 1–11, DOI: 10.1177/2056305116641343.

Todd, A. (2018) 'Virtual (dis)orientations and the luminosity of disabled girlhood', *Girlhood Studies*, 11(3), pp. 34–49, DOI: 10.3167/ghs.2018.110305.

CHAPTER 9

'Self, Self, Self': Masculine Modes of Sexual Self-Representation and the Disruptive Politics of Jouissance on OnlyFans.com

Gareth Longstaff

1   Introduction: Disruptive Desires

This chapter will focus on the tension between the psychoanalytic concept of jouissance and the politics of masculine sexual self-representation on the website OnlyFans.com. To do so it will focus on the rise of both the production *and* consumption of sexual content on OnlyFans.com during the 2020 pandemic and how this specific platform and its 'vernacular' (Gibbs et al, 2015) has worked to disrupt the fields of gay male pornography and self-representation from the standpoint of neoliberalism and late capitalism (Hennessey, 2000, Fisher, 2009, Hakim, 2018). It attempts to situate the complex politics of jouissance and its ascription to OnlyFans.com as something that is both culturally and unconsciously 'most powerfully held together by the common rationale of market mobilisation' (Brockling, 2016, p. 59) and as a form of governance that is fuelled by incentives, competition, and 'the innate addiction to self-aggrandisement'(ibid). More so it uses this foundation to understand self-representational pornography on OnlyFans.com as 'a field of labour, technological innovations, monetary exchange, carnal acts and sensations, regulatory practices, verbal definitions, and interpretations' (Paasonen, 2011, p. 8) disrupted and buttressed by jouissance.

In the context of the 2020 pandemic (and subsequent lockdown), where physical intimacies and desires were sanctioned, this move to a space of entirely digital and networked sexual pleasure is also allied to how desire connects to the tensions which endure between capitalism, desire, and sexuality. More so and during the 2020 pandemic the curation of this self on social and user-generated media platforms increased and intensified the ways in which self-representational and amateur porn coalesced with broader socio-political relations of how sexual pleasure, desire, labour, and entrepreneurialism were tethered to a neoliberal sensibility. Using this as a bedrock and re-evaluating Rosemary Hennessey's claim that 'sexualities which participate in the logic of the commodity help support neo-liberalisms mystifications' (2000, p. 109) and in what follows I will scrutinise how the construction of white cis-gendered masculine content creation on OnlyFans.com is both ensnared to and enabled by 'profit and pleasure' from the precarity of the pandemic and these techniques of hegemonic, subjective, and corporeal labour. By analysing the persona of Josh Moore, it will provide both a critical overview and analysis of how everyday lives transect with pornographic identities and how OnlyFans.com facilitates and maintains this. Whether this is through paid subscription, purchasing from wish lists, live requests, or private hires with fans (which are often filmed and uploaded for sexual pleasure and consumption), Moore and thousands of others like him manipulate these constructs as fetishes to retain the fan as a consumer / subscriber. They do this by urging them to invest sexually, emotionally, and pleasurably in an enigmatic construction that oscillates between modes of distance and proximity, public and private, and reality and fantasy (Longstaff, 2013).

This chapter uses the context surrounding Onlyfans.com and the contours of pornographic content allied to cis-gendered male performers. These are men who signify and capture an ideological discourse of sexualised masculinity in the context of neoliberalism and its capacity to facilitate and sustain agile and adaptable levels of self-ambition, self-promotion, and self-mobilisation through the monetisation of sexual desire. The politics of how these men are self-signified and how they manage their own self-signification can be aligned to the tensions between unconscious drives (in this instance the concept of jouissance) and the content-focused labour of them as neoliberal 'content creators' and 'content collaborators' ostensibly in charge of their own sexual agency, sexual labour, and self-defined desires. Here the diverse possibilities of how jouissance might manoeuvre sexual pleasure, intimacy, isolation, and sex-work begin to coalesce with the proficiency of neo-liberal capitalism. It is here that content creation, strategic collaboration, and entrepreneurial self-management are informed by a perceptive and tactical awareness of their own bodies, dicks, allure, spatialisation and more broadly the assimilation and use of authentic, mundane, ordinary, and domestic space undergirds an aesthetics of amateurism that arouses and sustains 'fans' as subscribers. The chapter will use these instances and a specific focus on the gay male porn-star / content creator Josh Moore to consider how practices of labour, self-representation, and entrepreneurial agency are aligned and commodified across digital, networked, and pornographic media.

I argue that these conditions form disruptive *and* affirmative tensions which can be aligned to Jacques Lacan's psychoanalytic concept of jouissance, and the construction of an online sexual self. In many ways, the responses to the pandemic echoes and resonates with Lacan's theoretical concept and the ways in which jouissance disrupts the performativity of sex, morality, normativity, and our precarious grasp of desire. In the shadow of jouissance desire, is always disruptive and is intensified by the operational possibilities that might occur when jouissance and a digitally networked sexual self are amalgamated and fused together. Just as an orthodoxy allied to psychoanalysis remains both impossible and injurious, we also see that something like an ethics of (Lacanian) psychoanalysis is just as problematic to pinpoint. Fink (1995) asserts that psychoanalysis, like jouissance, 'is not pragmatic in its [ethical] aims' (p. 146) in that it defies and subverts 'compliance with social, economic, and political norms and realities' (ibid). In a chapter that undertakes a psychoanalytic and cultural critique of gay masculinity and desire, an (un)ethical and (non)methodological approach is better positioned through a 'praxis of jouissance' (ibid). In turn, this account also repositions and attempts to transgress accepted ethical and methodological frameworks of how desires are represented and read. It is through jouissance and the potentials in re-conceptualising how analytical positions are realised and carried forward that the ways in which 'jouissance is anything but practical' (ibid) can be used prolifically. It is because 'the techniques that psychoanalysts must use to deal with jouissance wreak havoc' (ibid) that psychoanalysis is able continually to re-evaluate and re-position the discursive rubric of approaches to sexual desire and signification. Leo Bersani (2011) sums this up in the stately claim that 'the heroically impossible project of psychoanalysis is to theorise an onaldizable psyche' (p. 13), which, through jouissance allows 'unreadable pressures to infiltrate the readable, thus creating a type of readability at odds with how we have been taught to read' (ibid). Here, the impossibility of psychoanalysis as a methodological or ethical doxa is expressed in how it 'performs the blockages, the mergings, the incoherence inherent in the discipline Freud invented' (ibid). It is also through these impasses in language, and through this affirmative form of disruption that psychoanalysis makes possible, that some of the problems allied to working with the production and consumption of sexually explicit images of the self are raised across OnlyFans.com and Josh Moore's mediated persona.

The articulation of desire on Onlyfans.com is facilitated via boundless and disruptive practices of subscribing, filming, editing, messaging, watching, pausing, posting, and commenting. Here, the public display and affirmation of the 'ordinary' sexual self via sexually explicit self-representations is instantaneously connected to, and dislocated from, a particular individual and/or groups of users. This is a space where those who are seeking out desire through forms of jouissance are persuaded into associating with a yearning for proximity, intimacy, and reciprocity. Isolation, anxiety, financial austerity and precarity contour the sexual excess and domestic ordinariness of OnlyFans.com and its huge popularity. Here, the powerful allure to create and sustain sexually explicit self-promotional and mediated content means that fans 'are pushed toward being conscious of pleasure as itself a type of work, a realization that seems particularly critical in the case of pornography in which what we are seeing, and taking pleasure in, is bodies at the work of pleasure' (Patterson, p. 118, 2004).

This accumulation and rating of mediated content online industriously position and legitimate sexual desirability as verification and rateable evidence of entrepreneurial success in capitalism and within this pornographic sphere a simultaneously affirming and troubled ethics of neoliberalism are performed and embodied. Here this strain of 'successful' sexual selfhood and citizenship is measured by a tactical blend of self-reliance, awareness, resilience, reinvention, and a public persona that resituates sex work, sexual risk, and the self-affirmation of 'sex-positivity'. In these spaces where fan communities and fans as individual consumers invest in the porn performer we find that figures such as Moore strategically 'turn the image of the self into a commodity that is made public and consumable by others, projecting personal images into collective space' (Iqani and Schroeder 2015, p. 411). In turn, this kind of content 'as desire' urges the expedition of jouissance to become more enigmatic and the management of desire for profit and ego more productive.

2   Situating Jouissance

The theoretical concept of jouissance disrupts the indices of how sex, desire, and pleasure are articulated and experienced. Jouissance is never fulfilled, inscrutable and unfathomable. Its qualities inflect and reflect not only the disruptive aspects of sex and sexuality but also the unforeseen conditions of the pandemic and its effect on sexual desire. Furthermore, the inconsistency of what jouissance actually refers to and how it can (and cannot) be used allows for a consideration of how particular modes of male sexual self-representation on OnlyFans.com sway between what Bruce Fink (1995) claims 'might be understood as involving the attempt to present, represent, symbolise, and thereby subjectify' (p. 117) jouissance, whilst also being open to the fact that jouissance is at the core of what will 'not have been spoken, written, represented or subjectified' (ibid). Here, self-representation connects to the ways in which jouissance defies signification and meaning because it also exists and remains as 'the part that has effects without signifying' (ibid). This kind of disruption links to the work of Jacques Lacan and its queering by Tim Dean

(2000) where the psychoanalytic configurations of the Imaginary other, the Symbolic Other, and the Real can be connected and examined through the vulnerability of the Phallus and the precarious formation of jouissance. It is also in this psychoanalytic space that the excessive aesthetics of sexual self-representation (Longstaff, 2020) disrupt the politics of desire to suggest that a re-engagement or queering of psychoanalysis, and particularly the work of Lacan, may be where a new method or, indeed, a new way to situate psychoa-nalysis, sexuality, and the exigence for pornography is located. Dean points out that the very action of asking 'How?' to move beyond rhetorical versions of sex-uality and desire form an ambiguity, in that the frameworks, methodologies, and academic literature for such an inquiry are themselves rhetorical. Seeing sex through the queer prism of Lacanian psychoanalysis and the enigmatic possibilities of jouissance (and psychoanalysis more generally) may also allow us to read and interpret desire beyond the terms that ensnare it as desire.

Understanding how these shifts and intersections are articulated through psychoanalysis requires a more detailed consideration of the Imaginary 'other' and Symbolic 'Other' in relation to the register of the Real in Lacan's tripartite structure of the 'Real-Symbolic- Imaginary'. The most accepted way of grasp-ing how the Imaginary and Symbolic are mapped in relation to the Real (and its allegiance to jouissance) is to understand that Imaginary intersubjectiv-ity is constructed through a subject-to-other relation whilst Symbolic inter-subjectivity occurs through a subject-to-Other relation. In this exchange the 'Other' differs from the 'other' in that it occupies an asymmetrical space that is 'strictly divested of subjective status' (Dean, 2000, p. 43). Although desire is formed through an unconscious desire of the Other (that is the Symbolic force of language beyond an individual's control), it is done so because the Imaginary other is often visualised and signified as spuriously coherent. For instance, in self-representational pornography where we are privileged and seduced into interacting with desirable, authenticating, and ordinary others engaging in sexual acts, we see a potent way of repetitively enhancing and affirming an Imaginary rhetoric of desire. In this pornographic context we also see that the Imaginary other is ensnared by the big Symbolic Other and vice-versa. More so, the multiplicity of exchanges between fan and performer at the level of an inter-subjective and Imaginary other create and sustain modes of sexual arousal and recognition that are understood to be the desires of subject and other. Yet, when these interactions are considered as Symbolic through an 'Other', and the underlying power of the 'rules that I follow [and] mean-ings that haunt me' (Zizek, 2006, p. 9), we see that the 'Big' (ibid) Symbolic Other allows and even encourages subjects and others to (mis)recognise and doubt the substance of their desires. In turn, this may be where the operation of jouissance begins to emerge to suggest that desire can only be manifested *as* desire through complex and unstable inter-relations which disrupt and falter. Paradoxically, it is also when these sexual exchanges are turned 'into signifying form' (Lacan, 2003, p. 316), and, in this instance, sexually explicit images (such as those of Josh Moore examined here and thousands of other men who are performatively and visually akin to him) that a precariously phallic language of signification allied to gay pornography, sexuality and masculinity emerges.

In terms of sexuality the Imaginary and Symbolic are constituted and mediated by the Real and its power to push desire towards its own 'limits, impasses and dead ends in acceding to symbolic mediation' (Watson, 2017, p. 465). Like jouissance, the Real is impudently ahistorical to language and representation; it is 'both the hard, impenetrable kernel resisting symbolization *and* a pure chimerical entity which has in itself no ontological consistency' (Zizek, 1989, p. 190). It also establishes 'the gap that separates us from the image' (Lewis, 2008, p. 194) and, in so doing, convinces the subject that 'the Symbolic needs the Imaginary (the fantasy) because it is not complete, and the Imaginary needs the Symbolic [...] because it is not complete' (p. 195). This relation is both a mutual encounter and a rutted conflict and it is here that the capricious possibilities of the Real and the knotted impossibilities of attaining jouissance and anxiety begin to emerge. The Real is that which seems to resist, fall outside of, or fails to articulate signification in the Imaginary and Symbolic because 'the real is not an effect of symbolic and imaginary orders; at most it is a theoretical construct that explains negatively the function and limits of these two orders' (Dean, 2000, p. 88). Whilst it is beyond the limits of these two orders that the 'Real' of jouissance and anxiety exists, it seems that to begin to articulate something, indeed anything, of jouissance and anxiety as Real, we need to acknowledge that the Imaginary-Symbolic relation also has the capacity to open us up to the potential signification of the Other's / other's Real jouissance and anxiety.

It is also important to note here that the use of Lacan's triadic formula (Imaginary other, the Symbolic Other, and the Real) align themselves to the ways in which the contexts of pornography, subjectivity and online media converge and intersect. In all of these conceptual and visual paradigms, how desire is configured as both a useless and useful construct is always underpinned by Lacan's emphasis on 'the nonsensical nature of the signifier' (Fink, 1995, p. 118) and how it 'exceeds its symbolic function' (ibid). Lacan sees the relationship between this claim balanced precariously between language (speech) and jouissance (non-speech) or, as he also suggests, between law (droit) and jouissance, or utility and pleasure (Lacan, 1999, p. 3).

In the networked spaces of Onlyfans.com there is a wrenching and pulling between jouissance and the self. This suggests that performers sway between states of desire both enigmatically and productively because exchanges of self-curation, self-surveillance, self-promotion, and self-worth act as capitalist tools that reify desire whilst also intimately arousing the Real and displacing the Imaginary other/ Symbolic Other. It is in the subject's unconscious that this relationship to jouissance is (or indeed is not) mapped as desire. In this Real setting jouissance is something that can't ever be cogently captured, articulated, or expressed is thus positioned as a '"non-specular" component' (Hook, 2015, p. 119) in specular forms (such as pornography and more specifically Onlyfans.com) where we begin to see also how it imbues desire. Here the confluence of jouissance and mediated space catalyses a productively disruptive force that impalpably destabilises the Imaginary imaging and experience of the sexual subject with a prolific and mutable level of power. It is also through the erratic force of jouissance that the subject's precarious desires with the Symbolic Other and the allure of the Real are in some way managed and mapped out as inscrutable traces of a jouissance that cannot be represented or released.

Psychoanalysis, and its connections to Symbolic structures and topographies of jouissance, yields the power to destabilise and thus rearrange the relationship between desire and the self. OnlyFans.com is also connected to this kind of disruptive tension and here we find desiring subjects that are split in terms of the signifier, jouissance, and the exchanges between Imaginary others and Symbolic Others. In this way and in an excessively visual setting like OnlyFans.com we find that the Imaginary 'signifier takes the subject's place, standing in for the subject who has now vanished' (Fink, 1995, p. 41) in the Symbolic. As a result, we may well suggest that when desire is constructed as an Imaginary other of desire, there is the potential that the Symbolic Other of jouissance has already been eliminated. Also, and when sexual desires are self-mediated and 'the subject appears only as a pulsation, an occasional impulse or interruption that immediately dies away or is extinguished' (ibid), then there is also the possibility that speech, language, and the operations of the desire reenergise jouissance's pleasurable self-destruction. Within a space such as OnlyFans.com and through the persona of a figure like Josh Moore the precarious mediation of practices such as public-sex, online sex-work, barebacking within their online personas capture some of the enigmatic slippages of jouissance. Paradoxically, this also suggests that whilst sexual desire has intensified in terms of how it is expressed, it has also become less dissident and itinerant through paradigms of excessive participation, visibility, and accessibility of pornographic self-representation in late and neo-liberal capitalism. On OnlyFans.com the sexualised self-representations that take porn 'beyond the studio' (Mercer, 2017) are reorganised into an enigmatic form of jouissance that relies upon and is reified as a commodity fetish with a complex compound of 'occlusion, displacement, concealment and illusion' (Munoz, 2009, p. 78). In turn this is allied to how economic and subjective processes of self-surveillance and self-promotion converge with fandom and subscription. It is here that desires are principally positioned as neo-liberal commodities (Ryan, 2019) and more provocatively this is where jouissance is negated by the superficial 'reality that capitalism presents to us' (Fisher, 2009, p. 18) as authenticating and familiar.

To think about how the operations of jouissance might work in these net-worked and pornographic spaces Mark Fisher's observations in *Capitalist Realism* (2009) are incredibly provocative and insightful. He states that neo-liberals are 'the capitalist realists par excellence' (p. 2) in that they are defined by capitalism as both 'a monstrous, infinitely plastic entity, capable of metab-olising and absorbing anything with which it comes into contact' (p. 6) whilst accepting that it is also 'the only viable political and economic system' (ibid) that they know. As Fisher also observes and a lot like the topology of jouissance 'what needs to be kept in mind is *both* that capitalism is a hyper-abstract imper-sonal structure *and* that it would be nothing without our cooperation' (2009, p. 15). Capitalism as an unspeakable or abstract ontology is also explored by Slavoj Zizek who aligns it to Lacan's Real register. For Zizek the Real sets the limits and informs the surplus and excessive production of jouissance in a cap-italist context. More so, the Real kernel of capital also relies upon an 'economy of *jouissance* to the extent that it involves the circulation of surplus as [...] an essentially human mark: the production of a surplus' (Pinto de Góes, C. R. and C.A. Santana Pereira, 2015, p. 7). Connecting this to what we know about sexual self-signification on OnlyFans.com we see just how forcefully users are inter-pellated and regulated by this surplus jouissance. Users move towards a form of jouissance that 'reifies man transforming him into factor of production' (ibid) and as a result this desire is forced to exist from within a capitalist sys-tem where repetitious and limitless forms of jouissance underpin and define the surplus self-production and self-promotion of that desire. For instance, if we pay the $15 per month fee to subscribe to an OnlyFans.com account the subject 'as subscriber' begins an excursion which positions the relationship between jouissance as one reinforced by promotional capital yet one which does not trouble the user who is part of a system that is 'able to fetishize money in our actions only because we have already taken an ironic distance towards money in our heads' (Fisher, 2009, p. 12).

3   Onlyfans.com, Josh Moore and Sexual Self-Representation

Onlyfans.com is a UK based company that was founded and launched by Tim Stokely in 2016. It urges anyone to 'Sign up to make money and interact with your fans!' and enables performers or more specifically 'content creators' to receive monthly income and more so tips and tokens on the HD streaming and PPV (pay-per-view) facility. The 'subscriber as fan' can only view the content of a content creators' profile if they pay a monthly membership fee of which 80% goes to creator and 20% to Onlyfans.com. As of June 2021, the site has 1.5 million content creators, 170 million registered subscribers and claims to have paid out approximately $2 billion to its 'content creators'. More so, and on its login page there are options to login as 'performer' or 'fan' and performers are also referred to as 'models' so that their individualised and commodifiable desires are aligned to their self-representational appeal. Performers are organised around a rhetoric of promotional display and desires are actualised through economic visibility; the performers are self-advertised as 'today's sales' and 'promotional pricing' which also allows them to self-brand and self-promote as products with a '10% 25% 50% or 100% discount' or a 'free 3-day trial'. Here the emphasis is focused on the fact that this platform offers 'more ways to make money than any other platform' and that it boldly positions sexual modes of desire in terms of an economic freedom that is cohesively achieved 'by peoples individual choices [with] the help of prices' (Brockling, 2016, p. 60) and the principle that entrepreneurial competition and individual difference will trigger and facilitate the preferential agency of sexual desire through competitiveness (ibid).

This is the kind of setting where men like Josh Moore thrive. Here they can self-mediate and self-commodify their bodies, they can capture, crop, edit and share their abundant sexual encounters with other men, and most perceptibly they can monetise their dicks as sites of desire where jouissance is reified and transformed into self-representational and pornographic content for profit and reward. These networked spaces also allow users the tools to create a politics of self-definition via the self-promotion of a sexually constructed body and its sexual competence through a fusion of 'erotic capital and social capital' (Hakim, 2018, p. 236). Here his body is self-branded and self-presented as an aspirational tool that has accumulated the required forms of discipline, pleasure, and knowledge to enable and sustain a user's individual success and self-fulfilment.

Moore also exploits this perfectly whilst also leaning towards the well-worn tensions that align his life before porn to the ordinary and banal. In a 2019 online interview he references this stating that;

when I was 22, and I was tired of working a boring office job, I decided to say 'fuck this' – I signed up to my favourite studio at the time to see if they would cast me. Two weeks later, I was in Greece filming my first film! I've never looked back. This has now been my full-time job for four years'. Moore revealed that 'I've always looked at porn, since I was about 14, and I always thought to myself that I'd love that to be me.

JOHNSON, 2019

Here the notoriety primarily offered by studio work (he is a highly rated 'star' on Pornhub.com, and the only UK 'exclusive' performer signed to the popular US studio Falcon) have informed and enabled him to create and sustain his own pornographic content for his followers and fans. Moore states on his Twitter xxx account that he is in the top 0.2% on OnlyFans.com and in the 'top 0.2% of worldwide creators' and in this same interview goes on to state that 'I use JustFor.Fans and onlyfans within the gay porn industry, I'm actually one of the top content creators in the world. I create lots of different content – I always like to mix it up, which I think is what my subscribers love'. Moore's ability and willingness to do this as a gay male porn performer is in no way unique. Online gay male porn performers with enormous influence and in some cases who have collaborated with Moore such as Gabriel Cross. Along with Moore, there is a community of 'top content creators' who use their networked authority, bodily assets, dynamic promiscuity, and collaborative agency to both arouse and 'influence their audience' (Khamis and Welling, 2017, p. 193) through the 'heterogenous pursuit of a hedonistic, narcissistic form of individuality and pleasure' (van Doorn, 2010, 426).

Moore's Imaginary identity politics are also connected to and capitalise on the emergence of a 'sporno-sexual' body in contemporary culture. This a desirable male body that amalgamates the ideological ambitions and aspirations allied to the bodies of male sports stars and porn stars vis-à-vis the legacy of metrosexual masculinity. This is the ideological body of a 'young, white, middle class, cis-gender man' (Hakim, 2018, p. 233) framed from within a perspective of male dominance and privilege. This male body self-disciplines and maintains a 'developed muscular body and highly groomed appearance' (Mercer, 2017, p. 31) and confidently displays 'overt and assertive sexual desirability' (ibid) as monetised pleasure and self-defined profit. In mediated discourses of bodily anxiety and aspiration it is often the type of body 'men are striving to achieve' (Hakim, 2018, p. 233) reliant on 'high musculature and low body-fat' (ibid). The signification of this type of gay masculine desire forms a key emphasis within a signifying chain that also enigmatically locates private accessibility and personal intimacy with Moore as the energiser of gay desire, and also its causal index. Whilst his posts on OnlyFans.com seem to form and construct a highly personal discourse of desire specific to Moore they are constantly shared and re-blogged from multiple online spaces. Here they converge with Moore's self-managed and self-defined content across platforms such as Instagram, Twitter xxx, and Pornhub's gay communities to create and sustain a sophisticated awareness and aesthetics that is informed by authenticity, surveillance, ordinariness, and amateurism (Mercer, 2017, pp. 170–171). Moore uses his porn stardom and celebrity to manipulate, assimilate and amplify desire through this kind of approach. In turn, this positions him through the guise of 'symbolic amateurism' (Hamilton in Mercer, p. 182) which adopts 'the pose of the amateur even while inhabiting the sphere of the professional' (ibid). Here there is an affirmation of amateurism, but one which is knowingly performed and manipulated strategically by Moore to signify amateurism. This strategic amateurism is reliant upon corporate and symbolic elements as well as the core tensions 'between the professional (embodied in the gay porn star) and the non-professional (embodied in the amateur)' (ibid) that Moore clearly exploits on his OnlyFans.com platform. The sexual desires of an ordinary and authentic Moore coalesce with Moore the international porn star to cultivate and sustain a self-assured, self-produced and self-aggrandised awareness of how his every day and domestic experiences powerfully compound with the porn industry, porn stardom and pornographic distribution across various platforms. Moore exploits the ideological and aesthetic qualities of 'professional amateurism' in porn which support a broader 'vocabulary that many men use to construct their sexualised bodies for consumption online' (ibid) so that the subtleties of everyday life seem to be authentically disrupted and enhanced by the object of sexual fantasy.

The individual choices and agency bound to this way of subscribing to desire via the self-representations shared on Onlyfans.com work towards augmenting the veracity of the sexual and desiring body as an accessible, intimate, immediate, and satisfying version of itself; albeit one that is always regulated at a technological distance. Here the combined meritocracy and mutability of subscribing to a user such as Moore's 'self' are both enabled and ensnared by the digital tools and networked platforms he utilises, and which utilise him. In this way OnlyFans.com and its technological capacity work to facilitate a way of algorithmically marketing, promoting, monetising, and commodifying the desires of the users and their 'fans' through an enigmatically and productively reified composite of desire and pleasure. It is at this juncture that the conceptual potential of jouissance becomes 'fundamentally a refusal of the demands of the Other, a rejection of its signifiers, or some of them [...] which effectively negates the subject' (Leader, 2021, p. 78).

Contextually we see how this is ambivalently brought to bear via the signi-fier and in Moore's case through the primacy and size of his '9-inch penis'. He uses this a central signifier on OnlyFans.com and we find that within many of the videos that he posts its visibility and size are privileged and promoted. In various clips we see him playing with his dick at a public urinal, his dick pro-truding from his shorts as he sits on a train platform or as he masturbates it in the train station, and others where he riskily masturbates in front of mirrors at the gym or in public toilets. As they intersect, the metaphorical and Imaginary essence of Moore 's phallus can only be deciphered on the basis of its symbolic representation as a metonymic Other which inexorably urges desire towards the place of jouissance and the Real. Whilst it is more convenient to see him and his phallus as an Imaginary metaphor, he is sexually alluring because he is metonymic, in that he has been dislocated from his origin and repositioned as a trope that stands in the place of the big 'Other' and the ideological discourses of Moore's phallically sexual beauty, ability, and vivacious proclivity for pub-lic, promiscuous, precarious, and exhilarating sex. The dimensions of this are complex, in that any representation of desire (a photograph, a video, a tweet …) only manage to represent desire on the basis of how that representation has been assembled, caused, and articulated *as* desire in language. To the extent, therefore, that the unconscious is structured, like language, so a content crea-tors' such as Moore's self-surveillance cannot be separated from the operations of jouissance via language and the unconscious.

Here jouissance can be positioned through the dominant ideology and thus signification of the gay male phallus and its correlation to Lacan's theory of phallic jouissance. Tim Dean observes that Lacan himself supplants, and then almost completely displaces, the certainty of the phallus. As he suggests, this concept (which has formed the foundation for many theorisations of jouis-sance), should be considered as 'provisional rather than foundational' (2000, p. 45) and less concerned about the ways in which Moore actually has sex using his dick and more troubled with the actual problem of how sexual desire itself is activated, pursued and satisfied as jouissance. Throughout Lacan's *Seminar XX* (1973) the subject (that is the sexual subject) is configured in operational terms so that the sexual self is always a disrupted and shattered self, decep-tively articulated through the enigma of a jouissance that guarantees sexual 'subjectivity is focalized in the falling-way of the phallus' (Lacan, 2016, p. 168). On OnlyFans.com the Symbolic and metonymic dimensions of phallic mas-culinity and its temptation to seek a reflection in the Imaginary other are everywhere. As users and their mediated content compete and jostle with one another they both betray and display evidence of their divergent phallic jou-issance in the pursuit of sexual pleasure that reaches a particular point, but a point that ultimately brings jouissance to a temporary halt. Through these kinds of images which seem to authenticate Moore's sexual allure through the size of his dick we see how the incoherence and transposition of meaning of that sexual organ offer up a new potential, whereby the phallic signifier unfetters itself from its significatory meaning and, quite literally, 'exceeds its symbolic function, to signify' (Fink in Lacan, 1999, p. 19). More broadly and across these sexually explicit narratives of self-promotion, the processes of paying to subscribe, logging in and out, watching and sharing, clicking and typing, filming and uploading, as well as waiting and anticipating for Moore (or indeed any performer you choose to subscribe to) to appear, to masturbate, to fuck, to piss, to cum, to speak, etc ... indicates that the subject is looped into a continuous Symbolic exchange of jouissance and its capacity to disrupt desire.

Moore's videos demonstrate an awareness of how to charismatically self-produce and persuasively urge his 'fans' to invest in the impossible jouissance of the other's body and dick economically and sexually. At an Imaginary level this situates Moore as a commodity and object of desire and as he states 'I get so bored of seeing guys in the same bed with the same static camera angle. It's boring, so that why I'm always doing new, exciting, and risky things on my platforms – that keeps people excited and hooked' (Johnson, 2019). Yet, when we begin to locate this at the level of jouissance it becomes apparent that Moore does not exist in relation to a specific or singular mode of desire. Rather, the vectors of unconscious jouissance and subjectivity are formed and reformed in relation to an asymmetrical tryst whereby Moore exists as a mode of desire that '"accompanies" the signifier yet remains detached from it' (Chiesa, 2007, p. 185) and as a consequence this energises an enigmatic process of jouissance that 'emerges *in* the signifier itself' (ibid) and nowhere else.

4   Enigmatic Jouissance and Interpassive Desires

This formation of jouissance thwarts, frustrates, and destabilises desire because it is balanced on the breach of its own signification and meaning through the fractures that exist between self and Other / other. The content creator functions as a form of desire that demands in a ceaseless and selfish cathexis; never giving up, or as Lacan states, 'demanding it (*ne cesse pas*)' (1999, p. 5). Here, jouissance demands a jouissance of the Other / other in retro-active cycles that enigmatically rise and fall at uneven gaps which generate an insight into the failure of desire itself. In the context of this gap in jouissance, Jean Laplanche's concept of the 'enigmatic signifier' affirms the enigmatic potential of jouissance's rise and fall. He initiates the concept by invoking Lacan's 'distinction between a signifier *of* – a specific meaning or signified – and a signifier *to* – addressed to and interpellating a specific subject' (Fletcher in Laplanche, 1999, p. 12). This 'enigmatic signification' symbolically undercuts the power of an enigmatic jouissance that fails to articulate desire in that it controls, sanctions, and also compels jouissance to behave itself through signification. Just as pornographic images force desires to repeat and, thus, reiterate jouissance, they do so through 'a knowledge [that] they are at once willfully withholding from me and using [me] in order to invade my being' (Bersani, 2001, p. 356). To the gay male user these images of Moore are both distant and, somehow, at the kernel of how gay desire is signified and unfulfilled as an enigmatic form of jouissance between subjects. As Laplanche observes

> An enigma, like a riddle, is proposed to the subject by Ir subject. But the solution of a riddle in theory is completely in the conscious possession of the one who poses it, and thus it is entirely resolved by the answer. An enigma on the contrary, can only be proposed by someone who does not know the answer, because his message is a compromise-formation in which his unconscious takes part.
>
> 1999, p. 254–55

Here, the force of enigmatic jouissance possesses 'the very formula of desire of which I myself am ignorant' (Bersani, 2001, p. 356), and, thus, splinters both self (the gay male fan) and other (the 'content creator' and in this instance Moore) through the duplicitous *and* reciprocal pursuit of pleasure. In the pornographic and self-representational content that Moore produces and posts a reified form of jouissance steers the subject towards an enigmatic space in which sexually arousing and explicit 'signifiers fit together, combine and concertina' (Lacan, 1999, p. 37) as pornographic content. Here the enigmatic breaks in jouissance are necessary for this jouissance to occur and for the enticement of a desire 'for' or 'with' a figure like Moore to continue. It is through this enigmatic form of signification that the pornographic performer is allowed to 'signify something [...] and can be read in an infinite number of different ways' (ibid) by a potentially limitless number of fans. More generally, it is how the images on OnlyFans.com are posted, as analogous reproductions and repetitively arousing representations of a boundlessly 'porned' identity, lifestyle, work, and pleasure, which allow them to be allied to the thwarted reification of gay male jouissance. Therefore, and in terms of a 'gay' male self-representation, we are confronted with the key problem of psychoanalytic discourse, which, as Lacan observes, always 'give[s] a different reading to the signifiers that are enunciated (*ce qui s'enonce de signifiant*) than what they signify' (ibid). Because there is the fantasy of corresponding relationship between the performer and the desire, between the signifier and referent, this allows reality and jouissance to deceivingly blend and manifest *as* desire. This is instilled because Moore's location on the site, the subscription process, and the posts and blogging tools which may allow for encounters to happen synchronously can only be understood through inter-passive lapses, inhibitions, and asynchronous struggles to make conscious the unconscious and the impersonal personal.

As this is traversed by Moore and his subscribers, we find that aspects of self-representational display, self-promotion, strategic amateurism, ordinariness, liveness, public and private spheres of desire, self-surveillance, and the tensions between how sexual desire as a fantasy are transposed and sustained through the creation of an 'intimacy with', and 'authenticity of' the porn performer all converge together. This is also defined by a disruptive form of desire that was amplified during the covid-19 pandemic and from within the late capitalist and neoliberal inevitability of having to pay for the 'free choice' (Patterson, 2004, p. 116) to interact with Moore's (and indeed any OnlyFans.com) account / profile. Here, there is the assurance of excessively and explicitly seeing Moore and the thrill of engaging and participating in a form of sexual exchange with him through interactivity that shapes a disruptively arousing process of cultural and economic engagement. Here the interactive element is buttressed by a level of interpassivity (Pfaller, 2017) and its powerful allure to situate interactive exchanges as illusory forms of vicarious pleasure between performer and fan so that it is 'unclear how much substantive interaction is taking place and whether we want it if it were there' (Patterson, p. 117).

Inter-passivity is a state of passivity that is allowed and sustained by interactivity and here it suggests that fans enjoy seeing the other (Moore) enjoying in their place. On Onlyfans.com interactivity is augmented by a displaced interpassivity between Moore as a 'performer as content creator' and his 'subscribers as fan'. Inter-passive exchanges indicate that the subject to other relation is 'one in which the other not only does the work for the viewer but also enjoys and believes in the viewers place' (ibid). In this instance both Moore's OnlyFans.com posts function as a vessel and/or composite space where the camera / camera-phone, the computer, the image, and the self simultaneously conflate and permit an artifice of desire to mix. In these self-representational and networked spaces of sexual desire there is both 'an ensuing confusion about the specificity of tasks and labour' (p. 118) and the affirmative 'pleasures of the technology itself, and the particular fantasies it has to offer' (p. 119) all happening at the same time.

Here, we are confronted with an exchange that is 'simultaneously subject and object, and simultaneously passive and active' in its endless pursuit of jouissance (p. 118). Moore is performing, enjoying, and working for the subject, as is the camera that he films himself with, and the website he uploads the content to. In this way both Moore and his place on OnlyFans.com align to 'the affective charge of pornography, linked to, and redoubled by, the affective charge attached to new and perpetually renewed computer technology' (p. 119) as well as 'the new possibilities for subjectivity that [the] technology seems to offer' (ibid). It is within these monetised and subscripted forms of exchange that the unconscious vectors of jouissance as enigmatic proffer a form of desire that can only be performed, embodied, and subsumed as a neo-liberal commodity. In this way the enigmatic distribution and consumption of jouissance splinters the subject-to-other relation (Dean, 2000, p. 43) that upholds an Imaginary ego. Here we see how 'performer-to-fan' or 'fan-to-performer' desires falter to indicate that the jouissance of either configuration can only ever be enunciated as a break in desire. In this 'active-passive / passive-active' encounter jouissance productively pivots desire away from the subject and other and towards the Real. As a result, this renders the desiring subject as perpetually displaced, disrupted and absorbed by a vigorous, dysfluent and seductive jouissance they can't maintain or control. This is always outside of their reach *in* language yet, also, *of* the language through which they are subsumed and constituted.

More specifically, the use of self-representational technologies and the immediacy of how clips can appear on OnlyFans.com are also formed in relation to how desire and jouissance surround an individual's 'anxious' subjectivity and sexual desire. As the individual searches for meaning through the Symbolic Other their subjective desires coalesce, disavow, embrace, and assimilate their Real jouissance in the name of the Imaginary other. It is in this powerful yet illusory realm of the Imaginary that the individual subject is directed towards modes of identification and recognition with the 'other' which seem to temporarily defer anxiety and jouissance and falsely satisfy desire. More complexly and because jouissance as an enigmatic and furtive form 'does not point to anything, nor does it serve any purpose whatsoever' (Braunstein, 2003, p. 106) – the subject is forced to locate or search for desire through the 'Other' which ultimately fails to fulfil desire and urges them towards the Real. When desire fails, anxiety productively arrives because the individual subject can 'only answer with his or her own lack. And in dealing with his or her lack, as well as with the lack in the Other, the subject encounters anxiety' (Salecl, 2004, pp. 22–23). That said, lack does not necessarily equate to a desperate or distressing form anxiety. The assumed vacuity that comes from lack is also connected to the subject's inscrutable pursuit of jouissance. By attaching desire to both jouissance and anxiety we find it is 'not the lack, but rather the absence of the lack, i.e., the fact that where there is supposed to be lack, some object is present' (ibid) that perpetuates anxiety as a productive state of desire. In this way, the idea that we have come to comprehend anxiety (vis-à-vis Lacan) as the 'lack of the lack' acknowledges that where there is lack, there is also desire. In this context, and more specifically if we think of the self-representational and ideological desires allied to Moore, we see that this tension between anxiety and desire is captured when sexually explicit and networked content is produced to both manage or defer his own jouissance and the jouissance of the Other.

It may be here that the viewer's anxiety and expectancy for arousing, and often strategically authenticating and amateur content *of* a persona such as Moore is also exploited and capitalised upon *by* Moore. An example of this is when he utilises his knowledge and access to pornographic discourse to produce and participate in videos that work around the repetitive fantasy and realisation of gay group sex and/or the gay orgy. On OnlyFans.com there are a vast range of videos where Moore sexually 'collaborates' with established porn performers as well as a range of 'ordinary' fans and followers. The fantasy of group sex for both performers and fans functions as a way of deferring an unconscious and disruptive anxiety and 'anchoring the social and subjective identifications that allow the subject to experience themselves, and their surrounding world, as coherent' (Hook, 2015, p. 117). That said, this is also where states of anxiety are not necessarily performed or embodied in diagnostically 'anxious' ways connected to clinical and medical discourses. Rather, the boundless search for jouissance through pornographic modes of interpassivity and in this case the excessive and affirming promiscuity of the group orgy provides a setting where the simultaneity of sexual self-representation and consumption are as much about the excess of sexual desire as its lack. Here the visual 'frenzy' (Williams, 1989) of sex and sexuality, which is mediated as a pornographic commodity, indicates that in this context anxiety is not about the absence or lack of sex, rather it is about the productive ubiquity and pervasiveness of it.

In kind of these group settings Moore and several men have sex in various configurations which seem to follow the accepted conventions of group sex between men in porn; they are muscular, young, virile and demonstrate physical skill and confidence in relation to how they kiss, fuck, suck, and rim one another. Yet this is also informed by the self-manipulation and self-presentation of their bodies through technological devices that we also see within the scene. Laptops with webcams, cameras on tripods, tilted lighting devices, and mobile phone camera devices are persistently visible and generate a sense of their strategically pitched amateurism and the 'do it yourself' authenticity that connects to the urgency and awkwardness of filming group sex as mediated promotional content. The visibility of these self-representational tools is a key trope that defines these sexual encounters and with his 'fans' in mind Moore also uses them to ensure that 'the process of intimacy and identification is cemented by the somatic identification of one body experiencing sexual pleasure and sexual arousal with another body experiencing the same thing' (Patterson, p. 119, 2004) on a mobile device and/or computer. Here (and in a limitless number of clips and scenes) the pursuit of jouissance affirms and captures something of anxiety, yet this is mediated as 'an incitement for subjective identification with the performer, for this ever-fuller sense of participation with that performers life, and that it is this ever-elusive relationship, in effect, that itself becomes the obscure object of desire' (ibid). This object is ultimately a fragile and fallible signifier and, in its attempts, to express jouissance it only partially generates a productively anxious signifier of desire which 'signals a failure onald reality, [and] a disappearance of the fantasy support of desire' (Palacois, 2013, p. 51). It is here that the self-led promotion and representation of promiscuous group sex as well as the excess of jouissance are textured by a productively anxious lack aligned to Lacan's claim that 'anxiety isn't about the loss of an object but its presence. The objects aren't missing' (2016, p. 54).

5   Conclusion

Gay male pornographic self-representations seen online, and, specifically, on Onlyfans.com offer up the paradox of being able to manage and contain desire between men whilst also allowing it to unravel and disperse in limitless ways. The rhetoric of promiscuity, freedom, self-assurance, large dicks, alluring orgies and idealised male bodies are not new, they are standardised and repetitive tools that have amplified and aroused gay male desire in pornography for decades. Yet it is the ways in which they are mediated and reified through jouissance that potentially steers us towards a way of seeing them in alternative and disruptive ways. As an inevitable result, the subject searches for and defers the unconscious vectors of jouissance by attempting to locate and sustain through the visual prism of capitalism. Individuals such as Moore using their networked visibility seem to supply an inexhaustible image bank of Imaginary desire that is reliable, germane, synchronous, sexually explicit, self-representational, and/or pornographically arousing; however, the compound of clips, profiles, users and images and their circulation as markers of desire between men rely upon a far more complex network of queer exchange. This is because desire is entrenched in a Symbolic Other capable of extricating it through any combination of enigmatic and productive identifications spurred on by the Real conditions of jouissance as an affirmative disruption to established forms of hegemony, homonormativity and individuated forms of agency and responsibility. More provocatively this way of conceptualising jouissance as a reified capitalist and neo-liberal way of orienting sex and sexuality suggest that in this a reification there might be the possibility for new, abstruse and persistent modes of sexual desire. Just as 'jouissance is put at its own service in a kind of incessant self-indulgence' (Pinto de Góes, and Santana Pereira, 2015, p. 7) it also forces us into thinking about how 'switching to another production mode implies changing this jouissance economy, this way of producing. It implies regulating the pleasures of the body in some other way' (ibid).

How and why users choose to self-promote and commodify their sexual practices and desires are multiple but they in some way demonstrate how capitalist agency and the illusions of neo-liberal freedom as self-worth flourish in their attempts to affirm and disrupt the inexorable failure of desire. If sexual pleasure if derived from the circulatory moments of jouissance it is done so through the 'habitual and repetitious delay of satisfaction' (Kielty, 2012, p. 44). Jouissance operates on the principle that it is impossible to fulfil desire. In fact, the purpose of desire in capitalism is for desire to remain unfulfilled. Capitalist systems continue to reify and attenuate the inscrutability of jouissance and human commodities such as Moore on OnlyFans.com capture this. If desire is satisfied it ceases to function as desire or more so as a commodity that can speak desire. This is why the enigmatic and productive dynamics of jouissance resurface and haunt the subject so assiduously in these neo-liberal and capitalist spaces of desire.

References

Bersani, L. (2001) Genital Chastity. In: T. Dean, and C. Lane (eds.) *Homosexuality and Psychoanalysis*. Chicago and London: University of Chicago Press, 351–367.

Bersani, L. (2011) "Ardent Masturbation" (Descartes, Freud, and Others). *Critical Enquiry* 38 1–16.

Braunstein, N. (2003) Desire and Jouissance in the Teaching of Lacan. In: J.M. Rabate *The Cambridge Companion to Lacan*, Cambridge University Press, 102–115.

Brockling, U. (2016) *The Entrepreneurial Self: Fabricating a New Type of Subject*, London: Sage.

Chisea, L. (2007) *Subjectivity and Otherness: A Philosophical Reading of Lacan*. Cambridge, Massachusetts. Massachusetts Institute of Technology.

Dean, T. (2000) *Beyond Sexuality*. Chicago and London: University of Chicago Press.

Fink, B. (1995) *The Lacanian Subject: Between Language and Jouissance*. Princeton, New Jersey: Princeton University Press.

Fisher, M. (2009) *Capitalist Realism – Is there no alternative?* Winchester, Zero Books.

Gibbs, M., Meese, J., Arnold, M., Nansen, B., and Carter, M. (2015) #Funeral and Instagram: death, social media, and platform vernacular. *Information, Communication and Society*, 18:3, 255–268.

Hakim, J (2018) *Work that Body – Male Bodies in Digital Culture*. New York and London: Rowman and Littlefield.

Hennessy, R. (2000) *Profit and Pleasure: Sexual Identities in Late Capitalism*, London and New York: Routledge.

Hook, D. (2015) Mapping Anxiety. *Psychology in Society*. (48): 114–120.

Iqani, M., and Schroeder, J.E. (2015) #selfie: digital self-portraits as commodity form and consumption practice. *Consumption Markets & Culture*. 19(5), 405–415.

Johnson, G (2019) Josh Moore is here to mix things up. *Interview with Josh Moore*, 19th November 2019. https://meanshappy.com/josh-moore-is-here-to-mix-things-up.

Khamis, S. Ang, L., and Welling, R. (2017) Self-branding, 'micro-celebrity' and the rise of Social Media Influencers. *Celebrity Studies*, 8(2), 191–208.

Kielty, P. (2012) Embodiment and Desire in Browsing Online Pornography. *Proceedings of the iConference*. Toronto, ON, Canada. 41–47. https://tspace.library.utoronto.ca/bitstream/1807/78145/1/p41-keilty.pdf.

Lacan, J. (1999) *The Seminar of Jacques Lacan – Seminar XX Encore: On Feminine Sexuality, The Limits of Love and Knowledge 1972–73*. Edited by J.A. Miller, Translated by B. Fink. New York: Norton.

Lacan, J. (2003) *Ecrits: A Selection*. Trans. by Sheridan, A. 1977. London: Routledge.

Lacan, J. (2016) *Anxiety – The Seminar of Jacques Lacan – Book X*. Edited by J.A. Miller, Translated by A.R. Price. Cambridge: Polity Press.

Laplanche, J. (1999) *Essays on Otherness*. London: Routledge.

Leader, D. (2021) *Jouissance: Sexuality, Suffering and Satisfaction*. London: Polity.

Lewis, M. (2008) *Derrida and Lacan: Another Writing*. Edinburgh: Edinburgh University Press.

Longstaff (2013) From Reality to Fantasy: Celebrity, Reality TV and Pornography. *Celebrity Studies*, 4:1, 71–80.

Longstaff (2020) Selfies and Sexual Identity. In: Ross, K. (ed.). *The International Encyclopaedia of Gender, Media, and Communication*. Wiley-Blackwell Publishing.

Mercer, J. (2017) *Gay Pornography: Representations of Sexuality and Masculinity*. London: I.B. Tauris.

Munoz, J, E. (2009) *Cruising Utopia: The Then and There of Queer Futurity*, New York and London: New York University Press.

Paasonen, S. (2011) *Carnal Resonance: Affect and Online Pornography*. Cambridge, MA: Massachusetts Institute of Technology.

Palacios, M. (2013) *Radical Sociality: On Disobedience, Violence and Belonging*. London and New York: Palgrave.

Patterson, Z. (2004) Going On-line: Consuming Pornography in the Digital Era. In: L. Williams, (ed.) *Porn Studies*. Durham and London: Duke University Press.

Pfaller, R. (2017) *Interpassivity –The Aesthetics of Delegated Enjoyment*. Edinburgh: Edinburgh University Press.

Pinto de Góes, C.R., and C.A. Santana Pereira. (2015) Notes on the Implications of the Psychoanalytic Concept of Subject in Marxist Communism. In, *The International Journal of Zizek Studies*, 5(1): 1–9.

Ryan. (2019) *Male Sex Work in the Digital Age*, London and New York: Palgrave.

Salecl, R. (2004) *On Anxiety*. London and New York: Routledge.

Van Doorn, N (2010) Keeping it Real: User-Generated Pornography, Gender, Reification and Visual Pleasure. *Convergence: The International Journal of Research into New Media Technologies*, 16(4), 411–430.

Watson, E. (2017) Reflections of the Encounters between Psychoanalysis and Queer Theory. In N. Giffney, and E. Watson, (eds.) *Clinical Encounters in Sexuality Psychoanalytic Practice and Queer Theory*. New York: Punctum Books, 445–473.

Williams, L (1989) *Hardcore: Power, Pleasure and the "Frenzy of the Visible"*. Berkeley and Los Angeles: University of California Press.

Zizek, S. (1989) *The Sublime Object of Ideology*. London: Verso.

Zizek, S. (2006) *How to Read Lacan*. London: Granta Books.

CHAPTER 10

Pandemic Dating: Masculinity, Dating Practice and Risk within the Context of Covid-19

Abbey Couchman

1   Introduction

Situating socio-cultural and discursive constructions of behavioural practice is fundamental for understanding, navigating and promoting any form of behavioural change. Arguably the global pandemic context, and subsequent public health campaigns/policy have led to the largest set of behavioural restrictions in modern Western history. These restrictions have had very real implications for everyday life and social interaction, particularly any form of close contact with those outside of our own 'household', including dating. Pandemic notwithstanding, the practice of dating has itself been undergoing seismic shifts in terms of behavioural, technological and cultural change. This chapter explores the intersection of masculinities, dating practices and risk, against the backdrop of regulatory measures imposed by the pandemic context. Discussion addresses how men navigate risk in relation to aspects of Covid-19 and digital dating throughout the pandemic. Attention focuses upon how men have been pursuing dating practices throughout the social distancing restrictions and the associated risks involved. Given men's sensitivity is often masked by portrayals of heterosexual gendered behaviour, such as asserting dominance and preoccupation with sex, the reality of the fragility of masculinity is often overlooked. Such tensions provide insight to the extreme lengths that men may go to secure intimacy, and equally extreme responses in the face of rejection. The interplay between health policy, government interventions, and gendered behavioural dispositions provides context from which to understand discursively constituted subjectivities and 'risky' behaviours among men. It is therefore critical that Covid-19 and its implications within the contemporary understanding of masculinity be considered. As the chapter unfolds, three main themes are explored in relation to men's dating practices and behaviours during the pandemic: the greater likelihood of men to resist and subvert safety measures such as mask-wearing and limiting social contact (Duarte, 2020; Ruxton and Burrell, 2020; Hearne and Niño, 2021; Mahalik et al., 2022); the adaptations and 'disruptions' to dating during this time, including the technological developments in dating apps' user experience which have encouraged users to continue to date, despite the pandemic; and finally, the negative manifestations of masculine 'fragility', such as rejection-sensitivity (Hanby et al., 2012) and networked misogyny (Banet-Weiser and Miltner, 2016), that appear to be heightened in times of crisis (Faludi, 1999). Before we consider the more specific nuances of socially distanced dating and contemporaneous masculinities pre/post Covid-19, it is worth laying some foundations in terms of the progression of the dating landscape and the development of technological affordances of mobile dating applications which have facilitated and encouraged dating during the pandemic.

2   Just Keep 'Swiping' ...

Mobile dating apps are a direct result of a cultural shift which has seen modern dating become more of a casual activity that celebrates free choice and personal fulfilment, and where the notion of traditional romantic courtship and commitment seems something of a distant past (Haywood, 2018). Massa (2013) suggests that we have moved into an era of "post-dating" where dating for love is said to have expired, replaced with "booty calls, unnecessary miscommunications and failed maybe-almost-relationships" (Massa, 2010) and indicating a breakdown in traditional dating conventions. This is deemed to be facilitated by what we have come to understand as "swipe culture" (Acton, 2017); a prominent and arguably dissociative feature instilled in many millennial matchmaking mobile applications. This process of swiping through profiles has become akin to how one would shop online for goods; engaging with what is thought to be an affective experience, using filtering as a means of excluding undesired items (Haywood, 2018; Tiffany and Fetters, 2020) or indeed personal features in the context of online dating. This empowerment within online dating practices allows hook-up culture to thrive, changing the social and sexual scripts of Western culture (Gagnon and Simon, 1987) as a range of sexual behaviours become dislocated from a more traditional, romantic relationship (Garcia et al., 2013; Heldman and Wade, 2010). Therefore, "cheap thrills are becoming the new norm" (Miller, 2019) as there is less pressure for men to demonstrate compassion and chivalry to maintain an active sex life (LalalaLetmeexplain, 2022). Such developments are highlighted in the rise of no-strings-attached (NSA) sex, catering to varied sexual preferences and fantasies (Haywood, 2018).

Within the mediated experience of the mobile dating application, the construction of self-identity has become a ritualized and routinized endeavour (Butler, 1990; Haywood, 2018). Continuously scrutinised, this takes place in "the context of multiple choice as filtered through abstract systems" (Giddens 1991, p. 5); choice in how the platform can be utilised for one's needs, but also how oneself can be constructed and portrayed in a fragmented and boundaryless sense of identity, perceived in an abundance of representations (Illouz, 2012). As such, Hall (1997) depicts representation within the mediated experience as being a negotiation, taking into consideration the intended meaning by its producers as well as its deconstruction and analysis by audiences. This formation of identity online is interconnected with one's experiences of media use, as well as how its construction involves the differing negotiation of identity among varied media (Fornäs and Xinaris, 2013; Nava, 2007).

Within this new era of post-dating, courting rituals include the act of sending and receiving flirtatious messages and suggestive emojis; acts which often coincide with a pre-emptive fear of being ghosted and subsequent rejection (Porter, 2021). With digitalisation's obsession with personalisation and individual choice then, comes an inherent rise in social, emotional, health and physical risks associated with contemporary dating practices, as well as a subversion of the traditional gender scripts which correspond with conventional dating norms. This includes the uncoupling of sex from traditional 'courtship' and romantic relationships within a broader 'hook-up' culture and user interface restrictions on mobile dating apps (such as Hinge) where women have the power to initiate conversations with men first. Within the context of the Covid-19 pandemic however, the following sections highlight the ways in which aspects of hegemonic masculinities and public safety measures produce a friction that can become challenging for men. Conversely, these tensions can also become a way for us to perhaps understand the reactions of some men who become more aggressive, 'toxic' and misogynistic in dating apps, during a time of such immense social upheaval (Faludi, 1999).

3   'Un-mask-uline'? Physical Risk and Male Bodies

Despite some progressive shifts in how we see masculinities in mass culture, there can often remain a residual essentialism in discourses and perceptions of men, encapsulated in phrases such as 'real man' (Connell 1995, p. 45), comprised of physical strength, independence and mental and emotional resilience. These performative masculine traits are a socially prescribed set of ideas around what it means to be a man, whereby men must perform in a certain way in order to appear masculine. These characteristics were difficult to maintain throughout the pandemic, as collective safety measures limited the scope to meet such expectations. Such tensions in the construction and performance of masculinities and pandemic regulatory health measures may help to understand resistance to rules among men that has been documented in terms of men's lack of cooperation in adhering to personal hygiene practices, social distancing regulations (Ruxton and Burrell, 2020) and mask-wearing (Duarte, 2020; Hearne and Niño, 2021; Mahalik et al., 2022). Prior to the vaccine, face coverings were one of few control measures available for protection against the virus, serving as a physical barrier to protect against the spread of infection (Haischer et al., 2020). However, mask-wearing can be explored as a political landscape. A terrain which reveals various socio-structural relations and discursive power dynamics along racialised, classed and gendered axes. In the early pandemic, the act of mask-wearing was associated with Asian countries and often dismissed because of racist assumptions about those countries (North, 2020; Leung, 2020). Later, as many cities began to require residents to wear masks, police began targeting Black men for covering their faces (Cineas; 2020; Thomas, 2020), profiling them as criminals rather than as citizens abiding by health guidelines. And for a certain subset of mostly white, conservative men, not wearing a mask seemed to have become a hallmark of manliness (Petter, 2020; White, 2020; Willingham, 2020). The subject of mask-wearing has therefore become a highly controversial and politicised issue (Haischer et al., 2020), and attitudes towards mask-wearing remain polarised (Palmer and Peterson, 2020). Not only are men highlighted to be less likely to wear a mask than women (Haischer et al., 2020) but, among men, it is indicated that wearing a face covering is "shameful [...] and a sign of weakness" (Glick, 2020; Petter, 2020). This has been compared to widespread resistance by men in wearing a condom (Victor, 2021; Willingham, 2020) both in general and in relation to the HIV/AIDS 'crisis' during the 1980s and associated sexual health campaigns (Elan, 2020); another instance where masculine ideology has driven resistance to public health protection.

This macho bravado has been demonstrated throughout the pandemic, with previous U.S President, Donald Trump, publicly removing his mask on the steps of the White House following his hospitalisation by the disease (Smith et al., 2020). The Guardian also declared former UK Prime Minister, Boris Johnson, a "super-spreader" (Grace, 2020), as he made a point of handshaking prior to both the pending lockdown and Mr. Johnson's eventual hospitalisation with the infection. Furthermore, Brazil's President Jair Bolsanaro professed that his athletic past would prevent him from falling ill with the disease (Marshall, 2020), and so deemed himself to not require a mask. Whilst the trends between gendered mask-wearing throughout the pandemic has brought the subject of mask-wearing to the forefront, particularly among global leaders, it is clear that the broader, societal issue pertaining to the ideology of masculine leadership and the pressures this instils, continues to prevail to a dangerous extent where it is willing to neglect public health safety. In the UK, the Secretary of State for Health and Social Care at the time, Matt Hancock, was also caught breaking the very social distancing measures he had helped to put in place, to pursue an extra-marital affair during the pandemic. These overt performances of hegemonic masculinity by world leaders in neglecting to follow restrictions resonate with notions of heterosexual male bodies as impenetrable in a physical and immunological sense (Kanzama and Kawaguchi, 2002). Such masculine displays of defiance in relation to risk could have reinforced this logic among male populations, encouraging them to break lockdown restrictions themselves, should they have wished to continue dating. In light of the above intersections between masculinity, mask-wearing and risk-taking in terms of intimate encounters (Elan, 2020; Willingham, 2020; Victor, 2021), we can begin to unravel the reluctance of men to wear face coverings during dates and/or negative reactions when these topics arise in online dating or in-person contexts. However, as we will see in the next section, mobile dating applications became incredibly agile in adapting to the pandemic context and integrating the political economy of ethical citizenship. Various technological and cultural affordances were made to facilitate and sustain dating during the seismic disruption to everyday life and enable people to carry on pursuing intimacy. At the same time, users were encouraged to actively promote public health campaigns and codify their 'pandemic dating preferences' through their profile.

4   Post-dating in a Pandemic

Haywood (2018) identifies how new forms of digital dating practices influence men, particularly those with a more fragile masculinity, in terms of changes in dating behaviours; encouraging the portrayal of archetypal, masculine characteristics. These behaviours are therefore reborn, with sexual aggression and dominance being rife in these dating contexts. This has come to be more widely known as toxic masculinity (Hess and Flores, 2018), or networked misogyny (Banet-Weiser and Miltner, 2016) in its application within digital spaces. As a result, men must consistently self-reflect both in terms of their profile and performance within these new dating practices, given that heteronormative masculinities are very much reinforced within these environments. It is noted that those whose heterosexuality fails to meet these expectations (in that they may remain celibate, live alone or are unsuccessful in securing sex) are subject to ridicule, moral disapproval and condemnation given such perceived feminine (Kimmel, 2007), 'perverse' (Foucault, 1978) or queer (Hubbard, 2000) behaviours. Sexual aggression is therefore considered a defensive effort to prevent one's emasculation (Kimmel, 2007) and protection against negative perceptions or labels. One recent example of these mechanisms and potential after-effects is the 'incel' (a portmanteau of involuntarily celibate). Often stereotyped as demonstrating violent, aggressive and misogynistic behaviour because of alienation and lack of sexual success (O'Malley et al, 2022), the 'incel' represents a community-based manifestation of misogyny in light of female rejection. The concept of self-image therefore "exerts considerable power over young men" (Haywood 2018, p. 156), producing "a recognition of potential masculine vulnerability" (Cosma and Gurevich, 2020) and highlights the perpetual instability and risks of performatively constituted subjectivities (Butler, 1990).

However, as individuals begin to navigate the norms of a post-dating scene, the sudden health threats caused by the Covid-19 pandemic transformed the ways in which we consider romantic interactions and formulate our understanding of appropriate dating behaviours. Whilst the global lockdowns and restrictions were adhered to, for the most part, it is indicated that a significant amount of citizens continued to pursue intimate relationships during this time. As relationship initiation practices continue to be disrupted, particularly given the social distancing restrictions caused by the pandemic, the expectations which normalise men's behaviours are also in transition. The pandemic has also stimulated previously identified "reconfigurations of gender protocol, expectations and normalization" (Haywood, 2018) in dating practices. Subsequently, an array of methods have evolved in which relationships can be pursued, depending on the extent of risk participants are willing to take, in terms of one's personal safety or the extent of one's fetishization of risk (Döring, 2020). For instance, PornHub, a popular porn website, reported the first coronavirus search at the end of January 2020, followed by a worldwide increase in searches for coronavirus-themed pornography – pornography which is noted to include "sex with masks, surgical gloves and hazmat suits" (Zattoni et al. 2020, p. 829).

In the period of lockdown, there was a decrease of 'in-person' casual sex during the pandemic (Li et al., 2020) and a rise in telephone and online sex (Döring, 2020; Callander et al., 2021). Simultaneously, there was a rise in the number of subscriptions for *OnlyFans*; an online platform for adult content creators to post material that can also be monetised through subscriptions and pay-per-view. The platform now boasts over two million content creators (de Gallier, 2022) and 170 million users worldwide (Spire, 2022). Alongside the pandemic, Callahan (2021) notes a sexual revolution and a collision in technology being the cause of a shift in attitudes towards utilising these platforms, for both content producers and subscribers. For instance, 'sexting', previously considered deviant behaviour (Döring, 2014), was actively recommended as a legitimate method of sexual interaction throughout the pandemic, when close contact with strangers and abstinence from casual sex was encouraged (Peck, 2020). We therefore need to consider how the pandemic has perhaps encouraged and facilitated a pre-existing evolution towards technologically enhanced and digitally structured intimacy and sexual practices. The pandemic has framed such shifts in terms of necessity but also provided a narrative for justifying specific behaviours that may previously, or currently, be defined as risky or deviant. While we navigate these areas surrounding shifts in dating practice, it is also crucial to explore how the discursive threats to masculinity posed by the pandemic may intersect with adaptation, risk and heteronormativity. This could be as a result of adhering to the lockdown restrictions or, conversely, breaching these protective measures as a means of pursuing what were once considered 'normal' dating practices and re-affirming masculinity through resistance strategies.

5   Dating from a Distance

For many members of the public, the decision was made to pursue or continue romantic relations remotely as a means of adhering to the lockdown restrictions. The early stages of dating are typically understood as a time where new partners gather context cues which help to make sense of one another, be that information about friends, family and interests, for example. Of course, the coronavirus protocols meant that the opportunity for this to occur organically in person was made impossible, given that elements of the 'real' world allow these observations to be made achievable (Fetters, 2020). Nonetheless, messaging on Tinder has increased globally by 52% in April 2020 since the start of March 2020 (Seabrook, 2021), 44% of UK Hinge users have been on a video date since the function was installed in the summer of 2020 (Seabrook, 2021) and OkCupid has seen an 83% increase in new users setting their location preferences to 'anywhere' since the beginning of the pandemic (Burns, 2021). The nature of the pandemic has therefore encouraged a willingness to engage in these platforms and practices, as well as liberating its users (albeit temporarily perhaps) from geo-spatial limitations for intimacy. All of this transpired despite the intrinsic anxieties that emanates from the presentation and critique of one's depiction of self, associated with contemporary online dating practices. The next section considers some of the adaptations of digital dating platforms in response to the pandemic context.

6   Technological Affordances: Covid-19 Features

As a result of the pandemic, there has been a significant rise in activity on dating applications. For instance, Tinder boasted a record number of 3 billion swipes in one day (Fortune, 2021) during the pandemic, and an 11% increase in user engagement across 2020 (Dietzel, Myles and Duguay, 2021). Furthermore, the Match Group (comprised of forty-five dating brands, including Tinder, Hinge, Match and OKCupid) reported more people using its apps in 2020 than prior to the pandemic. The company ended its second quarter with ten million subscribers, six million of which are Tinder users. In fact, OkCupid noted that only 6% of its users were prepared to wait until after the pandemic to begin dating again (OkCupid, 2020).

Because of this, dating applications have seen amendments and updates to the setup in terms of functionality and pricing (Thor Jensen, 2020) in alignment with the increased usage, as a means of meeting user demand. For example, dating applications in the Match Group portfolio launched new features which encouraged safe dating practices such as the opportunity to video date (Meisenzahl, 2020), with Tinder specifically offering its 'Passport' feature for free (Tinder, 2020); a paid feature which allows users to choose a city to match in, as opposed to using current location (Thor Jensen, 2020). Furthermore, Plenty of Fish launched live streaming for its daters (Johannson, 2020), similar to Facebook Live in its functionality in that the user broadcasts a live video stream for others to watch as it happens in real time. Grindr, the most popular gay-dating app, even offered phone sex tips to its users (Brown, 2020).

Popular dating app, Bumble, was ahead of the curve, offering its users voice and video calling since 2019, seeing a spike in use of 93% between 13th March and 27th March 2020 (Brown, 2020). The restraints of the pandemic acted as a catalyst for further developments including 'Bumble Night In' in the US and Canada, allowing users to play games on virtual dates (Porter, 2021). The pandemic has further influenced the construction of user profiles given that, since the social distancing restrictions began to lift, Bumble and Hinge have allowed daters to make their "Covid-related dating preferences" (Link, 2021) public, such as how they would like to meet – "virtually, socially distanced, or distanced with a mask" (Seabrook, 2021). Prior to this, OkCupid (2020), in particular, saw a 900% increase in its users utilising 'coronavirus' and 'social distancing' wording in their profiles between February and March 2020, as well as self-proclaiming their preferences in terms of preparedness for dating in the context of Covid-19. Similarly, others included disclaimers in their profiles to provide a "pre-emptive rejection" (Link, 2021) to those not willing to abide by social distancing restrictions and safety standards. Such codification of 'preference' and 'status' is reminiscent of online profiles already documented on gay 'hook-up' sites where users have profile options in terms of preference for 'safe' sex (i.e. with condom, and/or regular STI testing), listing HIV status and pre-exposure prophylaxis (PrEP) use (Medina et al, 2018).

During the pandemic, in partnership with the UK government (Match Group, 2021), Tinder, Match, Hinge, Bumble, Badoo, Plenty of Fish, OurTime and Muzmatch all began allowing users to indicate whether they have received a Covid vaccination with a badge which can be displayed on their dating profiles (Kleinman, 2021), following its inception amongst U.S. dating applications in May 2021 (Elan, 2021). Dating sites and applications further permitted additional incentives and features for those with vaccination badges and stickers which would usually cost a fee, such as profile boosters and free "super" likes (Marris, 2021), allowing users to show potential matches that they are particularly interested. However, the admission that the user has had the vaccine is self-reported and is not independently verified or guaranteed by any of the apps offering this feature. The government partnership further involved in-app display advertisements and banners which promote the NHS' 'every vaccination gives us hope' campaign (Stubley, 2021), timed alongside the beginning of the eligibility for under 30's to have the vaccination.

The above indicates a possible attempt to interpellate (Althusser, 2014) dating application users as citizen-subjects through maintaining responsible behaviour. This becomes codified through embedding Covid-19 and related public health measures into a set of categories and preferences that become visible and meaningful through the user-interface. The use of vaccine status and 'covid preferences', as 'citational subjectivity' (Boyne, 1999) devices, illustrates the intersection between technology, culture and identity. Mobile dating applications, in this way, become sites where gendered selves, sexual relations, scripts and behaviours, become discursively constituted against wider socio-structural notions of normativity and 'deviance' (Foucault, 1978). Through the creation of a set of profile options that are coronavirus-related, the user-interfaces of these mobile dating applications bring into existence a set of social relations that can subsequently be observed, named, and performed.

Undoubtedly during the pandemic and associated lockdown restrictions, dating app behaviours began to change. Cox (2020) suggested that those possessing fear of coronavirus demonstrate less interest in prospective dates, even if individuals deemed their date to be highly attractive, given the potential additional health risks associated with in-person encounters. As a result, individuals have spent more time getting to know each date, or match, as opposed to persistent evaluation and serial-swiping. Tinder, for example, reported that the average conversation facilitated on the app now lasts 10 – 20 times longer than prior to the pandemic (Varsity, 2021). Subsequently, in contrast to pre-pandemic practices, individuals are much more cautious to date in person given the risks associated with coronavirus. It is therefore important to consider the intricacies of these digital dating practices, given their accessibility during the national lockdown, and how masculinity is enacted in these environments.

7   Post-Covid Masculinity

Both prior to the pandemic and to this day, there exists an unspoken expectation and resulting pressure for men to meet, often Western, standards of masculinity. This can be better understood through the notion of hegemonic masculinity (Connell, 1995; Connell and Messerschmidt, 2005); the dominance and maintenance of a particular ideology (Gramsci, 1971), such as patriarchy (Connell, 1995). Argued to legitimise unequal gender relations between men and women as well as among masculinities (Messerschmidt, 2018), hegemonic masculinity refers to a preferred, 'normative' state of masculinity in which men embody their manhood by positioning themselves in relation to the ideological legitimation of the subordination of women (Connell and Messerschmidt 2005, p. 832). Hegemonic masculinities are noted to take form through "endorsing sexist attitudes, traditional gender roles, and a tendency to objectify women" (Mescher and Rudman 2014, p. 1063), through "consensus building" (Blackmore, 1997; Mac an Ghaill, Haywood and Bright, 2013). Whilst the internet has permitted a space for the empowerment of women, particularly where dating apps such as Bumble endorse a female-first approach to dating (Bumble, n.d.), hegemonic masculinity continues to have an increased prominence online (Banet-Weiser and Miltner, 2016).

This unwavering hostility towards women, often sexualised in nature, in online environments has become referred to as "networked misogyny" (Banet-Weiser and Miltner 2016, p. 171). Indeed, as women build self-confidence and self-esteem, succeeding women's rights movements such as #MeToo, some men deem this to be an attack on their manhood and threat to their place in the social hierarchy (Banet-Weiser and Miltner, 2016). As such, women globally experience harassment in the form of abusive and insulting language, deliberate embarrassment, body-shaming and threats within the online sphere (Davey, 2020), and this has become a normalised affair in online dating practices (Gillett, 2018). Networked misogyny therefore needs to be considered in relation to the mobile dating app's heteronormative networked public spaces (Light, 2013).

Regardless of gender, online dating users have been reported to have lower levels of self-esteem, increased self-body shaming and comparison to others in terms of appearance (Strubel and Petrie, 2017). Individuals are therefore encouraged to continuously self-critique and consider their online presence in terms of marketability and potential for success. This becomes a form of risk for users given that success or failure in online dating can determine an individuals' physical and emotional wellbeing (Finkel et al., 2012). Whilst mobile applications are promoted as an accessible way to connect with potential love interests or casual sex partners without the fear of "rejection" (Tinder Inc, 2017), ultimately, success in these pursuits validates or discourages sense of self-worth (Warren, 2008). Those striving for validation and acceptance must therefore engage in risk practices synonymous with the dating landscape. The following section begins to unravel the navigation and negotiation of risk facing heterosexual men who use mobile dating apps. Three specific areas form the basis of discussion – the 'dick pic' (un/solicited images of male genitalia); fear of rejection; and aggression towards women who exhibited fear/reluctance to meet in real life. These examples highlight the complexities and nuances of challenges to masculinities in relation to dating-specific 'risk' across digital platforms and in-person contexts framed within the global pandemic.

8   Risks and Dick Pics

The online dating sphere offers a challenging landscape to navigate, particularly with an added expectation that an element of risk must be taken in these dating pursuits to be successful. There has been a rich body of literature examining the correlation between masculinity and engaging in risk practices (Mellström and Ericson, 2014; Robinson and Hockey, 2011; Robinson, 2019) particularly within the mediated experience, and there are a number of ways in which risk-taking can occur in mobile dating. Given that the mobile dating sphere offers the opportunity for the sharing of eroticism and sexual intimacy, literature focuses largely on more literal instances of risk culture, such as sexting and sending "dick pics" – (Peters, 2017; Ravn et al., 2019; Waling and Pym, 2019; Waling et al., 2020). We are only just beginning to understand these practices and, specifically, how a cultural economy of sharing sexually explicit images through mobile technology and social media now exists. This cultural economy was initiated through earlier developments in mobile phone technology that allowed for taking photographs and sharing via text message (sexting). However, the development of social media applications which include the functionality to upload private albums (where many users store 'xxx' pics and 'nudes'), share video content instantly, and live stream contribute to the 'pornographication' (McNair, 1996) of modern dating apps and their users. Dick pics are fraught with tensions – public/private, anxiety/desire, risk/reward. These tensions are structured in terms of context, and researchers have pointed towards the complexities of this phenomenon. Previous work has highlighted how dick pics are: a form of 'technology-facilitated sexual violence' (Powell and Henry, 2017); used to gain the attention of the recipient (Paasonen et al, 2019); provide a way for men to brag about their penis (Mandau, 2019); a form of compliment for the recipient, or to encourage the sharing of explicit images between users (Gulla, 2020). However, a host of factors frame the recipient's interpretation and response in equally complex variations that render the sharing of sexually explicit images risky for men – although, as some note, not in the same way that women experience risk and shame in the same context (Paasonen and Sundén, 2021). Sharing sexually explicit images through mobile dating applications exposes men to potential ridicule (Mandau, 2019), disgust and rejection (Amundsen, 2021) or even revenge porn (Hearn and Hall, 2019). At the same time, others note how engaging in risk-taking practices is a means of conforming to masculine norms, given that "gendered configuration has traditionally been conflated with acts of courage, mastering fear, and risk 'management'" (Mellström and Ericson 2014, p. 147). The increase of sharing sexually explicit images during the pandemic has been documented elsewhere (Döring, 2020; Thomas et al 2021). Consequently we can propose that lockdown provided a heightened context of pressure and risk for male dating app users as social isolation contained men within the domestic sphere, constructed a variety of Covid-specific risky behaviours (such as non mask-wearing and close contact with those outside of the household), as well as increasing the scope through which men could or would engage in technologically-mediated sexual activity.

9   Rejection and Resisting Restrictions

However, the subtler nuances with regards to perceived risk-taking in the wider online dating context are also beginning to be acknowledged. For instance, there is an expectation that men actively pursue sexual relationships to prove a masculine, sexual assertiveness, thus concealing motives "incompatible with an idealized version of himself" (Goffman 1959, p. 56). Although, in modern dating, Couch and Liamputtong (2007) highlight that those who engage in online dating practices consider the risks involved and can become skilled, autonomous risk-managers.

Hanby et al. (2012, p. 1868) further highlight how many online daters experience 'rejection sensitivity'; defined as "an individual's tendency to anxiously expect, readily perceive, and emotionally over-react to perceived threats of rejection by close socials". Being rejected can impact upon self-esteem and may undermine one's need to belong (Baumeister and Leary, 1995) and, as such, rejection acts as a "precursor of male hostility and aggressive responses against women" (Andrighetto et al. 2019, p. 572). Romantic rejection can range from an individual ending an existing relationship through to unrequited love (Baumeister, Wotman, and Stillwell, 1993), and subsequently jilted love interests, may display hostility and aggression (Twenge et al., 2001) as an attempt to "restore their threatened masculinity" (Andrighetto et al. 2019, p. 578; Vandello and Cohen, 2008).

Kelly et al. (2015) note that men demonstrating higher levels of social dominance are more likely to respond with aggression in the face of female rejection, which provides further intricacies to the understanding of masculinity in the online dating sphere. Given that rejection and resulting anti-social behaviour by men is widely acknowledged, perhaps greater support should be offered to online daters in order to steer men away from this type of emotional response in the first place. Similarly, Andrews (2020) documented examples in which men acted aggressively towards women, not when advances were rejected, but when women explained that they would feel uncomfortable breaking lockdown restrictions when potential dates were persistent to meet in-person. This became a recurring behaviour throughout the pandemic with men belittling the perspectives of women who adhered to social distancing and lockdown restrictions. Examples including the deprecation of Covid-19 in its comparison to the flu or statements that it's a hoax, as well as suggestions to prioritise pleasure over risk, were used as excuses to tempt dates to break restrictions. Other men were documented to deliver outright expletives in retaliation such as 'crazy bitch' (Andrews, 2020); an example of the hostility following romantic rejection. Haywood argues that mobile dating applications reinforce the notion of toxic masculinity in that mobile dating promotes "transactional relationships" (Haywood 2018, p. 169) in the sense of choosing a quick, sexual fling over the development of more deep, meaningful relationships, epitomising the standard of "manliness" in heterosexuality, control and the exploitation of women. This heteronormativity is further reinforced in men's resistance to change and greater likelihood of breaking social distancing rules (White 2020, p. 19). Even throughout the pandemic, women were recorded as more likely than men to have been pressured for sex (42% vs. 19%) (Barroso, 2020).

Despite this, the pandemic has heightened a sense of isolation which was already present for many men. Throughout the pandemic, the UK emotional support helpline, Samaritans, saw a significant increase in male callers talking about a lack of human connection (Lyons, 2021). Monella and Martínez (2021) note how this may be due to conventional understandings of masculine norms being challenged, whether this be in the form of challenges to identity through the imposition of restrictions as well as disruption to everyday practices and financial instability/insecurity. As a result, men are more likely to externalise any emotional difficulties, evidenced in the pandemic, such as in anger, alcohol or substance abuse and risk-taking in comparison to women (White 2020, p. 22). This may manifest through forms of exhibitionistic display, conflict or risky health and sexual behaviours (Levant and Wimer, 2014; Mahalik et al., 2022; Pawlowski, Atwal and Dunbar, 2008).

10   Conclusion

The explorative discussion above has highlighted the need for a continued focus upon gendered dimensions of interaction and digital technology. Mobile dating applications exist as a specific ecological landscape in which behaviours and practices operate within, and outside of, previous norms and social structures. Within the sphere of heterosexual dating and associated mobile apps, the pandemic can arguably be seen as expediting a shift towards increased use of digital platforms for intimate, romantic, and sexual gratification. The combined contextual elements of the Covid-19 pandemic and mobile dating applications allows us to examine the relationships between digital technology and the constitution of identities.

The pandemic restricted our scope for social contact and consequently disrupted the traditional, or regular, strategies for identity formation and management which we were familiar with. In some contexts this was more extreme. In terms of heteronormative masculinity, the pandemic provided the backdrop against which risk was constitutive of gendered selfhood. This operated across a range of activities from mask-wearing to observing hygiene regimens and social distancing rules. In the sphere of dating, risk itself is managed, felt, suffered, negotiated, and resolved in various ways. Mobile dating applications offered the chance to maintain intimate connections and, in some cases, even broadened the intimate horizons of users who began to explore new global and digital intimacies. Mobile dating applications facilitated this shift towards increased use of digital platforms through signposting users towards particular digital pandemic intimacy strategies such as video call dates, and even phone sex. Online and mobile dating platforms also became a key site through which the pandemic was discursively constituted into dating practice as 'Covid-preferences' became 'profile options', and 'vaccine status' an incentivised citational device for the signification of users as 'citizen-subjects' or 'healthy'/'safe' intimate others.

However, these contexts also situate the heightened risk and associated risk-management strategies that may be embedded in notions of hegemonic masculinity and sense of self. These relate to the increased scope of 'risk' within the pandemic context whereby men may display physical prowess or invulnerability, in face of coronavirus by reluctance to wear face-coverings. Within the dating sphere, the pandemic also resulted in a shift towards greater levels of digital interaction. Although data above suggests that this may encourage dating app users to spend more time getting to know their prospective dates virtually and build on emotional connections rather than meeting to engage in sexual practices, residual anxieties and common issues remain. In some cases, these anxieties and risks have been exacerbated such as the risk of ridicule, humiliation, disgust, and revenge porn that can happen after sharing dick pics. Alternatively, while mobile platforms may facilitate the maintenance of intimate connections under social distancing and even lockdown, research mentioned earlier suggests that mobile dating application users exhibit greater levels of vulnerability in relation to low self-esteem, body-shaming and social comparison. As a population with reportedly higher levels of such vulnerabilities, issues such as rejection-sensitivity may help us to understand the increased aggression, over-reactions and networked misogyny exhibited by men on dating apps throughout the pandemic. This also connects with the trend for men to pressurise women to meet in person for dates during the pandemic. The navigation of risk intersects here with the construction of a hegemonic masculine identity – as physically invulnerable, risk-taking and sexually assertive. While this pressure may be as a result of an attempt to avoid the 'perverse' label as a result of not being sexually active, the frustration of the blanket abstinence approach which was enforced during lockdown could have also contributed to this dynamic.

References

Acton, A. (2017) *The Innovative Dating Apps Challenging Tinder 'Swipe' Culture.* Available at: https://www.forbes.com/sites/annabelacton/2017/11/22/the-innovat ive-dating-apps-challenging-tinder-swipe-culture/?sh=2bd5dc237916 (Accessed: 16 January 2021).

Althusser, L. (2014) *On the Reproduction of Capitalism.* London: Verso.

Amundsen, R. (2021) 'A Male Dominance Kind of Vibe': Approaching Unsolicited Dick Pics as Sexism', *New Media & Society,* 23(6), pp. 1465–480.

Andrews, T. (2020) *9 Examples of Men Acting Aggressively Because Women Won't Break Quarantine to Go Out With Them IRL.* Available at https://www.cosmopolitan.com /sex-love/a32732628/men-acting-aggressive-because-women-reject-them-during -coronavirus/ (Accessed: 12 September 2021).

Andrighetto, L., Riva, P., and Gabbiadini, A. (2019) 'Lonely hearts and angry minds: Online dating rejection increases male (but not female) hostility', *Aggressive Behavior,* 45(5), pp. 571–581.

Banet-Weiser, S., and Miltner, K.M. (2016) '#MasculinitySoFragile: culture, structure, and networked misogyny', *Feminist Media Studies,* 16(1), pp. 171–174.

Barroso, A. (2020) *Key takeaways on Americans' views of and experiences with dating and relationships.* Available at: https://www.pewresearch.org/fact-tank/2020/08 /20/key-takeaways-on-americans-views-of-and-experiences-with-dating-and-relati onships/ (Accessed: 12 June 2022).

Baumeister, R.F., and Leary, M.R. (1995) 'The need to belong: Desire for interpersonal attachments as a fundamental human motivation', *Psychological Bulletin,* 117, pp. 497–529.

Baumeister, R.F., Wotman, S.R., and Stillwell, A.M. (1993) 'Unrequited love: On heartbreak, anger, guilt, scriptlessness, and humiliation', *Journal of Personality and Social Psychology,* 64(3), pp. 377–394.

Blackmore, J. (1997) 'Institutional Schizophrenia: Self-Governance, Performativity and the Self-Managing School', paper presented to the Annual Conference, Australian Association of Research in Education, Brisbane, pp. 1–4.

Boyne, R. (1999) 'Citation and Subjectivity: Towards a Return of the Embodied Will', *Body & Society,* 5(2–3), pp. 209–25.

Brown, A. (2020) *Coronavirus Is Changing Online Dating – Permanently.* Available at: https://www.forbes.com/sites/abrambrown/2020/04/05/coronavirus-is-changin gonline-dating-permanently/?sh=408c2c4b3b22 (Accessed: 17 September 2021).

Bumble (n.d.) *About: Make the First Move.* Available at: https://bumble.com/en/about (Accessed: 14 April 2021).

Burns, H. (2021) *Can a Long Distance Relationship Work in a Pandemic?* Available at: https://www.nytimes.com/2021/02/05/well/long-distance-dating-coronavirus. html (Accessed: 12 September 2021).

Butler, J. (1990) *Gender Trouble: Feminism and the Subversion of Identity.* New York: Routledge.

Callahan, M. (2021) *OnlyFans, COVID-19 pandemic have spurred a new sexual revolution.* Available at: https://nypost.com/2021/04/14/onlyfans-covid-19-pandemic-have -spurred-a-new-sexual-revolution/ (Accessed: 14 April 2021).

Callander, D., Meunier, É., DeVeau, R., Grov, C., Donovan, B., Minichiello,V., Kim, J., and Dustin, D. (2021) 'Investigating the Effects of COVID-19 on Global Male Sex Work Populations: A Longitudinal Study of Digital Data'. *Sexually Transmitted Infections,* 97(2), pp. 93–98.

Cineas, F. (2020) *Senators are demanding a solution to police stopping black men for wearing – and not wearing – masks.* Available at: https://www.vox.com/2020/4/22 /21230999/black-men-wearing-masks-police-bias-harris-booker-senate (Accessed: 14 September 2021).

Connell, R.W. (1995) *Masculinities.* Berkeley, California: University of California Press.

Connell, R.W., and Messerschmidt, J.W. (2005) 'Hegemonic Masculinity: Rethinking the Concept', *Gender and Society,* 19(6), pp. 829–859.

Cosma, S. and Gurevich, M. (2020) 'Securing sex: Embattled masculinity and the pressured pursuit of women's bodies in men's online sex advice'. *Feminism and Psychology,* 30(1), pp.42–62.

Couch, D., and Liamputtong, P. (2007) 'Online dating and mating: Perceptions of risk and health among online users', *Health, Risk & Society,* 9(3), pp. 275–294.

Cox, D. (2020) *Coronavirus: Why dating feels so different now.* Available at: https://www .bbc.com/worklife/article/20201116-how-the-pandemic-has-changed-our-roman tic-relationships (Accessed: 13 July 2021).

Davey, M. (2020) *Online violence against women 'flourishing', and most common on Facebook, survey finds.* Available at: https://www.theguardian.com/society/2020 /oct/05/online-violence-against-women-flourishing-and-most-common-on-faceb ook-survey-finds (Accessed: 26 October).

de Gallier, T. (2022) *People turned to online sex work in the pandemic – then had their images stolen.* Available at: https://www.bbc.co.uk/bbcthree/article/4dbbe2ca -bd9d-42b0-b3ea-22407c09e85c (Accessed: 22 March 2022).

Dietzel, C., Myles, D., and Duguay, S. (2021) *Relationships during a pandemic: How dating apps have adapted to COVID-19.* Available at: https://theconversation.com/relati onships-during-a-pandemic-how-dating-apps-have-adapted-to-covid-19-160219 (Accessed: 14 September 2021).

Döring, N. (2014) 'Consensual sexting among adolescents: Risk prevention through abstinence education or safer sexting?' *Cyberpsychology: Journal of Psychosocial research on Cyberspace,* 8(1).

Döring, N. (2020) 'How Is the COVID-19 Pandemic Affecting Our Sexualities? An Overview of the Current Media Narratives and Research Hypotheses' *Archives of Sexual Behavior* 49(8): pp. 2765–778.

Duarte, F. (2020) *Coronavirus face masks: Why men are less likely to wear masks.* Available at: https://www.bbc.co.uk/news/world-53446827 (Accessed: 14 September 2021).

Elan, P. (2020) *The data is in: men are too fragile to wear Covid-19 masks. Grow up, guys.* Available at: https://www.theguardian.com/commentisfree/2020/jul/03/covid-19 -masks-men-masculinity (Accessed: 13 September 2020).

Elan, P. (2021) *Hot vax summer? Dating apps encourage vaccination.* Available at: https:// www.theguardian.com/fashion/2021/may/22/hot-vax-summer-dating-apps-encour age-vaccination (Accessed: 14 September 2021).

Faludi, S. (1999) *Stiffed: The Betrayal of the Modern Man.* London: Vintage.

Fetters, A. (2020) *The New Relationship That Fizzled Out in Quarantine.* Available at: https://www.theatlantic.com/family/archive/2020/05/new-relationships-coro navirus-pandemic/612352/ (Accessed: 12 September 2021).

Finkel, E., Eastwick, P., Karney, B., Reis, H., and Sprecher, S. (2012) 'Online Dating: A Critical Analysis from the Perspective of Psychological Science', *Psychological Science in the Public Interest*, 13(1), pp. 3–66.

Fornäs, J., and Xinaris, C. (2013) 'Mediated Identity Formation: Current Trends in Research and Society', *Journal of the European institute for Communication and Culture*, 20(2), pp. 11–25.

Fortune (2021) *Activity on dating apps has surged during the pandemic.* Available at: https://fortune.com/2021/02/12/covid-pandemic-online-dating-apps-usage-tin der-okcupid-bumble-meet-group/ (Accessed: 14 September 2021).

Foucault, M. (1978) *The History of Sexuality: Volume 1: An Introduction.* New York: Pantheon Books.

Gagnon, J.H., and Simon, W. (1987) 'The sexual scripting of oral genital contacts', *Archives of Sexual Behavior*, 16, pp. 1–25.

Garcia, J.R., Reiber, C., Massey, S.G., and Merriwether, A.M. (2013) *Sexual hook-up cul-ture.* Available at: https://www.apa.org/monitor/2013/02/ce-corner.

Giddens, A. (1991) *Modernity and Self-Identity: Self and Society in the Late Modern Age.* Cambridge, England: Polity Press.

Gillett, R. (2018) 'Intimate intrusions online: Studying the normalisation of abuse in dating apps', *Women's Studies International Forum*, 69, pp. 212–219.

Glick, P. (2020) *Masks and Emasculation: Why Some Men Refuse to Take Safety Precautions.* Available at: https://blogs.scientificamerican.com/observations/masks -and-emasculation-why-some-men-refuse-to-take-safety-precautions/ (Accessed: 27 July 2021).

Goffman, E. (1959) *The Presentation of Self in Everyday Life.* Doubleday.

Grace, J. (2020) *Boris fails to convince with sanitised take on coronavirus.* Available at: https://www.theguardian.com/politics/2020/mar/03/boris-fails-to-convince-with -sanitised-take-on-coronavirus (Accessed: 27 July 2021).

Gramsci, A. (1971) *Selections from the Prison Notebooks.* New York, International Publishers.

Gulla, E. (2020) *An ultimate guide to dick pics: taking them, asking for them, and what recipients really think.* Available at: https://www.cosmopolitan.com/uk/love-sex /sex/a34087539/dick-pics-ultimate-guide/ (Accessed: 7 August 2022).

Haischer, M.H., Beilfuss, R., Hart, M.R., Opielinski, L., Wrucke, D., Zirgaitis, G., Uhrich, T.D., and Huntre, S.K. (2020) 'Who is wearing a mask? Gender-, age-, and location-related differences during the COVID-19 pandemic', *PloS ONE*, 15(10), pp. 1–12. DOI: 10.1371/journal.pone.0240785.

Hall, S. (1997) *Representation: Cultural Representations and Signifying Practices.* London: SAGE Publications Ltd.

Hanby, M.S.R., Fales, J., Nangle, D.W., Serwick, A.K., and Hedrich, U.J. (2012) 'Social Anxiety as a Predictor of Dating Aggression', *Journal of Interpersonal Violence*, 27(10), pp. 1867–1888.

Haywood, C. (2018) *Men, Masculinity and Contemporary Dating.* London: Palgrave Macmillan.

Hearn, J, and Hall, M. (2019) "This Is My Cheating Ex': Gender and Sexuality in Revenge Porn', *Sexualities,* 22(5–6), pp. 860–82.

Hearne, B.N., and Niño, M.D. (2021) 'Understanding How Race, Ethnicity, and Gender Shape Mask-Wearing Adherence During the COVID-19 Pandemic: Evidence from the COVID Impact Survey', *Journal of Racial and Ethnic Health Disparities*, 9(1), p. 176–183.

Heldman, C., and Wade, L. (2010) 'Hook-Up Culture: Setting a New Research Agenda', *Sexual Research and Social Policy*, 7(4), pp. 323–333.

Hess, A., and Flores, C. (2018) 'Simply more than swiping left: A critical analysis of toxic masculine performances on Tinder Nightmares', *New Media & Society*, 20(3), pp. 1085–1102.

Hubbard, P. (2000) 'Desire/disgust: mapping the moral contours of heterosexuality', *Progress in Human Geography*, 24(2), pp. 191–217.

Illouz, E. (2012) *Why Love Hurts.* Cambridge: Polity Press.

Johannson, C. (2020) *What is the Live! Feature on Plenty of Fish?* Available at: https://blog .pof.com/2020/03/what-is-the-live-feature-on-plenty-of-fish/ (Accessed: 14 September ber 2021).

Kanzama, T., and Kawaguchi, M. (2002) 'HIV risk and the (im)permeability of the male body: representations and realities of gay men in Japan', in J.E. Robertson, and N. Suzuki (eds.) *Men and Masculinities in Contemporary Japan.* London: Routledge, pp. 198–215.

Kelly, A.J., Dubbs, S.L., and Barlow, F.K. (2015) 'Social dominance orientation predicts heterosexual men's adverse reactions to romantic rejection', *Archives of Sexual Behavior*, 44, pp. 903–919.

Kimmel, M. (2007) 'Masculinity as Homophobia: Fear, Shame, and Silence in the Construction of Gender Identity', in N. Cook (ed.) *Gender Relations in Global Perspective: Essential Readings.* Ontario: Canadian Scholars Press, pp. 73–83.

Kleinman, Z. (2021) *Covid vaccine stickers come to dating apps in UK.* Available at: https://www.bbc.co.uk/news/technology-57379034 (Accessed: 14 September 2021).

LalalaLetMeExplain (2022) *Block, Delete, Move On.* London: Transworld Publishers Ltd.

Leung, H. (2020) *Why Wearing a Face Mask Is Encouraged in Asia, but Shunned in the U.S.* Available at: https://time.com/5799964/coronavirus-face-mask-asia-us/ (Accessed: 14 September 2021).

Levant, R.F., and Wimer, D.J. (2014) 'The relationship between conformity to masculine norms and men's health behaviors: Testing a multiple mediator model', *International Journal of Men's Health*, 13, pp. 22–41.

Li W., Li G., Xin C., Wang Y., and Yang S. (2020) 'Changes in sexual behaviors of young women and men during the coronavirus disease 2019 outbreak: A convenience sample from the epidemic area', *Journal of Sexual Medicine*, 17(7), pp. 1225–1228.

Light, B. (2013) 'Networked Masculinities and Social Networking Sites: A Call for the Analysis of Men and Contemporary Digital Masculinities and Social Change', *Masculinidades Y Cambio Social,* 2(3), pp. 245–265.

Link, J. (2021) *Dating During COVID: How Dating Apps Evolved in the Age of Social Distancing.* Available at: https://builtin.com/design-ux/dating-apps-social-distancing (Accessed: 14 September 2021).

Lyons, E. (2021) *The Covid pandemic is highlighting men's mental health and how they can seek help.* Available at: https://edition.cnn.com/2021/05/10/world/pandemic-mens-mental-health-wellness/index.html (Accessed: 13 September 2021).

Mac an Ghaill, M., Haywood, C., and Bright, Z. (2013) 'Making Connections: Speed Dating, Masculinity and Interviewing', in B. Pini, and B. Pease (eds.) *Men, Masculinities and Methodologies. Genders and Sexualities in the Social Sciences.* London: Palgrave Macmillan, pp. 77–89.

Mahalik, J.R., Bianca, M.D., and Harris, M.P. (2022) 'Men's attitudes toward mask-wearing during COVID-19: Understanding the complexities of mask-ulinity', *Journal of Health Psychology*, 27(5), pp. 1187–1204.

Mandau, M.B.H. (2019) 'Directly in Your Face': A qualitative study on the sending and receiving of unsolicited 'dick pics' among young adults', *Sexuality & Culture*, 24(1), pp. 72–93.

Marris, S. (2021) *COVID-19: Dating apps are going to offer perks for users who get a vaccine.* Available at: https://news.sky.com/story/covid-19-dating-apps-are-going-to-offer-perks-for-users-who-get-a-vaccine-12326685 (Accessed: 14 September 2021).

Marshall, E. (2020) *Brazil's Bolsanaro says athletic past would protect him from coronavirus symptoms.* Available at: https://www.telegraph.co.uk/news/2020/03/25/brazils-bolsonaro-says-athletic-past-would-protect-coronavirus/ (Accessed: 27 July 2021).

Massa, J. (2010) *How Are We Finding Love in a Post-Dating World?* Available at https://
www.huffpost.com/entry/how-are-we-finding-love-i_b_614720 (Accessed: 5 September 2021).

Massa, J. (2013) *The Gaggle: How to Find Love in the Post-Dating World.* New York: Simon and Schuster.

Match Group (2021) *Match Group Partners With the UK Government To Promote COVID-19 Vaccinations.* Available at: https://mtch.com/single-news/591 (Accessed: 14 September 2021).

McNair, B. (1996) *Mediated Sex: Pornography and Postmodern Culture.* London: Routledge.

Medina, M.M, Crowley, C., Montgomery, M.C., Tributino, A., Almonte, A., Sowemimo-Coker, G., Nunn, A., and Chan, P.A. (2018) 'Disclosure of HIV Serostatus and Pre-exposure Prophylaxis Use on Internet Hookup Sites Among Men Who Have Sex with Men', *AIDS and Behavior,* 23(7), pp. 1681–688.

Meisenzahl, M. (2020) *These charts from Match Group show more people are turning to online dating during the pandemic.* Available at: https://www.businessinsider.com/tinder-hinge-match-group-dating-apps-more-users-coronavirus-2020-8?r=US&IR=T (Accessed: 14 September 2021).

Mellström, U., and Ericson, M. (2014) 'Masculinity at risk', *NORMA: International Journal of Masculinity Studies,* 9(3), pp. 147–150.

Mescher, K., and Rudman, L. (2014) 'Men in the Mirror: The Role of Men's Body Shame in Sexual Aggression', *Personality and Social Psychology Bulletin,* 40(8), pp. 1063–1075.

Messerschmidt, J.W. (2018) 'Multiple Masculinities', in B.J. Risman, C.M. Froyum, and W.J. Scarborough (eds.) *Handbook of the Sociology of Gender.* (2nd ed). Switzerland: Springer, pp. 143–153.

Miller, E. (2019) *Stripping Down the Hookup Culture: The Need for Emotional Visibility.* Available at: https://www.ted.com/talks/erin_miller_stripping_down_the_hookup_culture_the_need_for_emotional_visibility (Accessed: 14 May 2022).

Monella, L.M., and Martínez, M.R. (2021) *Pandemic creates 'historic moment' to end macho culture.* Available at: https://www.euronews.com/2020/09/24/pandemic-creates-historic-moment-to-end-macho-culture (Accessed: 14 September 2021).

Nagy, P., and Neff, G. (2015) 'Imagined Affordance: Reconstructing a Keyword for Communication Theory', *Social Media + Society,* 1(2), pp. 1–9.

Nava, M. (2007) *Visceral Cosmopolitanism: Gender, Culture and the Normalisation of Difference.* New York: Berg Publishers.

North, A. (2020) *What Trump's refusal to wear a mask says about masculinity in America.* Available at: https://www.vox.com/2020/5/12/21252476/masks-for-coronavirus-trump-pence-honeywell-covid-19 (Accessed: 14 September 2021).

O'Malley, R.L., Holt, K., and Holt, T.J. (2022) 'An Exploration of the Involuntary Celibate (Incel) Subculture Online', *Journal of Interpersonal Violence,* 37(7–8), pp. NP4981–NP5008.

OkCupid (2020) *Love in the Time of Corona: Massive Spikes in Matching, Messaging and Virtual Dates Around the World.* Available at: https://theblog.okcupid.com/love-in-the-time-of-corona-massive-spikes-in-matching-messaging-and-virtual-dates-around-the-ec12c49eab86 (Accessed: 14 September 2021).

Paasonen, S., Light, B., and Jarrett, K. (2019) 'The Dick Pic: Harassment, Curation, and Desire', *Social Media + Society,* 5(2), pp. 1–10.

Paasonen, S., and Sundén, J. (2021) 'Shameless Dicks: On Male Privilege, Dick Pic Scandals, and Public Exposure', *First Monday,* 26(4). https://doi.org/10.5210/fm.v26i4.11654.

Palmer, C.L., and Peterson, R.D. (2020) 'Toxic Mask-ulinity: The Link between Masculine Toughness and Affective Reactions to Mask Wearing in the COVID-19 Era', *Politics & Gender,* 16, pp. 1044–1051.

Pawlowski, B., Atwal, R., and Dunbar, R.I.M. (2008) 'Sex Differences in Everyday Risk-Taking Behavior in Humans', *Evolutionary Psychology,* 6(1), pp. 29–42.

Peck, P. (2020) *Sex in Isolation? Maybe Not. Sexting? Definitely.* Available at: https://www.vogue.com/article/sexting-in-isolation (Accessed: 17 May 2022).

Peters, J. (2017) *"Welcome to the generation of fuckbois": Postfeminist masculinities and gender discourses in the social media era.* MA Thesis. Tilburg University. Available at: http://arno.uvt.nl/show.cgi?fid=144913 (Accessed: 14 September 2021).

Petter, O. (2020) *'Real men don't wear masks': The link between masculinity and face coverings.* Available at: https://www.independent.co.uk/life-style/face-masks-men-masculinity-coronavirus-lockdown-boris-johnson-b1077119.html (Accessed: 17 July 2021).

Porter, J. (2021) *Bumble's new Night In feature is an attempt to break the ice on virtual dates.* Available at: https://www.theverge.com/2021/3/11/22325404/bumble-virtual-date-trivia-quiz-social-distancing (Accessed: 14 September 2021).

Powell, A., and Henry, N. (2017) *Sexual violence in a digital age.* London: Palgrave Macmillan.

Ravn, S., Coffey, J., and Roberts, S. (2019) 'The currency of images: Risk, value and gendered power dynamics in young men's accounts of sexting', *Feminist Media Studies,* 21(2), pp. 315–331.

Robinson, V. (2019) 'Masculinity and/at risk: The social and political context of men's risk taking as embodied practices, performances and processes', in L. Gottzén, U. Mellström, T. Shefer, and M. Grimbeek (eds.) *Routledge International Handbook of Masculinity Studies.* London: Routledge, pp. 488–497.

Robinson, V., and Hockey, J. (2011) *Masculinities in transition.* Basingstoke: Palgrave Macmillan.

Ruxton, S., and Burrell, S. (2020) *Masculinities and COVID-19: Making the Connections.* Washington, DC: Promundo-US. Available at: https://promundoglobal.org/wp-cont ent/uploads/2020/09/BLS20254_PRO_Masculinities_COVID19_WEB_005.1.pdf (Accessed: 13 July 2021).

Seabrook, V. (2021) *Love in lockdown: How the COVID-19 pandemic has changed the world of dating.* Available at: https://news.sky.com/story/love-in-lockdown-how -the-covid-19-pandemic-has-changed-the-world-of-dating-12215385 (Accessed: 4 July 2021).

Smith, D. Gambino, L., and Sullivan, H. (2020) *Contagious Trump removes mask for photos upon return from hospital.* Available at: https://www.theguardian.com /us-news/2020/oct/05/donald-trump-walter-reed-hospital-covid-19 (Accessed: 14 September 2021).

Spire, J. (2022) '*7 OnlyFans Statistics 2022: Users, Top Earners & Market Growth*' Available at: https://jonathonspire.com/onlyfans-statistics/ (Accessed: 30 June 2022).

Strubel, J., and Petrie, T. (2017) 'Love me Tinder: Body image and psychosocial function- ing among men and women', *Body Image*, 21, pp. 34–38.

Stubley, P. (2021) *Covid: Dating apps offer benefits to vaccinated users in new government jab campaign.* Available at: https://www.independent.co.uk/news/health/covid -vaccine-dating-app-campaign-b1860718.html (Accessed: 14 September 2021).

Thomas, A. (2020) *I'm a black man in America. Entering a shop with a face mask might get me killed.* Available at: https://www.theguardian.com/commentisfree/2020/apr /07/black-men-coronavirus-masks-safety (Accessed: 14 September 2021).

Thomas, M.F., Binder, A., and Matthes, J. (2021) 'Sexting during Social Isolation: Predicting Sexting-related Privacy Management during the COVID-19 Pandemic', *Cyberpsychology*, 15(3) Article 3.

Thor Jensen, K. (2020) *How COVID-19 Is Changing Dating Apps and Relationships.* Available at: https://uk.pcmag.com/dating/125562/how-covid-19-is-changing-dat ing-apps-and-relationshipshttps://uk.pcmag.com/dating/125562/how-covid-19-is -changing-dating-apps-and-relationships (Accessed: 14 September 2021).

Tiffany, K., and Fetters, A. (2020) *The 'Dating Market' Is Getting Worse.* Available at: https://www.theatlantic.com/family/archive/2020/02/modern-dating-odds -economy-apps-tinder-math/606982/ (Accessed: 29 December 2020).

Tinder (2020) *Passport Feature Now Available For Free to All Tinder Members.* Available at:https://uk.tinderpressroom.com/2020-03-31-Passport-Feature-Available-For-Free -All-Members (Accessed: 14 September 2021).

Tinder Inc. (2017) *Tinder on the App Store.* [online] App Store. Available at: https://itu nes.apple.com/us/app/tinder/id547702041 (Accessed: 8 December 2017).

Twenge, J.M., Baumeister, R.F., Tice, D.M., and Stucke, T.S. (2001) 'If you can't join them, beat them: Effects of social exclusion on aggressive behavior', *Journal of Personality and Social Psychology*, 81, pp. 1058–1069.

Vandello, J.A., and Cohen, D. (2008) 'Culture, gender, and men's intimate partner violence', *Social and Personality Psychology Compass*, 2(2), pp. 652–667.

Varsity (2021) *The Rise of Online Dating Apps Amid Pandemic*. Available at: https://www.varsity.co.uk/sponsored/the-rise-of-online-dating-apps-amid-pandemic (Accessed: 17 July 2021).

Victor, D. (2021) *Coronavirus Safety Runs Into a Stubborn Barrier: Masculinity*. Available at: https://www.nytimes.com/2020/10/10/us/politics/trump-biden-masks-masculinity.html (Accessed: 14 September 2021).

Waling, A., and Pym, T. (2019) "C'mon, no one wants a dick pic': Exploring the cultural framings of the 'dick pic' in contemporary online publics', *Journal of Gender Studies*, 28(1), pp. 70–85.

Waling, A., Kerr, L., Bourne, A., Power, J., and Kehler, M. (2020) "It's nice to be appreciated': Understanding heterosexual men's engagements with sexting and sharing Dick Pics', *Sexualities*, 25(3), pp. 198–221.

Warren, C. (2008) The influence of awareness and internalization of Western appearance ideals on body dissatisfaction in Euro-American and Hispanic males. *Psychology of Men & Masculinity*, 9(4), pp. 257–266. DOI:10.1037/a0012472.

White, A. (2020) 'Men and COVID-19: the aftermath', *Postgraduate Medicine*, 132(4), pp. 18–27.

Willingham, E. (2020) *The Condoms of the Face: Why Some Men Refuse to Wear Masks*. Available at: https://www.scientificamerican.com/article/the-condoms-of-the-face-why-some-men-refuse-to-wear-masks/ (Accessed: 17 July 2021).

Zattoni, F., Gül, M., Soligo, M., Morlacco, A., Motterle, A., Collavino, J., Barneschi, A.C., Moschini, M., and Dal Moro, F. (2020) 'The impact of COVID-19 pandemic on pornography habits: a global analysis of Google Trends', *International Journal of Impotence Research*, 33, pp. 824–831.

CHAPTER 11

Post-lockdown Sex: Uncertain Intimacies, Cultures of Desire, and UK Sex Clubs

Chris Haywood

The social area is crammed full of people sitting around drinking. The atmosphere is like an upmarket pub, with sporadic peals of laughter climbing above the noise of the drinking and chatting. Most women wear sophisticated dresses, often small black numbers, with chic shoes. Men, almost like high street mannequins, wear flowered shirts, smart-looking jeans and dark shoes. There are exceptions. Two women have their t-shirts off tucked into their jeans pockets and walk around in their bras. A man with a gimp mask, leather braces, tight-fitting shorts with a tail attached walks around talking to groups of people. As there is nowhere to sit, I casually hover by tables, overhearing their conversations. One person had recently bought a new car, another talked about their holidays, another, the school they were trying to get their kids entry into. In front of them, just to their side, is a huge television streaming live footage from a private room; a room that is located beyond the social area of the club. A black woman is sitting on an older white man fucking him hard and fast.

> "Before lockdown, we went to Majorca".
> "Magaluf?" another man mockingly shouted.
> "No, not the commercial side; we hired a villa".
> The couple on the screen had switched positions and he was now going down on her giving her oral sex.
> "Did it cost much?"
> "Not bad, no more than what a place in the UK costs at the moment. You have to rent a car though, that makes it a little more costly".

The volume on the screen is either turned down or drowned out by the constant noise of people drinking and chatting in the bar. I overhear the barman pleading to a member of staff, "Get them out of here. Get them to go to the rooms!" The barman flits around, trying to casually say that the playrooms are open (they were never shut), but no one moves. The laughter, the talking and the fucking on the screen continue.

1   Introduction

The global pandemic of Covid-19 did a number of things to sex. Sex outside of governmentally regulated bubbles became illegal, we visited strangers' bedrooms without sleeping with them, online forums for anonymous sex thrived, then bombed, as the novelty of the virtual sex nights soon wore off. Sexual abstinence was recommended with masturbation, OnlyFans increased its users from 7.5 million to eighty-five million, creative sex between partners was on the rise and sales of sex toys (especially the silent ones) rose by 160% (Harman 2021). At the same time, news reports and press conferences teased an eagerly awaiting public with the sexological language of waves, plateaus, peaks and troughs. Even the term 'firebreak', a sexual health intervention designed to disrupt the spread of HIV (Parkhurst and Whiteside 2010), was recommissioned to refer to a broader practice of social abstinence. In short, the pandemic produced a range of cultural disruptions and fractures to sex, pleasure and leisure that we are still trying to understand and come to terms with (Ashford and Longstaff 2021). This is partly because the pandemic initiated an 'epistemological jolt', or what could be understood as a 'counterintuitive' texturing of reality (Killeen 2017, p. 4). Whilst much work continues to be done on what happened to sex during Covid (Pennanen et al. 2021; Lehmiller et al. 2021), the permanent impact of the pandemic on post-lockdown sexual intimacy is now being contoured and discussed. It is argued that the lifting of lockdown and the signalling of the 'post-pandemic' for some people resulted in the emergence of an 'uncertain intimacy', '... a kind of intimacy that is a derivative of fear of involvement' (Paprzycka 2018, p. 56). It is in the aftermath of this epistemological jolt and the residual effects of an uncertain intimacy impacting upon the repairing and reconnecting of sexual relationships, practices and places that this chapter explores.

As the pandemic begins to be sedimented in cultural memories, competing media responses are emerging that attempt to make sense of this moment of uncertain intimacy. On the one hand, media narratives talk of a post-Covid world characterized by a momentous orgiastic fuckfest (Jones, K. 2021). On the other hand, it is argued that forging new sexual intimacies is becoming problematic as the interruption of the pandemic is disrupting the ways in which sexual connections are being made (Jones, A. 2021). These narratives are not new. Rather it appears that the post-lockdown context has exacerbated and thrown into sharper focus pre-pandemic cultural anxieties about sex. Politicians, activists and moral entrepreneurs continue to target sexual deviancy that includes, but is not exclusive to, online sex-seeking; friends with benefits and 'sex with an ex'; hypersexual Black men and lack of family commitment; over(t)ly-sexual gay men, Grindr culture and Chemsex parties; transgender MtF and their use of female-only spaces. The recurrent theme embedded in this moral hysteria is that such deviance is often coded as being disconnected from normative, honest, caring, mutually supportive and emotionally rewarding monogamous (preferably heterosexual) sex. Furthermore, as Furedi (2020) points out, prior to the pandemic, there was a social and cultural trend to reduce physical contact and touching (unless between established partners). The pandemic has simply accelerated an existing trend where social distance is becoming increasingly regulated. Thus, as Nofre (2021a) has suggested, nightlife since the pandemic has become a synonym for 'vice, sin, immorality, and a "perilous agent" for the socio-economic recovery in a post-pandemic world' (Nofre 2021b). In a similar way, those engaging in 'sex for sex's sake' (Schwartz and Rutter 1998, p. 45) are becoming a focus for the projection of pandemic related social, economic and cultural vicissitudes.

By drawing upon ethnographic research in sex clubs collected in England before, during and after the pandemic, this chapter explores how disrupted knowledges become folded into the negotiation and practice of sexual encounters. Disrupted knowledges draws upon Rogoff's (2013, p. 1) exploration of the 'dislocation of subjects, the disruption of collective narratives and languages of signification' and epistemologies of difference. The result is that in this chapter, disrupted knowledge is not simply about the limits of cultural rationalities, rather, disrupted knowledges should be understood as an affectivity; a combination of anxiety, excitement, uncertainty and pleasure. Furthermore, prior to the pandemic, sexual encounters were "...focussed on self-pleasure and fun; characterized by 'adventurism', 'experimentation', 'choice', 'variety' and 'sensation' (Illouz, 1999 p.176)". (Attwood and Smith 2013, p. 334–335). Existing work suggests that post-lockdown, people may, in some extremes, experience what has been called Covid-19 Stress Syndrome, which involves a fear of touching, infection and fear of unknown others (Bacon et al. 2022; Taylor et al. 2020). Others have suggested that there is less hesitancy and increasing demand for hedonistic sex (Jia et al. 2022).

This chapter explores how a broader fear, anxiety and frustration prompted by the pandemic may be articulating itself in the context of sex clubs. It does this by first briefly highlighting how the pandemic impacted sex clubs and their initial responses as commercial enterprises. It then explores ethnographically how the pandemic appeared to exacerbate particular cultures of desire (Cornwall 1997) that were manifested in increased forms of social intimacy, scopophilic touching and visceral physical connections. The chapter concludes by arguing that disruptions can often operate productively in that through a process of emersion, new forms of sexual knowing and being can emerge.

2   Disrupting Methodologies: Sex Clubs and the Emergence of
     Uncertain Intimacy

This draws upon research entitled '*High risk sex in hard-to-reach places*', a
project that had been developed in response to the emergence of older heterosexuals, being one of the fastest-growing groups transmitting sexual infections. More recently, heterosexuals are the main source of the transmission of
HIV, overtaking men who have sex with men. By focusing on spaces that were
high risk in the heterosexual community, it explored how clubs marketed to
heterosexuals as a place for anonymous sex, might be useful to understand
how meaningful and effective sexual health interventions could be developed. Overall, the project undertook ethnographies in eighteen sex clubs, a
number that represents nearly half of all sex clubs in England. These sex clubs
are not strip clubs, pole dancing clubs or bordellos; these are clubs that have
been traditionally associated with 'swingers' or those engaging in Consensual
Non-Monogamy (CNM). However, such thinking tends to heteronormalize
such clubs by underplaying the diversity of sexual practices that take place on
the premises. Having already conducted research in twelve clubs, a further six
clubs formed part of the methodology post-lockdown. In this project, covert
research was adopted as a means to 'getting in and staying in' (Arber 2001).
Sex clubs market themselves on their discreteness and anonymity offered to
patrons within the club. The covert nature of the ethnographies was not only
necessary to secure access to the club, but it also interestingly supported the
anonymous and non-intrusive ethos cultivated by clubs and their participants
(see Haywood 2023 for a fuller discussion of the ethical challenges). As such,
and as part of formal ethical approval for the project, the names, identities and
geographical locations have been adjusted in this chapter to protect the clubs
and participants.

    The fieldwork used in this chapter takes excerpts from the ethnographies
and in themselves can be troubling and disruptive as, at times the style of
writing can resemble the 'ethnopornographic'. The 'ethnopornographic' refers
to '... a cluster of concerns about the meanings of pornographic representation, the plurality of sexualities, the legacies of colonial representation' (Sigal
et al. 2019, p. 9). Being mindful of the potential readings fieldwork can incite,
it deliberately moves beyond empiricist ethnographic forms and recognizes
the importance of creativity in capturing the atmosphere, the feelings, the
being-there-at-that-moment sense of the research practice. Berry (2017, p. 18.)
talks about the use of 'multi-sensory and thick description to create emotional
resonance and empathy', an approach that is adopted in this chapter. Thus,
the chapter interweaves the ethnographic fieldnotes with social and cultural

theory, in a way that disrupts social scientific approaches to knowledge generation and analysis. In this sense, the ethnographic and the analysis, touch each
other by puncturing the limits of the empirical and the conceptual and enabling them to mutually inform one another. The result is that it is also methodologically by adopting principles of evocative autoethnography without being
wholly autoethnographic (Gergen and Gergen, 2018). Disruptions occur also
because the encounters within sex clubs draw upon the 'intense here and now'
(Jonasson, 2018, p. 12) and as such are inflected by realist ethnography. So not
only is there an appeal to ethnographies as poetic, it also wants, as Ellis and
Boschner (2006, p. 433) suggest, to 'put culture and society in motion' and at
the same time 'freeze frame' and 'tame' ethnographic encounters.

Sex clubs are unusual and ordinary places. Marketed towards the fulfilment
of men and women's heteroerotic fantasies, such clubs enable men and women
to have (often anonymous) sexual encounters outside of the private space of
the home and the normative bonds of a relationship. As Hubbard (2001, p. 51)
puts it, "public spaces are constructed around particular notions of appropriate sexual comportment which exclude those whose lives do not centre on
monogamous, heterosexual, procreative sex". However, sex clubs also exclude
themselves. Clubs acknowledge the stigma that surrounds an erotics of desire
and pleasure that stands outside of heteronormativity and, as a result, promote
themselves as safe, discreet and anonymous places. One of the ways they do
this is by using forms of architectural camouflage (Zhou et al. 2019). By day sex
clubs are hidden by masquerading as hotels or pubs that have previously been
closed down, factory lock-ups on industrial estates or faceless buildings at the
back of shopping precincts. At night sex clubs come alive, often with constant
streams of people emerging from the cloak of darkness into the glare of the
motion-triggered security lights. The promise of anonymous sex, group sex,
partner swapping, bukkake, same-sex practices, cuckolding, threesomes, 'bareback sex', gang bangs, BDSM, and interracial and intergenerational sex, draws
people from all over the UK, often being attracted to, what has been termed in
male-on-male contexts, 'erotic oases' (Tewkesbury, 2002). Such practices are
promoted as part of a themed evening or daytime event. There is a constant
reminder that sex clubs are a commercial venture '... that produce and usually look to profit from the provision of memorable or stimulating experiences,
such as theme parks, strip clubs and role-play adventures' (Alston 2013, p. 5).
In short, sex clubs offer the opportunity to display their desire through the
pursuit and the staging of their fantasies (Žižek, 1991).

As the pandemic took hold, the ability of like-minded people to meet up for
anonymous sex, was disrupted as sex clubs were legally required to close. In
response, sex clubs and their patrons began to adapt, an experience that was

collectively shared with people uniting to overcome the situation (Marzana et al. 2021; Amoah and Amoah 2021). Whilst most clubs did close their doors, a number of others focused on providing *social* spaces for like-minded people to meet. Other clubs kept their doors open but only allowed play to take place between those who had arrived together, resulting in people maintaining their own sex bubbles. In some cases, clubs surreptitiously kept their doors open and tried to navigate the lockdown restrictions by opening when they said they were closed. Some clubs attempted to migrate online and staged online events. However, attendees at such events were quite low. Certain forms of sexual intimacy had always been restricted in some clubs, such as no sex in the jacuzzi, no sex in the social area and no high heels on the beds. Some clubs also displayed 'no anal sex' serving to highlight tensions between queer discourses of sex and a commodified forms of heteroeroticism. However, at times, it did appear that such signage encouraged the very sex it was designed to outlaw. However, some clubs began to introduce additional signage of 'No sex' throughout the club alongside strict entry and exit guidance. As found in nightclubs in London, sex clubs became 'barely recognizable from their core identity' (Assiter 2022). However, as restrictions began to be lifted, clubs slowly began to operate along similar lines to pre-Covid conditions but often maintained measures such as temperature checks, PCR tests and sometimes showing vaccination passports. At the same time, two prominent clubs in the South of England, who had initially moved to cashless online entrance fees to manage numbers, have maintained the system. Such changes have implications 'relating to a "culture of surveillance", which might be contentious to a significant proportion of potential visitors, concerned about their privacy or simply unwilling to endure extra bureaucratic burdens' (Mazierska and Rigg 2021 p. 82; also see Ashford and Longstaff 2021 on the evasion of such sexual surveillance).

Whilst work on the impact of the pandemic on post-lockdown leisure activities has focussed on how businesses are reviewing and developing their business strategies, it is important to understand how experiences of those engaging in leisure sex began to take shape. As clubs began to open up, rather than a slow arrival of people in a club that was characteristic of sex clubs before the pandemic, post-lockdown meant that some clubs were witnessing what appeared to be an exponential rise in the number of visitors. For example, rather than the usual pattern of no more than twenty people arriving in the first thirty minutes, one club had at least eighty people arriving within the space of ten minutes of opening. Other clubs began to see traditionally slow weekdays suddenly becoming sold out. One club that typically had no more than forty or fifty cars on a weekday afternoon had, in a month of opening, over two hundred and twenty cars stationed in their car park for one afternoon. After eighteen months where anonymous sex was effectively outlawed, when sex clubs re-opened with no restrictions, they became a place where it appeared that more people than usual began to visit. In response, some clubs held re-launch and re-opening parties that were initially sold out within days but then were extended and spread over a number of days. Thus, there appeared to be a strong demand for a sex club experience. However, it was not self-evident what that experience would look like. Through the use of ethnographies, it was possible to capture how disruptions caused by the pandemic were shaping post-lockdown sexual encounters.

3   Cultures of Desire and Uncertain Intimacies

In order to understand the experiences of sex clubs in a post-lockdown context, the concept 'cultures of desire' is used to understand how sex is experienced, practised and felt. Cultures of desire are made up of two elements, erotic hierarchies and affective atmospheres. Green (2014) uses the concept of erotic hierarchies to refer to the way that contexts are being shaped by a system of shared norms and values. In such systems, various identities, social characteristics or practices carry different amounts of erotic capital. Thus, in UK sex clubs, women, Black men and young men are more desirable and more sought after than older, larger white men. Green suggests that this ordering constitutes a structure of desire, where 'Structures of desire eroticize and assign value to certain bodies, affects, and practices while rending others neuter or undesirable' (Green 2014, p. 28). As a consequence of the structure of desire, certain bodies are ascribed a particular sexual capital that both authorizes and refuses access to shared practices. However, where a structure of desire is in place within clubs, it is also subject to variability, fluidity and change. One of the dynamics that produce such change is affective atmospheres. Affective atmospheres are instances where erotic hierarchies break down, do not make sense, or exceed the categories that contain their agency. Methodologically, this means not only recognizing shared meanings, texts, emotions and practices that contradict and challenge the historical structures of desire but also including what Bissell (2010, p. 271) considers as the 'pre-cognitive, pre-discursive and affective'. This may include the narratives spoken by the room such as the sense of abandonment in dark rooms on a bi night, the air of exclusion by cliques in social areas, the inclusiveness of the jacuzzi on a couples night, and the solemnness of a dungeon. Following Michels (2015), such atmospheres emerge from an interplay between the human and the inhuman. Quite simply, affective atmospheres encapsulate more than individual networks but point to an intensity of space and place that exceeds an individual subjectivity. It is therefore argued that within sex clubs, erotic hierarchies and affective atmospheres provide the scaffolding for the emergence of cultures of desire.

It is argued that in a post-lockdown context, sex clubs could be characterized as places where uncertain intimacy presents itself. Uncertain intimacy is not a new concept. Eldridge's (2014) work on HIV highlights how components of intimacy such as closeness, openness, trust, affection and mutuality become problematized when the virus impacts men's relationships. Such an impact can involve, according to Eldridge, the slowing down of intimacy, the threat to sexual intimacy and barriers to being intimate. In a similar way, Dawson and Dennis (2020), in their special double issue of *Anthropology in Action* on 'Covid-19 and the Transformation of Intimacy' identify numerous ways across various spheres such as love, families, states and citizens, nation-states and temporality, how the pandemic has created uncertainty. They suggest that this uncertainty not only operates as personally transformative but also 'how the new forms of intimacy produced by the pandemic are in and of themselves transforming society more broadly' (2020, p. 7). Importantly, such transformations may not always be progressive. In their discussion of social communication, Paprzycka (2018) also discusses how transformations in intimacy are creating a fear of involvement. Although this work uses Illouz's (2007) suggestion for heterosexual men and their fear of commitment, such work highlights that post-lockdown sex might take place in a number of different ways. It is these different ways that are explored further.

3.1   *Social Sex*

One of the post-lockdown responses in sex clubs was the increasing visibility of a shift towards *social* rather than sexual closeness. More specifically, people are meeting people in sex clubs that were not simply driven by a desire for sexual encounters. Instead, people are visiting sex clubs as a place to engage in particular forms of sociality. Whilst the lockdown experience of isolation often resulted in a greater sense of a collective shared understanding of the challenges posed by the pandemic, it is argued that post-lockdown, there is a greater feeling of isolation (Cocco et al. 2020; Marzana et al. 2021). As such, sex clubs are places where social ties, contacts and connections are being made and re-established. However, this re-establishing is often connected to the spatiality of the club and how it promotes particular forms of public intimacy. The concept of public intimacy draws upon Kaplan's (2018) approach that highlights how institutions bring people together socially in particular ways. More specifically, Kaplan argues that 'In many modern social institutions, strangers negotiate modes of cooperation through face-to-face or mediated interpersonal interactions. As a form of a social club, each institution embodies a particular version of a common underlying logic of strangers-turned-friends' (ibid., p. 12). From the spatial dynamics of the club, its ethos, the cost of entry and membership, its self-presentation inside and online, the role of staff and the clientele visiting, and their sexual practice and demeanour, clubs promote specific forms of sociality. It appears that sex clubs in the UK have grafted existing templates of leisure and recreation into the fabric of their sociality that often takes the shape of a social club, a bar, a jazz bar, a karaoke bar or a nightclub.

At the centre of most clubs is the social area. This is a place where people gather before they engage in the playrooms that are often situated away from the social area. The social area, and specifically in a post-lockdown context, resonates with Tim Dean's characterization that British culture is somewhat repressed (Dean, 2015). Often the mundanity of the social area almost operates as a façade that is gently unwilling to acknowledge the sexual nature of the club. Some clubs prohibit sex or refuse to play porn in the social area, with an emphasis on sexual restraint and inhibition; characteristics "deeply ingrained in the (British) national character" (Leach 2004, p. 133). In one club, sexual play was explicitly discouraged in the social area, and unlike most clubs across the UK, the TV didn't show pornography; it played muted re-runs of reality TV that featured the police and crime and home and gardening upscaling. The 'no sex in the social area' policy also pointed to the ways that class repertories reflecting socio-sexual dynamics were also inflected by particular forms of race and ethnicity. More specifically, there could also be something very English (and white) about the social area. In some clubs, this appears to mimic what would be common in an everyday English living room; slightly faded sofas, comfy chairs, unbalanced lampshades, plants, and coffee tables. In the corner of one club, there were two board games of Twister and Trivial Pursuit (Classic Edition), underneath a pile of swimming pool inflatables (presumably for the jacuzzi). It should be added that though there were displays of sexualized dancing on the dance floor and the presence of nearly naked bodies (of more women than men), the social area in some clubs tends to be a non-sexual sphere. The emphasis on a de-sexualized space corresponds with D'heer and Courtois's (2016) claim that the living room is a traditional social hub; the use of space here is more communal and less privatized. Such a distinction between the sexual and the non-sexual tells us that sex itself, even in some clubs, is cordoned off and bounded. In this context, this bounding reinforces the (in)visibility of heterosexuality supporting the view that heteroerotics is distinct from heterosexuality. As such the normative structures that establish heterosexuality as natural and 'asexual' (Phillips, 2006, p. 167).

Before the pandemic, the sharing of pizza and chips over a pint of beer or glass of Chardonnay before dipping into the large jacuzzi for group sex was not unusual. Thus, socializing became the space to identify people for potential sexual encounters later in the night. However, in a post-lockdown context, sociality became *the* reason for being at the club. The fieldnotes used at the beginning of the chapter highlighted how people attending the club wanted to engage in a form of sociality, a culture of desire, that was not dependent on sexual encounters. As a result, it is important not to see the social and sexual in opposition but intrinsically connected. As Sjoberg (2017, p. 73) explains:

> By seeing the "the social" as sexual, I mean seeing the ways that "the sexual" regulates "the social" and "the social" regulates "the sexual" in a way that makes *sociality* and *sexuality* conceptually inseparable.

By seeing the sexual and the social as imbricated, we may even push the argument further and see the socializing within the social areas at a time of uncertain intimacy as being a safe, less risky erotic practice. As Jia et al. (2022) have pointed out, "... it is hard to build trust and bodily intimacy with strangers in the post-pandemic era". It is argued, therefore, that conversations in this social space have become increasingly eroticized. The reason for reframing the social element of the club as erotically pleasurable is not simply because conversations take place in a club that facilitates sex. There are conversations that take place in clubs that discuss anything from cancer to car engines. However, what tends to remain out of the conversations are indicators of personal identity. Names, addresses and workplaces are generally not a part of the conversations. As such, there is a distinct playfulness of anonymity and non-revelation and a limit to talk. In the context of the sex club, such talk can often become erotized as 'Erotic pleasure arguably requires a kind of momentary annihilation or the suspension of what normally counts as "identity" ...' Waldby (1995, p. 226). In this way, some conversations operate metonymically, not only displaying the cultural order within sex clubs but standing in as the activity within that place (Musson and Tietzse 2004). Thus, at the beginning of this chapter, the talk of the holiday in Spain became another means of engaging in an eroticized activity without the risk and anxiety of close physical intimacy. An eroticized activity that took place with the exciting possibility of a sexual encounter that wasn't going to be pursued.

At the same time, this sociality also filtered into sexual encounters. For example, in one club, as I wandered upstairs to a playroom, I was quickly joined by four other single men watching what appeared to be three sets of couples and a single woman having sex. The stable door style entrance remained half-closed, a mechanism that restricted physical access but welcomed people to watch. Initially, the couples appeared to be with their established partners and the woman on her own sat on the floor at the bottom of the three red PVC beds. From the doorway, you could see each of the couples slowly peel away from each other quietly and slowly to sexually engage with other couples. For example, one man moved across to another couple and started to touch the woman between the legs as her partner was fucking her. This carried on for around five minutes and eventually, as her partner got off, she invited another man to climb on top of her. Her partner was then given oral sex by another of the women. However, what was most intriguing was the younger woman on her own, sitting on the floor by the door, who began to provide a running commentary.

The woman sitting on her own began shouting out and laughing, 'Can't you get hard then?' or 'Have you come yet?' As one woman was going down on a male partner, she got up, stood behind the couple and began slapping his buttocks, exclaiming, 'Don't cum too quickly', making the people having sex laugh, 'He's holding on, he don't wanna cum, too quickly'. This encounter felt much like a scene from a local pub underpinned by a strong working-class gendered coding. In some pub culture scenarios, men make comments about women playing pool, trying to put them off with crude and sexualizing remarks as women try to make shots. Such a scenario is captured by Jones (2018), who suggests that in pub culture, such humour is used by men to reduce women's playing of the pool as not a real game and just a bit of fun. Jones argues that this is a means of maintaining control of women in a male-dominated culture. It could be seen that a similar mirroring effect is in place that within a space where women hold more erotic capital than men, men's bodies become subject to control, review, and commentary. Whilst it is the case that she was ridiculing and mocking the tropes through which sexual masculinities establish themselves, such humour should also be understood as a creative practice sustaining and consolidating the relationships within the encounter. As Plester and Sayers (2007) point out, the use of humour speaks to forms of social acceptance and the reinforcement of relationships. At the same time, they also draw attention to the negativity that is often involved in 'taking the piss' as a means of 'deflating the ego' but also creatively maintaining and establishing the contours of relationships within a group. In spite or even because of the humour, the men and women carried on having sex regardless, sometimes laughing or sometimes completely ignoring the humour.

It became apparent that the humour reconfigured the sexualized atmosphere of encounters within the room. This was not a space for the living out of middle-class erotic aesthetics; rather, it was the creation of a culture of desire inflected and reconfigured a working-class masculine humour into a form of sociality and connectedness. It was a moment where in a post-lockdown context, experiencing the social and the sexual together was of growing significance in the club. The camaraderie, the safety, and the pleasure of their encounter seemed to establish a way of doing sex that was not simply erotically driven.

3.2   Scopophilic Touching

One of the consequences of the disruption caused by the pandemic was the intensification of the pleasure of the scopophilic. It appeared that the disruption caused by the pandemic resulted in people who visited the club becoming more hesitant, tentative and cautious in initiating and taking part in sexual encounters. Fear, anxiety the potential risk of being too close to someone in a sexual encounter became lived out through cultures of desire that operated and worked through a scopophilic positionality. This hesitancy is built on an erotic routine that pre-existed the pandemic. More specifically, the spatial dynamics of clubs encourage and prioritize the pleasure of seeing sexual encounters. Open doorways, rooms with windows on all sides, couches and chairs around PVC mattresses and chaise lounge nudge club visitors into the experiencing of sexual encounters. As such, patrons of the club freely move around these rooms, surveying, watching, moving on or joining in with an expectation and anticipation building between rooms. As Hammers (2009) points out: 'Spaces thus provide a road map (Weinberg and Williams 1975)—that is, the contours and parameters for certain behaviors, encouraging particular actions while discouraging and inhibiting others'. Some rooms witness waves of onlookers, erotic tourists, edging themselves closer to the 'action' through doorways and mirrors; brushing up close to strangers, where the act of looking becomes a simultaneous act of doing, with quick glances and exchanged smiles, sometimes enabling reciprocal touching and (in) advertent rubbing.

Whilst this scopophilic staging of desire was evident before the pandemic, in a post-lockdown context, it became more conspicuous. In one club, there was a taste of tentativeness in the air, a paralyzed urgency, impelling women, men and couples to wander through the cinema room, the windowed torture room, the dark rooms and glory holes, past the private rooms to the shared purple beds. Casually dressed, people nervously giggle as they peer into the rooms and stand for a while in the doorway (being careful not to block the view of those before them). They watch, for example, a man's head being thrust between the legs of a woman, who is uneasily perched on the edge of the bed. Seizing his slightly balding black hair, she forces him into her. She looks up and gazes at those watching her. Holding their drinks a little tighter than before and closer to their faces, those watching wait a while. In previous research 'The Gaze' has often been understood as a metaphor for patriarchy (Evans and Gamman 1995). However in this context, the power embedded in the gaze is reversible. As Church (2014, p. 8) points out in relation to adult movie theatres, '... distinctions between exhibitionism and voyeurism are impossible to maintain: not only does theater play depend on the very publicness of sexuality for its erotic charge, but (male) theater patrons can quickly become participants and observers of each other'. This transitory connection contains circuits of desire transversing in multiple directions, not simply between those in the playroom and those being watched but also between those watching and between those being watched. It is a visually driven indulgence, where the "The erotic relationship is one in which we're constantly feeling our skin *from the inside and out*, feeling ourselves being touched in the act of touching" (Barker 2009, p. 36). For those watching, this is a transitory moment, driven by a consumption of bodies as commodities, a consuming that moves with the crowd from one room to another and to another.

Those watching then drift towards the next room, a thin snaking line of spectators, come across the torture room; a room doused in a dim purple light. A man and a woman, dressed in tight black leather shorts, take turns using their hands to lightly paddle a naked woman tied to a St Andrews cross. The crowd watched, transfixed. The couple within the room kneel to find the right kind of tools, paddles, whips, clamps and wheels, to be used as part of the experience inside a small leather holdall. The spectators continue to watch. There's a shared fascination emerging as more and more people gather around the windowed room. Just as Maina reflects in the context of online porn sites, '... we skip feverishly ... from site to site, fantasy to fantasy, searching for the perfect image, succumbing more to the seduction of the search than to the pleasure of the result' (Maina, 2009, p. 131). There's an anticipation of the next room that often drives audiences to move swiftly on in anticipation of the next potential erotic encounter to be watched, to be part of. Whether watching or being watched such co-created encounters throughout the club are often temporary, with few people staying on to consume the experience. Waves of men and women, 'interact with one another in the mode of spontaneous communitas become totally absorbed into a single, synchronized, fluid event' (Turner, 1982, p. 48). Move to one room, watch, then move on, to the next. And the next.

It is thus argued that the scopophilic practice present in the club prepandemic, was post-lockdown, being reconfigured as part of a broader concern about social and sexual distancing. Rather than sheltering from risk through sociality or capturing reconnections through sexual encounters, in this section, the emphasis has been on distance as becoming an eroticized practice. This culture of desire, which shifts from room to room without touching, enables a doing of sex, from a distance. Within this erotic visuality, there is no being viewed and there is no one simply viewing; all are watching and being watched. As Zizek points out, 'When I am looking at an object, the object is always already gazing at me and from a point at which I cannot see it: ...' (ibid. p. 35). For Zizek, it is the gaze that is being captured by desire, a desire that is cultivated and produced by the object wherein the subject is retroactively entangled. This mutual gaze can be characterized at the point where the scopophilia and the exhibitionism meet, entwine and produce an atmosphere of mutual and individualized zones of pleasure, and in this case, at a distance.

3.3   *Physically Compelled*

The final expression of desire that became more intense after the lockdown was lifted was captured by desperation and an immediacy to touch. The pre-pandemic structure of desire in clubs tended to be based on norms of consent and respectfulness. Men would often display their respectfulness through being polite and demonstrating a responsible masculinity (Elliott, 2014) that takes care not simply in what it is doing but what it is being *seen* to do. As a result, the sex club, on the surface at least, appears to promote particular forms of sexually respectful masculinities that prioritize and show care towards women's experiences. Pasura and Christou's (2018) work on respectable masculinities highlights the ways in which migrant men, in order to gain status, aspire to demonstrate a sense of respectability. They argue that respectability is conveyed through conformity to socially agreeable values. In the sex club, men attempted to do something similar by using respectfulness to differentiate between groups of men, a differentiation that becomes extremely important when negotiating sexual encounters. The alternative to respectability are men who were often called 'opportunists', desperates' or 'wank zombies'; men who would be too insistent and demanding. Prior to the pandemic, such individuals were always a minority in clubs and club management was always keen to stop behaviours that made women, in particular, feel uncomfortable.

Post-lockdown, rather than an uncertain intimacy characterized by a careful sexualized sociality, a culture of desire emerged that was erotically charged with an urgency to be involved in physical, sexual encounters. For example, at the end of one evening, a man sat with a younger woman in a black bikini laced top and leather PVC knickers. They were watching a woman fucking a man on a massage bench. At the same time, they were chatting to a man across from them, a man that was wearing red PVC shorts, braces and a red dog collar. The couple stopped fucking and wandered downstairs. In their place, the man in the shorts walked up to the other man's partner, lifted her off the chair and laid her down on the bench. They began kissing, and she started to dry fuck him, pushing herself against him, tightening her legs around his back. Apart from the kissing, there was no touching inside the clothing, no genital contact, just rubbing, a frisson across each of their bodies. They constantly changed positions, arranging their bodies in ways that would maximize their pleasure. It was a form of unspoken eroticism, a shifting, twisting around of bodies, using one another, urging each other on through touching, all on the outside of their clothing. They moved to another massage table on the other side of the room; she was clinging with her legs around his waist as he laid her down. This time, a number of men and women stood around them, watching this intense writhing of bodies, searching and seeking out pleasure. The man buried his face in her hair, kissing and tasting her neck; she lurched upwards, forcing herself against the hardness of his cock beneath his shorts. She moaned as the man switched sides, tasting her again with an urgency and a frenzy. An older man leaned over, close to her face, and shouted, 'Are you enjoying that?'

3.3.1   The Spell Was Broken

Perhaps it was the presence of a different kind of sex within this club night that was most noticeable. The atmosphere and the experience all interwove into the experience of the evening. Besides the group sex, the use of huge sex toys, the hard flogging on the St Andrew's cross and the multiplicity of sex between a T-girl and two women, this felt transgressive. However, more generally, there is something about the erotic energies of the club, something that was picked up by Pini (2001) in their discussion of dance clubs and raves. They discuss a way of being erotic that exceeds the categories of straight, gay and lesbian, which operationalize the sexual. The result is that what appears, for example, to be heterosexual becomes more blurred, fragmented and queered. More specifically,

> This is not about a sexual longing directed towards a specific or individual 'target', but about a far more dispersed and fragmented set of erotic energies which appear to be generated within the dance event. This new form of 'jouissance' has little to do with 'pick-up' or even with something outside the self (and this becomes particularly clear when several of the women use the term 'autoerotic').
> PINI 2001, p. 175

It is these energies, this sense of moving away from the individual to a sense of encounters and moments, that signals how sexual encounters within a club can be experienced. However, in a post-lockdown context, there appeared to be a greater need for this shared pleasure to be physically accessible. In other words, there was a desperate need to connect and join in. As Martinkova et al. (2021) suggest, 'Unfortunately, during the pandemic, handshakes, hugs or other touching gestures have become dangerous because of an invisible and not immediately known danger'. As a result, '... the absence of traditional touching during handshakes and other kinds of touching—feeling the texture of the skin of others, tactile manifestations and the persistence of affects— could lead to a certain deprivation of internal sensations, emotions, and felt proximity to others'. It is argued that the uncertainty generated by the absence of touching, for example, meant that when people began to re-visit clubs, there was a discernible earnestness to physically engage and connect with people. In many ways, this led to bypassing of the sexual routines and rituals that had previously been established.

In the above encounter, the old man leaning over the couple shouting, 'Are you enjoying that?' prompted the woman lying down to move her head away. Another man intervened and pushed the man away, then tried to put his hand on her. She moved the hand away. The couple tried to continue and then another oldish, short man in shorts and braces leaned into them with a bottle of poppers, trying to get the man to sniff the bottle. The man on top of the woman didn't see this, but he flung his head around and knocked the amyl nitrate all over his face and the face of the woman lying underneath him. It went into her eyes and hair and over her neck. She instantly cried out as it stung her. Everything immediately stopped. The man with the poppers bottle faded into the background and the group of people around the couple began to disperse. The couple both ran to the toilets to bathe their eyes; amyl nitrate in the eye can cause irreversible damage and loss of sight. The difference between the pre and post lockdown desperation to touch in clubs could be character- ized as a move away from being calculated and respectful to one that was urgent and demanding. Prior to the club, those men (and they usually were men) who were more insistent in sexual encounters tended to be selective and targeting of opportunities to engage with women or couples. Post-lockdown, there appeared to be an immediacy, an urgency to be physical that was con- testing the previously embedded pre-Covid culture of desire.

4   Conclusion

The pandemic produced an 'epistemological jolt' that has resulted in people re-evaluating the relationship between the social and the sexual. This chapter has used ethnographic fieldwork in sex clubs to reflect on how such re-evaluations are taking place in post-lockdown sexual encounters in the sex club. Whereas clubs in the past were characterized by immersing consumers in club rituals and routines, the pandemic has witnessed an increasing prevalence of emersion, where sexual practices are being cultivated in response to uncontrollable events. Existing work on leisure usually associates emersive experiences based as involuntary experiences produced through unpredictable relationships between the body and the physical environment (Andrieu and Nobrega 2020). In this way the pandemic is creating a social context where sexual experiences and encounters are being re-evaluated and reflected upon. It has been argued that responses to the pandemic appear to manifest themselves in three emerging cultures of desire – the social as sexual, an intensified scopophilic touching and a need to be involved in physical encounters. It is possible that as a 'new normal' settles into sex clubs, these cultures of desire may disperse with eroticism re-articulating itself closer to something that resembles the pre-pandemic scenarios, new configurations of eroticism and intensity or a combination of both. What is more certain is that the disruptions generated by the pandemic have resulted in attempts to resume, repair and reconnect with others in existing and innovative experiences often characterized by enigmatic hesitation, excitement and pleasure.

References

Andrieu, B., and da Nobrega, P. (2020) 'From Slowness to Deepening: The Way of Emersive Awareness', *Sport, Ethics and Philosophy*, 16(2) pp. 1–13.

Alston, A. (2013) 'Audience participation and neoliberal value: Risk, agency and responsibility in immersive theatre', *Performance Research*, 18(2), pp. 128–138.

Assiter, B. (2022) 'From dancefloors to tables: socially distanced clubbing, temporary urbanism, and the gentrification of London's nightlife', *Annals of Leisure Research*, DOI: 10.1080/11745398.2022.2027252.

Arber, A. (2001) 'Getting in and staying in: Negotiating and maintaining access to a hospice setting'. In *Ethnography and Health Care Conference*. 8th December, 2001, London: Royal College of Nursing.

Amoah, A., and Amoah, B. (2021) 'The COVID-19 pandemic lockdown: a buzz of negativity with a silver lining of social connectedness', *Journal of Economic and Administrative Sciences*, 38(1), pp. 178–197.

Ashford, C., and Longstaff, G. (2021) '(Re) regulating gay sex in viral times: COVID-19 and the impersonal intimacy of the glory hole', *Culture, Health & Sexuality*, 23(11), pp. 1559–1572.

Attwood, F., and Smith, C. (2013) 'Leisure sex: More sex! Better sex! Sex is fucking brilliant! Sex, sex, sex, SEX', in T. Blackshaw (ed.) *Routledge handbook of leisure studies,* London: Routledge. pp. 347–358.

Bacon, A.M., Krupić, D., Caki, N., and Corr, P.J. (2022) 'Emotional and Behavioral Responses to COVID-19', *European Psychologist*, 26(4), pp. 334–347.

Barker, J.M. (2009) *The tactile eye: Touch and the cinematic experience.* London: University of California Press.

Berry, M. (2017) *Creating with Mobile Media.* London: Palgrave Macmillan.

Bissell, D. (2010) 'Passenger mobilities: affective atmospheres and the sociality of public transport', *Environment and Planning D: Society and Space*, 28(2), pp. 270–289.

Church, D. (2014) 'Heterosexuality, Recreational Sex, and the Survival of Adult Movie Theaters', *Media Fields Journal*, 8. Available at: http://mediafieldsjournal .squarespace.com/this-thing-of-ours/.

Cocco, E., Mines, A.F., and Salvatore, R. (2020) 'Dreaming of Remoteness, Coping with Emptiness in Post-Lockdown (Under) Tourism Scenarios for the Inner Areas of Southern Italy: a Fieldwork Based Reflection', *Fuori Luogo. Rivista di Sociologia del Territorio, Turismo, Tecnologia*, 7(1), pp. 53–68.

Cornwall, R. (1997) 'The Social Articulation of Desire', in A. Gluckman, A., and B. Reed. (eds.) *Homo Economics:Capitalism, Community, and Lesbian and Gay Life.* New York: Routledge, pp. 89–123.

Dawson, A., and Dennis, S. (2020) 'Microbial intimacy', *Anthropology in Action*, 27(2), pp. 1–8.

Dean, T. (2015) 'No Sex Please, We're American', *American Literary History*, 27(3), pp. 614–624.

D'heer, E., and Courtois, C. (2016) 'The changing dynamics of television consumption in the multimedia living room', *Convergence*, 22(1), pp. 3–17.

Eldredge, S. A. (2014) *Intimacy Uncertainty and Identity in Gay Male Couples Dealing with a Serodiscordant HIV Status.* PhD Thesis. University of Tennessee.

Ellis, C. S., & Bochner, A. P. (2006) Analyzing analytic autoethnography: An autopsy. *Journal of contemporary ethnography, 35*(4), 429–449.

Elliott, S. (2014) "Who's to blame?" Constructing the responsible sexual agent in neoliberal sex education. *Sexuality Research and Social Policy, 11*(3), 211–224.

Evans, C., and Gamman, L. (1995) 'The gaze revisited, or reviewing queer viewing', in P. Burston, and C. Richardson (eds.), A *queer romance: Lesbians, gay men and popular culture*. London: Routledge, pp. 13–57.

Furedi, F. (2020) 'Social distancing, safe spaces and the demand for quarantine', *Society*, 57(4), pp. 392–397.

Gergen, K. J., & Gergen, M. M. (2018) Doing things with words: toward evocative ethnography. *Qualitative Research in Psychology*, 15(2–3), 272–286.

Green, A.I. (2014) 'The sexual fields framework', in Green, A.I. (ed.), *Sexual Fields: Toward a Sociology of Collective Sexual Life*.Chicago: University of Chicago Press, pp. 25–56.

Hammers, C. (2009) 'An examination of lesbian/queer bathhouse culture and the social organization of (im) personal sex', *Journal of Contemporary Ethnography*, 38(3), 308–335.

Harman, L. (2021) 'Silent vibrator sales have rocketed during lockdown', *Woman & Home*, February 23.Available at: https://www.womanandhome.com/health-wellbeing/silent-vibrator-sales-have-rocketed-during-lockdown/ (Accessed: 16.08.2022).

Haywood, C. (2023) *Sex: Clubs: Recreational Sex, Fantasies and Cultures of Desire*. London: Palgrave.

Hubbard, P. (2001) 'Sex zones: Intimacy, citizenship and public space', *Sexualities*, 4(1), pp. 51–71.

Illouz, E. (1999) 'The Lost Innocence of Love: Romance as a Postmodern Condition', in M. Featherstone (ed.) *Love and Eroticism*, London: Sage. pp. 161–187.

Illouz, E. (2007) *Cold intimacies: The making of emotional capitalism*. Cambridge: Polity.

Jia, J.S., Yuan, Y., Jia, J., and Christakis, N.A. (2022) 'Risk perception and behaviour change after personal vaccination for COVID-19 in the USA', *PsyArXiv*. Available at: https://psyarxiv.com/afyv8/download.

Jonasson, K. (2018) 'What [I] talk about when [I] am running': Revetment Running, Ethnography and Econarratological Poetry. *The Ethnographic Edge-Contemporary Ethnography Across the Disciplines*, 2(1), 9–20.

Jones, A. (2021) 'The new summer of love: 'People are desperate to have sex – it's been a long year'', *The Guardian*, 5th June. Available at: https://www.theguardian.com/lifeandstyle/2021/jun/05/new-summer-of-love-people-desperate-to-have-sex-its-been-a-long-year (Accessed: 16.08.2022).

Jones, K. (2021) Carefree or Careless: What Will You Be in the Post-Pandemic Fuck Fest? *Erotic Review*, 12th Feb. Available at: https://ermagazine.com/relationships/carefree-or-careless-what-will-you-be-in-the-post-pandemic-fuck-fest/ (Accessed 16.08.2022).

Jones, S. A. (2018) *Women can't play dominos: an ethnographic study of working class life in a Midlands pub*. Doctoral Thesis. University of Birmingham.

Kaplan, D. (2018) Social club sociability as a model for national solidarity. *American Journal of Cultural Sociology*, 6(1), 1–36.

Killeen, K.J. (2017) 'Scrutinizing Surfaces: Microscopy, Surfaces and the Unknowable in Seventeenth-Century Natural Philosophy (from Lucretius to Margaret Cavendish)', *Journal of the Northern Renaissance*, 8, pp. 1–22.

Leach, J. (2004) *British film*. Cambridge: Cambridge University Press.

Lehmiller, J.J., Garcia, J.R., Gesselman, A.N., and Mark, K.P. (2021) 'Less sex, but more sexual diversity: Changes in sexual behavior during the COVID-19 coronavirus pandemic', *Leisure Sciences*, 43(1–2), 295–304.

Maina, G. (2009) Pornscapes. Re-enacting Porn Film in the Landscapes of Contemporary Pornography. *Cinéma & Cie*, 9(1), 127–0.

Martínková, I., Andrieu, B., & Parry, J. (2022) Slow Sport and Slow Philosophy: Practices Suitable (Not Only) for Lockdowns. *Sport, Ethics and Philosophy*, 16(2), 159–164.

Marzana, D., Novara, C., De Piccoli, N., Cardinali, P., Migliorini, L., Di Napoli, I., ... and Procentese, F. (2021) 'Community dimensions and emotions in the era of COVID-19', *Journal of Community & Applied Social Psychology* 32(3), 358–373.

Mazierska, E.H., and Rigg, T. (2021) 'Challenges to British Nightclubs During and After the Covid-19 Pandemic', *Dancecult: Journal of Electronic Dance Music Culture*, 13(1), pp. 69–87.

Michels, C. (2015) 'Researching affective atmospheres', *Geographica Helvetica*, 70(4), pp. 255–263.

Musson, G., and Tietze, S. (2004) 'Places and spaces: The role of metonymy in organizational talk', *Journal of Management Studies*, 41(8), pp. 1301–1323.

Nofre, J., (2021a) 'Nightlife as a source of social wellbeing, community-building and psychological mutual support after the Covid-19 pandemic', Annals of Leisure Research, DOI: 10.1080/11745398.2021.1964991

Nofre, J. (2021b) 'The Touristifcation of Nightlife: some theoretical notes', *Urban Geography* Vol.42(10): pp1552-1561.

Paprzycka, E. (2018) 'Discursiveness of intimacy-sociological conceptualizations and perspectives of analyses', *PRO COMMUNIO*, University of Presov.

Parkhurst, J. and Whiteside, A. (2010) 'Innovative responses for preventing HIV transmission: the protective value of population-wide interruptions of risk activity', *Southern African Journal of HIV Medicine*, 11(1) pp. 19–21.

Pasura, D., and Christou, A. (2018) 'Theorizing black (African) transnational masculinities', *Men and Masculinities*, 21(4), pp. 521–546.

Pennanen-Iire, C., Prereira-Lourenço, M., Padoa, A., Ribeirinho, A., Samico, A., Gressler, M., and Girard, A. (2021) ' Sexual health implications of COVID-19 pandemic', *Sexual Medicine Reviews*, 9(1), 3–14.

Phillips, R. (2006) Unsexy geographies: Heterosexuality, respectability and the travellers' aid society. *ACME: An International Journal for Critical Geographies*, 5(2), 163–190.

Pini, M. (2001) *Club cultures and female subjectivity: The move from home to house.* Hampshire: Springer.

Plester, B. A., & Sayers, J. (2007)"Taking the piss": Functions of banter inthe IT industry. *Humor: International Journal of Humor Research*, 20(2), pp. 157–187.

Rogoff, I. (2013) *Terra infirma: Geography's visual culture*. London: Routledge.

Schwartz, P., and Rutter, V. (1998) *The gender of sexuality*. Oxford: Rowman & Littlefield Publishers.

Sigal, P., Tortorici, Z., and Whitehead, N.L. (2019) 'Ethnopornography as Methodology and Critique Merging the Ethno-, the Porno-, and the -Graphos', in Sigal, P., Tortorici, Z., and Whitehead, N.L. (eds.) *Ethnopornography: Sexuality, Colonialism, and Archival Knowledge*. Durham: Duke University Press, pp. 1–41.

Sjoberg, L. (2017) Queering IR Constructivism. In H. D. Gould (Ed.) *The Art of World-Making: Nicholas Greenwood Onuf and His Critics*. London: Routledge. pp. 68–77.

Taylor, S., and Asmundson, G.J. (2020) 'Life in a post-pandemic world: What to expect of anxiety-related conditions and their treatment', *Journal of Anxiety Disorders*, 72, 102231.

Tewksbury, R. (2002) 'Bathhouse intercourse: Structural and behavioral aspects of an erotic oasis', *Deviant Behavior*, 23(1), 75–112.

Turner, V. (1982) *From ritual to theater: The human seriousness of play*. New York: Performing Arts Journal Publications.

Waldby, C. (1995) 'Boundary erotics and refigurations of the heterosexual male body', in E. Grosz & E. Probyn (eds) *Sexy Bodies: The Strange Carnalities of Feminism*. London: Routledge.

Weinberg, M. S. and Williams, C.J. (1975) Gay baths and the social organization ofimpersonal sex. *Social Problems*, 23(2): 124–36.

Zhou, R., Zhu, K., and Liu, Y. (2019) 'Analysis of the design of military building skin under the guidance of camouflage concept', *Journal of Physics: Conference Series*, 1237(2) pp. 1–6.

Žižek, S. (1991) Looking Awry: An Introduction to Jaques Lacan through Popular Culture. London: October Books. pp. 31–55.

CHAPTER 12

Pain and Suffering, Uterus Trumpets and the Wild Ride: Autoethnographic Aca-fandom, Para-social Relationships and *Diane* Podcast

Michael Waugh

Overwhelmed by mental stresses brought on by conditions of lockdown, I increasingly sought comforting escapism, especially within the discourse surrounding the television series *Twin Peaks*. I lost myself in YouTube videos, blog-posts, forums and podcasts. Of these, the *Diane* podcast (2016-present) – an episode-by-episode breakdown of *Twin Peaks'* three seasons (1990–1991; 2017) and the film *Twin Peaks: Fire Walk With Me* (1992), as well as all epitextual materials – provided my most intimate para-social experience. Philosophers of digitality debate the intimacy of on/offline interaction, interrogating the legitimacy of formulating emotionally beneficial relationships through digital platforms (Jamieson, 2013). Some (e.g. Beck and Beck-Gernsheim, 2002; Bauman, 2003; Berardi, 2011) remind us how illusory our virtually negotiated connections are: we must, we are told, never forget that these manipulative spaces fuel the culture industry; that their sugar-rush stimuli are impoverished stand-ins for real-world sociality. Others (Jurgenson, 2012; Giddens, 1991) contend that 'the identity foundations on which new relationships are built can be every bit as sturdy online as off' (Baym, 2010, p. 121).

The affiliation I felt listening to *Diane* for the first time, mediated though it was, seemed *real* to me, and the solace it afforded in a time of isolation and adversity was invaluable. As I listened, I developed a kinship with people I had never met, who did not even know I was tuned-in; my daily lockdown routines became intertwined with the voices of these knowledgeable individuals. Further to this, as time went on, the podcast's contents also began to contribute significantly to my own academic practice. I had produced little during those first months of lockdown, wallowing in the demotivation and writer's block wrought by such a disruptive event. Listening to *Diane*, though, I slowly found my thoughts returning to research. This was partially due to the more positive emotional state the podcast put me in, but also because the ideas presented by its hosts felt as thoroughly researched and visionary as much published scholarly work. Why did this specific podcast realign my focus and stimulate me back into research and scholarship with renewed vigour?

Through an autoethnographic examination of my para-social *Diane* fandom, I reflect on my subjective experience to investigate why podcasts offer such supportive familiarity, especially in times of crisis. Within this, I consider the value of *Diane*'s 'fan labour', examining how its hosts' scholarly but accessible exchanges manifest the methods central to 'aca-fandom' and thus might act as inspirational tools for teaching and research within popular culture studies. To understand fully the practicalities involved in the production and presentation of *Diane*, I have combined the autoethnographic and critical components with interviews with three of the four hosts (Adam, Rosie and Bob), querying the research and effort that goes into preparing for their conversations, the discursive dynamic on the show, and their interactions with the *Twin Peaks* fandom. This chapter does not exist to critique *Diane*; if that were the case, I would analyse the podcast in a more 'traditional' academic format than the disruptive and reflective autoethnographic style that animates this chapter. The depth of psychological and intellectual sustenance that its hosts (inadvertently) provided is fundamental in studying why this podcast reinvigorated me and my academic practice. From the outset, therefore, I make no apologies for the celebratory attitude of my autoethnographic account of the para-social relationship I established with *Diane*.

I begin by briefly clarifying the process of 'autoethnography'. Manning and Adams define it as a 'research method that foregrounds the researcher's personal experience [as] it is embedded within, and informed by, cultural identities, [...] popular texts, and a community's attitudes, beliefs, and practices. [Autoethnographers] often use storytelling devices such as narrative voice, plot, and character development to represent their experiences' (2015, p. 188–189). The method has been necessarily linked to transgressive cultural studies, enabling scholars writing from subjugated racialised, gendered, classed, or sexualised perspectives to speak of their experiences in a format unsuppressed by the aggressively formal (and historically white, patriarchal) prose of the academic establishment. Writing 'about these often-private experiences [allowed these scholars] not only to better understand those events themselves, but also to show others how they make sense of and learn lessons from them' (Manning and Adams, 2015, p. 191). More recently, its application has filtered into popular culture studies, especially relating to fandom (and, in many powerful cases, continuing to foreground those with marginalised voices). 'Aca-fans', pop culture devotees operating in a scholarly context, 'have been the object of much theoretical debate' by influential figures such as Jenkins (2007) and Hills (2002), 'regarding both their positioning towards [...] fan communities and their scientific legitimacy' (Cristofari and Guitton, 2017, p. 714). They typify a conflicted tension between objective scholarly observation and fervent fan participation: can academics realistically detach themselves from texts into which they invest so much to analyse them impartially, and should they even hope to do so? Responding to this, autoethnographic aca-fandom embraces the notion that 'personal experience cannot be [...] definitively separated from social and relational contexts' (Manning and Adams, 2015, p. 190). Authors conducting autoethnographic studies of their subjective fandoms 'develop narrative accounts of what it means to take up these subject positions and use them to create a sense of self as a lived experience' (Evans and Stasi, 2014, p. 15), combining 'thick description' of themselves and the popular cultural text(s) that shaped them with relevant theoretical materials (Manning and Adams, 2015, p. 193). Evans and Stasi paraphrase Hills' claim that fan-driven autoethnography 'avoid[s] common-sense notions through continuous self-reflexive questioning; [does] not use theory to disguise personal attachments; challenge[s] academic power and/or convention; and treat[s] the self and others identically' (Evans and Stasi, 2014, p. 15). In so doing, it has 'the potential to avoid a position of the single text and [...] instead respond to the fandom's intertextuality' (ibid). Several excellent aca-fan autoethnographies that have informed this chapter include Monaco's examination of memory work's worth to the method (2010); Cuellar's reflection on the links between developing sexuality and para-social relationships with celebrities (2015); Herrmann's study of the connections between selfhood and his popular musical passions (2013); and Greenfield's measured overview of how his love of hip hop might allow for nuanced pedagogical discourse around topics of race and racialisation (2007).

There is controversy surrounding autoethnography, with some scholars maintaining that they can 'recognise their own status as members of a community but still observe the community, and not themselves' (Cristofari and Guitton, 2017, p. 718). Debates persist about whether the self-reflexivity deployed to 'interrogate sociocultural forces and discursive practices that inform personal experience and the research process' is an adequate replacement for the 'objectivity' and 'researcher neutrality' of 'traditional social scientific studies' (Manning and Adams, 2015, p. 190), not to mention fundamental ontological contentions about how we might define, and distinguish between, 'selfhood', 'subjectivity', and 'narrative'. Despite this, and considering the pertinence of my own experiences as a fan of *Diane* to the broader concerns of this chapter, I remain convinced that the method is hugely beneficial for the discipline of aca-fandom and acutely potent for the purposes of this project. Manning and Adams list five strengths of autoethnography that have contributed to my belief in its appropriateness, including

the ability for researchers to 1) use personal experience to write alongside popular culture theories and texts, especially to show how personal
experiences resemble or are informed by popular culture; 2) use personal
experience to criticize, write against, and talk back to popular culture
texts; [...] 3) describe how they personally act as audience members; [...]
4) describe the processes that contribute to the production of popular
culture texts; and 5) create accessible research texts that can be understood by a variety of audiences.

2015, p. 199–200

Each of these points (excepting, perhaps, the second) can be related to my
reflections here; as such, I will now progress to the 'thick description' of the
events and repercussions of my *Diane* fandom.

During the first UK lockdown, I struggled – as so many did – with the psychological and emotional pressures of being stuck indoors, facing isolation from
and concern for relatives and friends, confusion and anger from disenchanted
students, and the disappointment of a long-postponed wedding, alongside
longstanding underlying mental health concerns. I am under no illusions
about my privileged position here: these are, no question, minor obstacles to
have faced at a time when so many have lost those close to them. Nonetheless,
and uncomfortable though it is to spotlight so publicly, the impact on my
mental health was substantial, and I consequently retreated from academic
research. Intellectual work seemed difficult, trivial. I escaped instead into pop
culture, leaning particularly on my love of *Twin Peaks* and the participatory
discourses of its passionate fan community. I re-binged the entire third season
in two days, numbing my mind to the suffocating reality by diving into the
ocean of online fan conjecture and lore surrounding the show. This sufficed
as a temporary distraction, but it exacerbated two problems: I was still avoiding work, and I was not alleviating my feelings of isolation and disconnected-
ness. Eventually, seeking more 'human' contact than that found on television,
social media, and forum threads, I began digging through the vast quantity
of podcasts about *Twin Peaks* to locate one that appealed. This was done on
something of a whim. While I had dipped into podcasts on various topics spo-
radically in the past, listening over an extended period had never previously
appealed to me. I hesitantly tried out a handful, switching some off halfway
through their first episode and giving others the benefit of three or four before
dropping out. Ready to move onto other pursuits, intuiting podcasts were
simply not what I needed, I decided to try one more: *Diane*. Its first episode,
featuring Bob, Adam and Rosie analysing the pilot of *Twin Peaks*, grabbed me
instantaneously. I listened during that day's morning run, jogging through the

nature reserve near my home in the middle of a spring heatwave, and the hosts
had me transfixed within the first ten minutes. I devoured its episodes over
the next week, hastily consuming all one hundred-plus hours and relistening
immediately. I clung onto this podcast more than any other fan-text; here, in
the 'company' of these intelligent individuals with whom I shared so many
interests, was the intimate connection lacking elsewhere. The conversations
of Adam, Rosie, Bob, and Mark (who debuted in the second episode) were my
anchor in a bleak and challenging period, with my *Diane* fandom growing to
practically usurp my love for the television series that had inspired it. I note,
though, that unlike the other texts I turned to – *Twin Peaks* itself, alongside
many films, comics, videogames, music, etc. – *Diane* did not serve as a mere
distraction from my situation. Instead, its presenters and their insights were
stimulating and motivating. Listening intently, clichéd though it seems, I felt
genuinely refreshed. Ideas for teaching and research quickly started to perco-
late, breaching the disruption that lockdown pressures had created. I became
fascinated by the reasons why *this* podcast had resonated with me in such a
deep and productive way.

A 'para-social relationship', as coined by Horton and Wohl, is 'intimacy at
a distance'; an intense connection with individuals we do not actually 'know'
(1956). This 'illusion of [a] face-to-face relationship' promises 'pervasiveness
and closeness' but 'is inevitably one-sided' (1956, p. 216–217). Audiences come to

> 'know' such a persona in somewhat the same way they know their cho-
> sen friends. [...] The persona offers, above all, a continuing relationship.
> [Their] appearance is a regular and dependable event, to be counted
> on, planned for, and integrated into the routines of daily life. [In] time,
> the devotee – the 'fan' – comes to believe that [they 'know'] the persona
> more intimately and profoundly than others do.
> ibid

Theorisation of the para-social has inevitably centred on the issue of how 'real'
or 'illusionary' this connection is (cf. Turner, 2004, p. 92–93), but for the purposes of this chapter I am more interested in the reasons *why* fans develop
such intimate relationships with people that they have never met and the
impact that these can have.[1] Horton and Wohl demonise the phenomenon,

---

1 I am aware of a possible contradiction here involved in interviewing the individuals with
   whom I shared a para-social relationship for a project about the very 'illusionary' nature of
   that relationship. Once the hosts of *Diane* became aware of my existence and agreed to talk
   to me about their podcast, we had of course immediately established a connection that was

operating within the early media studies milieu that scorned a perceived docile passivity in fandom, but later scholars identify more positive effects of contemporary para-social dynamics. Podcasts have been analysed within this context, including in articles by Zuraikat (2020), McGregor (2019) and Savit (2020). The latter, writing about the *Friends* (1994–2004) podcast *Best of Friends* (2015-present), notes that as episodic television 'podcasts grow in popularity, they develop fandoms of their own [and become] fan objects, turning the hosts into subcultural celebrities within the larger fandom' (Savit, 2020). The potent relationship we foster with podcast hosts stems from the medium's effortless penetration into our everyday lives, as we have

> our favourite podcasts in our headphones while we complete daily tasks. [...] Earbuds transmit [hosts'] voices inside [our] head[s] – they roost there, rubbing shoulders with [our] own thoughts. No wonder [we] feel as if [we] know them; that the sound of their voices comes to fire precisely the same neurons, arouse the same feelings, that the voices of [our] closest friends do.
>
> MCGREGOR, 2019, p. 383

Confined to the house, leaving only to go for a run or to walk my dogs (headphones notably in for both), the effect of this was magnified; my 'daily tasks' were completed without the comforting 'voices of [my] closest friends' and family, replaced by those of four individuals at the opposite side of the country.

Zuraikat argues that the 'potentially consistent and repetitive nature' of para-social relationships is 'one of [their] main appeals', so the fact that 'the consumption of a new podcast episode can become part of the listener's daily routine [means that] "interaction" with the [host] becomes integrated into the listener's life to the extent that listening becomes almost a habit' (Zuraikat, 2020, p. 44). The medium's para-sociality becomes a disruptive force, with these 'interactions' penetrating the tedium of everyday life – particularly potent during such a challenging and socially isolating period as lockdown. The serialisation of episodic television podcasts exemplifies this, with growing recognition of the hosts' tastes and vocal tics, intrigue about the progress

---

no longer one-sided and mediated; I had, to paraphrase an anthropological phrase frequently deployed by Rosie on *Diane*, 'gone native'. However, the autoethnographic segments of this chapter refer to a period prior to the interview taking place, while the interview data provides supplementary (rather than foundational) material specifically about the podcast itself. As such, its contents serve a function separate from the analysis of my intimate para-social relationship with Adam, Bob, and Rosie.

of their unfolding theories, and the recurrence of running jokes cultivating audience familiarity. The title of this chapter contains three such examples from *Diane*, evocative for any repeat listener, whose (re)appearances offered me moments of stability amidst the uncertainty of the first lockdown. The first of these, 'pain and suffering', comprises the show's sign-off, a catchphrase inspired by *Twin Peaks: Fire Walk With Me* that concludes each episode. It is, however, an accidental misquote (the original line being 'pain and sorrow'), a mistake amusingly acknowledged by the hosts several episodes into the podcast. The self-deprecating and humorous embarrassment of this all-too-late realisation, coupled with the continuing employment of the erroneous version for future episodes, becomes a frequent in-joke shared between the presenters and their audience.

Para-social relationships are amplified by the 'super-fan' status often afforded to podcast hosts. Savit asserts that episodic television podcasts are examples of 'fan labour', 'a form of labour situated directly within the realm of leisure [that is] distributed and shared among an online fan community entirely for free' (Savit, 2020). *Diane* is no exception, educating, entertaining, and expanding listeners' participation in a manner that enhances fans' experiences of the urtext that is *Twin Peaks*. During our interview, Adam conceded that 'quite a lot of work' goes into podcasting, but he and Rosie were self-deprecating when discussing the amount of research they do for each episode: 'it doesn't take that long', says Rosie; 'a few hours a week', suggests Adam (personal interview, 2021). 'A few hours' of weekly 'fan labour' is, nevertheless, a hefty time investment, and a glance at the lengthy show notes made available to Patreon subscribers is testament to this. Add in Rosie's technical role as the editor of the episodes (assisted by her partner and *Diane*'s proverbial 'fifth Beatle' Soundwave Dave, described as the show's 'structuring absence' [Rosie, personal interview, 2021]) and Adam's upkeep of their Twitter presence, and the level of effort becomes substantial. Considerable labour undoubtedly went into fashioning a professional and systematic format for the podcast during its early days, especially once a listenership was established:

ADAM: As soon as people started to take notice, I think that was part of where it suddenly became less of just chatting with some beer on Tuesday and suddenly started to gel a little bit more as a thing which we wanted to do well I suppose. [...]

BOB: It took us a while to work out whether we would have four voices or three, whether that meant that one of me or Mark would rotate in and out. I think we established that as we were recording the first one which didn't feel right. [...] Then it basically was like, 'OK, well hang on. We can have a bit of a structure to this', and there was a bit of rotation to it. [...] Once we started recording, [...] I would always listen very intently to what Mark was saying and be like, 'right, the third voice here has to work in a certain way. I can't do it like Mark does'.

personal interview, 2021

One result of this 'fan labour' is the development of an (unintended) hierarchy within the para-social podcaster/audience dynamic. By broadcasting their expertise, podcasters like Team *Diane* amass a subcultural fanbase of their own, as listeners 'project any knowledge they may have of the series onto [the] hosts, rendering themselves casual viewers who are less informed than [them], regardless of whether this is actually true' (Savit, 2020). Their *Twin Peaks* perspectives come to carry an air of greater validity than those of less objectified or laborious fans, who in turn request supplementary authoritative assessments about the series from the presenters. This can be a mutually beneficial relationship, as Bob attests: 'I didn't want to be a *Twin Peaks* super-fan but now that I am one, I find that it is a big part of my identity and I'm quite attached to it and it's quite valuable' (personal interview, 2021). The hosts of *Diane* become objects of fandom in much the same way as *Twin Peaks*, or its creators David Lynch and Mark Frost; I certainly consider myself a *Diane* fan.

Of course, these observations could describe many pop culture podcasts, depending on the listener's tastes and needs, and this chapter is concerned with why *Diane* resonates so intimately with *me* where others did/do not. While I do appreciate other podcasts, I would not deem myself a habitual listener and do not have a fervent connection to any of them. Yet I hang on *every* word of *Diane*, and have located comparable virtues in its hosts' adjacent podcasts. Zuraikat posits that 'the diversity of podcasts and their hosts allows for listeners to determine to an extent what role the host will play for them, [...] depending upon what emotional release they may be seeking' (Zuraikat, 2020, p. 45). *Diane* offered the psychological salve that I required during that specific period, and there are several components of the show's makeup that I can pinpoint as appealing directly to me. One of those, undoubtedly, is the camaraderie of its hosts, something that both McGregor and Savit stress as crucial for generating a connection with audiences. Rosie quotes Soundwave Dave's assessment that they are 'all sort of slightly on wedding behaviour' on the podcast: 'you're being yourself; you're showing up as yourself, and you're showing up in a mode actually that's quite sincere but a bit well-behaved' (personal interview, 2021). This constrained 'wedding behaviour' accentuates the professionalism of the presenters' 'fan labour', but it also vitally endows their conversations with an aura of authenticity. 'Authenticity', of course, is a complex and loaded idea that has been heavily debated in fields such as cultural studies and popular music studies, preoccupying scholars such as Goffman ([1959] 2009), Moore (2002), Trilling (1972), Ferrara (1998), and Guignon (2004). Authenticity is equated with ideas of 'sincerity', 'honesty', 'truth', the unfiltered 'self': for us to perceive someone as authentic, we must believe that we are seeing the 'real' them, a 'realness' illustrated through unguarded and unambiguous behaviour. An authentic individual will 'express [their] inner traits in [their] actions in the external world'; they will 'actually be what [they] are in [their] ways of being present in [their] relationships, careers, and practical activities' (Guignon, 2004, p. 6). Ferrara's interpretation of the 'authentic' as 'being somehow connected with, and expressive of, the core of the actor's personality' (1998, p. 5) is perhaps the most 'straightforward' definition for the purposes of this chapter, although it is crucial to emphasise that each of these scholars highlights the performative and socially constructed nature of the concept. We regard some characteristics (vocal, bodily, costumed, political, etc.) as more authentic than others (these vary depending on context), and we make distinctions between 'truthful' and 'fake' individuals on this basis. Consequently, those with a public presence are often seen to 'act up' these tropes, ironically 'performing' the 'real' person that their audience desires. According to Moore, '"authenticity" is a matter of interpretation that is made and fought for from within a cultural and, thus, historicised position. It is ascribed, not inscribed. The question of whether a performance is authentic, then, depends on who "we" are' (Moore, 2002, p. 210). Meserko's (2015) investigation of 'authentic' podcasters both foregrounds some of the contradictions inherent in the notion of constructing an 'expression of the self' and convincingly defends the legitimacy of the term. He claims that the performance of authenticity 'tells us much about what attributes we value in others', as it 'is at once an exclusively inward-looking meditative exercise, but it is also one that becomes observable and manifest through human actions. [It is] both something that individuals grasp on their own through introspection and also something that is judged socially. [It] is therefore inwardly evoked and outwardly observed' (Meserko, 2015, p. 798). While I use the term relatively lightly here, recognising its contentiousness, I identify an authenticity in the conversations of Rosie, Mark, Bob, and Adam. This authenticity, most evident in their relaxed and unforced affability, aided in the foundation of my intimate para-social relationship with them.

This organic quality is attributable to both their real-world closeness (Mark, Rosie and Adam are siblings, and Bob is a close friend) and social conscientiousness, with Bob reflecting on the 'the family vibe' of his co-hosts and the significance of having 'a woman's voice as the central voice' given the dominance of male perspectives in cult fan communities (personal interview, 2021). The collective vibe was clearly important when putting the team together: during our interview, each interviewee was full of praise for the contributions of their co-presenters, recognising their academic talents but primarily foregrounding the ways their distinct but complementary personality tropes make the podcast successful. Bob says he is 'help[ed] immensely' by Adam's grounded presence and philosophical leanings and builds many of his thoughts on Rosie's ability to balance her academic knowledge with her understanding of the 'emotional truths' of *Twin Peaks* (ibid). Mark is described as 'so funny' while 'quietly com[ing] up with the best ideas. [...] He has got a wonderfully creative brain and he has a wonderful way of spotting poetry in things' (Rosie and Adam, personal interview, 2021). Both Adam and Rosie emphasise that Bob, in 'bringing the fun', is 'a necessary' counterbalance to the relationship of the three siblings (ibid). The podcast was founded firstly as a forum for these close-knit individuals to 'make our friendships and personal relationships strong and consistent and productive' (Bob, personal interview, 2021), and that purpose is borne out in compulsively listenable conviviality. This amicability renders the tangents and in-jokes that emerge from their chats remarkably inclusive and genuine. The references to 'The Wild Ride' and 'uterus trumpets' in this chapter's title exemplify this. The former, an invention of Mark, is especially indicative of the cordiality and thoughtfulness of the four hosts. It alludes to a much-derided sequence of *Twin Peaks*' second season during which the increasingly marginal character James Hurley travels to a nearby town, meets an older woman named Evelyn Marsh and becomes inexplicably wrapped up in a clichéd and infuriatingly drawn-out film noir plot. Dubbing this storyline (which stretches over five or six episodes but feels much longer) 'The Wild Ride' granted an element of levity to the overview of a run of narratively dry episodes, presenting an entertaining platform from which to analyse parts of the text that otherwise may have been of less interest to listening *Twin Peaks* fans. In contrast, 'uterus trumpet' was borne out of the widely lauded 'Part 8' of Season 3, with Adam grasping for a suitable name to express the strangeness of a device in the episode. Rather than making a dreary storyline more enjoyable, the 'uterus trumpet' was instead a humorous but apt instance of the hosts' evocation of the confusion and excitement that their audience was similarly feeling during the airing of *Twin Peaks*' highly experimental third season in 2017. The approachability implicit in these in-jokes (other examples of which include 'sexy velociraptors', 'hot Dougie love' and the 'bunnymoth'), coupled with my rapt attention over an extended period, contributed to the para-social intimacy of my listenership: I had desired 'human' contact, and instinctively began to engage in the process of what Zuraikat dubs 'mindreading', 'infer[ring] the mental states [of and developing] intuitive feelings and assumptions about' these individuals despite having no 'actual' links to them (Zuraikat, 2020, p. 42–43).

This para-social 'mindreading', however, is a trend that resonates with many listeners of many different podcasts. Plenty of podcasts feature likeable presenters with obvious chemistry. What uniquely enabled *Diane* to disrupt my lockdown malaise, as an aca-fan, was the lucidity with which I found they wielded complex critical concepts, applying them to their text of choice in an intellectual mode that importantly did not abandon the wonderment and sensuality so vital to fan communities. When asked to define the 'USP' of *Diane*, all interviewees extolled its 'constrained informality' (Adam, personal interview, 2021). The podcast is not a 'completely casual' opportunity for a few close acquaintances to simply 'shoot the breeze' about a television show (Rosie, personal interview, 2021). Instead, while there is a 'conversational free flowing element', it remains 'chained to that central text [and therefore gives] us some degree of structure' (Adam, personal interview, 2021). The scholarly capabilities exhibited by the hosts can be attributed to their varying backgrounds in sociocultural criticism: Rosie is a Doctor of Social Anthropology with extensive experience of academic lecturing and research, and Bob, Adam and Mark are founders of the influential comics blog/fanzine *Mindless Ones* and contributors to other publications. The 'fan labour' of these four individuals transcends the typical expectations of television podcasting, as their detailed research has seen them integrate a wealth of theoretical materials from fields as diverse as philosophy, anthropology, sociology, cultural studies, theosophy, film studies, and beyond without ever drifting into inaccessible pretension. That they pair these perspectives with examples from fairy tales, comics, Fortean lore, videogames, and popular music absolutely aligns with my 'tastes', and I confess that this has had some undeniable influence on my admiration for *Diane*. Really, though, this eclectic mix functions so effectively because of the balanced conversations of its presenters, with the layout of the podcast enabling them to meld their measured scholarly inquisitiveness organically and skilfully with their passion for *Twin Peaks*. This was, according to Adam, an initial motivation for the podcast, as they had 'an interest in *Twin Peaks* as a text amongst texts, [and wanted to] bring a more consistent level of critical analysis to it but [...] do it in a fun way. I was certain that we would not be dry. [We wanted] accessibility, but [also] critical analysis and diversity of thought' (personal interview, 2021). As academically articulate fans that love the show, the exchanges are neither intellectually exclusionary (as is almost inevitably the case with scholastic discourse) nor naively celebratory (as with many explicitly 'fannish' texts). When Rosie introduces the works of Claude Lévi-Strauss, Marina Warner and Angela Carter, Adam applies Jacques Lacan,

Mark Fisher and Slavoj Žižek, Mark weaves intricately poetic interpretations of soundscapes and abstract imagery, or Bob 'hits the Foucault button', it is not isolatingly highfaluting. It is enlightening, articulate, fascinating – disruptive in the most potent and productive way.

Reinhard and Olson's educational aca-fandom podcast *The Pop Culture Lens* (2014-present) aims to 'keep the tone conversational yet informational, [bringing a] scholarly conversation about media and pop cultural texts to people other than academics but in a way that does not "dumb [it] down"' (Reinhard and Olson, 2017). While I confess to having never listened to *The Pop Culture Lens*, I believe that *Diane*'s approach fulfils these criteria. This quote from Bob encapsulates the 'conversational yet informational [...] tone' of the podcast:

> The bits that are the most fun and I think might be most valuable to the listeners is when the three of us or when Mark and the guys are conversating, just when we're picking up on each other's points and asking each other to tease them out and unpack them a little bit. The bits that we haven't rehearsed and that are just about us chatting, that often throws up a lot of the best stuff that we say.
>
> Bob, personal interview, 2021

Lest anyone think that this has only been exhibited in relation to a single televisual text, thus limiting its potential generalisability, I note that the hosts' auxiliary podcast projects, in addition to indulging further passions of mine, continue to demonstrate their skill in analysing pop cultural formats confidently and accessibly in relation to numerous critical contexts. Rosie has been especially prolific in this respect, co-founding a variety of podcasts about diverse topics and consistently illustrating her nuanced combination of academic and fannish interests. For the now-concluded *getObject* (2020), she (with co-host Paul Walker-Emig) used anthropological, literary, and theological ideas to examine videogames, in each episode aiming to 'find the spirit' of a particular in-game object, and the ambitious and compelling *The Shadow Trap* (2017-present), co-presented by Bob, applies comparable strategies to monsters from cinematic and mythical histories. Indulging their creative sides, Adam and Rosie have experimented with innovative scenarios for tabletop RPGs on the *Gelatinous Cube* podcast (2021-present) and, with Bob again onboard, have widened their scope with *Eleven Past Midnight* (2020-present), which employs 'crimes' in films, videogames and comics as routes into contextual and aesthetic analyses of their case studies. However, there is audibly less pressure involved in the production of these other podcasts, with Bob revealing that *Diane*'s prominence in the *Twin Peaks* community leads to enlarged audience (and self-) expectations about its quality, so their style is overall weighted more toward good-humoured camaraderie than intensive academic research (Bob, personal interview, 2021). *Diane* remains the presenters' main focus, with Bob insisting that 'we are better when we're all together, I think. I don't think any of the side projects, as valuable as they are [to] us as individuals and to the people who listen, [...] none of them have clicked in the same way' (ibid). Though I must admit that I – a media and cultural studies lecturer by profession – am probably not best-placed to judge the universality of these podcasts given my foreknowledge of the concepts therein, I am nonetheless always looking for novel ways to negotiate the ambiguous boundaries between intellectualised and fan-driven popular cultural dialogues in my teaching. Perhaps, in hindsight, I should simply feel grateful that such an unpleasant experience brought me to *Diane*, given it provided such pleasure and inspiration as I languished in the house in the breaks between delivering lectures on Zoom.

As mentioned, a major consequence of the early days of lockdown disruption was the collapse of my motivation to do research. As *Diane*'s aca-fandom became part of my daily routine, however, I found myself increasingly brimming with ideas. I crucially do not regard the podcast as one I consume passively, setting it apart from more escapist pursuits that I had sought initially, and the intent with which I absorbed it impacted heavily on my subsequent return to research and writing. It is no coincidence that, in just a few weeks after discovering *Diane*, I wrote abstracts for two *Twin Peaks*-related conference papers, sketched the outline for a new module about Popular Culture & Identity at my university, and of course came up with this very chapter. Each of these is informed by *Diane*, directly or indirectly; the elation accompanying this fruitful burst stands in sharp contrast with the despondency of the stagnant stasis that had preceded it. On my second listen-through, with the seeds of these projects planted, I obsessively took page after page of relevant notes for inspiration, building theoretical frameworks from ideas that sprouted from the hosts' musings. An episode that proved acutely important was 2017's '*Twin Peaks: The Return* – Closing Thoughts'. An hour-long conclusion to the most frenetic period of *Diane*'s existence (*Twin Peaks: Season 3*'s weekly broadcast schedule), it is primarily comprised of Adam and Bob's ruminations on the series' ergodic and fractal nature. I expanded on these exact themes in a paper for 2021's 'It is in our house now: *Twin Peaks: The Return* first online conference', my argument for which would not have existed if not for *Diane*. Admittedly, the ease with which I was able to translate their dialogue into academic work is partially attributable to this being one of the most 'formal' conversations on *Diane* (being, as it is, distinct from the more typical episode-by-episode design), somewhat uncharacteristically isolating theory from fan enthusiasm, and it is therefore not the best exemplar of the hosts' ability to balance the scholarly and the approachable. However, when they revisited analogous topics during their 2019–2021 Season 3 're-watch', they capably and humorously integrated these complex over-arching ideas, particularly in their overviews of 'Part 4' and 'Part 5' (titled 'In Detail – Brings Back Some Memories' and 'In Detail – Case Files' respectively). In the latter, Adam's frequent amused interjections about the excesses and superfluity of the episode are simultaneously funny and deceptively perceptive, analysing the series in terms under-considered in other *Twin Peaks*-adjacent fan texts.

I end with an evaluation of the disruptive and productive influence that *Diane* had on my work. Leading fan studies scholar Booth endorses freeing teaching and research in popular culture from institutional restrictions, fostering aca-fandom that is not trapped within privileged educational structures but which instead actively 'gets involved' with fan communities and thus 'benefit[s] from more fandom enthusiasm' (Booth, 2015). He regards fandom as 'the classroom of the future' because it 'encourage[s] critical thinking and deep discussion in a way that the neoliberal university [seems] increasingly averse to. [...] It is our role as educators to listen to fandom; and it is our responsibility as fans to promote critical fandom in all our work' (ibid). From my experience, *Diane* presents a perfect encapsulation of this 'critical fandom', exemplified in the space that its hosts locate between theoretical/philosophical and fannish discursive practices. From their objectified position of 'super-fans', the presenters encourage their listeners to 'talk back' in both populist *and* academic spaces (answering questions on the podcast, responding to tweets/emails, participating in conference panels, etc.) while remaining slightly withdrawn from the fandom at large in order that their ideas can flourish uncontaminated. As Adam stresses,

> It's actually really quite a warm community and it is possible for us to be anonymous in it as well. [...] I'm conscious of the place we fill because I see our impact, [...] but at the same time, [...] I think maybe that distance is, in a way, one of the strengths of the podcast because my identity isn't maybe wrapped up in it in the way that some people's are.
>
> Adam, personal interview, 2021

This aptitude for interacting with fans while preserving a 'distance' is precisely the type of balance that is crucial to aca-fandom as a discipline, with the hosts of *Diane* maintaining a degree of objectivity within the *Twin Peaks* community despite their 'super-fan' status. The supplementary content that Rosie, Bob, and Adam provide for their supporters on Patreon demonstrates these fan engagement techniques acutely as well as granting insight into the diverse component parts that come together in the 'critical fandom' of 'parent' podcast *Diane*. *Rosie Plays …*, a set of videogame playthroughs (2017-present), are less formal than *Diane* but increase its communicative potential. As she explains, 'there's five or six people who chat away in the comments on the videogame playthroughs [and] that's the *Diane* listenership as far as I'm concerned. […] They're the only people I have ongoing interaction with' (Rosie, personal interview, 2021). Counterbalancing the relaxed atmosphere of these playthroughs, both Rosie and Adam have produced audio essays for their subscribers (the former's *The Moral of the Story* [2017–2019] and the latter's *Twin Peaks Tarot* [2018], *A Blue Velvet Minute* [2019-present], and other projects), highlighting their intellectual strengths in a more explicitly 'writerly' format. Bob's contributions are two dense video essay series: *The Invisible Podcast* (2018-present) and *The Bookhouse Bloke* (2021-present). The former is an issue-by-issue dive into the conspiracy lore of Grant Morrison's 1990s comic *The Invisibles* (1994–2000), while the latter takes the same thorough approach to every *Twin Peaks* tie-in novel. His analysis in both is forensic and enthralling, as with *The Moral of the Story*, and his performance is mesmerisingly unpredictable and impulsive. Although less immediately accessible than *Diane*, and perhaps with smaller appeal, both are still extraordinarily extreme examples of 'fan labour'. As Bob describes it, the preparation for these endeavours is 'difficult and obsessive', but their 'rhizomatic lines of flight' allow his 'mind to unfurl' (Bob, personal interview, 2021). In many ways, Bob's 'rhizomatic' and 'unfurling' monologues are reminiscent of *actual* YouTube conspiracy theory videos, with the host sitting in a room chatting directly to his webcam for anywhere between one and four hours at a time. Witnessing the two types of Patreon material in isolation – the chilled-out playthroughs contrasting with the more intense scholarly audio/video essays – illuminates the place between these poles that the more publicly available *Diane* intricately occupies.

In conclusion, while *Diane*'s hosts are not working academics (Rosie's PhD research and previous role as a lecturer have, of course, given her significant insights into scholarly practice), they openly engage in both the detached interactivity and diversity of investigative method that should be standard for lecturers and researchers in popular culture. To return to Booth,

> Fandom may be one of the only places where one is encouraged to think critically, to write, to discuss deeply, and to make thoughtful and critical judgments about hegemonic culture. […] Scholars, educators, and fans [must] support, nurture, and maintain these critical fandoms against

[an] encroaching turn to neoliberal education and corporate-focused fandom.

BOOTH, 2015

Diane does not force a singular fan agenda on listeners, nor is there a refusal to scrutinise a line of enquiry due to subjective biases. Rather, the presenters' independence allows them to deliver critical evaluations divorced from a hyper-corporatised contemporary pop culture that favours certain fan voices and suppresses others (a corporatisation that has impacted on the *Twin Peaks* fan community since the 2017 release of Season 3, with production company CBS flexing its intellectual property muscles and cancelling fan-organised festivals [Dom, 2019; @twinpeaksukfest, 2020]). As Rosie asserts, 'I think of *Diane* as quite a closed sphere in a way and it benefits from that, the fact that we can all chat with each other and come up with these very specific ways of talking about media that makes sense in our group of friends and family' (Rosie, personal interview, 2021). Their objective receptivity enables them to discuss the show, its creators, and its context analytically, often unpacking issues examined predominantly within university spaces in easily graspable terms that emphasise their love for the series. I believe that we can see Booth's 'critical fandom' crystallised in this, and that those of us invested in studies of popular culture can learn from and draw on such a methodological and pedagogical style both inside and outside the classroom.

When I pressed play on the first episode of *Diane* I was hoping for intimacy, companionship and comfort, and I was not disappointed. I had not anticipated, however, that the podcast would have such a profound influence on my scholarly output. My *Diane* fandom is personal and complex, and my goal in writing this autoethnography has been to signal how the emotional and practical implications of this connection, aligned with the podcasting techniques of Adam, Bob, Rosie, and Mark, could perhaps be more widely applied within aca-fandom. Nevertheless, even if I have overestimated its universality, the impact of this para-social relationship on my own psychological wellbeing and academic practice during a period of hardship, distress and disruption has absolutely merited such a reflection.

References

Bauman, Z. (2003) *Liquid Love*. Cambridge: Polity Press.
Baym, N.K. (2010) *Personal connections in the digital age*. Cambridge: Polity Press.
Beck, U., and Beck-Gernsheim, E. (2002) *Individualization*. London: Sage.

Berardi, F. (2011) *After the future*. Chico: AK Press.

Booth, P.J. (2015) 'Fandom: The classroom of the future', in A. Kustritz (ed.) 'European fans and European fan objects: Localization and translation' (special issue), *Transformative Works and Cultures*, Vol. 19. DOI: https://doi.org/10.3983/twc.2015 .0650.

Cristofari, C., and Guitton, M.J. (2017) 'Aca-fans and fan communities: An operative framework', *Journal of Consumer Culture*, Vol. 17(3), pp. 713–731.

Cuellar, M. (2015) 'The makings of a boyfriend: Doing sexuality through parasocial relationships', *The Popular Culture Studies Journal*, Vol. 3(1/2), pp. 270–298.

Dom, P. (2019) 'Fan-run *Twin Peaks* festival in Washington State discontinued after 26-year run', *Welcome To Twin Peaks*. Available at: https://welcometotwinpeaks.com /news/twin-peaks-festival-discontinued/ (Accessed 23 July 2021).

Evans, A., and Stasi, M. (2014) 'Desperately seeking methods: New directions in fan studies research', *Participations: Journal of Audience and Reception Studies*, Vol. 11(2), pp. 4–23.

Ferrara, A. (1998) *Reflective authenticity: Rethinking the project of modernity*. London: Routledge.

Giddens, A. (1991) *Modernity and self-identity: Self and society in the late modern age*. Cambridge: Polity Press.

Goffman, E. ([1959] 2009) 'The presentation of self', in D. Brisset, and C. Edgley (eds.) *Life as theater: A dramaturgical sourcebook*. New Brunswick: Transaction Publishers, pp. 129–141.

Greenfield, D. (2007) 'What's the deal with the white middle aged guy teaching hip hop? Lessons in popular culture, positionality and pedagogy', *Pedagogy, culture and society*, Vol. 15(2), pp. 229–243.

Guignon, C. (2004), *On being authentic*. London: Routledge.

Herrmann, A.F. (2013) 'Daniel Amos and me: The power of pop culture and autoethnography', *The Popular Culture Studies Journal*, Vol. 1(1/2), pp. 6–17.

Hills, M. (2002) *Fan cultures*. London: Routledge.

Horton, D., and Wohl, R. (1956) 'Mass communication and para-social interaction: Observations on intimacy at a distance', *Psychiatry: Interpersonal and Biological Processes*, 16(3), pp. 215–229.

Jamieson, L. (2013) 'Personal relationships, intimacy and the self in a mediated and global digital age', in K. Orton-Johnson, and N. Prior (eds.) *Digital Sociology*. London: Palgrave Macmillan, pp. 13–33.

Jenkins, H. (2007) 'Transmedia storytelling 101', *Confessions of an aca-fan*. Available at:http://henryjenkins.org/blog/2007/03/transmedia_storytelling_101.html (Accessed 20 December 2020).

Jurgenson, N. (2012) 'The IRL fetish', *The New Inquiry*. Available at: http://thenewinqu iry.com/essays/the-irl-fetish/ (Accessed 17 June 2021).

Manning, J., and Adams, T.E. (2015) 'Popular culture studies and autoethnography: An essay on method', *The Popular Culture Studies Journal*, Vol. 3(1/2), pp. 187–222.

McGregor, H. (2019) 'Yer a reader, Harry: *HP* Reread Podcasts as digital reading communities', *Participations: Journal of Audience and Reception Studies*, Vol. 16(1), pp. 366–389.

Meserko, V.M. (2015) 'The pursuit of authenticity on Marc Maron's *WTF* podcast', *Continuum*, Vol. 29(6), pp. 796–810.

Monaco, J. (2010) 'Memory work, autoethnography, and the construction of a fan-ethnography', *Participations: Journal of Audience and Reception Studies*, Vol. 7(1), pp. 102–142.

Moore, A. (2002) 'Authenticity as authentication', *Popular Music*, Vol. 21(2), pp. 209–223.

Morrison, G. (1994–2000) *The Invisibles* (New York: DC Vertigo).

Reinhard, C.D., and Olson, C.J. (2017), 'Podcasts for public intellectualism: *The Pop Culture Lens* and public discourse', *Playing, with research*. Available at: https://play ingwithresearch.com/2018/11/15/podcasts-for-public-intellectualism-the-pop-cult ure-lens-and-public-discourse/ (Accessed 4 August 2022).

Savit, L. (2020) 'Examining the fan labour of episodic TV podcast hosts', *Transformative Works and Cultures*, Vol. 34. DOI: https://doi.org/10.3983/twc.2020.1721.

Trilling, L. (1972) *Sincerity and authenticity*. Cambridge, Massachusetts: Harvard University Press.

Turner, G. (2004) *Understanding celebrity*. London: Sage.

@twinpeaksukfest (2020) 'An announcement x', 15 May 2020. Available at: https:// twitter.com/TwinPeaksUKFest/status/1261355753769545728?s=20 (Accessed 23 July 2021).

Waugh, M. (2021) '"Make sense of it": Information overload, fan participation and an excess of meaning in *Twin Peaks: Season 3*', from the conference 'It is in our house now: *Twin Peaks: The Return* first online conference' (online: 19 June 2021).

Waugh, M. (2021) 'Personal interview with Adam, Bob and Rosie of *Diane* podcast' (online: 10 April 2021).

Zuraikat, L. (2020) 'The parasocial nature of the podcast', in J.A. Hendricks (ed.) *Radio's Second Century*. New York: Rutgers University Press, pp. 39–52.

Filmography

Friends (1994–2004) Created by Crane, D. and Kauffman, M. [Television Serial] USA: NBC.

Twin Peaks (1990–1991) Created by Frost, M. and Lynch, D. [Television Serial] USA: CBS.

Twin Peaks: Fire Walk With Me (1992) Directed by Lynch, D. [Feature Film] USA: New Line Cinema.

Twin Peaks: Season 3 (2017) Created by Frost, M. and Lynch, D. [Television Serial] USA: Showtime.

Podcasts Cited

Blue Velvet Minute, A (2019-present) [Patreon Subscription Podcast] Available at: https://www.patreon.com/dianepodcast (Accessed 10 May 2020).

Bookhouse Bloke, The (2021-present) [Patreon Subscription Video Series] Available at: https://www.patreon.com/dianepodcast (Accessed 4 August 2022).

Diane (2016-present) [Podcast] Available at: https://diane.libsyn.com (Accessed 2 April 2020).

Eleven Past Midnight (2020-present) [Podcast] Available at: https://diane.libsyn.com /eleven-past-midnight-1-the-siege-of-nakatomi-plaza (Accessed 15 January 2021).

getObject (2020) [Podcast] Available at: https://podcasts.apple.com/gb/podcast/get object/id1496675080 (Accessed 29 April 2021).

Gelatinous Cube (2021-present) [Podcast] Available at: https://gelatinouscube.libsyn .com (Accessed 4 July 2021).

Invisible Podcast, The (2018-present) [Patreon Subscription Video Series] Available at: https://www.patreon.com/dianepodcast (Accessed 10 May 2020).

Moral of the Story, The (2017–2019) [Patreon Subscription Podcast] Available at: https:// www.patreon.com/dianepodcast (Accessed 10 May 2020).

Pop Culture Lens, The (2014-present) [Podcast] Available at: https://playingwithresea rch.com/pop-culture-lens-podcast/ (Accessed 5 February 2021).

Rosie Plays ... (2017-present) [Patreon Subscription Video Series] Available at: https:// www.patreon.com/dianepodcast (Accessed 10 May 2020).

Shadow Trap, The (2017-present) [Podcast] Available at: https://shadowtrap.libsyn. com (Accessed 1 May 2020).

Twin Peaks Tarot (2018) [Patreon Subscription Podcast] Available at: https://www.patr eon.com/dianepodcast (Accessed 10 May 2020).

CHAPTER 13

'Standing in Your Cardigan': Evocative Objects, Ordinary Intensities, and Queer Sociality in the Swiftian Pop Song

James Barker, Richard Elliott and Gareth Longstaff

1 Introduction

Popular music thrives on the articulation and amplification of little, telling details: the cigarette that bears a lipstick's traces, the half-drunk cup of coffee, the scarf you keep because it reminds you of me. These little but crucially important things can be thought of as 'evocative objects' (Bollas, 1987, 2009; Turkle, 2007) that also create and reflect 'ordinary affects' and intensities (Stewart, 2007). Songs articulate things, feelings, and atmospheres by attaching words to very particular forms of motivated affect, creating what one scholar of Greek rebetiko has called 'sonic-lyrical regimes' (Tragaki, 2020, p. 185) and what we might think of also as song worlds. Any established song genre is likely to have its own evocative atmospheres, created by lyrical tendencies, singing styles and the timbre of voices and other instruments. Evocative objects are part of these atmospheres and country music has its favoured objects, as do rebetiko, fado, blues, hip-hop, and aspects of pop. Furthermore, songs themselves become evocative objects, part of the broader atmosphere or climate associated with song forms, genres, artists, the sonic worlds of listeners and their own subjective desires and memories.

In this chapter, we focus on the potential of these disruptive and evocative objects, ordinary intensities, and atmospheres in the work of US music artist Taylor Swift as we seek to identify the ways in which lyrics use objects to intensify and evoke memories, regrets, and desires in the world of the 'Swiftian' pop song. Despite the dominant narrative regarding Swift's move from country to pop, her use of evocative objects and atmospheres and her identification with the ordinariness and universality of human emotion and experience connect her strongly to the genre of country music and its traditional reliance on a kind of imagery that is as important as singing or instrumental style. Our approach takes as given the importance of song lyrics, hearing them as the vital stuff of popular songs and hearing songs as ways of understanding our situatedness in a world of objects, identifications and relations. Furthermore, we suggest that

Swift's lyrics connect evocative objects to an intensity that is felt as both ordinary and uncanny and that it is here that she merges a poignant and intensive level of subjective desire to an intensive form of neoliberal capitalism.

Taylor Swift's *folklore* and *evermore* (Swift 2020a, 2020b) were interpreted by some listeners as queer albums, in part due to the use of different gendered speakers and the fan response to the song 'betty'. Country music is a genre not often associated with LGBTQ+ representation and queer expression, despite the longstanding presence of LGBTQ+ performers and listeners in the genre that scholarship is increasingly recognising (Hubbs, 2014). There is a tension with 'betty' being Swift's first single since 2013 to be promoted within country music radio formats (Reuter, 2020). Yet, through an analysis of 'betty', we will demonstrate the potential for LGBTQ+ listeners' practices of queer reading to rework and recuperate (Sedgwick, 2003, pp. 149–51) the genre of country music to represent their experiences. In this way, the song becomes a particular kind of evocative object as we consider the way this text has a materiality and sociability interlinked with the sociability of its listeners' lives (Ahmed, 2017, p. 17). In this focus on LGBTQ+ listeners within the country music genre, the 'ordinary intensities' described previously take on a particular character and are deployed for a specific purpose. For LGBTQ+ fans of Swift the encounter with these songs evokes a particular kind of emotional intensity. Songs resonate with ordinary experiences of coming out, queer longing and 'unrequited love' (Kircher, 2020), aspects which some journalists and queer scholarship have identified as running through narratives of contemporary LGBTQ+ experience. Drawing on Sara Ahmed's work on the 'circulation' of texts and their role in sustaining feminist and queer 'communities' (Ahmed, 2017, p. 17), we argue that Swift's songs can, and in fact do, circulate among and 'sustain' (Sedgwick, 2003, p. 151) LGBTQ+ listeners. At the same time there is a tension of how these affective intensities are commodified and how the strong attachment Swift's fans have to these songs are monetised as a particularly lucrative asset allied to Swift's other commercial strategies and position as a commodified cultural form.

2   Evocative Objects in the Swiftian Song

Certain themes, experiences and referential strategies emerge in Taylor Swift's songwriting to the extent that they evoke what Dafni Tragaki calls 'sonic-lyrical regimes' (Tragaki, 2020, p. 185). This regime or song world allows us to speak of 'the Swiftian song' with a reasonable level of stability. A representative but not exhaustive list of features of the Swiftian song would include: extensive references to memories and recollections (some nostalgic, some painful); yearning, longing or wishing to change things from the past (often articulated via conditional phrases or terms such as 'should've' or 'what if'); desire for revenge and a sense of songwriting as a form of revenge; reflection on the life course (whether celebratory or rueful); reference to romantic tales and mythology (especially in the early work); a desire to capture moments and the strategies that can be used for doing so (memorising, taking pictures, recalling sounds); mining experiences for moral lessons and shareable wisdom. These themes have waxed and waned over the course of Swift's songwriting career, with some commentators noting a maturity from a songwriter intent on revenge and reaction in earlier work to one showing greater reflection in later albums. The move from revenge to reflection should not be overstated, however; while one could certainly place 2008's 'Picture to Burn' against 2020's 'happiness' in support of the maturity/reflection thesis, it would be necessary to recall the mature reflection in Swift's early 'Tim McGraw' (Swift, 2006) and to recognise the presence of 'early lateness' (Elliott, 2015, pp. 31, 221) that signalled a consistency in the work to come. That consistency can be found in the Swiftian song's repeated invitation to consider rupture and the reflection and learning that comes from it. This is underlined by the commentary Swift has provided for her fans with each album release, whether in the form of traditional liner notes within physical releases or in messages posted on social media. These commentaries have invariably given an account of what Swift has learned since her last set of songs, simultaneously suggesting the layering of experience that attends the life course and identifying fresh concepts around which to build a new collection of songs.

Everyday objects play an important role in creating the lyrical regime of the Swiftian song. Swift has repeatedly referred to objects that recall experiences, evoke memories or stand in for things, people and moments that have passed. This was evident from her debut single 'Tim McGraw' (also the opening song of her first album in 2006), the narrative of which is framed around a series of resonant objects: blue eyes, the Georgia stars, a Chevy truck, a little black dress, a box beneath a bed, an unsent letter, the moon, a lake, faded jeans. Most resonant is the 'favourite song' by country singer Tim McGraw that the song's protagonist hopes will remind a former lover of her. In the chorus, the singer McGraw is conflated with the song he sings so that just thinking of McGraw will act as a reminder of the song and of the dress, the faded jeans and the other memories recalled in the song. It's important, given the marketing of Swift as a country artist at this stage of her career, that the objects listed in 'Tim McGraw' can be easily connected to the US South, to the sonic-lyrical regime of country music and to an assumed class identification for its audience. As Kathleen Stewart observed in the decade preceding Swift's debut,

> In country music, an inhabited, negating space of desire challenges the class codes of ideologically marked objects: Cadillacs versus pickup trucks, diamonds versus rhinestones, champagne in fancy glasses versus beer in the can, people who pay their bills by home computer versus those who get their coffee already ground.
>
> STEWART, 1996, p. 125

While such city/country binaries might well be challenged as the new millennium dawned, and while such adherence to 'country objects' would not be a mainstay of Swift's songwriting, the connections between commodified objects and people would remain a feature of her work. In this way, even as Swift moved away from country music towards pop, the ways in which she continued to use mundane objects in poetic ways arguably helped to connect the Swiftian song to the 'metanarratives of loss and desire' that Aaron Fox (1992, p. 54) identified as central to country music's engagement with the everyday. Fox traced the ways in which 'commodified "objects" become speaking "subjects", and heartbroken "subjects" consume themselves as commodified "objects"' via country's lyrical narratives (1992, p. 53). Nate Sloan builds on Fox's work to argue that Swift, far from being an 'interloper' in country music during the early part of her career, instead 'evinces mastery over the formal language of country, how a song is structured and tells a story on a macro level' (Sloan, 2021, pp. 4–5). Sloan uses the example of Swift's 'Our Song' (2006), to highlight how 'the pedestrian is made holy' in a lyric that find's the couples' special song not in a pre-existing recording (like 'Tim McGraw'), but in the slamming of a screen door, tapping on windows and the sound of 'real slow', late night phone conversations (Sloan 2021, p. 4).

The lyrics of 'Our Song', like those of 'Tim McGraw', can be parsed as a list of everyday objects or experiences: the car radio, 'the slamming screen door', 'tapping on your window', 'the way you laugh', front porch steps, roses, a note on the bed, the napkin and pen on which the images finally move from abstract ideas to lyrics on their way to song. These are evocative objects, understood here not only in the sense deployed by Sherry Turkle's (2007) intervention into material culture studies, but also via the concepts developed by the psychoanalyst Christopher Bollas (1987, 1992, 2009). Bollas (2009) connects the 'evocative object world' to the free association and trains of thought identified by Freud as ways of understanding psychic life, taking his interpretation outside the analytic session to consider our everyday interaction with the world around us and the objects we encounter. In Bollas's work (which takes examples from art as well as from analysands' experiences), these encounters with worldly objects are vital to our understanding of ourselves and our ability to attach descriptive and analytical narratives to our life experience. Objects have an 'integrity' or relative stability which help us fix points in the flux of our lived experience, marking points in our past, present and future. Evocative objects may recall past experiences, as in the examples we have seen in Swift's songs, or they may represent sites of desire, opening up the promise of new experience. Bollas speaks of nostalgia and 'the nostalgic object' (2009, p. 80) but is also keen to highlight the ever-present nature of evocation, which can be as much about the future and present desires as it is a calling back to the past.

Objects in Taylor Swift songs work on multiple levels of evocation. One of the most commented-on examples can be found in 'All Too Well' (Swift 2012), where a failed romance is narrated via a series of evocative objects and scenes: 'singing in the car', 'autumn leaves falling down', 'wind in my hair', 'plaid shirt days and nights', a photograph of 'a little kid with glasses', lovers 'dancing 'round the kitchen in the refrigerator light', and the 'crumpled up piece of paper' with which the protagonist identifies as the relationship breaks down. Most famously, there is the scarf that is used at each end of the song, firstly as an item of clothing left by the protagonist in her lover's sister's house and later as the 'old scarf [that] reminds you of innocence and … smells like me'. The scarf revives the past for both the protagonist and her ex, while acting as a suitably evocative object for the songwriter tasked with condensing the ups and downs of a relationship into a handful of poetic images. While a narrative can be picked out by the listener (a 'story of us', to quote another Swift song), it is the song's imagery that forces its way to the foreground, repeating a process common to country songs where, as Stewart notes, 'narrative action comes to a full stop in the face of the lyric' (Stewart, 1993, p. 222).

Swift's fans, often keen to make connections between lyrics and performer, wasted little time in connecting the scarf in 'All Too Well' to one that Swift was seen wearing while walking with actor Jake Gyllenhaal. The story of the scarf has been wrapped around the story of Swift and Gyllenhaal to such an extent that, five years after the release of the song, *The Verge* saw fit to run a story about the 'mystery' of this particular piece of clothing. Journalist Kaitlyn Tiffany summed up the enduring appeal:

> It's hard to explain exactly why the scarf is so fascinating, but to hazard some guesses: "scarf" is a funny word to say over and over. Everyone relates to the experience of assigning outsized significance to the debris of a relationship. Everyone relates to the experience of a very short

relationship having an inexplicably large emotional impact, its brevity forcing you to pick something silly to cling to from a meager selection of objects related to it. Everyone likes a good mystery. Autumn in New York is a fantastic setting for a mystery. Autumn in New York is a fantastic setting for a failed love story; Jake Gyllenhaal is famous and compelling in his own right.

TIFFANY, 2017

This passage gets at the multiple layers of evocation that a song may contain, whether in lyrical imagery, sonic pleasure, or the recognition that celebrities such as Swift and Gyllenhaal are themselves objects distributed for consumption. This condensation of evocative imagery works to make the song itself an evocative object, one that has taken on a life of its own among Swift's fans.

If the foregoing has started to delineate the ways in which evocative objects form part of the sonic-lyrical regime of the Swiftian song, we must also consider how songs become evocative objects with their own trajectories and destinies. Swift has shown this in her songwriting by using songs as evocative objects in 'Tim McGraw', 'Our Song' and elsewhere. She turns that realisation on her own work too, as in the following introduction of 'All Too Well' to a concert audience in 2018:

In my brain, there's the life of this song, where this song was born out of catharsis and venting and trying to get over something and trying to understand it and process it. And then there's the life where it went out into the world and you turned this song into something completely different for me. You turned this song into a collage of memories of watching you scream the words to this song, or seeing pictures that you post to me of you having written words to this song in your diary, or you showing me your wrist, and you have a tattoo of the lyrics to this song underneath your skin. And that is how you have changed the song 'All Too Well' for me.

SWIFT, 2018

This fits with Bollas's conception of 'the evocative object world', where objects can be transformational (meaning that we can use them to transform our experience and ultimately ourselves) and aleatory (meaning that objects can take us by surprise and on unexpected journeys). We both select objects for our strategic use (or according to our desires) and also become subject to 'aleatory objects' which catch us unaware, surprise us and entice us (Bollas, 1992). This is not an either/or situation: we seek out those objects which, having arrested us in their aleatory trajectory, make us long to return to them. And we hope for the aleatory, the unexpected, even as we revisit our most cherished and seemingly familiar objects. Applying this to music, we can think of songs as being transformational objects for listeners, a process which operates independently of authorial intention.

Evocative objects are the subject matter of many songs and among those evocative objects are songs themselves. In any consistent artist's work there will be some replication, in which constellations of objects, atmospheres and affective climates create the possibility for, and the desire for, further such constellations. That is why we can even speak of something like the 'Swiftian song'; we need the recurrence and recognition of patterns to identify otherwise disparate objects as a connected, coherent style. This is not to deny Swift's creative agency, nor to issue accusations of standardisation, repetition, cliché, and so on. Rather, it is to think of human agents attuning to the atmospheres in which they find themselves. Atmospheres and climates are created by multiple elements, while multiple elements find themselves disposed and oriented towards each other and their environment by atmospheres and climates. To join a song (to join in singing) is to attune oneself to the atmosphere of that song, to let the agency of the song reorient singer and audience.

While recognising consistency in the lyrical (and sometimes in the sonic) regime of the Swiftian pop song, we must note a dynamism to the process too, where larger and smaller shifts become notable with each album project or concert tour. It is this idea of change within Swift's output that allows fans and critics to read new messages into older songs or to hear newer songs as containing messages that unfold a new, more revealing or somehow truer side to the performer. This is both part of, and distinct from, the evolution of the Swiftian song in that reading messages about the singer into the songs has much to do with how musical personas work (Auslander, 2006; Hansen, 2019). While multi-authored construction of musical personas by artists and audiences should arguably be distinguished from the identification of commonalities in a song corpus, it is inevitable with an artist of Swift's stature and with her kind of persona that lines will be blurred. If, on the one hand, it is only to be expected that listeners are going to read Swift's songs as revealing something about her, it is also useful to reiterate the essentially fabricated relationship between persona and song narrative. We may read the songs as evocative song objects that exist in a world that is intimately connected to, but also separable from, the worlds of celebrity, fame, persona, and fandom. This forms a central paradox in the Swiftian song and its positioning as an evocative object. On the one hand, the perfectly crafted, poignant and affirmative song and lyric can affectively, nostalgically, and evocatively move the listener to identify subjective subconscious and unconscious associations; yet on the other, this is aligned with an objectively efficient organized and strategized world of Swift's identity as a global brand and the ways in which the distribution and maintenance of her celebrity persona and individual wealth through profit are intertwined.

3   'Something That Feels Like Something' – Ordinary Intensities and
       Intense Commodities in *folklore* and *evermore*

The connections between the Swiftian world of evocative objects and their commodifiable and affective potential are also aligned to the formation of what might be termed 'ordinary intensities'. It is through the incidental moments in Swift's music that 'ordinary intensities' appear and the potential of being caught up in 'something that feels like something' bears the potential for 'a something coming together' (Stewart, 2007, p. 2). Katheen Stewart's concept of 'ordinary affects' (2007) energises and informs the emergence of these ordinary intensities in the lyrics and song-world of *folklore* and *evermore*, the pair of albums Taylor Swift recorded and released during the pandemic in 2020 (Swift 2020a, 2020b). Stewart primarily situates the ordinary affect through the 'emergent present' and 'immanent force' (p. 1) of 'neoliberalism, advanced capitalism and globalisation' (ibid.) and how these conditions are imbued with the ordinary and intense intimacy of 'a pleasure and a shock, an empty pause or dragging undertow, as a sensibility that snaps into place or a profound disorientation' (p. 2). As well as this the 'disparate scenes and incommensurate forms and registers' created by Swift (p. 4) underpin a 'something' that is produced by the intensity of listening to her and the evocative, uncanny, aleatory, and ordinary experiences that her music captures.

    This is also associated with what Bollas terms the 'thing-ness' (2009, p. 80) of evocative objects and their capacity to 'have an integrity of their own' (ibid). Yet this evocation and intensification of the object and/or the affect can't exist in isolation. Rather, the feelings and intensities that are connected to the evocative object are only possible because we also have the potential to become 'evocative objects – living things – that bring about textures of inner experience with the other' (p. 94) through commodified objects. How these evolve and emerge in Swift's music is closely tied to the lyrics and songs as assemblages of public and private subjectivities, memories, and temporalities. More so, and across both *folklore* and *evermore*, we find that lyrics which capture an ordinary intensity often involve an evocative object and that the relationships between them are located 'in the intensities they build and in what thoughts and feelings they make possible' (p. 3).

For instance, we see this in the song, lyrics and positioning of the 'cardigan' as an intensive and evocative 'thing'. As Swift writes and sings 'and when it felt like I was an old cardigan under someone's bed, you put me on and said I was your favourite', we see that the cardigan, as both object and subject, moves 'through bodies, dreams, dramas, and social worldings of all kinds' (Bollas, 2009, p. 93). Throughout both *folklore* and *evermore* Swift tethers an intense 'thing-ness' to ordinary and mundane objects and situations. Once again in 'cardigan' she recounts a vivid memory and moment of her lover ('Dancing in your Levi's drunk under a streetlight'). In 'seven' she contours a familiar yet mysterious childhood longing ('Pack your dolls and a sweater we'll move to India forever'). And, perhaps most movingly, in 'marjorie' (an elegy to her grandmother) she expresses how grief and loss are formed through a series of ordinary and routine actions ('watched as you signed your name marjorie', 'kept every grocery store receipt' 'long limbs and frozen swims, you'd always go past where our feet could touch'). In Swift's work these ordinary intensities are linked to the impersonality of socio-cultural, economic, and political structures as well as through intensely intimate, subjective, and personalising modes of identification or affirmation. It might also be via named individuals (Betty, James, Dorothea, Marjorie), the objects they are associated with (a cardigan, a magazine, a grocery store receipt) or the spaces and times that they inhabit (the gym, the summer, the autumn, a lake, the car ride) that we experience 'something' of their misty experiences. Here Betty, James, Dorothea or Marjorie become involved in an aleatory and anticipatory exchange of desires as 'those who encounter us as evocative objects [and ...] register us in the world of their inner experience' (Bollas, 2009, p. 94). In this tryst the qualities of an object or a person's 'something-ness' generate intangible desires and affective memories for individuals to cling to, wrap themselves up in and share with others. It is through the intensity and ordinariness of the object and its experiential connection to human experience that a 'something-ness' occurs.

Within this Swiftian world the permutation of country, pop, queer desire, evocative objects and ordinary intensities produces a queer 'something' that elicits a moment of ordinary and commodifiable intensity. For instance, a feeling of queer longing can only be triggered, expressed, and realised through the evocation of a lyric and the associated images and representations of how longing and queerness have already been culturally constructed and represented. Consequently, Swift's lyrics both locate and manifest something of that queer longing in reference to an evocative object and an ordinary intensity working in conjunction with one another. This both locates and dislocates the evocative objects and ordinary intensities on *folklore* and *evermore*, so they shift between the past and present, the here and there, and the then and there.

José Esteban Muñoz's work, which considers the contours of queer temporalities, utopias and futurities, suggests that 'a posterior glance at different moments, objects, and spaces might offer us an anticipatory illumination of queerness' (2009, p. 22) and in doing so nurture a 'queerness as something that is not yet here' (ibid). This is queerness based on the premise that 'queerness is a structuring and educated mode of desiring that allows us to see and feel beyond the quagmire of the present' (p. 1) and by offering a glimpse into the 'not-yet-hereness' of queer worlds. As it is expressed by Swift, this may also be allied to queerness as a transitory, fleeting and ethereal moment of affect that is both present and absent. This is a queer way of longing and sociality that both strives towards grasping how evocative objects and the intensity of ordinary experience might 'stave off the ossifying effects of neoliberal ideology and the degradation of politics brought about by representations of queerness in contemporary popular culture' (p. 22).

As well as this, these moments of ordinary intensity are connected to the listeners' subjective and affective experiences which simultaneously falter, embody and enigmatically trigger Swift's lyrical representations in divergent and capricious ways. A queer theorisation of this transient 'something' through the prism of queer experience allows the listener to stray from, disrupt, and subvert the universality and uniformity of neoliberal capitalist experience. It also allows them to use the atypicality or inauthenticity of queer to reshape those innate conditions of what has been situated as 'capitalist realism' (Fisher, 2009) and the shaping of a 'cruel optimism' that Lauren Berlant describes as deceptively bringing subjects closer to a 'moral-intimate-economic thing called "the good life"' (Berlant, 2011, p. 2) and its illusion of a 'satisfying something that you cannot generate on your own but sense in the wake of a person, a way of life, an object ...'. This 'good life' and the happiness that it seems to promise are also linked to the emergence of 'cottagecore' as a dominant aesthetic and discursive feature of both neoliberalism and the politics of the 2020 pandemic. Both albums folded into this perfectly and some of the tensions between the affective and the commodified aspects of this 'Swiftian' world permeate through the idealised rurality and nostalgia that *folklore* and *evermore* capture.

Here, neoliberal queerness is combined with millennial femininity into an intensive and commercial evocation that we also see in the music and lyrics of Swift's recent contemporaries – artists such as Olivia Rodrigo, Lorde and Billie Eilish – who explore and exploit tensions between anxiety, desire, privilege, trauma and pleasure, and do so in ways which are eloquently and atmospherically unravelled through poetic and confessional reflection. This exploration is only made possible through the materiality of capitalism and its capacity to allow deeply individual forms of desire, intimacy and agency to be marketed, promoted and monetised. In this way we see that 'cottagecore' is 'in part a reaction against capitalism and our increasing time spent in front of a screen, but also related to ongoing interests in social justice, wellness and sustainability, and more broadly the idea of an informed social conscious-ness' (Reggev, 2020). Swift fits perfectly into this space and both albums con-struct and construe an aesthetic and ideological mixture of rurality, nostalgia and modes of social advocacy and individual desire. Cottagecore also offers a hauntological (Coverley, 2020) aperture into a distinctly Swiftian world to capture the tensions more widely allied to queer experiences of temporality, futurity and loss. Yet this distinctly Swiftian portal into the something-ness of 'cottage-core' always transforms and positions these experiences into transac-tional, monetised, marketed, branded and legal paradigms. In this way Swift's work is compatible with the 'forms of consciousness encouraged by neoliber-alism' (Hennessy, 2000, pp. 80–81) and the official merchandise allied to both *folklore* and *evermore* use lyrics from key songs in subtle and nuanced ways to brand and sell 'evocative objects' to fans. Once again, the evocative object that seems to capture some of this ordinary intensity is the cardigan. Just as Swift references the evocative objecthood of the cardigan in 'betty' ('standing in your cardigan'), and just as it is 'under someone's bed' in the eponymous song, it also becomes a key merchandisable object that fans desire and that Swift profits from. The cardigan's metonymic and metaphorical qualities shift as it is repositioned yet always understood as a piece of merchandise linked to a song lyric, an ordinary intensity, an evocative object, a queer signifier, a neutrally gendered piece of clothing, a comforting and a safe thing to nest, hibernate and isolate in. The lexical ambiguity of the cardigan also uses a lyr-ical trope common to Swift's work, whereby evocative objects (in this case, a cardigan) are used as ways of connecting people to moments, experiences, and shared memories, while also suggesting there is a possibility to adopt a sub-ject position via an object. Swift indirectly selling cardigans as merchandise and the cardigan itself offer up a ubiquitous space of ordinary safety, security, and familiarity with Swift. The cardigan as an intensive and evocative object becomes the 'thing' and the object of desire that the fans can feel connected to Swift through.

This is the enigmatic and mystifying commodity fetishism that Marxism is concerned with, and which Kevin Floyd (2009) develops as a form of queer reification. Here 'reification identifies the very process of social differentiation within capital as fundamentally and objectivity mystifying' (p. 17) so that the merchandisable and branded cardigan as an evocative object is powerfully connected to Swift's lyrics as a moment of ordinary intensity. Here the cardigan as an object, a lyric and a feeling are riven by a complex form of reified commodity fetishism that speaks to and comfortably sits within a neoliberal and advanced capitalist context. Here the cardigan produces and sustains 'a way of seeing whereby the definite social relations at capitalism's core assume the fantastic relation between things' (Hennessy, 2000, p. 95). This tenders a Swiftian mode of production that is distinctly neoliberal in that it facilitates and supports the illusion of individual agency and expectant desire through consumption. Here the listener as consumer can use the cardigan to cultivate their own desires and do so in ways which reinforce how 'dynamic, productive social relations between people take the form of (exchange value) relations between static, autonomous things, things that appear to be independent of people' (p. 17). Citing Jean Baudrillard, Turkle asserts that 'commodities cultivate desires that support the production and consumption capitalism requires' (2007, p. 313). More so, this process allows for the ordinary intensity and/or Swiftian evocation to be conceptualised and converted into an affective commodity so that a 'material culture [that] carries emotions and ideas of startling intensity' (Turkle, 2007, p. 6) is a consequence of a capitalism in which we are 'invited to know the value of commodities as if it [... capitalism ...] were lodged in things themselves' (Hennessy, 2000, p. 95).

These tensions also disrupt and enhance Swift's persona as a global pop star and commodity whilst cultivating a sonic space for modes of relational and affective intimacy across Swift's voice, lyrics, songs and her listeners. Some of the encounters between Swift's branded, commodifiable and celebrity persona and the pathos of her distinctly 'Swiftian' evocations are also distilled and captured across the songs and lyrics on both the *folklore* and *evermore* albums. Here the confluence of Swift's songs, lyrics and the merchandise associated with both albums have produced a range of uncanny, evocative, and ordinary objects which are simultaneously mass-produced objects that use the lyrical content from Swift's songs to produce a kind of 'evocative merchandise' that Swift profits from. This upholds Swift's branded and monetised persona whilst also capturing the subjective, affecting and enigmatic nature of her 'sonic-lyrical regimes'. Just as *folklore* and *evermore* connect to the precarity of intimacy, futurity, self-reflection, isolation, and fear allied to the contours of the 2020 pandemic, they also produce a range of objects that listeners and fans can always purchase as evocative, ordinary, and emotional commodities.

4   'betty' as a Queer Evocative Object

In thinking about this tension between albums and songs as both commodities and evocative objects with ordinary intensities we might also consider them as material texts that circulate both as 'texts' and as 'material objects' (by text we are referring to the sonic and musical elements as well as linguistic or lyrical aspects) (Ahmed, 2017, p. 17). Sara Ahmed, when describing her 'killjoy survival kit', outlines her idea of a 'companion text' (2017, pp. 16–17) to refer to feminist books that help 'sustain' (Sedgwick, 2003, p. 151) feminist communities. The affective function of sustaining a marginalised community is rooted in the materiality of these objects, which have qualities that Turkle describes in relation to 'evocative objects' as 'life companions' (2007, p. 9) and 'provocations to thought' (2007, p. 5). 'Feminist community' is also sustained through the 'circulation' of these texts between its members, which Ahmed describes as a 'sociability' and where the exchange of books enacts a change in the collective 'body' of these feminist communities: 'the sociability of their lives is part of the sociability of ours' (Ahmed, 2017, p. 17). For Ahmed, these feminist books have been a companion to her 'as a feminist and diversity worker' and she describes some of the evocative affects as having 'enabled [her] to proceed on a path less trodden' (2017, p. 16). Evocative objects have a particularly potent affective function as companion texts and enable marginalised people to 'survive' (Ahmed, 2017, p. 17) unwelcoming and hostile circumstances as these objects provide them the 'sustenance' to 'sustain' themselves and 'communities' (Sedgwick, 2003, pp. 150–1).

Taylor Swift's songs and albums are particularly suited to this kind of affective work, in large part because of the sonic-lyrical regime highlighted earlier where recurring tropes and features of Swiftian song become the basis for providing this sustenance amongst LGBTQ+ listeners. This combination of continuity and dynamism in Swift's discography provides both comfort and possibility for Swift's listeners to interpret the songs in different ways. In this way Swift's songs can be considered not only as evocative objects with ordinary intensities and affects but also as forms of companion texts for feminist and LGBTQ+ communities, particularly within country music. Country music is a genre that is often perceived to lack LGBTQ+ participation. 'betty', as Swift's first single to be released to country radio formats since 2013 whilst being described by various media outlets as a queer anthem (Kircher, 2020), brings these issues to the fore.

One way of thinking about these kinds of LGBTQ+ communities is the role of fandoms. Previous research on Taylor Swift fandoms has explored the way in which teenage female audiences have engaged with lyrics as part of their identity formation (Chittenden, 2013); the way Swift's increased political advocacy has been received by her fanbase (Nisbett and Dunn, 2021; Driessen, 2020); the way fans interact with Swift through different social media platforms including TikTok and Twitter (Avdeeff, 2021; Kehrberg, 2015). Some of this research has acknowledged Swift's LGBTQ+ fans (Driessen, 2020; Avdeef, 2021; Smialek, 2021). There is also research around the commodification of fandom and community building within Taylor Swift's fandom (Carroll, 2021). Carroll (2021) argues that Taylor Swift fandom presents 'consumer loyalty [as] participatory fan culture', drawing on Matthew Guschwan's (2012) term 'brandom'. Here the tension between Swift's public and celebrity persona is obscured through the ordinary intensities of fans' engagement with the star. As Carroll (2021) argues: 'inherent and impersonal power structures become acceptable to fans when presented in a commercial package as a personalised object and a "potential best friend"'.

LGBTQ+ experiences become articulated and embedded in this participatory fan culture. This participatory aspect in many ways takes on a speculative aspect, which is stimulated by Swift herself, through for example featuring hidden clues ('Easter eggs') throughout her promotional material and music videos, such as in 'You Need To Calm Down' (Romano, 2020). The cryptic nature of these 'Easter eggs' mean that it is ambiguous the extent to which interpretations of these hidden messages are about Swift's authorial intention and which are from active fan readings. This tension becomes particularly pronounced around 'You Need To Calm Down' which featured LGBTQ+ celebrities and, as Romano points out, 'a scene where she dyed her hair in what appeared to be the colors of the bisexual flag' (2020). If this is intentional by Swift this would suggest a purposeful commodification of fans' intense emotional engagement with her, and possibly support social media discourse claims of 'queerbaiting' (the 'luring of fan and media intrigue by hinting at her possible bisexuality' (Smialek, 2021, p. 12)). A less cynical interpretation would be that this discourse of speculation invites alternative and queer readings of Swift that enable LGBTQ+ fans to actively identify themselves within these texts (both Swift herself and her songworld). This research around Taylor Swift fandoms demonstrates that comparable communities to the communities formed by passing books around described by Ahmed are developing around Swift and her music as 'companion texts' (2017, p. 17).

It is through the active listening practices around 'betty' within Swift's LGBTQ+ fanbase that the potential for queer or LGBTQ+ identification can be found. Throughout *folklore* the songs have different protagonists of potentially different genders, and the album features three songs as part of a teenage love triangle: 'cardigan', 'august' and 'betty', narrated from the perspective of

Betty, the unnamed other woman and James respectively. Journalists writing in media outlets including *Vulture* (Kircher, 2020), *Pitchfork* (Mapes, 2020), *bitchmedia* (Lewis, 2020), and LGBTQ+ publications *Advocate* (Reynolds, 2020) and *Country Queer* (Barker, 2020) have all discussed 'betty' as being (or having the potential to be) a song about a lesbian relationship. Madison Malone Kircher (2020), writing in *Vulture*, argues that, as Taylor Swift is named after James Taylor, 'when she's singing as James, telling a story about James, she's telling a story about herself'. Therefore, Kircher (2020) argues that, when Swift sings 'Slept next to her [another woman], but I dreamt of you all summer long', the first-person protagonist 'is still a woman'.

In addition to this kind of 'evidence' (Barker, Harper, Hubbs and Wilson, 2021) as a justification for a queer reading of the song, Kircher (2020) describes the affective and evocative qualities and features of the song that for her lend even more support for reading the song in this way: 'Longing. Unrequited love. Skateboards. Gender bending. Rumors. A harmonica! Everything about this song screams queer'. It can be noted, as elsewhere in Swift's discography, that in Kircher's reading of 'betty' these ordinary intensities elicited by the song are in connection or proximity with evocative objects: the 'harmonica', 'skateboards' and even 'rumours' and 'gender bending' as items in Kircher's list become objects on which to hang the more affective qualities she describes of 'longing' and 'unrequited love'. 'Unrequited love' can be associated with LGBTQ+ narratives around coming out where the feelings of desire may be directed to someone who is straight, closeted or otherwise prevented from openly reciprocating those feelings. The idea of 'longing' has been associated by scholars such as Muñoz as a particular kind of queer affect: 'Queerness is a longing that propels us onwards, beyond romances of negative and toiling in the present' (2009, p. 1). Longing, for Muñoz, is not a nostalgic (as defined as a movement backwards into the past (Elliott, 2014, p. 132)) or necessarily regretful affective mode, but one that 'propels' subjects forward and to experience texts and objects in different ways. As Susan Sontag has described in her notes on camp, this queer longing has 'the power to transform experience' (2018, p. 5) and gain an alternative 'experience' of an object beyond 'the "straight" public sense in which something can be taken' (2018, p. 13). These kinds of affect can function within the ways listeners actively experience the object, in this case the song 'betty', but also the song's own aesthetic qualities can produce these kinds of affects.

'betty' is structured as a disruptive and enigmatic collection of memories with a first-person narrator. The narrator's commentary gives these memory fragments some sense of narrative flow, at times trying to piece these fragments together into some narrative coherence, whilst at other times embracing the unpredictable blur and flow of memories and getting stuck in storytelling loops of 'the worst thing that I ever did' and 'If I just showed up at your party'. These acts of recollection often relate to feelings of regret and a situation or choice the song's protagonist made and longs to fix. The chorus performs this longing for a different ending to this narrative: 'If I just showed up at your party'. The chorus in its first two iterations is tentative and speculative, with the use of the conditional tense ('if') and the questions conveying the protagonist's ponderings of what would happen: 'Would you have me? Would you want me?'. The succession of questions gives the chorus a sense of propulsion, building a narrative of James showing up at the party, being 'potentially' (Barker, Harper, Hubbs and Wilson, 2021) welcomed in and led to the garden where James and Betty reconcile and rekindle their relationship.

'betty' performs and evokes this sense of longing, making it a particularly evocative object that, when contextualised through fan listening practices within affective logics and histories of queer longing, fits within the claims made by Kircher and others of 'betty' being generatively read as a queer, lesbian or LGBTQ+ song. Kircher (2020) supports her argument further by alluding to the way other Swift fans have interpreted the song: 'If you don't believe me please go directly to Twitter or Tumblr and search "betty gay"'. Whether or not 'betty' is or is not a definitive lesbian song is beside the point; what is more of note and undeniable is the way that listeners have responded to the song. Listeners have used 'betty' as a companion to their emotional lives and have found the song a useful object for the way in which they understand their own lived experiences, LGBTQ+ identities and use this to articulate and assert their presence within the 'dominant culture' (Dyer, 2002, p. 153), of which *folklore* as a mass culture commodity is a product. In thinking of these companion texts as deriving their impact not just from the experience of the individual listener, but collectively in the way that they affect the formation, development and sustaining of LGBTQ+ subjects and communities, it is important to think of these as social and circulating objects. This 'sociability', to use Ahmed's term, is evident through the media reception and fan response on social media sites that demonstrate that 'betty' is circulating amongst LGBTQ+ fans and thereby being treated as a queer evocative object.

It is important not to romanticise the idea of LGBTQ+ community forming around Swift, particularly not to overlook its role as a commercial product aimed at profit. In this way the intense affective attachments LGBTQ+ fans form around 'betty' can be commodified into a financial asset for Swift. The extent to which it can be argued that 'betty' is contributing to the building of LGBTQ+ communities depends on how far this 'exceeds the logic of the market' (Edwards, 2009, p. 7) and this has impacts beyond building a loyal fanbase who will spend their money on Swift's music and merchandise. One way to consider this kind of impact is to think of the sociability of the object ('betty'). In thinking of its 'circulation' or 'sociability' as a 'companion text' (Ahmed, 2017, p. 17), and evocative object with ordinary intensities, this can also be thought of as where this song travels and where this song does not travel to. It is notable that the publications mentioned as having identified 'betty' as potentially queer are publications with a broader focus than country music. The coverage around 'betty' within more country specific publications (Liptak, 2020; Taylor Swift's 'betty' will Challenge Radio Programmers, 2020) gave comparably less attention to the potential queer or lesbian readings of the song. This indicates that 'betty' has successfully built and strengthened the affective and commodifiable attachment of LGBTQ+ fans to Taylor Swift. Within the current music industry and streaming context, where albums and artist brands struggle to gain traction compared to individual songs, this is a particularly lucrative commercial asset to Swift. Perhaps less cynically, Swift resonating with LGBTQ+ audiences with an aesthetically country song could be evidence of an alternative country music culture to the Nashville establishment, challenging Nashville as the 'center' (Laird, 2018, p. 572) and the key determining authority over the genre. In this way the intense and ordinary affects, with potentially extraordinary implications that exceed profit making 'logic of the market' (Edwards, 2009, p. 7), are in tension with maintaining the commercial viability of Swift's fandom.

5   Conclusion – a Disrupted World?

The tensions that make up this 'Swiftian' world capture a series of disruptive and affirmative narratives and experiences of love, desire, and loss which underpin both pop and country music. They also provide a way for the listener and fan to interpret and identify with the meanings that the writer and performer evoke. Swift's music and lyrics also form the symbolic and emotional constituents of the everyday rituals and customs that we all experience. In moments of celebration, inexplicable grief or through the uncanny shock that the pandemic instilled, these two albums and their songs articulated and captured our 'ordinary affects' (Stewart, 2007) in response to unforeseen events and ways of being in the world. In this way they also provided a mode of emotional intensity to seemingly trivial encounters so that the potential for the ordinary to become an intense encounter functioned on both an individual and collective level of remembering and forgetting (Brainard, 1975; Adair, 1986). We also find in this 'Swiftian' space the amplification and magnification of often transient, incidental or 'small' glimpses into a 'moment'. Just as her lyrics weave together the 'ordinary' lives and memories of others (Marjorie, Rebecca, Betty, Doreatha), geographies (The Lake District, Rhode Island, Tupelo, Coney Island), and objects (a cardigan, a wallet) we can't detach them from Swift's 'extraordinary' persona as a global pop celebrity and the commodified 'cottagecore' narratives allied to both albums and their neoliberal qualities. In 'betty' LGBTQ+ country fans might use Swift's song as a tool to build an alternative country community, however, just as utopian narratives of greater democracy in the music industry as a result of streaming services are problematic (not least in their overlooking the financial instability this creates for musicians in terms of royalty payments), a utopian reading of a liberation from Nashville or from discriminatory forms of governance, government and neoliberal greed is also overly simplistic.

Swift is one of the most commercially successful celebrities of the 21st century and is also more able to navigate, negotiate and circumvent industry dynamics and gatekeepers. With 90.5 million Twitter followers (as of July 2022) Swift could announce both *folklore* and *evermore* through the platform, meaning she is less reliant on older media outlets such as radio and TV to promote her work. Many country and pop artists, including LGBTQ+ artists, do not have this size of platform. Additionally, Swift to an extent gained her platform through the country music industry and its traditional gatekeepers, including radio. Therefore, Swift cannot be just read as a figure that evokes and captures the poignancy, beauty and melancholia of the pandemic. Nor can she be read as one that completely democratises and challenges the structures within the country or pop music industry. Whilst the queer uses (Ahmed, 2019) of Swift and a song such as 'betty' as an evocative object yield the power to sustain ordinary and intense forms of queer sociability and community, Swift's branded persona and global sway do indicate that there are other agents at play which continually evoke and disrupt the 'Swiftian' world she has created and which she profits from.

References

Adair, G. (1986) *Myths and memories*. London: Flamingo.
Ahmed, S. (2017) *Living a feminist life*. Durham: Duke University Press.
Ahmed, S. (2019) *What's the use?* Durham: Duke University Press.
Auslander, P. (2006) 'Musical personae'. *TDR: The Drama Review*, 50(1), pp. 100–119.

Avdeeff, M.K. (2021) 'TikTok, Twitter, and platform-specific technocultural discourse in response to Taylor Swift's LGBTQ+ allyship in "You Need to Calm Down"'. *Contemporary Music Review*, 40(1), pp. 78–98. DOI: 10.1080/07494467.2021.1945225.

Barker, J. (2020) 'From 'Fifteen' to folklore: growing up queer with Taylor Swift'. *Country Queer* https://countryqueer.com/stories/article/from-fifteen-to-folklore-growing-up-queer-with-taylor-swift/ [Accessed 27 August 2021].

Barker, J., Harper, P., Hubbs, N., and Wilson, I. (2021) 'I don't want you like a best friend: a Gaylor Swift panel discussion'. Conference Panel, Taylor Swift Study Day: Eras, Narrative, Digital Music and Media, online, 18 July.

Berlant, L. (2011) *Cruel optimism*. Durham: Duke University Press.

Bollas, C. (1987) *The shadow of the object: psychoanalysis of the unthought known*. London: Free Association Books.

Bollas, C. (1992) *Being a character: psychoanalysis and self experience*. London: Routledge.

Bollas, C. (2009) *The evocative object world*. London: Routledge.

Brainard, J. (1975) *I remember*. London: Notting Hill Editions.

Carroll, G. '"It gets ugly really fast": social media and community building within the online Taylor Swift fandom' (Conference Paper), Taylor Swift Study Day: Eras, Narrative, Digital Music and Media. 18 July 2021.

Coverley, M. (2020), *Hauntology: ghosts of futures past*. London: Oldcastle Books.

Chittenden, T. (2013) 'In My Rearview Mirror'. *Journal of Children and Media*, 7(2), 186–200.

Driessen, S. (2020) 'Taylor Swift, political power, and the challenge of affect in popular music fandom'. *Transformative Works and Cultures*, 32. DOI: https://doi.org/10.3983/twc.2020.1843.

Dyer, R. (2002) 'In defence of disco', in *Only entertainment*. London and New York: Routledge, pp. 151–160.

Edwards, L.H. (2009) *Johnny Cash and the paradox of American identity*. Bloomington: University of Indiana Press.

Elliott, R. (2015) *The late voice: time, age and experience in popular music*. New York: Bloomsbury Academic.

Elliott, R. (2014) '"Time and distance are no object": holiday records, representation and the nostalgia gap'. *Volume!* 11(1), pp. 131–143.

Fisher, M. (2009) *Capitalist realism*. Winchester: Zero Books.

Floyd, K. (2009) *The reification of desire: toward a queer Marxism*. Minnesota: University of Minnesota Press.

Fox, A. (1992) 'The jukebox of history: narratives of loss and desire in the discourse of country music'. *Popular Music*, 11(1), pp. 53–72.

Guschwan, M. (2012) 'Fandom, brandom and the limits of participatory culture'. *Journal of Consumer Culture*, 12(1), pp. 19–40.

Hansen, K.A. (2019) '(Re)reading pop personae: a transmedial approach to studying the multiple construction of artist identities'. *Twentieth-Century Music*, 16(3), pp. 501–29. DOI: 10.1017/S1478572219000276.

Hennessy, R. (2000) *Profit and pleasure: sexual identities in late capitalism*. London and New York: Routledge.

Hubbs, N. (2014) *Rednecks, queers and country music*. Berkeley: University of California Press.

Kehrberg, A.K. (2015) '"I love you, please notice me": the hierarchical rhetoric of Twitter fandom'. *Celebrity Studies*, 6(1), pp. 85–99.

Kircher, M.M. (2020) 'Taylor Swift's 'betty' is queer canon. I don't make the rules'. *Vulture*, 24 July, https://www.vulture.com/2020/07/taylor-swift-betty-folklore-lyrics-queer.html [Accessed 27 August 2021].

Laird, T.E.W. (2018) 'A new century', in Malone, B.C., and Laird, T.E.W. (eds) *Country music U.S.A: 50th anniversary edition*. Austin: Texas University Press, pp. 545–572.

Lewis, R.C. (2020) 'Does Taylor Swift have to be queer for "folklore" to be a lesbian album?' *bitchmedia*, 30 July, https://www.bitchmedia.org/article/is-taylor-swifts-folklore-a-gay-album [Accessed 27 August 2021].

Liptak, C. (2020) 'Taylor Swift makes a triumphant return to the ACM Awards stage with "betty"'. *The Boot*, 17 September https://theboot.com/taylor-swift-betty-2020-acm-awards/ [Accessed 27 August 2021].

Mapes, J. (2020) 'Taylor Swift folklore'. *Pitchfork*, 27 July https://pitchfork.com/reviews/albums/taylor-swift-folklore/ [Accessed 27 August 2021].

Muñoz, J.E. (2009) *Cruising utopia: the then and there of queer futurity*. New York and London: New York University Press.

Nisbett, G. and Dunn, S.S. (2021) 'Reputation matters: parasocial attachment, narrative engagement, and the 2018 Taylor Swift political endorsement'. *Atlantic Journal of Communication*, 29(1), pp. 26–38.

Reggev, K. (2020) What Exactly Is Cottagecore and How Did It Get So Popular? *Architecural Digest*, 21 October, https://www.architecturaldigest.com/story/what-exactly-is-cottagecore [Accessed 14 December 2022].

Reuter, A. (2020) 'Can Taylor Swift's "betty" help country radio's gender imbalance?' *Sounds Like Nashville*, 17 August, https://www.soundslikenashville.com/news/taylor-swift-betty-radio-return/ [Accessed 6 July 2022].

Reynolds, D. (2020) 'Taylor Swift sings queer anthem "betty" at Country Music Awards', *Advocate*, 17 September, https://www.advocate.com/music/2020/9/17/taylor-swift-swings-queer-anthem-betty-country-music-awards [Accessed 27 August 2021].

Romano, A. (2020) 'The queering of Taylor Swift'. *Vox*, 30 July https://www.vox.com/21337354/folklore-taylor-swift-kaylor-betty-gay-lesbian-subtext [Accessed 27 August 2021].

Sedgwick, E.K. (2003) 'Paranoid reading and reparative reading, or, you're so paranoid, you probably think this essay is about you', in *Touching feeling: affect, pedagogy, performativity*. Durham: Duke University Press, pp. 123–153.

Sloan, N. (2021) 'Taylor Swift and the work of songwriting'. *Contemporary Music Review* 40(1), pp. 11–26, DOI: 10.1080/07494467.2021.1945226.

Smialek, E. (2021) 'Who needs to calm down? Taylor Swift and rainbow capitalism'. *Contemporary Music Review*, 40(1), pp. 99–119, DOI: 10.1080/07494467.2021.1956270.

Sontag, S. (2018) *Notes on 'camp'*. London: Penguin.

Stewart, K. (1993) 'Engendering narratives of lament in country music', in Lewis, G.H. (ed.), *All that glitters: country music in America*. Bowling Green, OH: Bowling Green State University Popular Press, pp. 221–25.

Stewart, K. (1996) *A space on the side of the road: cultural poetics in an 'other' America*. Princeton: Princeton University Press.

Stewart, K. (2007) *Ordinary affects*. Durham: Duke University Press.

Swift, T. (2006) *Taylor Swift* [CD. Big Machine Records, BMR120702].

Swift, T. (2012) *Red* [CD, Big Machine Records, BMR310400A].

Swift, T. (2018) *Taylor Swift: Reputation Stadium Tour*, directed by P. Dugdale [Netflix Movie, released 31 December].

Swift, T. (2020a) *folklore* [CD, Deluxe Edition, "In the Trees", Republic Records, 00602435034805].

Swift, T. (2020b) *evermore* [CD, Deluxe Edition, Republic Records, B0033405–02].

Tiffany, K. (2017) 'With the return of fall comes the return of a fantastic pop culture mystery'. *The Verge*, 17 October, https://www.theverge.com/tldr/2017/10/17/16488476/taylor-swift-scarf-mystery-jake-gyllenhaal-all-too-well [Accessed 20 August 2021].

Tragaki, D. (2020) 'Acoustemologies of rebetiko love songs', in Riedel, F. and Torvinen, J. (eds), *Music as atmosphere: collective feelings and affective sounds*. London: Routledge, pp. 184–201.

Turkle, S. (ed.) (2007) *Evocative objects: things we think with*. Cambridge, Massachusetts: The MIT Press.

'Taylor Swift's "betty" will challenge radio programmers' (2020) *The Boot*, 30 July, https://theboot.com/taylor-swift-betty/ [Accessed 27 August 2021].

CHAPTER 14

My Doubtful Cézanne

*Assembling Emergent Knowledges of Matter and Mattering
through Painting-by-Numbers and Autoethnography during Covid*

Briony A. Carlin

In March 2020, as the full threat of the pandemic escalated in the UK, I moved
from London to Newcastle. I was also moving into the 'writing up' phase of
my PhD, already living and working in an unstructured and somewhat solitary
fashion before the onset of the pandemic. PhD life is plagued with loneliness
and insecurity (Mackie and Bates, 2019; Brown, 2013; Pagan, 2019): even without social distancing, I felt intellectually isolated. Global uncertainty collided
with personal doubt.

Building out of this specific, situated position of knowledge-making
(Haraway, 1994), in this chapter I explore how the isolation and disruption
of the pandemic enacted a disjuncture from previous mental and social patterns that produced new knowledges and forms of knowledge-making about
(my) self and the world. Through autoethnographic writing about my experience doing a paint-by-numbers of a landscape painting by the French post-
Impressionist painter Paul Cézanne (1839–1906), I chart plural knowledges and
forms of knowledge-making that emerged through embodied activity within
the affective atmosphere of heightened introspection enacted by lockdown
(Sumartojo and Pink, 2019).

The autoethnography acts in the first instance as data for a feminist new
materialist analysis of the more-than-human agencies of lockdown that enabled a shift towards a more *careful* knowledge-making, producing insights on
topics relating to nature, epistemology, artistic labour and the commodification of art (Dee, 2018). After several drafts that re-vision my recollected experience, the more-than-human status of the autoethnography itself emerges as an
artefact of materialised knowledge and mattering (Barad, 2007; Bennett, 2010).
Following María Puig de la Bellacasa's argument that "caring" foregrounds "a
way of speaking of the critical engagements of knowledge producers beyond
the polarised divisions around the meanings of social and politically "useful"
research" (2017, p. 16), I explain how the atmosphere of thinking deeply and
feeling intensely through lockdown disrupted patterns of academic knowledge-
making and produced an ethico-political commitment to alternative modes of

thinking, feeling and knowing with care as a central mode of academic practice.The next paragraphs provide theoretical context to concepts of affective atmospheres and feminist new materialist theory. The chapter is then structured in two parts. Part 1 uses a narrativized writing style to weave theory into situated moments of knowledge-making, with some of the tangents I followed along the way. My decision to retain some less focussed text is intended to capture "the actual more laborious and situated conditions in which care [in knowledge-making] takes place and by which its agencies circulate in interdependent more than human relational webs" (ibid., pp. 18–19, 24). These meta-autoethnographic accounts are organised through two 'stories'[1]: i) doing the paint-by-numbers, then ii) subsequent encounters with texts that deepened my onto-epistemological understanding. The analysis uses care to attune to the *matter* of these assembled activities and the *mattering* they discursively acquired in relation to each other. Part 2 seeks to disentangle some agencies and knowledges that emerged through the autoethnographies, contextualise them in relation to questions of more-than-human mattering, care and my role as researcher in the assemblage.

1   Theoretical Signposts

This chapter draws on a range of theoretical work to make sense of comings-together of things, thoughts and beings. The first of these is the concept of affective atmospheres, a metaphor in cultural studies that expresses configurations of factors in our material, physical, social and political landscape which, according to Shanti Sumartojo and Sarah Pink, affect "how we constantly encounter and make sense of our surroundings, what we do in them and with whom and how we ascribe value and meaning to this" (2019, p. 3). To notice and analyse affective atmospheres requires "sensory and imaginative forms of understanding" that "evade capture" (ibid.), bridging analyses of personal and collective meaning-making. For example, through social and physical restrictions, and metaphysical sensations of fear and panic, the pandemic enacted affective atmospheres on global, local and individual scales.

Although not articulated in explicitly more-than-human terms, an affective atmosphere is founded on the understanding that nonhuman entities can have meaningful agency in directing our experiences. Jane Bennett calls this

---

1   So-called because it is a generic word, but one that also has prior application in feminist enquiries into visualising pluralistic knowledge production – see Haraway (1994); Smith (2012).

"impersonal affect" (2010, p.xiii): it is not a "spiritual supplement or 'life force'" added to independent bodies of insentient matter, such as a stubby paint brush or a patch of grass, but a way to describe the relational affect that issues forth in interactions between people and things, as well as configurations of inanimate things without human intervention. This highlights the importance of human and more-than-human situational factors as they come together in a temporary "political ecology of things" (ibid.).

The interdependent, *configured* sense of more-than-human agency is central to thinking about the agency of more-than-human phenomena in how we make meaning and knowledge from experience. Atmospheres and ecologies are impermanent: each affective atmosphere of lockdown only held for a limited amount of time, in a correlation between factors such as restrictions, unfamiliarity, fear and stocks of toilet paper. Karen Barad's "agential realism" captures this impermanence in stating that affect, materiality, meaning and discourse are performatively co-constituted, because matter and discourse emerge through dynamic "material-discursive intra-action" between entities (2003, p. 810). Barad's ethico-onto-epistemology extends the notion of affective atmospheres through querying the intra-actions through which affect arises.

For Barad, knowing, being, feeling, mattering and ethics are inseparable. Instead of portraying phenomena such as 'politics', 'environment', 'toilet paper', or 'social interaction' as distinct, *a priori* objects and actions, these things appear as fluid configurations of matter and meaning with variable agencies, to be differentiated or 'cut' into disparate bodies through how they come to signify in discourse (Barad, 2007, p. 337). For example, loo rolls did not mean panic, until their bulky mass was missing from shops; a few months later, the matter of well-stocked shelves constituted meanings of security, joking, and meme (Sikka, 2021). These transient configurations, ecologies or coming-togethers are imprecise and not limited to the terminology used to visualise them. They are imperfectly described in this chapter as "assemblages", a term I borrow from assemblage theory (Deleuze and Guattari, 2004; De Landa, 2007) to describe not a fixed structure of things, but an expression of dynamic self-structuring linkages between agencies that assemble in situated moments, then disperse. It is with this more-than-human, temporal, agential thinking that I have approached the analysis of my modes of knowledge-making during the Covid-19 lockdowns.

To study how meaning emerges from impermanent assemblages requires thinking and knowing, which María Puig de la Bellacasa states are "essentially relational processes that require care" (2017, p. 19). Thinking and knowing are so embedded in our lived and haptic experience and temporalities of the everyday world, that to survey them is a situated and non-innocent practice.

I will return to discuss this notion of posthuman care in knowledge practices throughout. For now, it suffices to say my acts of care in knowledge-making have required interrogating my own standpoint (Harding, 2004; Haraway, 1992) in order to perceive small affects and subtle configurations of more-than-human agencies with which to construct notions of affective atmosphere and relationality. To this end, I use autoethnography and phenomenology as tools for accessing experiential and critical detail.

Autoethnography consciously engages the self in ethnographic enquiry, using autobiographical data to explore cultural analysis. The data in this chapter is primarily drawn from journaling, photographs and voice memos made across a 12 month period between March 2020 and March 2021. Autoethnographic research offers an alternative to positivist, objectivist research paradigms and can produce a greater plurality of knowledges. Instead of presenting ideas as an impersonal argument, autoethnography offers a means for exploring the research process as an authentic, unfolding and idiosyncratic narrative (Adams, Holman Jones and Ellis, 2021). However, autoethnography often presumes a bounded self as the centre of interpretation, which leaves it vulnerable to accusations of solipsism and valorising the experiences of the self over other people or things.

In this chapter, I mitigate these concerns through using autoethnography from the feminist epistemological position thus outlined. Knowledge production is dependent on a researcher's standpoint and on specific epistemic, historical and cultural perspectives (Keller and Longino, 1996). The pandemic has significantly shifted how we understand our culture and place in time and history, and therefore also our epistemic structures of knowing the world. With this in mind, the bounded, subjective account typical to autoethnography, which describes responses to an exterior world, is critiqued here as the product of intra-acting forces and flows. I am not a hermetic being: instead, my experiences and embodied actions unfold as part of an assemblage of shifting things and phenomena. In this autoethnography, I attempt to de-centre my own agency through visualising the more-than-human, intra-active assemblage in which these knowledges are co-produced.

My use of Barad's relational ontology for purposes of autoethnography and my understanding of affective atmospheres are additionally influenced by phenomenology, which not only studies how experiences in and with the material world appear to common sense, but describes how physical phenomena arise, disrupting "our perceptual faith in the independent solidity of objects" (Dreyfus and Dreyfus, 1964, p.xiii). I build on this notion that boundaries between the self and the material world are imprecise cognitive constructions, to mobilise phenomenology's attention to embodied experience as a means for understanding the world as dynamic configurations of more-than-human matter and perceptual meaning, or as Barad puts it, "mattering" (2007). It is from this combined theoretical and methodological foundation of matter and mattering the research has been constructed.

2   Part One: Autoethnographies of Being and Knowing

2.1   *First Story: Being with Nature through Cézanne-by-Numbers*

Can nature be reduced to numbers? This story considers how doing my paint-by-numbers landscape within the affective atmosphere of lockdown constructed, mediated and transformed my ideas about being in nature, by visualising how technologies, images and other impersonal affects intra-acted with phenomenological perception. I revisited memories and diaries to map a genealogy of more-than-human factors that led me to begin the paint-by-numbers, the matter and mattering of my experiences whilst completing it, and the knowledges that emerged from this socio-material assemblage.

I bought the paint-by-numbers in April 2020 after my friend sent me a link to a video artwork by Heather Phillipson called *put the goat in the goat boat* (2014). It's a neon-coloured, somewhat hallucinatory cogitation on the nature of nature, human beings' place as part of and within nature, and the strange essentialising distinctions we nevertheless make between 'us' and 'animals' and other nonhuman beings. When I visited my local park that afternoon, through the effect of the video, everything seemed sharper, more saturated with movement, showing the matter and mattering of my experiences in the park were discursively shaped by an extended temporality of events that preceded and succeeded them.

In Phillipson's dream-like film, amidst a soundtrack of trippy melodies that sound like the flowers in *Alice in Wonderland*, an image appears of Mont Sainte-Victoire in the South of France, which Paul Cézanne painted almost obsessively in his later life. The image depicts an experience with nature mediated by an artist, and then by my laptop browser, then screen. In the first weeks of lockdown, while procrastinating over my doctoral thesis, the video directed me towards an old printout of an essay called *Cézanne's Doubt,* by Maurice Merleau-Ponty (1964, p. 9). According to my diary I read the essay "enthusiastically", but I quelled my initial, outrageously overambitious musings about wanting to "see and feel the world through painting it like Cézanne". Instead I Googled, found and ordered a paint by numbers kit copying one of Cézanne's many landscapes of Mont Sainte-Victoire on eBay. It took a bit longer to locate the saturated image as derived from a Wikimedia Commons file of the original 1902–4 work now hanging in the Philadelphia Museum of Art.

As I waited for the paint-by-numbers to arrive from China, knowledges emerged through the sense of expectation that amplified the lockdown affective atmosphere of introspection, doubt and inactivity caused by social restrictions and disrupted routines. I thought about flows of capital, flows of viruses, and my globalised experience of buying something from the other side of the world when I couldn't visit my local shop.

When my kit arrived and I began painting, my thoughts looped back to the video and the essay that led me to that moment of doing. According, to Merleau-Ponty, for Cézanne, "painting was his world and his way of life" (ibid.). By this, he means that the act of painting became Cézanne's actual mode of existence, a way of seeing, feeling and being in the world. Cézanne is best known for painting landscapes and still-lifes – things in space – which Merleau-Ponty argues played a key role in how the artist configured his understanding of the things around him and his place within the world.

Paint-by-numbers kits, by contrast, were first manufactured in North America from the 1940s as productive past-times for military troops, becoming widely popular through the twentieth century. The makers of paint-by-numbers were once skilled artists themselves, but in the digital age, any image can be easily rendered into a paint-by-numbers format. An existing image is submitted through algorithmic imaging software to reduce the complex colour palette of pixels into a range of 20 or so colours. This is printed, then subjected to another, less reliable transformation as the user paints colours by hand (more or less clumsily). Rendering a digital photograph into contoured planes for painting-by-numbers is a transformation of perceptual space. From Cézanne's painting to mine, the natural landscape represented has been further mediated, as the artwork was made, photographed, processed, printed, then repainted in a reduced, artificial selection of colours and textures. Each technological mediation is a material-discursive intra-action between the apparatus and the image formed, which alters the shape and interpretation of what is represented.

In my journal, I described my paint-by-numbers as a "cruel irony" to Cézanne's authentically phenomenological attention. His multi-dimensional world had been pushed through stages of digital and manual interference to become a non-coherent body of wiggly, flat, green lozenges. By filling the colours, I had expected "the landscape would suddenly loom towards me, as if through clearing fog, from the headache of squiggles". This did happen, at first, as darker paint colours intra-acted with form, surface and my Gestalt-y perception to pick out the contours of the mountain. As I progressed through each number in the midtones, the landscape became a soupy camouflage that failed at space and depth. It could only represent the superficial configuration of shapes and colours I had assembled. The sense of the 'picture' emerged and receded in relation to each shade added, and the tension of seeing more as we become accustomed to a form and seeing less because we become *too* accustomed (Merleau-Ponty, 2009). I mused what kind of image I was making, if it was an image at all or merely a pattern invented by a computer, transposed to material form. Each technical mediation from Cézanne's canvas to mine left a residue of distortion, resulting in what my boyfriend described as a "Chinese whispers of a picture".[2] My eventual phenomenological understanding of the artefact I had produced was an object whose primary representational value was, simply, a canvas painted-by-numbers.

However, for a short amount of time, the act and object of painting shaped my "world and mode of existence" in other ways. I carried its landscape subject into my interactions with nature. I thought about how Cézanne might have seen the world when I stepped into the park and watched the blustery wind shaking the trees. I found my relation to nature – lived, real-life, living nature, not painted or approximated – appeared as overlapping articulations of self, landscape, my place within it, my feelings about it, as a configuration of socio-political, geographical and corporeal sensibilities (Wylie, 2005). I journaled about the total, initial, embodied experience of the park (e.g., "sunny", "breathless"), then learned details of its natural landscape with time (noticing "tiny leaf buds"). As I coloured in a reproduction of a representation of a French mountain, I thought about the walk I went on that morning, the nature on my doorstep, and the faraway landscape of my family home, which I longed for through iPhone Live Photos, pressing the screen to make contact with the shimmering mirage of familiar country fields. How I perceived nature in the paint-by-numbers was more like a magic eye; I had to adopt a soft focus until this kind of mindful absence let the picture emerge as something experiential, seeing more with an imagined, embodied memory.

The manual activity and mental detachment of the paint-by-numbers landscape therefore mediated between my real, imagined, and remembered

---

2   I acknowledge this phrase has sinophobic connotations, which is not in any way intended by my use. It was spoken in nostalgic reference to the game we played as children that has become idiomatic for messages that become distorted through a chain of transmission. I understand this is now sometimes called the "telephone game", but as this is not a term that was familiar to either person during the conversation, I'm reporting it as it was said, with this note of consternation. (Although the canvas was in fact purchased and shipped from China).

encounters with nature, enacting a material-discursive relation of matter and mattering across temporalities and technologies (Barad, 2007, pp. 234–242; Law, 2002, pp. 133–134). While paint-by-numbers are not, per se, a creative process, the time and concentration they require can offer meditation, relaxation, and foster a meaningful link to the life experiences of their painter during the time of completion (Rubin, 2000, p. 271). In hindsight, the paint-by-numbers was a memorable, reassuring activity undertaken during a time of stress and uncertainty, that simulated a sense of progress amidst the inertia assembled through the lack of physical, mental and social variety resulting from Covid precautions. In the weeks the paint-by-numbers took me to complete, I would sit, absorbed, "zoning in/out until the rest of the room wasn't there", finding another way to escape my home during the lockdown, and a different kind of respite to the park. Through this embodied activity, I attained a disembodied attention, as the task drew my focus away from the habitual agential cut that delineates the edges of our physical bodies (Barad, 2007, p. 155, 210).

This autoethnographic detail draws attention to a blurring of subject/object binary modes of being and perceiving with material and technical worlds, which was also evident in the video and essay that drew me to the paint-by-numbers. Philipson's film, Merleau-Ponty's writing, and Cézanne's painting all expressed preoccupations with the permeable boundaries of interiority and exteriority of self and the natural world. When we read, watch films, or use other kinds of technologies that help us perceive the world around us, our concept of where our physical, intellectual and sensory self ends and where the thing being perceived begins is less concrete, as we are absorbed in what has been described as a "feedback loop" or closed channel of perception and apprehension (Hayles, 2002, p. 75; Thrift, 2005, p. 238; Littau, 2006, p. 8). The paint-by-numbers, the ruminating park walks, the texts, autobiographical details and critical theory all collapsed into each other as entangled experiences clustering around a desire for nature and escapism, which characterised my sense of being and knowing within the extra-ordinary affective atmosphere of the early pandemic.

Ted Toadvine has written in response to *Cézanne's Doubt*,

> What we reach through seeing, touching, painting, or speaking about nature is obviously not a level of noumenal reality. But neither are our stylisation and creative appropriation a screen between ourselves and the world; they are, instead, the condition for anything whatsoever to appear, to be disclosed. Nature, therefore is precisely what discloses

itself *through* our expressive acts, and as requiring such expression for its disclosure.

2009, p. 15

Cézanne aimed to express nature on its own terms, yet this necessarily relied upon his human intervention and painterly expression (ibid., p. 48). In 2020, my interactions with and expressions of nature were mediated by varying cyborgian technologies (Haraway, 1991). In both instances, what signifies is not the *outcome* of these expressive attempts; it is the process of attempting, feeling, experiencing, and desiring expression. Cultural modes of expression rarely replicate exactly the experiential thing they signify: they mediate an expressive distance that allows us to grasp and understand it more expansively. However formulaic or faltering, my efforts to represent my general relation to nature in image and word are an articulation of my relation with it and within it, limited by my abilities and experiences. My onto-epistemological construction of nature, via the paint-by-numbers and daily walks in my local park, emerged through a lived experience that was specific to, and configured by social, environmental and emotional disruptions caused by the pandemic, and that occurred in multiple phenomenological modalities.

The intra-acting assemblage of more-than-human agencies that produced these knowledges also includes lockdown measures. Through limiting my actual experience of being in nature, I dwelled more on my relation *to* nature, meanwhile my desire to represent it was amplified by lack of other distractions. I cannot convey my total experience of being in and with nature, as plural, simultaneous real and imagined landscapes that crowd and collapse together, but I can seek to understand it through its expression in activities and conversations I engage in (Toadvine, 2009). My paint-by-numbers activity was a sufficiently unchallenging, repetitive, yet stimulating activity to allow for this important visual, perceptual, interpretive distance from which to make knowledge.

Cézanne's original painting of Mont-Sainte-Victoire has an aura of vivid, fleeting phenomenological experience of being in nature. As a key painter in the European art historical canon, his work also represents dominant views about culture, economy, creativity and academic knowledge. Doing my paint-by-numbers copy of this painting at that moment in time in the confines of my living room brought these conceptual ideas into contact with the mundanity of lockdown, showing how what is banal and ordinary can speak to more transcendent layers of possibility, experience and meaning-making. Now hanging on the wall in a different flat, in a different part of town, two years later, the paint-by-numbers emerges through my pandemic autoethnography as a focal point for the anxiety, boredom, desire, creativity, insecurity, isolation and frustration I experienced: a banal object through which I can still connect with fleeting experience of an unprecedented time. Making this object taught me about myself, and helped me assemble other knowledges about the immediate, vibrant world that surrounded me.

2.2   *Second Story: On Not Learning to Paint or Make 'Art', but Learning to Know Differently*

> The paint-by-numbers came with rubbish paintbrushes. Its warped balsa frame wobbled on the table and I had to prop it up on a laptop stand.

In this story about the matter and mattering of creative making, the autoethnography foregrounds the materiality of doing then viewing the paint-by-numbers as sites of emergent knowledge that challenged my preconceived notions of the socio-technical production of artworks, leading me to question the ontological and epistemological 'cuts' that signify how creative work is valued. I chart how the tools, time and social interactions assembled around making my painting produced insights into the histories and economies that shape its signification, and how they intersect with conventions of academic labour disrupted by the pandemic. This prompts imaginative thinking about what other, Othered knowledges could be re-valued through more careful research practice.

The materiality of the rudimentary technical apparatus that was the paint-by-numbers enacted more-than-human agency in my manual engagement. My journal frequently relays the frustration the brushes caused me: an embodied emotion, felt through the assemblage of painty parts in which I was enrolled, which pushed back against my desire to manipulate it into neat shapes. The brushes and stiff paint did not co-operate to fill the juts and angles of the design; brushes, paint consistency and outlines were an incompatible trio struggling to work together. I could have swapped in better paintbrushes I already owned. I didn't because I had an emerging sense that I needed to do the activity exactly as it came. I put this down to a conceptual, technological enquiry about the nature of media (and/or media of nature). I was aware my interest in the paint-by-numbers was more elaborate than a naïve craft activity to pass the time, as I initially linked it to phenomenology. Through the materiality of *doing* the paint by numbers activity, knowledge emerged as a subtle awareness of the onto-epistemological value of the exercise as a means of challenging the conventional 'cuts' made between what signifies as an artwork, and what doesn't.

When constructing my autoethnography, I considered how my choice of image and activity were entangled with my work as an art historian and curator. The video and essay had suggested Cézanne to me and amplified my Covid-regulated real and imagined encounters with nature. At the same time, there is a simultaneous, entangled narrative in which I recognised the irony of reproducing a masterpiece of intuitive, experience-based art through a reductive, commodified craft (Dee, 2018). Without this academic curiosity, I might have done a cross-stitch. Instead, as I painted, I wondered about creating more paint-by-numbers of famous paintings, or landscapes; what this technical mediation might say about the subjects reproduced and canvases produced; and what circumstances of cultural production might be required for these objects to be socially constructed as "artworks" (Benjamin, 1935/2008; Dickie, 1974).

This line of thought was fed by conversations with my curator/painter friend Dan Goodman. We questioned what would happen if I exhibited my paint-by-numbers in a gallery, framed by these conceptual interests. I chronicled my conversation with my artist friend thus:

> Would exhibiting the paint-by-numbers make it an artwork? Modernity invented the art commodity, the framed saleable canvas. Post-Duchamp, art was further commodified as it no longer required Skill or Time or even Effort but only Concept (and bravado). Placing an object (famously a urinal) in a gallery with a signature transforms it through some social alchemy into Art. Giving an artefact a lengthy explanation with big words makes it a materialised Idea. As a curator, I can envision an exhibition that displays objects like my paint-by-numbers to provoke debate on why art has to necessarily be 'good' to be 'seen'. What does this say about the labour of artists?!!!!!! Dichotomies of art and craft?

This conversation was informed by sociological theories of art production, such as Howard Becker's functional model (1982/2008) or George Dickie's institutional theory (1997), which argue there is no essential quality that makes something an artwork. Rather, an artwork is produced through a complex of social conditions, such as being made by a person who identifies it as an artwork, exhibited within a frame on a gallery wall, presented to a group of people (an "artworld" public) who also agree it is 'art', and might buy it. In these sociological accounts, artworks are socially constructed through processes ranging from the intention of the artist to the approval of its audiences. The gallery, pricing, audiences and conceptual narrative could be viewed as apparatuses that configure together to make an agential cut between what is and isn't art, thus signifying the economic, symbolic and cultural value of a creative endeavour.

These dichotomies, too, ('is/is not'; 'art/craft') are cuts: arbitrary boundaries constructed between interrelating practices.

This sociological view is complicated by the boundary status of the paint-by-numbers commodity. A boundary object is something whose ontological value shifts according to its enrolment in different activities (Star and Griesemer, 1989, p. 393). Paint-by-numbers kits are not devoid of skill; they take time, care and diligence to complete. Pre-Photoshop, they would be created by graphic artists who would divide the source image into contours and colours. The 'work' of creating the paint-by-numbers would then be distributed amongst manufacturers, supply chains, and ultimately, be completed hundredfold by the users who paint them, as the final step in a functional, technical production distributed across many actors in space and time. Despite the qualities of skill, aesthetic judgement and global collaboration involved in the total completion of a paint-by-numbers, many sociological accounts would not consider it art because they require artefacts to be produced within a certain discourse, with certain intent, and distinction that they are *good* art, which is often dictated by what commercial galleries designate as *saleable* art (Bourdieu, 1984; Bourdieu and Johnson, 1993). I read this as a more-than-human ecology that assembles capital, materials and ideology.

The question of whether something is 'art' or 'not art' appears to emerge through a tense dialectal relation with 'popular culture', being perceived as somehow superior or more expressive than other forms of material culture. Yet, as Dee has argued, the distinction between art and popular culture is untenable, and exists to maintain strict frameworks for creative expression within capitalist political economies (2018). Ultimately, there is no essential distinction for what is or isn't art, because this discursive label emerges through an agential relation between the maker, the matter (or market) of the thing made and the conditions of its continued (re)making wherever it is altered, displayed, encountered or remembered. All this thinking was rooted in the matter and mattering of making my painting.

As it happens, in December 2021 I exhibited the canvas in an open submission co-organised by my friend Dan, called 'Now That's What I Call Art' (nerdy aside – what a brilliant title to exemplify material-discursive mattering situated in time and spatial relation!). Submissions were accepted without selection until there was no room left, removing questions of taste or 'good' or 'bad' art. Through this inclusion, a collective of participating curators and artists not only validated my paint-by-numbers as an artwork, but they identified me as an artist. The paint-by-numbers' boundary position in creative economies enabled this reconfiguration of its ontological status, as well as my 'role' as its producer, according to different scenarios. The craft hobby was co-opted by the pre-existing academic interests of its owner/maker, through a configuration of human habitus (my identifying as 'curator') and socio-economic structures of art-making and art histories which are at odds with the simplicity of the materials and the task in question. From the assemblage of materials, tools, existing knowledges and resources, the paint-by-numbers is a boundary object which could be repositioned, or 'cut' to sit within various fields of cultural practice, from the amateurish to the overly conceptualised, depending on its material-discursive framing, which is to say both physical use and situation, and conceptual positioning. The inclusion in the exhibition reconfigured it as 'art' through physical juxtaposition with other artworks, in a site discursively framed as an art gallery, where I had conversations with other artists about our submissions. This coming-together of material-discursive elements made it matter more as an artwork and cut it apart from its former agency and status as a relaxing activity in my living room (Barad, 2007, p. 178).

To understand the matter and mattering in the production of creative artefacts from a perspective of care requires a more inclusive view of their agency and signification. The 'matter' is a sense of *doing*, configured through material/technical intra-action with stuff – paintbrushes, gallery walls – and its mattering, or *signification,* is constructed by ongoing socio-cultural discourse. Being an artist is also a material discursive label that hangs in the relation between self-identification, social agreement, material production. Being able to paint – being a painter – does not make one an artist, if one fails to self-identify with this label. In *On not being able to paint*, Marion Milner's quest for a personal sense of what it means to make art demonstrates a proto-autoethnography using the self as a site of exploration of craft, environment and psyche (1950). Although technically proficient at representational painting, for Milner, the essence of artistic activity required abandoning learned conventions to discover a more elusive sense of where painting comes from and how it feels. This knowledge was not located in technical ability, but emerged through engaging with the experience of painting, as an embodied, intellectual, sensual endeavour related to her surroundings and inner life. Milner's paintings, and her approach to creating and knowing through painting, were artefacts of situated intra-actions between skill, mood, body, environment and painterly materials.

As Milner explored the emergence of a painting practice, I am also interrogating my own developing research practice as a product of relations between body, environment, matter and meaning, through prowling the boundaries of the materials that have inspired it, testing their value as artefacts of experience, economy and agency. Recognising the cuts between 'artwork' and 'not artwork', 'artist', 'painter' or 'other', as arbitrary and unfixed has consequences for my enquiry into what counts as knowing. In lockdown, many traditional boundaries lost their distinction: 'labour'/'leisure', 'home'/'work-place', 'together'/'apart'. This added a fluidity and flatness to the affective atmosphere of lockdown that, in my case, encouraged deeper understanding of the non-hierarchical epistemologies pervading my theoretical interests.

What emerges is a sense of plurality that is more historically found in non-Western epistemologies. This was highlighted by my first (and only) visit to an exhibition in 2020, in between Covid lockdowns, to BALTIC in Gateshead. It showed drawings of rainforest plants, animals and ecosystems by Abel Rodriquez, a *sabedor* or 'man of knowledge' from the Colombian Amazon. Rodriguez learned knowledge of Amazonian flora and fauna through oral history and time spent in the forest. He made drawings and paintings from memory to share this knowledge with non-indigenous botanists and biologists, showing creative practice as a crucial part in producing and translating understandings of the world. His works are gaining acclaim for their artistic value and appearing in global activities of artworld economies, however Rodriguez does not make "contemporary art" in a Western sense. The concept doesn't exist in his native language Muinane. The closest comparison he could suggest was *iimitya,* which means 'word of power' or "all paths lead to the same knowledge, which is the beginning of all paths" (BALTIC, 2020).

I was impressed by Rodriguez's depictions of a felt, experiential understanding of his native natural world, at a point when the pandemic's disruption to ways of moving through the world left me preoccupied with my own relation to nature. Revisiting it a year later through writing, I regarded Rodriguez's pictures as confluence between different ways of making knowledges; different paths to explore similar questions. They have emerged from personal experience and Indigenous tradition to communicate to contemporary (Western) science and artworlds. There is no suggestion that Rodriguez's pictures or oral histories are in any way inferior to the scholarship of those scientists he has guided through the rainforest. They are different ways of understanding the immeasurably complex: one person's demonstration of a diversity of Indigenous modes of thinking about the material and more-than-human (Muñoz et al., 2015, p. 210, 232; TallBear, 2015), without the attempt to possess or oppress knowledges through the collection and classification that pervades colonial epistemologies (Parry, 2004). Even the terms "scientist" and "sabedor" are etymologically similar: the former, derived from Latin *scire,* 'to know', and the second, from the Spanish *saber* 'to know', but initially the Latin *sapere* 'to notice, to research, to be wise'. Knowing cannot come without noticing, science cannot come without research. The pictures therefore depict rainforest ecosystems, but they also show the co-dependence of structured forms of scholarship and lived, felt understanding.

I cannot pretend my fleeting engagements with nature, though heightened by lockdown, have revealed even a glimpse of the intimate understanding of a *sabedor* such as Rodriguez. My activities negotiated a blurry field of knowledge-making practices, some led by touch and sensation, some through observation, others through wider reading and criticism. Much like Rodriguez's ecological rainforest portrait, or Cézanne's planes of air, meadow and sky, the knowledge practices explored here have carefully sought to express an interconnectedness in which I am but one actor. This humility felt particularly relevant amidst the lockdown affective atmosphere, by recognising the smallness of my own role in more-than-human, global assemblages of everything from knowledge to contagion. Meanwhile, bodies with less power in conventional hierarchies still have important agency in wider ecologies (Bennett, 2010, p. 13, 98; Puig de la Bellacasa, 2017, p. 170), whether through acts of handwashing or writing. In my case, this transient assemblage is materialised and made to matter through the apparatus of autoethnographic writing.

3   Part Two: an Emergent Methodology

3.1   *Making Visible the More-Than-Human in Autoethnography*
This autoethnography has been constructed through many layers. First, I found relaxation and intrigue in an everyday craft activity. When I began to write about it, the country was still moving in and out of lockdowns, which gave me ample solitary thinking time to situate my critique of the paint-by-numbers in relation to phenomenology, affect, ontology, epistemology and posthuman care. During lockdown, the hours spent in my living room became an extension of the hours spent living in my head. I saw my introspective self spill into my material surroundings, so the paint-by-numbers became a vessel for thinking through the conceptual arguments I became interested in at that time. I have since moved house and with further distance from the pandemic, my local park and the act of painting, the autoethnography has also become an artefact in its description of a particular, intimate moment in my personal history. My individual narrative of subjectivity, folding into my self and my self-questioning, whilst folding into nature and my doubting Cézanne, is encapsulated by a particular cultural moment in local and global society, of which the acts of writing are trying to make sense.

In a diary entry from Spring 2021 meditating on painting and walking in the park, I appreciated the new spring leaf buds that reassured me through being "... blissfully ignorant of whatever analytical idea it provokes in my overactive, introspective mind". There is a cliché here of a cartoon "academic" who shrouds

simple phenomena in overcomplicated theory to produce some obscure article of little real-world relevance. And yet, my lived experience of simple phenomena *did* stimulate complicated reflection on the situatedness of human
encounters with the world, as real as I lived it. In lockdown, by noticing how
ideas emerged through small, everyday activities, I linked relational, embodied
experiences with the more abstract knowledges they produced.

Among these knowledges were insights into how my experiences altered
my sensoria and elicited relational insight. An earlier draft of this chapter
involved a third autoethnographic account about walking in the park. Critical
issues relating to my experiences with the paint-by-numbers emerged through
these walks. Then, when sitting down to paint, my imagination would picture
lived experiences of nature, near and far. The activities were intra-actively
linked through simultaneous critical engagement, showing these knowledges
emerged in complex, mutually-constitutive relations to each other within the
context of a fixed period of time with unusual physical and social conditions.
As with Rodriguez's paintings, which mediated between Indigenous knowledge and scientific research, my encounters with art and nature have mediated
both creative/personal exploration and more conventional knowledge outputs
(like this essay).

Earlier in this chapter, I described autoethnography as a more "authentic"
view (Adams, Holman Jones and Ellis, 2021) of the messy, relational world in
which we live. My autoethnography channels an ethical commitment to situated knowledge practice that feminist discourse has previously characterised
as "reflexivity" (Guillemin and Gillam, 2004). The idea that autoethnography
is reflective implies the world can be mirrored without distortion (Barad,
2003, pp. 802–806). In fact, understanding situated knowledge as emergent
from more-than-human worlds shows knowledges about the world are always
processual and co-produced. The technique of autoethnography diffracts
(Haraway, 1992, pp. 299–300; Barad, 2007, p. 72) the research assemblage by
selectively shaping the account of knowledge production. In writing and
making a text material (even in a digital Word document), autoethnography
makes an unreliable object that takes on a life of its own, which can be revisited, revised, and new connections made. As time and memory fluctuate, the
autoethnography has posthuman agency in mediating between present, past
and future self, meanwhile mythologizing my perception of each. The method
and the outcomes of autoethnography are therefore another apparatus in the
assemblage of matter and mattering.

By mobilising autoethnography through this mode of more-than-human
relational thinking, I could map how activities were in fact an intra-action
between local and global agencies, from first-hand materials, conversations

and walks, to local and national lockdown measures, and the progress of the pandemic around the world. Walking in the park and undertaking the paint-by-numbers were activities I approached with greater intensity because of the pandemic, yet they engaged imaginative faculties that enhanced my experience of the other, whilst eliciting critical thinking. The embodied experience of a stimulating activity, whether it was walking and looking around me, or concentrating my movements upon a small area, heightened my sensitivity to other relational factors and more-than-human agencies structuring those experiences, and the common threads of art and nature carried the train of thought between activities.

At points, my journals described a dissolving of boundaries of self, as I became less aware of the limits of my physical being as something separate from the being-with-nature activity of walking or painting/imagining landscape, with all their imaginative and embodied stimuli (Bennett, 2010, pp. 13, 30–31; Wylie, 2005, p. 236). I experienced a more seamless flow of action, sensation, perception and emotion between points of matter in contact, whether it was feet-concrete-grass-breeze-memory or hand-hunched-posture-paint-gloop-mountain. These descriptive configurations engaged with physical, historical, social, personal, political factors at once, yet they express a more diffuse attention that precedes a material-discursive cut between the limits of certain kinds of matter and meaning, contributing to deconstructing ontological distinctions between more-than-human actors in the research assemblage.

This is a crucial point of where my approach to autoethnography has become disrupted: a de-centred approach in which I did not regard myself as a bounded self, but open and porous to the agencies of other, more-than-human actants, enabled me to develop sensitivity towards the tangible, meaningful impact of things as mundane as cheap paintbrushes or iPhone memories. This "relational confrontation with the everyday maintaining of life" enables other forms of knowing, which, Puig argues, enables us to "deeply understand the importance of material mediations against the abstractions of 'masculine' thought established on detachment from these devalued activities" (Puig de la Bellacasa, p. 14). In feminist discourse, those labours that mediate with the material world can be described as care. In my autoethnographic account, each activity elicited a tangle of socio-political consciousness that impacted how I formed ideas about myself, my work, other people and things. Among these combined actants, the most significant is the Pandemic, without which I wouldn't have engaged with these activities, nor developed the quality of attention described.

The specificity of the assemblage from which these knowledges emerged is evidenced by a more recent paint-by-numbers activity, which I found to be far less stimulating. I ordered another kit based on a photograph I had taken in the park, with the agenda to explore whether mediating it through paint-by-numbers produced new understandings about my relation to nature on my doorstep. This more intellectually self-conscious activity remains incomplete. During the first lockdown, I was at a point with my PhD that allowed mental attention for other interests, yet other pursuits were unavailable; the more recent lockdown, with the new paint-by-numbers, coincided with a more intensive period of thesis-editing, showing the way I made knowledges during 2020 emerged as a specific relation to circumstances both personal and societal. The affective atmosphere of lockdown, as a configuration of unfamiliar rules, overfamiliar surroundings, physical distance from loved ones, over-exposure to technological devices and low-level fear pressurised my emotions and attentions. At once, this disruption from prior habits and norms liberated me from responsibilities of other social roles and demanded a more flexible, permissive approach to 'work', a point which will be revisited in the final section.

This latter paint-by-numbers also behaves as a counterargument to criticisms of solipsism, because the act I initiated with explicit scholarly interest proved less fruitful. This later effort to "make" knowledge, as opposed to noticing how knowledges emerged incidentally and organically, was less successful because I sought to provoke connections myself, diminishing the agency of the assemblage. This relational autoethnographic enquiry, therefore, was more successful in instances where my own personal experience was decentred as a means through which to explore broader agencies and insights, such as to question how the affective atmosphere of lockdown impacted academic labour more generally, to which this discussion now turns.

3.2   *To Conclude: In Support of Careful Knowledge Practices in Academia*

According to Garrett Bunyak, Puig de la Bellacasa's work *Matters of Care* "argues for the importance of caring as well as possible in a complicated material present shaped by imperfect histories and uncertain futures" (Bunyak, 2018, p. 247). My argument has explored this emphasis on care in the complicated material present of a scenario that juxtaposes imperfect histories of academic production that devalue knowledges coded as feminine, such as affect and embodiment, with uncertain futures of contemplating new ways of being and feeling in an unprecedented pandemic. The affective atmosphere of lockdown, in which time, work, socialising and domestic responsibilities became collapsed with feelings of insecurity and uncertainty, and the relative freedom afforded by doing a PhD (with flexible and trusting supervisors) assembled together with my own agency as a researcher to enact a different kind of *care* towards the agencies of tools, texts and conversations through which knowledge emerged, and the new approach to methodology that this eventually produced.

This affective atmosphere of lockdown was primarily felt within academic life in practical terms. The disruption of the pandemic caused a break from routines, limited access to services, and impacted patterns of academic labour, such as teaching, marking, fieldwork, meetings and conferences, which were quickly adapted or postponed. Lockdown interrupted academic 'business as usual', which prompted a longer-term disjuncture with what future academic work might look like (particularly to an early career academic). As the pandemic provoked a re-evaluation of how time is distributed and research is produced, by necessity it facilitated other kinds of knowledge-making that might not have been possible within the regular demands of the "metric-oriented", "time-compressed" regimes of the neo-liberal university (Mountz et al., 2015; Giroux, 2021). The pandemic also foregrounded principles of the slow scholarship movement, which argues for an "ethics of care" in "how we work and interact with each other" that allows greater time and space for academic labours (Mountz et al., 2015; Garey, Hertz and Nelson, 2014).

Caring in academia is more than care-giving among students and peers: while the pandemic inspired new online networks of peer-support, funding for research extensions and increased familiarity in professional relationships as Zoom gave insight into each other's homes, care also becomes a way of speaking more of the critical engagements of knowledge producers beyond the polarised divisions around the meanings of social and politically "useful" research (Puig de la Bellacasa, p. 16). The constant need to assess and justify *how* we work within prescribed academic conventions has historically reinforced notions of what is "productive work" and even "productive personhood", tacitly affirming certain gendered/racialised/ableist/classist/neuronormative hierarchies (Mountz et al., 2015). Instead, inviting fluidity towards what research looks like opens a pluralistic space with room for more diverse modes of thinking beyond convention.

Longer-term, iterative modes of research, as supported by slow scholarship, challenge what counts for "knowing" in the academic sphere, not only because they resist the objective-oriented structures of many funding schemes. Throughout producing this text, I experienced strong sensations of doubt and insecurity that what I am producing is "knowledge". I now recognise the presence of doubt and uncertainty in my own research practice are not dissimilar to the humility required to recognise more-than-human agency (Bennett, 2010, p. 11). As shown in the discussion of Abel Rodriguez, non-hegemonic modes of making knowledges that are other to those prevalent in academia are not necessarily inferior, simply "a different path". Slow scholarship advocates are usually academics at secure points in their career, with permanent research positions, when their creative academic labour has been overwhelmed by the university's administrative load. For researchers like myself, it seems imperative to enter into academic labour having *already* made a commitment to safeguard and trust this approach to slow and emergent knowledge, which I could only do through promoting its validity. Lockdown separated me from the progress updates of peers, which helped nurture a conviction that my own work can look however it needs in order to suit the thing studied – an iterative, responsive, itinerant methodology, that doesn't start out with a fixed plan, but makes valuable knowledges through ongoing intra-actions of wandering in the world, writing, connecting, rewriting (Barad, 2007, pp. 190–191).

Through allowing space and time, common themes emerged which could be interesting avenues for further research, for example, the artificial division of humans and nature explored in Phillipson's work and my own experiences, or the general modernist paradigm of cultural artefacts as commodities. These themes challenge capitalist and colonial onto-epistemologies, and are thus suited to modes of enquiry that go against the grain of the conventional, imperial knowledge practices for sorting and defining – for, as Audre Lorde reminds us, we can't dismantle the racist, sexist and capitalist regimes that oppress our societies using tools invented by those same regimes; we must seek alternative methodologies to critique those forces we perceive to be corruptive (1984, pp. 53, 110–111).

In summary, the absence of certain constraints and the adoption of certain modes of attention can reveal forms of knowledge making that emphasise fluidity and subtlety. This subtlety is inhibited by prescriptive boundaries of research proposals, calls for papers and precarious early-career research, but it's also hard to capture amidst the daily routine. The severance from known routines and responsibilities enacted by lockdown, and the initiation of new ones, created a liminal space of learning through providing flexibility and possibility that enabled new modes of connecting experience into knowledge (Land, Rattray and Vivian, 2014). Lockdown plunged me into a greatly reduced physical world, in which I could attune to the matter and mattering of the more-than-human agencies that pushed me to one interpretation or another. When I began my paint-by-numbers, I had no inkling it would become meaningful enough to challenge my ontological and epistemological awareness. These kinds of research take time and open-mindedness. They necessitate slow, attentive scholarship that is generous to noticing knowledges as they emerge. In this example the objects of knowledge production may not be of enormous academic significance, but a sensitivity to more-than-human, felt, intuitive ways of understanding matter and mattering is an essential part of a care-centred, inclusive scholarship.

References

Adams, Tony E., Stacy Holman Jones, and Carolyn Ellis (eds.). (2021) *Handbook of Autoethnography*. 2nd ed. Milton: Taylor & Francis Group.

BALTIC Centre for Contemporary Art. (2020) *ABEL RODRIGUEZ*. [Exhibition handout].

Barad, Karen. (2007) *Meeting the Universe Halfway: Quantum Physics and the Entanglement of Matter and Meaning*. Durham: Duke University Press.

Barad, Karen. (2003) 'Posthumanist Performativity: Toward an Understanding of How Matter Comes to Matter'. *Signs* 28(3): 801–31. https://doi.org/10.1086/345321.

Becker, Howard Saul. (1982/2008) *Art Worlds*. Updated and Expanded 25th Anniversary ed. Berkeley, Calif.; London: University of California Press.

Benjamin, Walter., and J.A. Underwood. (1935/2008) *The Work of Art in the Age of Mechanical Reproduction*. Great Ideas; 56. London: Penguin.

Bennett, Jane. (2010) *Vibrant Matter: A Political Ecology of Things*. Durham, N.C.: Duke University Press.

Bourdieu, Pierre. (1984) *Distinction: A Social Critique of the Judgement of Taste*. Cambridge, Mass.: Harvard University Press.

Bourdieu, Pierre., and Randal Johnson. (1993) *The Field of Cultural Production: Essays on Art and Literature*. Cambridge: Polity Press.

Brown P. (2013) 'Loneliness at the bench. Is the PhD experience as emotionally taxing as it is mentally challenging?'. *EMBO reports*, 14(5), 405–409. https://doi.org/10.1038/embor.2013.35.

Bunyak, Garrett. (2018) 'Matters of Care: Speculative Ethics in More Than Human Worlds by Maria Puig De La Bellacasa (review)'. *Configurations* 26(2): 247–49.

De Landa, Manuel. (2007) *A New Philosophy of Society: Assemblage Theory and Social Complexity*. London: Continuum.

Dee, Liam. (2018) *Against Art and Culture*. Singapore: Springer Singapore Pte. Limited.

Deleuze, Gilles, and Félix. Guattari. (1987/2004) *A Thousand Plateaus: Capitalism and Schizophrenia*. London: Continuum.

Dickie, George. (1974) *Art and the Aesthetic: An Institutional Analysis*. Ithaca, N.Y.: Cornell University Press.

Dickie, George. (1997) *The Art Circle: A Theory of Art*. Evanston: Chicago Spectrum Press.

Dreyfus, Hubert L., and Patricia Allen Dreyfus. (1964) [Translator's preface], in Merleau-Ponty, Maurice. *Sense and Non-sense*. Northwestern University Studies in Phenomenology & Existential Philosophy. Evanston, Ill.: Northwestern University Press.

Garey, Anita Ilta, Rosanna Hertz, and Margaret K Nelson. (2014) *Open to Disruption: Time and Craft in the Practice of Slow Sociology*. Nashville: Vanderbilt University Press.

Giroux, Henry A. (2021) *Race, Politics, and Pandemic Pedagogy: Education in a Time of Crisis*. London: Bloomsbury Academic.

Guillemin, Marilys, and Lynn Gillam. (2004) "Ethics, Reflexivity, and 'Ethically Important Moments" in Research'. *Qualitative Inquiry* 10(2): 261–80.

Haraway, Donna Jeanne. (1991) *Simians, Cyborgs, and Women: The Reinvention of Nature*. New York: Routledge.

Haraway, Donna Jeanne (1992) 'The Promises of Monsters: A Regenerative Politics for Inappropirate/d Others', in L. Grossberg, C. Nelson, and P.A. Treichler (eds.) *Cultural Studies*. New York: Routledge, pp. 295–337.

Haraway, Donna Jeanne. (1994) 'A Game of Cat's Cradle: Science Studies', Feminist Theory, Cultural Studies. *Configurations*, 2(1): 59–71.

Harding, Sandra G. (2004) *The Feminist Standpoint Theory Reader: Intellectual and Political Controversies*. New York: Routledge.

Hayles, N. Katherine. (2002) *Writing Machines*. Mediawork. Cambridge, Mass., London: MIT.

Keller, Evelyn Fox, and Longino, Helen. (1996) *Feminism and science*. Oxford, UK: Oxford University Press.

Land, Ray, Julie Rattray, and Peter Vivian. (2014) 'Learning in the Liminal Space'. *Higher Education* 67(2): 199–217.

Law, John. (2002) 'On Hidden Heterogeneities: Complexity, Formalism, and Aircraft Design'. In Law, John, and Annemarie. Mol (eds.). *Complexities: Social Studies of Knowledge Practices*. Science and Cultural Theory. Durham: Duke University Press.

Littau, Karin. (2006) *Theories of Reading: Books, Bodies, and Bibliomania*. Cambridge, UK; Malden, Mass.: Polity Press.

Lorde, Audre (1984) *Sister Outsider: Essays and Speeches by Audre Lorde*. New York: The Crossing Press.

Mackie, Sylvia Anne, and Glen William Bates (2019) Contribution of the doctoral education environment to PhD candidates' mental health problems: a scoping review, *Higher Education Research & Development*, 38(3), 565–578, DOI: 10.1080/07294360.2018.1556620.

Merleau-Ponty, Maurice. (1964) 'Cézanne's Doubt', in *Sense and Non-sense*. Northwestern University Studies in Phenomenology & Existential Philosophy. Evanston, Ill.: Northwestern University Press.

Merleau-Ponty, Maurice. (2009) *The World of Perception*. Routledge Classics. London; New York: Routledge.

Milner, Marion [pseudonym Joanna Field]. (1950) *On Not Being Able to Paint*. The Heinemann Education Series. London: William Heinemann.

Mountz, Alison, Anne Bonds, Becky Mansfield, Jenna Loyd, Jennifer Hyndman, Margaret Walton-Roberts, Ranu Basu, Risa Whitson, Roberta Hawkins, Trina Hamilton, and Winifred Curran. (2015) 'For Slow Scholarship: A Feminist Politics of Resistance through Collective Action in the Neoliberal University'. *ACME: An International Journal for Critical Geographies* 14(4), 1235–59. https://www.acme-jour nal.org/index.php/acme/article/view/1058.

Muñoz, José Esteban, Jinthana Haritaworn, Myra J Hird, Jasbir K Puar, Eileen A Joy, Uri McMillan, Susan Stryker, Kimberly TallBear, Jami Weinstein, and Judith Halberstam. (2015) 'Theorizing Queer Inhumanisms: The Sense of Brownness'. *GLQ* 21(2): 209–10.

Pagan, Victoria. (2019) 'Being and Becoming a "good" Qualitative Researcher? Liminality and the Risk of Limbo'. *Qualitative Research in Organizations and Management* 14(1): 75–90.

Parry, Benita. (2004) *Postcolonial Studies: A Materialist Critique.* Postcolonial Literatures. London: Routledge.

Puig De La Bellacasa, María. (2017) *Matters of Care: Speculative Ethics in More than Human Worlds.* Minneapolis: University of Minnesota Press.

Rubin, Lawrence C. (2000) 'The Use of Paint-by-number Art in Therapy'. *The Arts in Psychotherapy* 27(4): 269–72.

Sikka, Tina. (2021) 'Feminist Materialism and Covid-19: The Agential Activation of Everyday Objects'. *NORA: Nordic Journal of Women's Studies* 29(1): 4–16.

Smith, Laurel C. (2012) 'Decolonizing Hybridity: Indigenous Video, Knowledge, and Diffraction'. *Cultural Geographies* 19(3): 329–48. https://doi.org/10.1177/147447401 1429407.

Star, Susan Leigh, and James R. Griesemer. (1989) 'Institutional Ecology, 'Translations' and Boundary Objects: Amateurs and Professionals in Berkeley's Museum of Vertebrate Zoology, 1907–39'. *Social Studies of Science* 19(3): 387–420. http://www .jstor.org/stable/285080.

Sumartojo, Shanti, and Sarah Pink. (2019) *Atmospheres and the Experiential World: Theory and Methods.* London: Routledge.

TallBear, Kimberly. (2015) 'An Indigenous Reflection on Working Beyond the Human/ Not Human'. *GLQ* 21(2): 230–35.

Thrift, Nigel. (2005) 'Beyond Mediation: Three New Material Registers and Their Consequences'. In *Materiality*, ed. Daniel Miller. New York: Duke University Press, pp. 231–55.

Toadvine, Ted. (2009) *Merleau-Ponty's Philosophy of Nature.* Northwestern University Studies in Phenomenology & Existential Philosophy. Evanston, Ill.: Northwestern University Press.

Wylie, John. (2005) 'A Single Day's Walking: Narrating Self and Landscape on the South West Coast Path'. *Transactions – Institute of British Geographers* 30(2): pp. 234–47.

Conclusion

Tina Sikka, Gareth Longstaff and Steve Walls

1 Critical Disruptions

This collection emerged as an in-house project within the Media, Culture and Heritage section at Newcastle University. Borne from a recognition among ourselves, that despite varied interests and fields of expertise there was a potential for a definitive 'Newcastle School' of thought. Perhaps as an 'unintended consequence' (Giddens, 1984) of 'disruption' posed by the coronavirus pandemic, we began to look inward and towards each other's expertise and research interests. This introspection illuminated the central threads of our perspectives, approaches, attitudes and practice, seen here to weave together as an overall critical approach to media ecologies, everyday life, technology, political, cultural and health economies, events, phenomena, contexts, individualities and collectivities. These may remain static or subject to change (sometimes rapidly, or even violently so), but as a group, our raison d'être remains staunchly centred around the intersection of theory/practice when critically unravelling and exposing materialities of inequality, the power dynamics of the social construction of knowledge and the discursive constitution of narratives and subjectivities. In this sense we implore an embracing of the creative and critical potentialities of 'disruption'.

Disruption is defined as: 'a disturbance or problems which interrupt an event, activity of process' (Oxford English Dictionary); the 'action of preventing something, especially a system, process, or event, from continuing as usual or expected'; or 'the action of completely changing the traditional way that an industry or market operates by using new methods or technology' (Cambridge dictionary). In terms of a literal reading, many of the chapters in this collection speak to the myriad 'disruptions' allied to various contexts during the global Covid-19 pandemic. Lives, behaviours, interactions, intimacies, economies, political regimes, cultural spheres, industries and experiences were all subject to drastic disruption. However, disruption is not simply an act of 'interruption' but instead, can be a critically reflexive and evolutionary process, a chance to pause, review and evolve both from a critical disciplinary perspective but also culturally, socially, individually.

In another way, the materiality and ethos of the current collection also points towards a more inward-facing view of academic output and internal reflection. We believe this to be a firm USP for the book, as 'collective intellectual enterprises of an integrated kind' remain 'unusual in the history of the social sciences' (Bulmer, 1984, p. 1) rarely emanating from an institutional subject level. Instead, they generally bring contributors together in terms of areas of expertise from a variety of organisations, institutions and backgrounds. Our approach here has been to embed collegiality and collectivity through 'disrupting' the way academic outputs have become subject to the logic of capitalist production – mass-produced within a knowledge economy and marketplace governed by monitoring, quantifying, measuring and competing for impact, funding and citations. The book has therefore, also functioned as a vehicle to bring us together as a 'section' or group of academics, researchers and practitioners, within a specific higher education setting. As a 'school' of thought we share a collective resolve and ethos in terms of our approaches, viewpoints and ethics. Part of this includes the nurturing and mentoring of early career academics and postgraduate research students who often lack the opportunities to develop writing skills and publish outputs. The collection here also 'disrupts' the current publication model that places barriers in the way for those on the journey towards, or on the cusp of, an academic career. This has been a productive process in terms of realising the potential of our talented early career researchers and PGR students, providing an avenue to grow, speak and reflect.

This collective resolve may be viewed through various lenses. Cynics or pragmatists may do so through the logic of capitalism and building a 'brand' as part of the commodification of higher education, to enhance reputation, increase recruitment, and maximise earning potential. However, we suggest readers understand this 'disruptive process' as a creative endeavour, a return to earlier modes of developing critical thought made famous through the Chicago School of the 1920s, the Frankfurt School of 1920s-1980s and the Birmingham School for Cultural Studies in the 1960s. These movements focus more upon bringing academics, researchers, practitioners together instead of pitting us against each other. To realise the critical, creative and productive power of our theoretical dispositions, perspectives, affinities and conflicts. We may come from different backgrounds and follow diverging trajectories within a broad subject area of 'media, culture and heritage' studies. However, there are definitive theoretical patterns and threads that can be successfully interwoven to make sense of the rich tapestry of our perspectives. Writing around such diverse themes that include traditional Chinese medicine, Brexit, sex clubs, OnlyFans, and painting-by-numbers may seem sporadic and enigmatic but there is a synergy present that connects the entire volume and specific assemblages of chapters. As our book title suggests, the central thread throughout remains the activity of disruption. However, this disruption becomes a lens through which to view, scrutinise and magnify issues in contemporary media and cultural studies. The key overarching themes can perhaps be mapped in various ways, and the below is by no means a proscriptive schema of how the work should be interpreted or understood. The intention here is to, instead, provide a preliminary frame through which suggestive threads and fibres can be woven together. In the spirit of the collection and its theme of disruption we have held this until the conclusion so that the reader has hopefully encountered and navigated the themes and issues of the book in their own unique way. Furthermore, the following sections are not meant to define, categorise and confine disrupted knowledge – rather they are here to situate, guide and contour our approaches to it and its inter and transdisciplinary potentials.

2   Discourse, Materiality and Effect

Throughout our chapters there is a collective focus upon the constitutive and productive power of discourse. Discourse operates to create the conditions through which media, technologies, cultures, identities and behaviours are characterised, rendered intelligible and ultimately experienced. Discourse situates subjects of value and worth, structures the conditions through which medical paradigms and technologies are developed, categorises individuals and frames experiences, whether this be of eroticism and intimacy (online, in sex clubs), sociality, socio-political regimes of knowledge, ideas and history. Discursive regimes in this way co-ordinate the landscape of what can be known, who is a knowledgeable subject and what is even worth knowing in cultural and temporal contexts. These contexts and experiences are also mediated, and through this mediation they also become material. When speaking about discourse there is a temptation to think about it as some sort of vapourous force, in the air, all around us yet somehow intangible. Although this may be characteristic of some inner workings of discourse, ultimately our collection illustrates that discursive regimes have material effects (and affects). Discourse becomes inscribed upon technologies, bodies, behaviours, spaces, documents, art. Discourses materially constitute our experiences through affect. This affect is also structured around various cultural antinomies of desire/disgust, anxiety/comfort, public/private, digital/physical, in/visibility, distance/proximity, mobile/fixed, reality/fantasy.

3 Neoliberalism and Commodification

Throughout many of the chapters there is also a common theme emerging around neoliberalism and the consequent impact upon social relations. Within neoliberalism the logic of capitalism expands into aspects of everyday life. A value/exchange relationship exists at the very core of our being and in the way our identities may be mediated through technologies and specific behaviours or interactions. Within the current volume we can see this clearly through notions of the flexible sociality of the trans-domestic sphere, 'cool disabled girl', 'consumer-citizen', queer commodification, 'post-dating' and sex clubs. These dynamics share notions of the entrepreneurial or 'enterprising' self (du Gay, 1996) that form the basis of much neoliberalist thinking. However, there are two other connections here in the form of the 'object' and those who may not enjoy the same privileges to inhabit subject positions of flexibility or exhibit entrepreneurial selfhood. This includes those without the material resources to 'flex' around structural inequalities such as racialisation, racism, class inequality, gendered proscriptions or ableist prejudices. Within neoliberal cultures, anything can become a resource, everything can become a commodity and individual 'lack' is seen as a result of individual failure to capitalise upon the opportunities that a neoliberal society offers. This is quite closely tethered to the commodification of jouissance, object cathexis and marketing of self, commonly illustrated through chapters in the collection here. The literal and symbolic transformation of body parts, embodied activities and identities into objects or brands to be promoted for exchange remains embedded within the parameters of neoliberal cultural dynamics and subject-formation.

4 Media, Citizenship, Social Relations and Objects

Citizenship is another theme that weaves itself through the book's chapters wherein state-defined citizenship and economic neoliberalism function to co-produce ideal citizen subjects. These subjects are productive, rights bearing, agential, and emplaced. Technologies of citizenship, our contributors argue, reproduce autochthonous forms of identity construction that are simultaneously raced, gendered, classed. Moreover, these citizen identities are surveilled and policed and, when deemed acceptable, co-opted in-line with logics of neoliberal capitalism and hegemonic discourse. This modality of citizenship, as Turner argues, functions through the "adaptation of imperial and colonial logics" that are attuned to "the particular demands of white supremacy [as well as normative] familial order" (Turner 2020, p. 98; Walia 2021). Sikka, Peng, and

Couchman express this understanding of citizenship through the lens of medicine and health; Bates, Brown and Sayner via nationalism and memory; and,
for Walls, Longstaff, and Haywood through the pursuit of desire and pleasure
vis-à-vis the ideal consumer and 'entreporneurial' citizen subject. These are
also the networked and digital citizens who curate and maintain their lives
via social media. Whether this is via sexualised and pornified space such as
Onlyfans or the broader variables of distance and intimacy that a platform such
as Zoom has both enabled and commodified, we find that the ontological and
epistemological experiences of 'being' and 'becoming' a citizen is always disruptive. Citizenship relies upon an assemblage of pasts, presents, and futures
and folded into all of this collection we see how medicalised citizens, are also
those citizens that have been regulated by discourses of nationalism, haunted
by traumatic cultural memories and disrupted by the pandemic. A slightly
broader arc aligned to disrupted knowledge and which builds on the construction and disruption of citizenship is connected to how our relationships to
objects and to each other are somehow always mediated. Just as Marx situates
his ideas around capital and commodity fetishism in relation to the materiality of 'things' we find in a disruptive (and a pandemic) setting that our reliance on mediated relations, socially intimacy and material objects becomes
more acute and precarious. The construction of the 'Covidiot' as well as the
layers of neoliberal ideology that run through this collection draw attention to
this. In this space we find that excessive bodily pleasures and self-led modes
of conspicuous consumption exist alongside angry protest, genuine austerity,
and political displacement. David Bates captures this kind of tension in his
analysis of the BLM 'moment' and the tearing down of colonial statues; here
these historical objects and the loaded metaphors and metonymies of the past
that they bear take on new meaning and power. Disruption involves an active
process of rejection, calling out, repositioning established values and beliefs
and a move towards new social relations and interactions. Here the implicit
disruption of media, sociality and objecthood also subverts our approaches
to the self and the politics of docile assimilation that haunts neoliberal capital and the experience of disrupted and indeed dislocated citizenship that the
pandemic starkly and vividly captured.

5   The Cultural Politics of (In)Visibility, the Scopic and How We Do
     and Don't 'See'

This complex amalgamation of citizenship and its alignment to media, sociality
and objecthood and the construction of mediated subjects is also embedded

into regimes and practices of the visual and a politics of visual culture. In an age where visibility is frenzied and excessive, and where there is quite literally 'too much of everything', we find that any disruption to this yields the potential to undermine and perhaps make visuality a more precarious cultural form. Yet during the pandemic, visual politics and the scopic thrived and our reliance (and expectation) for visual pleasures and references became amplified. Here the cultural politics of turning our cameras on or off on Zoom twinned with the signifiers of our 'backgrounds' created a politics of seeing the subject(s) and other(s) in terms their social class, cultural, economic and intellectual capital as well as through their physical and cultural geography and its loaded semiotics of cultural difference, taste and judgement. All of this echoes Pierre Bourdieu's work and reflects a productively disruptive potential to critique the scopic formations of sociality, gender, race, class and the inequalities of seeing vs viewing the Other. How and what we 'see' is also reliant on how we do not 'see' and in our collection almost every chapter considers these tensions.

Tina Sikka's work examines this in relation to skin colour in medical technologies, David Bates in terms of BLM protests and discourses of racism and nationalism, Alexander D. Brown and Joanne Sayner consider through what can be seen in terms of national history, and how we 'see' the past. Sarah Hill's work discusses this in a way that uses the intersections of self-representation, disability, and drag to directly critique and situate the cultural politics of the 'stare' as a form of disabled 'gaze'. Longstaff's chapter is also concerned with the dynamics and possibilities between self and Other and the interpassive modes of seeing and not seeing on OnlyFans.com. In his work the concept of jouissance challenges us to question what we see and how we see it. He argues that jouissance and pleasure cannot be 'seen' and by using pornographic content creation and the visual excess of sexual self-representation as a very real fantasy (which invites us to see more than we should), he invites us to question the disruptive politics of visual pleasure and identification. Haywood's work also speaks to this so that the reversible gaze and stare in the sex club allies itself to broader socio-cultural modes of how we see and look in ordinary and extraordinary spaces and scenarios. In Barker et al there is also a consideration of how we 'see' emotion through lyrics whilst in Carlin's the focus is on affective and philosophical narratives connected to how we see 'art 'and 'nature'. Here we find a visual landscape where vision is blurred, half-awake and half-asleep. This is a visual culture of disruption where 'the subject is decentred, split, and comes to terms with its own incompleteness' (Jay, 1993 p. 363). In this way, an illusory form of reciprocity and recognition can be 'seen', via the presence of another (on OnlyFans, via a Zoom call, a swipe on a dating app) yet the unseen gaze of the Other is something that has not yet grasped the place of the subject. It is here that the subject remains stuck in what a disruptive or anamorphic gaze. It is only the subject using a specific social media platform or device who can capture the image – here the Other is distant, isolated, and displaced. In a pandemic space social distance, lockdown and regulatory governance intensifies visual desire, yet this desire can only be invigorated at a distance. In this way, the illusion of clarity that visual desire performs is disrupted and reformed into an 'anamorphic blotch' or 'stain' (Zizek, 2006, p. 69) that undercuts the 'seeing subject' through 'the gap between the eye and gaze' (ibid). It is in this instance that the subject is 'always-already gazed at from a point that eludes his eyes' (ibid). Once again, visual desire is disrupted and entrapped – it is seen, from one side, by the subject and, from the other, by the 'Other' yet it only 'belongs' in the image because it has the power to anamorphically capture the subject, and, thus, distort the Other's gaze. The commodity, which is in the neoliberal subject's grasp, is responsible for capturing the image we (the Other) see. Yet, it is also necessary for the subject to distort their coherent image by turning, editing, cropping, and sharing the camera with a culture or a person they will never grasp. Whilst the vantage point of the viewer seems to be guaranteed, because the subject is there for them to see, they are actually seeing him from within a disruption and a distortion.

6   Self-Reflexivity and Auto-ethnography

This distorted approach to seeing and visuality is also something that connects to our critical analyses of the self and the epistemological space that disrupted knowledge opens for auto-ethnographic and self-reflexive scholarship. In many ways the entire collection is an attempt to navigate and situate how auto-ethnographic and self-reflexive ways to research and write can disrupt and affirm the desires and anxieties we have all felt since 2020. In some chapters, this is more marked but the threads that run though this collection acknowledge and consider approaches to critical pedagogy (Bates and Hands), heritage and the past (Brown and Sayer), wellbeing and isolation (Waugh), self-realisation and art (Carlin), and music and emotion (Barker et al) which forced us to re-evaluate and re-position how the global Covid-19 pandemic has changed our everyday, ordinary and assumed privileges. The pandemic has provided the contextual frame for many of the chapters in this volume, but we argue that the connectivity between each author runs much deeper. As part of a wider critical discipline of media, culture and heritage studies the work presented here can be understood as part of the not-too-distant past, an aspect of the present, and a piece of the future.

References

Bulmer, M. (1984) *The Chicago School of Sociology: Institutionalization, Diversity, and the Rise of Sociological Research*. London: University of Chicago.

Du Gay, P. (1996) *Consumption and Identity at Work*. London: Sage.

Giddens, A. (1984) *The constitution of society: Outline of the theory of structuration*. Los Angeles: University of California Press.

Jay, M. (1993) *Downcast Eyes: The Denigration of Vision in Twentieth-Century French Thought*. Berkeley, Los Angeles, and London: University of California Press.

Turner, J. (2020) *Bordering intimacy: Postcolonial governance and the policing of family*. Manchester University Press.

Walia, H. (2021) *Border and Rule: Global migration, capitalism, and the rise of racist nationalism*. Chicago, IL: Haymarket Books.

Zizek, S. (ed.) (2006) *Lacan: The Silent Partners*. London: Verso.

Index

www.ingramcontent.com/pod-product-compliance
Lightning Source LLC
Chambersburg PA
CBHW070055030426
42335CB00016B/1892